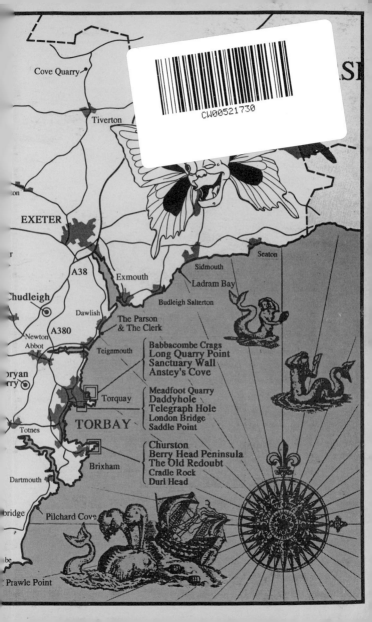

Cove Quarry

Tiverton

EXETER

A38

Exmouth

Chudleigh

Dawlish

Newton
Abbot

A380

The Parson
& The Clerk

Teignmouth

Sidmouth   Seaton

Ladram Bay

Budleigh Salterton

Babbacombe Crags
Long Quarry Point
Sanctuary Wall
Anstey's Cove

oryan
rry

Torquay

TORBAY

Totnes

Brixham

Dartmouth

Meadfoot Quarry
Daddyhole
Telegraph Hole
London Bridge
Saddle Point

Churston
Berry Head Peninsula
The Old Redoubt
Cradle Rock
Durl Head

bridge

Pilchard Cove

be

Prawle Point

Ian Vincent on Empire of the Sun (F7b) Photo: Nick White

South Devon
&
Dartmoor

By Nick White

Published by CORDEE

The Hand of Power

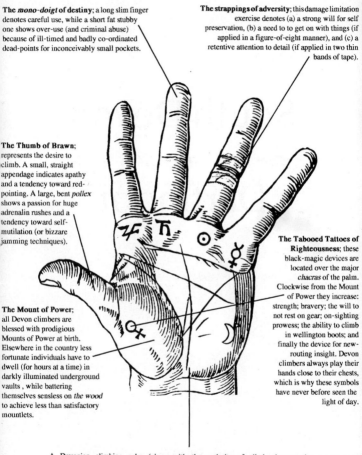

The *mono-doigt* of destiny; a long slim finger denotes careful use, while a short fat stubby one shows over-use (and criminal abuse) because of ill-timed and badly co-ordinated dead-points for inconceivably small pockets.

The strappings of adversity; this damage limitation exercise denotes (a) a strong will for self preservation, (b) a need to to get on with things (if applied in a figure-of-eight manner), and (c) a retentive attention to detail (if applied in two thin bands of tape).

The Thumb of Brawn; represents the desire to climb. A small, straight appendage indicates apathy and a tendency toward red-pointing. A large, bent *pollex* shows a passion for huge adrenalin rushes and a tendency toward self-mutilation (or bizzare jamming techniques).

The Tabooed Tattoes of Righteousness; these black-magic devices are located over the major *chacras* of the palm. Clockwise from the Mount of Power they increase: strength; bravery; the will to not rest on gear; on-sighting prowess; the ability to climb in wellington boots; and finally the device for new-routing insight. Devon climbers always play their hands close to their chests, which is why these symbols have never before seen the light of day.

The Mount of Power; all Devon climbers are blessed with prodigious Mounts of Power at birth. Elsewhere in the country less fortunate individuals have to dwell (for hours at a time) in darkly illuminated underground vaults , while battering themselves senseless on *the wood* to achieve less than satisfactory mountlets.

A Devonian climbing palm (along with the majority of climbers' paws the world-over) could be said to be composed of all thumbs and no fingers, especially when viewed in direct contrast with the flaccid hand of a "normal" human being. This state of affairs led Maria Callous (renowned gypsy palmist) to develop a specialised reading of the appendage in question. She reckoned that the left hand could be used to interpret the style of ascent to which a climber aspired, while the right hand showed what they made of themselves by their own efforts.

*"If you keep an open mind. . .
you will discover dark secrets"*

Climbing Guide to Dartmoor and South West Devon
by Keith Lawder, 1957 (RNSMC)

Rock Climbing in Devonshire
edited by Bob Moulton, 1966 (RNSMC)

First Edition, (South Devon)
by Pat Littlejohn and Pete Biven, 1971 (West Col)

Dartmoor Climbers' Guide
by Tony Moulam, 1976 (West Col)

Devon Rock Climbs
edited by Bob Moulton, 1978 (RN & RMMC)

Second Edition, (South Devon and Dartmoor)
by Pat Littlejohn and Pete O'Sullivan, 1985 (Cordee)

Third Edition, (South Devon & Dartmoor)
by Nick White, 1995 (Cordee)

ISBN 1 871 890 32 2

Produced by

Prepared for printing by Parker Typesetting Service, Leicester

Front Cover: Dave Thomas leading an E5 after one-too-many *Flaming Drambuie(s)*.(Photo. Pete Bull)

Back Cover: Ian Mountford bouldering on the Frog Boulder at Vixen Tor.(Photo. Nick White)

This guidebook is available from all specialist climbing shops and bookshops within the area, or direct from the publishers **CORDEE**, 3a De Montfort Street, Leicester, LE1 7HD.

CONTENTS

GUIDEBOOK DISCLAIMER

The inclusion of a crag or routes upon it, does not mean that any member of the public has a right of access to the crag, or the right to climb upon it.

Information on all climbing in the area is made available regardless of the access position for: historical purposes; for the sake of completeness; and so that the facts are available if access is permitted in the future.

Neither Cordee, the author, nor the editor of this guidebook accept any liability whatsoever for injury or damage caused to (or by) climbers, third parties, or property arising from this guide's use. Whilst the content of the guide is believed to be accurate, no responsibility is accepted for any error, omission, or mis-statement. Users must rely upon their own judgement and are recommended to insure against injury to person, property and third party risks.

This guide is probably as close as you would want to get to an exhaustive study of the recorded climbing in the South Devon and Dartmoor area. The inclusion of a route doesn't necessarily mean you are going to find it, although this area is not as bad as North Devon, where nine times out of ten your intended climb will have fallen down. The main factor to beware of is the deterioration of *in-situ* gear, be it for protection or belaying/abseiling. As seasoned rock-junkies you will all appreciate that ultimately the decision to climb (or not) is your own[1].

The author (unreservedly) makes no apology for the informal approach of the guide, or the screwball *bon mots* contained herein.

---

[1] *It has been statistically proven that more people are squeezed to death by their pet boa-constrictors, than die through rock climbing (so be careful. . . it's a jungle out there).*

ACKNOWLEDGEMENTS

First off I'd like to thank *Proper Job Breweries*, foremost artisans of Real Ale for the discerning tippler. Their continued sufferance of my penchant for Scruttock's Old Dirigible (responsible for the author tipping the scales at a rotund eighteen stones – *thank the Lord for liposuction*) helped to chill-out an otherwise overwrought hack.

Secondly, I'm indebted to Pat Littlejohn for being an inspiration, and a generous benefactor of vital anecdotal snippettes. Then of course, I can hardly draw my next breath without paying homage to the divine facetiousness of Alexei *Yuri Gagarin-glorious-five-year-plan-volga-tractor-sputnik* Sayle, without whom I'd have been seriously lost for words. While his philosophy of ". . .having the dolphins on my side" has helped considerably.

I have Clark Alston to thank for the "well-balanced" history section (*specifically requested by Martin Crocker, and vetted by Frank Cannings*). Clark was also insane enough to share a rope with yours-truly during the tertiary stage of guide-induced dementia, there can be no truer form of sacrificial masochism.

I'm obliged to both Pete Bull and Ian Smith (who proved to be a godsend in all aspects of guide production) for the use of their darkrooms, and I'm extremely grateful to Duncan Spilling and Exeter Art College for allowing me to grapple with their respective Graphic Design facilities.

I'd like to apologise to Dave Farrant for presenting him with the task of deciphering (and then translating) the gobbledygook computer language with which this guidebook was written. Many thanks to him and also to Mel White for supplying the relevant decoding software which made Dave's work possible.

I am beholden to both Chris Nicholson and Bruce Woodley (co-conspirator on the Inland Limestone Introduction) for a peculiarly Devonian apprenticeship. Without their candid appreciation of eccentricity, and modes of verbal expression incomprehensible to users of standard English (henceforth referred to as *furrineerz*), climbing in Devon could have been a severely limited experience.

Ken Palmer, Andy Grieve, and Nick Hancock together with a host of innumerable Plymouth-based phantoms, were responsible for the quantum breakthrough in undergrading at one stage rife throughout the Shire. They also bent over backwards to provide photos (of each other) for the guide.

Penultimately, I'd like to give my condolences to Bob Moulton. For twas he alone took upon himself the task of editing this tome, and with a stoicism heretofore unseen within the rarefied realm of guidebook-dom, elicited such sage-like comments as "I don't get it", "am I missing a Scandinavian pun here?" and "I give up!".

Finally, I'd like to mention a few, of the cast of thousands, without whom this guide just wouldn't be the same: Bjørn *the punch-bag* Aikman; the Arête Mountaineering Club; Nick *Don Juan* Biven; Mark Campbell and Charlie Woodburn *(aka Bill and Ted)*; Simon *Do you like sponge? I do!* Cook; Cliff Fishwick *(for turning a blind-eye to an apalling attendance record at college)*; Dom and Jon Gandy *The Dangerous Brothers*; Jenny Keith *(for oiling the wheels of the Exeter climbing scene)*; Ben Masterson and Joe Picalli *(for their vivid translation of a certain esoteric route)*; Theo Quant; Ken Robinson; Steve Thorpe; Dave *Tangent* Thomas; Paul *stumpy* Twomey; Ian *six pints of Stella* Vincent and Joe Healey *(for getting Ian to drink them)*. And at last, but by no means least, a big thank you to the proof-readers: Graham Lynch, Lizzie Payne, Neil Pearsons and Keith Sharples.

INTRODUCTION

South Devon plays host to clotted cream, chocolate-box scenery and fun in the sun, that is if and when it can be bothered to shine. For even the weather is prone to Devonitis (a malady often attributed to the longevity of the yokels and usually misconstrued as indolence). In a world of ever increasing violence, South Devon becomes an ever deeper reservoir of quietude. It is also a climbing area of immense diversity, which can be tailored to suit the most fastidious of palates. Both the franglais *racing-snake* and the most puritanical plus-foured arbiter of traditional values get what they deserve.

A brief look at the incomprehensible Geology notes, may give some indication as to the variety of rock types and geomorphology to be encountered; wind-swept granite tors, sunkissed limestone grottoes and the odd tottering stack of rubble. Thus armed with the brand new and third in the *aptly* named Hitchcock-ups guide to the South Devon and Dartmoor Trilogy, there is no excuse but to get out there and revel in it, whatever 'it' maybe. But before you do, remember that the words DON'T PANIC do not appear in large friendly gold letters on the back cover of this guide, as it is the considered opinion of the author that half the pleasure is in *the horror. . . the horror. . .*

Seeing as most of Britain lies to the north of South Devon (and that the few locals who practise the noble art of *'eel clamberin'* know where all the best grappling-hook placements are anyway), the guide has been laid out with the visitor in mind; ie. the crags within the Shire have been dealt with in a roughly north-to-south orientation. With this premise to the fore, the guide breaks down into four specific headings; Inland Limestone, Sea Cliff Limestone, Dartmoor Granite and Esoterica. These headings begin to sketch-in some of the more colourful aspects and practices of the indigenous climbing population, culture and myths. The main headings further breakdown into area headings which contain specific approach details as to how to get to that area, and what to expect when you get there. From there the actual crag details should enable you to find the route of your desire[2]. The routes are generally described in relation to your direction of approach to the crag. So on numerous occasions this occurs from right to left. If this is not mentioned in the text, then the omnipresent guidebook rule of ". . .all routes must be described from left to right. . ." is being enforced.

[2] *It has been proven (beyond any shadow of doubt) that you have a far greater chance of finding a crag in this region with this guide (without having to look out of the back window of the car), than you could ever hope to have of finding a single French crag using the relevant topo!!!*

The sheer number of climbs and the need to save space has at times necessitated a departure from the traditional approach of avoiding processional route descriptions (ie: route Z starts 10′ right of route Y, which starts 10′ right of route X,. . . which starts 10′ right of route A). This does not mean that you will have to walk the entire length of the crag identifying each route before you come across your chosen climb, as the crag diagrams and photo-diagrams have been carefully integrated into the text to speed up your orientation to the cliff layout. In this way it is possible to pin-point salient features at a glance and cross-reference them with the italicised notes (mentioning these features) which appear as linking passages between route descriptions. . . well that's the theory anyway. Putting theory into practice is a wholly different ball-game, and one that I will leave firmly in your court. Suffice it to say that the worst possible scenario would have you starting at Kerswell Quarry to find a route at Morwell Rocks.

☞: the use of hands (in the gutter margin of the running headfolio) indicates the direction of the relevant plan or photodiagram. If hands don't appear, refer back to the area map for the cliff or buttress in question.

There has been a deliberate policy to describe everything that has been done within the bounds of this guidebook area (and outside it in one exceptional case). Over the years the guide coverage to the Shire has come from many disparate sources, virtually all of them privately funded. All have taken different stances over what is worthwhile, to the extent that many of them have been of the Selected Climbs genre. So in the present retro-socio-political climate, this guide is pitched firmly in the record-just-about-everything category (which is as mealy-mouthed as you can get), because you wouldn't believe how much of the dross gets claimed over and over again. To make enough space for the recording of the crap, combined with the vast number of new routes, a fairly aggressive style of route description editing has been employed. This revolves around the abbreviation of common climbing terminology, and the odd route name.

Abbreviations: the inclusion of abbreviations severely curtails the sometimes epic length of certain route descriptions, and therefore saves paper (saves trees, forests and indeed the world. . . nuff said). Although there maybe an initial period of acclimitisation, this shouldn't last any longer than a couple of years. The abridged terminology that follows, appears in a variety of permutations throughout the main body of the text, while a further table of the same abbreviations appears in the end papers of the guide for easy reference.

L	-	Left	RH	-	Right-hand
LH	-	Left-hand	RWs	-	Rightwards
LWs	-	Leftwards	L/R	-	Left to Right
R	-	Right			

R\L	-	Right to Left *(Note: The stroke indicates the direction of the break, crack, or fault)*	PRs	-	Peg Runners
			PB	-	Peg Belay
			BR	-	Bolt Runner *(and so on, as for PR).*
OH	-	Overhang	TR	-	Thread Runner *(and so on, as for PR).*
OHing	-	Overhanging			
OHung	-	Overhung	NB	-	Nut Belay
†	-	Unrepeated	HWM	-	High Water Mark
PR	-	Peg Runner *(Note: If the word peg appears, you have to place it)*	N ↑	-	North(ern/*erly*)
			S ↓	-	South(ern/*erly*)
			E→	-	East(ern/*erly*)
			←W	-	West(ern/*erly*)

Route names of ten characters or more that are referred to else-where within the relevant section, are generally given abbreviations. This is indicated by an italicised entry in brackets after the route name in question. *Par example:*

29   Goddess of Gloom *(GOG)*   220′   HVS 5a,5a,5a   **(R)**   ★★

Route Numbers: the routes are numbered under each crag heading. These numbers are then used on the relevant diagram or map (if any), which is located as near as possible to the description.

(R) refers to the route being seasonally restricted by an agreed climbing ban. Berry Head is the only venue affected by such a ban. It extends from the 15th March to the 31st July, allowing the resident population of auks, cormorants, fulmars and kittiwakes to hatch and fledge their young without disturbance. If the stated reason for the ban is not persuasive enough, then the £1,000 fine should make even the most hardened nutter think twice.

Stars: these are merely a contrivance to lure you into some of the darkest, dankest places in creation. The system runs somewhere along the lines of: ★★★ equates to the notional idea of superior quality. A route generally receives this rating by either being a new router's wet dream, or by dropping the grade of an already established route; ★★ could be considered a profound meeting with normality (ie. every route deserves two stars, it's just that some are more two star than others); while ★ could have you laughing at the absurdity of it all. Those routes without stars are not to be sneered at. . . at least they're not polished.

Grading: the standard British grading system is used for most routes: ie. an adjectival (in capital form only: ie. E,M,D. . . through to E8) followed by a numerical grade ranging from S 4a through to E8 6c, thus far. However, sport routes are graded using the French system, followed by a British grade in brackets, *par*

Grade Comparison Table				
GB		**Fr**	**Oz**	**Alpine**
5a		5+	17/18	VI -
5b				
	E1	6a	19/20	VI+
5c	E2	6a/b	21	VII -
	E3	6b+	22/23	VII+
6a	E4	6c/7a	24/25	VIII -
	E5	7a/b	25/26	VIII+
6b	E6	7b/c+	27/29	IX
	E7	8a/+	30/31	X-
	E8	8b/+	32	X
6c/7a				

example 8a (E4 6a), for controversy's sake if nothing else. There are a few routes with Australian grades spattered about the place, by virtue of the fact that they sport *carrot* bolts. The Australians would probably argue that these routes are overgraded, thereby showing that they are all descendants of Plymouth stock[3]. Sea-level traversing has been taken to some quite heady-heights within the Shire. Many of the traverses described in the guide require a level of commitment and bravura far and above the sedentary pace of a day's cragging. This state of affairs has been reflected by the fact that the traverses are given Alpinesque grades. The same goes for a number of routes in the Esoterica section, most notably on the Sandstone nightmares and in one or two cases in the South Hams.

Bolting: a dubious activity at the best of times, this continental pestilence has been confined to very specific sites within the Shire[4].

---

[3] *Plymouth (under-)grading is an altogether different ball-game (probably played on stilts), and one which is impossible to fathom, except by means of the relatively simple equation of $E=MC^2$ (where E = the grade; M = the number of means by which the route is approached ie. cheat-stick, pile of rocks etc; and C = the number of car-jacks employed).*

[4] *ie. those areas twinned with eminent French places like Père Lachaise cemetery. You can imagine how pungent the exchange visitors are, and I'm not referring to the garlic.*

Failure to comply with the following guide-lines will bring down the ridicule, scorn and wrath of the entire Devon chapter of the Hell's Angels (or Satan's Slaves as they prefer to call themselves), which can become pretty intense if you are a paranoid lil' critter.

It is the policy of the BMC that the use of bolts and other drilled equipment is only legitimate on certain agreed quarried crags and agreed sections of certain limestone crags. Lists of agreed locations will be maintained by the local Area Committees.

BMC Policy May 1992

Bolt Free:

[1] - **Chudleigh Rocks**
[2] - **Cliffs north of Long Quarry Point** *(up to and including Petit Tor Point)*
[3] - **Sanctuary Wall**
[4] - **Cliffs south of Anstey's Cove to Sharkham Point** *(with the exception of Churston Quarries)*
[5] - **Dartmoor** *(without exception)*

Bolting Accepted:[5]

[a] - **Torbryan Quarry**
[b] - **Hazard Quarry**
[c] - **Long Quarry Point**
[d] - **Anstey's Cove**
[e] - **Churston Quarries**

The BMC is firmly opposed to retrospective bolting (ie. changing the character of a route by placing fixed equipment where none was previously used). Climbs should only be re-equipped on a basis of common consent established at open forum.

BMC Policy May 1992

The future re-equipping of routes is to be assessed under the auspices of the BMC South West Area Committee (SWAC)[6], in line with the final paragraph of the BMC fixed equipment policy (quoted above). The development of **new crags** within the area of this guide must be carried out within the guidelines quoted above – with the proviso that the venue dictates the style of climbing.

Chipping: Devonians say **NO** to chipping, only they express it in a less diplomatic fashion. It has been rumoured that a current deterrent is the vicious deployment of two pitch forks (selotaped either side of a fifty pence piece. This is a refinement passed on by some visiting Glaswegian climbers).

[5] *If it's not mentioned here, then reserve the bolt-gun for wet-dreams in your bedroom.*
[6] *SWAC is a not-too-distant cousin of the Federal Board of Investigations SWAT team. It is trained by MOSSAD, with ordnance supplied by the SAS, and it takes great pride in knowing that its acronym appears regularly in the Batman series.*

Stealing:
anyone caught stealing or interferring with legitimate *in-situ* gear will be strung up by their various nether regions and flogged until they scream "call me Gladys" in a voice five octaves higher than the one they were initially blessed with. Apart from being a particularly selfish act, the pilfering of pegs, threads and bolts is not only senseless but dangerous. The stuff is recognisable if it is used on other new routes (thereby proclaiming the first ascentionist *'as 'avin done the blag*, or been a third party). In most cases (especially with pegs) the original placement is invariably altered or destroyed, so what's the point?

Camping:
during the summer season there is no shortage of camping facilities. Just about all the farmers in the Shire turn their fallow fields over to the accruement of tourist *dinero*. However, there are few facilities during the spring, autumn and winter. This should not cause too much aggravation, as B&B or mobile home accommodation drops dramatically in price, so that the locals can eke out a meagre existence before they start raking it in again the following summer. For those of you who actively build the experience of a few nights under canvas into your climbing itinerary, there follows a list of campsites which are open 24hr a-day / 365 days-a-year.

Holmans' Wood: situated just off the A38, at Chudleigh's northern exit. Handy for both Chudleigh and Dartmoor.

Stover International: again just off the A38. Depending on your bent it has the added attraction/detraction of having the Trago Mills shopping complex en-suite.

River Dart Country Park: a further campsite just off the A38, this time residing on the fringe of Ashburton.

Ross Park: a very handy site for Torbryan Quarry, being just on the outskirts of Ipplepen (north of Totnes). Virtually all the other areas of the guide are within half-an-hour's drive.

Collaton St Mary: there is a gaggle of campsites just outside Paignton, on the Totnes road (A385).

Holly Gruit Campsite: situated just before the junction of the Torquay ring road (A380), with the A379.

Eating and Drinking:
the overall area notes give an indication of where to get that essential pre-route/redpoint cuppa and cream tea, or something a *tad* stiffer if courage is a prerequisite for your chosen route. However, some of the more delightful drink and eateries reside further off the beaten track, ergo this splendid résumé.

1 The Drew Arms   GR 734 908
Turn the clock back sixty years (cloth cap *de rigueur*), sit on one of two benches lining the walls. Order a ploughman's and a pint through a hole in the wall. Wait five minutes. One pint duly arrives with bird beak and twigs still in it followed by a lump of bread, a doorstep of cheese and a pickle of profound proportions.   (1934)

2 The Double Locks
GR 933 900

Traverse Marsh Barton Industrial Estate to cross over the canal via a clapper bridge. Follow the canal east to the *Locks*. Ask *Honest John* for a song while indulging in a pint from the menu and a home-made repast of devilled whitebait à l'orange. (1753)

3 The Bridge Inn
GR 979 884

Recorded as a licensed victuallers in the Doomsday Book, this watering-hole could be said to have a sense of history. It also has a bill of quaffable fare second-to-none. (1066)

4 The Nobody Inn
GR 855 867

Lost within the misty Haldon foothills, the rustic gem of *The Nobody Inn* could quite happily play host to any number of grim fairytales. *The Company of Wolves*-type aura pervading this sleepy hollow only goes to reinforce the yokel adage of "don't stray from the path". (1406)

5 The Warren House Inn
GR 674 809

Where most of the more far-fetched tales of the Moor are hatched. Notable for its freshly painted pentangle everyday and a fire that has not gone out since the dawn of history. (666)

6 The Cider Bar
GR 860 712

A sanctuary for cider-noses and hardened drinkers. If this were Newton Abbot's answer to one of Hugh Heffner's Playboy clubs, you would have to put up with half-skinned rabbit waitresses leaking blood into your pint-pot (apparently cider 'n'black is all the rage *par ce moment*). (1969)

7 The Hallsands Hotel
GR 817 386

A pan-galactic gargle-blasting venue, the indigenous population being mostly harmless. People wishing to enjoy the above estab-lishment had better hurry, as the sea is making large inroads towards the hostelry's foundations. (1901)

GEOLOGY (THE CHAOS THEORY)

It all started with a *butterflysaurus*. . . beating its leathery wings over a dreamy lagoon somewhere off the deltaic mass of Dumnonia (itself a mere spit off the big smoke of Pangaea). The water was literally teaming with the humdrum activities of local communities like the feisty brachiopods, arguing with the laconic crinoids over whose reef is it anyway (later to become Telegraph Hole). All this was taking place a long. . . long time ago, well to be exact it was a Thursday some 400 million years BC. The oldest Devonian beds of non-marine Dartmouth Slates had already been made (they were early risers). These beds still occupy an *axial* zone known as the *Watergate Anticlinorium*, a major East\West formation running from Dartmouth to Newquay. Above these snappily-coloured, *fluvio-deltaic* green and purple sand and siltstones, with *pyroclastics* no-less, came the marine Meadfoot Beds. These heralded the arrival of the Middle Devonian period. This was a complex era for South Devon, incorporating a mishmash of cross-bedded and interlocking slates, *intercalated lenticles* (reefs composed of various limestones, and often of considerable size) and volcanic activity. Unfortunately this caused more than a few ructions with the previously established Palaeozoic rock-types, who firmly believed in keeping South Devon a heterogeneous-free zone.

The larger carbonate masses that occurred at this point in time were Torquay, Berry Head and Plymouth – via lens-shaped reefs formed of raised banks in the sea which were gradually silted-up. This was the golden era of British Limestones, often referred to (by those in the know) as the Carboniferous era, roughly 300 million years ago. The Dumnonian deserts sank beneath the rising waves of the lagoon, well more a shallow, going-on not-so-shallow sea, leading to the Upper Devonian era. In South Devon this consisted of largely *ostracod*-bearing slates with thinner *cephalod*-bearing limestones and shales; it also witnessed the gestation of Chudleigh.

Another intruder to the Palaeozoic rock's status quo was the major granite *Armorican batholith*, *cupolas* of which outcropped as the separate *plutons* of Dartmoor, Bodmin, St Austell, Carnmenellis, Land's End and The Scillies (these six great *adamellitic* edifices are connected at great depth and it is thought that the whole *batholith* is L-shaped in vertical cross-section). Associated with Dartmoor's dramatic appearance was the rapid overdeepening of the surrounding river valleys, leading to the characteristic steep-sided gorges, of which Lustleigh Cleave is an eminent example.

However, the oldest intrusion was made by the *Greenstone*

**GEOLOGICAL SURVEY MAP:
SOUTH DEVON AREA**

Exeter

Plymouth

Schists, in the shape of dykes, sills and bosses. These were generally of *sodic plagioclase feldspar* and *pyroxene*, usually altered to *andesine* and *hornblende/biotite* within *metamorphic aureoles* (eg. Gammon Head and Bolt Tail). In climbing terms this rock ironically equates to a certain advertising campaign in that it is soft, (not that) strong and very long. These schists were faulted against the Devonian sediments to the north, where they became overlain by *New Red Sandstones*.

A lot of controversy surrounds the *New Red Sandstones*. They seem to be composed of indivisible, generally *unfossiliferous*, red-coloured *breccias, conglomerates, sandstones* and *marls*. They cover much of East Devon (giving the fields their characteristic red soil), and have perpetuated the title of the *New Red Sandstone Series*. On the South Coast they also form a large part of the colourful and locally grand cliffs between Paignton and Seaton, the most notable being the Ladram Bay Stacks, which bear a striking resemblance to the Twelve Apostles in Australia.

HISTORICAL
By Clark Alston

IN THE BEGINNING. . .
The first mention of rock climbing possibilities in the area was made by the redoubtable Victorian, Walter Parry Haskett-Smith, in the first volume of his "Climbing in the British Isles", published in 1894. Along with reference to the Dartmoor Tors, mention was made of the future possibilities at Anstey's Cove and Berry Head. The following years saw some sporadic activities, but the first real record of a climb was that of I.B.Prowse's three star Chudleigh classic *Wogs* in 1923.

Dartmoor had to wait until the mid-Thirties for David Cox, Rene Bere and Robin Hodgkin's ascents of the *Climbers' Club Routes*. Although subsequently adjusted in line these were amazing achievements, which attained standards of quality and technicality unsurpassed for at least ten years. Sir Bernard Jeram and Major Donald Romanis had visited the Dewerstone in the early Twenties. They left no record of their exploits, saying that they had climbed only on the subsidiary buttresses.

AFTER THE WAR
First ascent activity virtually ceased whilst the depression and Hitler were dealt with, but in 1946 Tony Moulam's *Aramis* at Haytor served as a pointer to the area's potential. 1948 saw the first stirrings of interest from the large military population which continues to this day, especially on the Western side of Dartmoor (interestingly most ascents on the Eastern side of the Moor seemed to come from civilian groups – a fact further highlighted by the military's use of the alphabet for route names at the Dewerstone! Imagine their quandary in having to name the hundred-or-so routes there now). In 1948 Jim Moulton, Commanding Officer of the Royal Marine Commando School at Bickleigh, and his Second-in-command *Skinner* Saunders made a joint solo of what later became known as *Colonels Arête*. It was an adventurous ascent in the best Boys-Own tradition! Wearing triple-hobbed boots and without a rope, Moulton set off up the crux third pitch, only to fall onto the small ledge below, where he was fielded by Saunders. Apparently the climb was completed without further excitement! Meanwhile, members of the newly-formed Royal Navy Ski and Mountaineering Club, including Keith Lawder and the brothers Bill and Bob Higgins produced a crop of routes taking obvious features at the Dewerstone and on the Tors. The best from this period was Jim Simpson's *Central Groove*.

The Fifties witnessed the climbing of *Raven Gully* on Haytor's Low

Man (which the Higgins brothers vehemently deny climbing), followed by the reappearance of Moulam in 1952 for his ascent of *Canis* on the Main Tor. Although Devon climbing did not have routes to compare with those of the Brown/Whillans era, one of Dartmoor's hardest routes was *Kistvaen Corner* at Hound Tor. This was thought to have been led by Geoff Sutton at HVS, although it turns out it was top-roped in the mid-Fifties by 'persons unknown'. This is still impressive as it had to wait until 1985 for Pete O'Sullivan's ascent at E3 6a.

By 1957 the area needed its first guidebook and the RNSMC obliged under the authorship of Keith Lawder. In the same year the legendary Scot, Tom Patey, appeared in the area, whilst serving as a Naval Doctor with the Royal Marines. He immediately set to work on some of the Dewerstone's finest routes including *Leviathan*, *Spider's Web* and other routes on the Upper Buttresses. Barry Page, who had partnered Patey on Spider's Web, left his own mark with the technical *Superdirect Start* to the Climbers' Club routes. Patey also explored some of the Tors and rediscovered the esoteric shale cliffs of Morwell Rocks. His last offering on Dartmoor was the bold *Outward Bound* at Haytor.

THE SWINGING SIXTIES
In 1960 the search for virgin rock led Patey to the then ivy-ridden Chudleigh (some would say it still is). The first fruits of this period being *Sarcophagus*, *Barn Owl Crack* and *Chudleigh Overhang*, the former is still an intimidating line. Onlookers at the time recall Patey hurling equal amounts of incredibly green ivy and outrageously blue invective earthwards!

Throughout 1961 Nev Hannaby and Eric Rayson, National Servicemen stationed at Honiton, commenced their explorations. *Loot*, *The Slot*, *Inkerman Groove* and *Great Western* were all excellent climbs following great natural lines. It was also in 1961 that Outward Bound instructors Dave Bassett and Alex Allen started seriously climbing in Torbay with their routes on Berry Head's Coastguard Cliffs. Bassett was also responsible for the great breakthrough on Haytor's Low Man, when in the same year, and with Harry Cornish, he climbed *Aviation*.

1962 marked the arrival on the Devon scene of the accomplished gritstone and Cornish granite climber, Pete Biven. He recorded a number of climbs on the South Face of Chudleigh, including the excellent *Combined Ops*, which was done in the company of his brother, Barrie. The latter forced the strenuous *Oesophagus*, a route which has claimed more than its fair share of scalps. Meanwhile, at the Dewerstone, activity continued with Brian Shackleton, Mike Rabley and John Jones to the fore. The first pair climbed *Valhalla Wall*, whilst Rabley teamed up with Jones for the first aided ascent of *Gideon*. Tragedy struck in 1963, however, when Rabley was killed in an accident at the Dewerstone, dealing a severe blow to the small band of local climbers.

Exonian Frank Cannings was the next to make his mark with several climbs on Chudleigh's North Face, along with Biven's trilogy *Nexus, Sexus* and *Plexus*. Throughout 1965 Cannings pushed himself to the forefront of Devon climbing with a series of fine leads including *Nimrod* and *The Track*. The outstanding events of the year were the final complete ascents of *The Fly*, and *The Spider* by Cannings (both routes had complicated histories, separate pitches being climbed at different times by different personnel). The Spider remained the most difficult and prestigious climb in Devon for a long time. At about this time Biven strayed from the inland limestone to visit the cliffs at Long Quarry Point where he climbed *Grey Tower*, but explored no further. Cannings subjected Dartmoor to the same rise in standards and in 1964 had climbed two difficult routes on Haytor, *Interrogation* and the *Low Man Girdle*. He also directed his considerable energies on the Dewerstone, establishing *Cyclops* with Shackleton.

By 1966 more strong climbers were emerging from Exeter to develop the local Chudleigh cliffs. Ian *Mac* McMorrin climbed *Perseus* on Garden Wall along with the difficult *Panga*, whilst Andy Powling did *Bolero* on which he was accompanied by a keen fifteen-year-old by the name of Pat Littlejohn. The following years were to see the emergence of Torbay as a climbing ground of importance. As well as producing many routes of individual merit, the area proved to be a perfect training ground for the skills needed to develop the big, serious crags of the North Devon and Cornish coastline.

THE MAGICAL MYSTERY YEARS
In May 1967, at Daddyhole Main Cliff, a tremendous piece of route-finding by Steve Dawson and John Hammond gave the classic *Gates of Eden*. The gates were well and truly opened, although their speed of opening could have been truly miraculous, had ". . .Cannings and Biven not been quite so keen to get back to the beach to look at the birds[1]. I couldn't understand it, as there were more lines to go for! Obviously I was a late developer" (sic), quipped Littlejohn. In less than two months during that summer, Cannings, Biven and the apprentice Littlejohn established sixteen new routes in the Daddyhole and Telegraph Hole areas. These included some of the best and hardest in the county, such as *Last Exit to Torquay, Triton, Crinoid, Gargantua* and the serious *Pantagruel*. In July, Littlejohn climbed his first route on the slabs at Long Quarry Point, when he succeeded on *Coup de Grâce*, a line attempted earlier by Hammond. By August, however, attention had switched to the Old Redoubt at Berry Head, where Biven and Littlejohn ascended *Moonraker* in a seven-hour, on-sight epic

---

[1] *This point has been categorically denied by Cannings.*

(originally it started some way to the left of its modern equivalent, although just how far left is still a bone of heated contention). Modern climbers with their Rocks, RPs, Friends, TCUs, Sticht Plates etc, etc, contrast strongly with the following account from Littlejohn:

> "There was lots of loose rock and vegetation; we used two 120′ long #3 nylon cable laid ropes and had 7mm hemp waist bands, no harnesses. Protection was drilled out steel engineering nuts. It was the biggest and most serious crag I'd been on. A serious multi-pitch climb involving route finding and commitment. When we got to the top there was a reception committee, about a dozen or so people waiting, climbers, onlookers and the coastguard with rescue gear. We got a bollocking for not informing the coastguard."
>
> High Mountain Sports May 1992

Cannings was soon in on the action, and with Biven he attempted the line of *Dreadnought*. The attempt was foiled at the top of the hanging groove on the third pitch, and they exited rightwards to produce *Barbican* – still a magnificent achievement. The year closed with a visit from Dorset coasteers John Cleare and Rusty Baillie, who traversed the base of the Old Redoubt to produce the topically named *Magical Mystery Tour*. The following years saw Biven continuing the sea-level traversing craze as he explored every piece of worthwhile coastline in Torbay.

Interest swung to the Long Quarry Point area in 1968. Biven and Littlejohn traversed in to climb *Incubus*, whilst Cannings attacked the bulging arête of the Mitre Buttress to give an excellent technical climb (Cannings declared *The Mitre* to be one of his hardest-ever leads, and few modern E3 leaders would disagree!). In June Littlejohn and Hammond created *Grip Type Thynne* on the vast boiler-plate slabs of Long Quarry Point after a mammoth gardening session, a technique that was fast becoming more and more widespread. This year also saw some quality shorter climbs by Littlejohn: *Acheron* and *Moonshot* at Anstey's Cove, and *Blood* at Berry Head have all become very popular.

To compliment Torbay's big, intimidating lines, Chudleigh held its own as the forcing ground for technical standards. Although most new lines were eliminate in nature, they still produced excellent climbing; Littlejohn's *Penny Lane* and *The Spy* from this period being good examples. However, after twenty-five years of repression it can now be revealed that the major addition of the year was by Southern Sandstone aficionado Jim Collins. After much wrangling (and the wracking of age-fuzzed grey matter) Littlejohn has conceded that Collins did the first ascent of pitch 1 of *Rhinoceros* at Haytor (with the proviso that had Bob Moulton shown him Jim's letter at the time, the confusion could have been sorted a long time ago).

ONE SMALL STEP FOR MANKIND. . .

April 1969 saw Devon's strongest team yet, Littlejohn and Cannings, ready to direct their combined energies on several outstanding lines at the Old Redoubt. *Dreadnought, The Hood* and *The Seventh Circle*, all had their fair share of thrills and spills. The pair were justifiably intimidated by The Hood, to such an extent that Littlejohn jokingly considered press-ganging Joe Brown into leading it. Dreadnought, on the other hand, must have had them seriously considering that they were in over their heads, after a huge chunk of rock fell away (containing the greater part of their belay). Cannings recalled that they were left hanging (nose-to-nose) from a dubious and solitary peg. Surrounded by a tangible aura of hushed menace, they began to tentatively reconstruct their rickety stance. A couple of pegs later they stole a glance at each other and were overtaken by a bout of near hysteria. After welding just about everything they'd got into the rock, Pat commented that. . . "Frank chain-smoked three fags and sprinted up the (5b) pitch." Cannings lightning lead was made with only two runners, probably because that was all he had left! Littlejohn then turned to less well-developed areas, when he climbed the compelling *Iconoclast* and *Neophron* at Babbacombe, and *The Pinch* at Cradle Rock. All three are steep and uncompromising, with The Pinch being dubbed "the most extending and hair-raising lead in the South West".

1969 also saw the emergence of a strong group from the ever-active Exeter University Climbing Club, mainly headed by Ed Grindley. After minor routes on Daddyhole Upper Cliff, Meadfoot Quarry and Anstey's Cove, Grindley directed his attention to the large virgin quarried faces at Long Quarry Point and Berry Head. John Hammond left his mark at Long Quarry Point with his *Gilded Turd*, whilst Grindley grabbed the finer but rarely-climbed *Steppenwolf*. In 1970 Hammond and Littlejohn breached Berry Head Quarry's formidable walls with their on-sight ascent of *Booh-bah Plost*, followed by Biven's *Dust Devil*. Combinations of Littlejohn, Grindley and Hammond then did *Yellow Rurties, Beggar's Banquet* and *Paranoid*, while in 1971 Grindley's activities culminated in the huge girdle-traverse of *Opus Dei*.

Back on the igneous rock there were still lines remaining on the Dewerstone which were to fall to a strong Plymouth group headed by ex-Marine Len Benstead. As well as *Dangler* and *Imperialist*, *Gideon* was freed to give the crag its hardest route to date. Schoolboys Andy *Mac* McFarlane and Deryck Ball also added *Fruitflancase* and *Tarantula*, two quality routes. Littlejohn also directed his talents towards granite. He plucked the worthwhile *Plektron* at Vixen Tor and then added the difficult and serious direct start to *Interrogation* at Haytor.

Ben Rowe on Needle Arête (VD). Photo. David Hillebrandt

Dave Thomas & Nick White on Caveman (E6 6b) Photo. Pete Bull

Ken Palmer on Tuppence (F8a+) Photo. Nick White

MUD ROCK AND HEAVY METAL

The beginning of the Seventies also saw the rise in popularity of two slightly off-beat climbing developments. The first was the creation of virtually all the esoteric sandstone experiences on the South and East Devon Coasts. This small bout of exploration culminated in the ascent of *The Parson* at Dawlish by the irrepressible Keith Darbyshire, a route described by Littlejohn as "the neckiest piece of climbing I've ever chickened out of!!!". The second development was full blown aid climbing over the winter months. *Iron Butterfly* and *The Curse* at the Old Redoubt were climbed by separate teams over several weekends. Little did they know that both would metamorphose in varying degrees into free climbs within two decades.

1972 was a quiet year except for Littlejohn's and Steve Jones's ascent of *The Quaker* at Berry Head. But by 1973 the pace was hotting up again. In February Littlejohn and Darbyshire unearthed the superb *Black Ice*, whilst K.Bentham and C.Gimblett climbed four big lines on the slabs including *Ruby in the Dust*. Darbyshire then deserted his beloved Culm for the tough *Man Bites Dog*, whilst McFarlane and Ball embarked on the magnificent *Rainbow Bridge*.

ALL QUIET ON THE SOUTH DEVON FRONT

The next few years were again quiet due to concentration by the locals on the immense offerings to be had on the North Devon and Cornish Coasts. Minor routes were found on Dartmoor by Iain Peters, Littlejohn and Darbyshire, who weighed in with the more substantial *Widecombe Wall*.

In 1976 and 1977 the honours were mainly shared between Littlejohn and the emerging Pete O'Sullivan. After a flying visit to Bench Tor, where he grabbed *Hostile Witness*, Littlejohn then concentrated on Torbay. *Snakecharmer*, *Fear of Flying* and *The Wake* were followed by the instant classic of *Yardarm* and the inspiring *Zuma*. Littlejohn also began to ascend some of his older routes completely free; *Barbican* and *The Hood* being good examples. O'Sullivan concentrated mainly on the Dewerstone with several aid eliminations as well as the more substantial girdle of *Nibelung*.

The better routes from 1978 were *Feasibility Study* at Vixen Tor and *Energy Crisis* at the Dewerstone, both from O'Sullivan. However, the ever-enthusiastic Brian Wilkinson did discover some worthwhile routes all over Torbay, mainly in the company of Andy Gallagher. The rarely-visited Morwell saw a sporadic burst of development over the winter of 1978/79, with O'Sullivan and his band of merry men being responsible.

Throughout the Sixties and Seventies many limestone first ascents did use the occasional aid point (due to the majority of routes being attempted on-sight). Thus it was not considered to be bettering an ascent by reducing the aid of a route, in deference to the sheer physical effort and exposure involved in hanging on to get the peg placed in the first place. However, by the end of the Seventies the quest for totally free routes was beginning in Devon, with local lad Steve Bell to the fore. He notched up success on *The Mitre* and *Neophron* in Torbay and *Penny Lane, Panga* and *Concerto* at Chudleigh. Bell also visited the Dewerstone to solve *Dragon Song*, one of this much explored crag's 'last great problems', and now a classic. Two lines which didn't scoop up were Nipper Harrison's brutal *Torture* at Vixen Tor and Littlejohn's technical *Rough Diamond* on the North Face of Haytor.

OUT OF THE BLACK AND INTO THE BLUE

Autumn 1979 also saw Londoner Mick Fowler visiting Torbay. A multi-talented climber with an eye for totally outrageous lines, he had his sights firmly set on the inverted and nightmarish world lurking above the Great Cave at the Old Redoubt. His first foray, in the company of the forceful Arnis Strapcans, produced *Depth Charge*, a magnificent-looking route which both before and after the first ascent rebuffed some very strong teams. Fowler sequelled this with his *Lip Trip* across the roof of the cave, in the company of Andy Meyers, so preparing mind and body for the delights waiting below. At the same time on the other side of Torbay, Steve Monks and Ed Hart hung on where Littlejohn couldn't, to complete the soaring groove-line of *Call to Arms* on the Sanctuary Wall. Not to be left out, O'Sullivan's contribution was the spectacular *False Alarms*, on the Old Redoubt.

The early Eighties saw the discovery of several good routes. Local ne'er-do-well Chris *Flinger* Nicholson made his first major contribution to the area with *Buzby* at Telegraph Hole. Yorkshireman Paul Dawson left the serious *Docker's Dilemma* at Vixen Tor, while O'Sullivan made a good find at Luckey Tor (previously entitled Eagle Rock – an outcrop some two miles south-east of this buttress) with the arête of *The Eyrie*. Mick Fowler also contributed to Dartmoor, when he freed *Interrogation Direct* while on the Low Man Girdle.

It was at the Old Redoubt, however, where Fowler was to further enhance his reputation. In 1982 after many attempts (well documented in Extreme Rock), and climbing with Meyers again, Fowler forced the awe-inspiring *Caveman* through the roofs above the Great Cave. Littlejohn also had old scores to settle in the area, and after a free ascent of *Black Death* at Chudleigh in 1982 he returned a year later to Torbay. *Madness*, climbed with Tony Penning, was a characteristically bold on-sight traverse across the Sanctuary Wall. *Blonde Bombshell* at Anstey's Cove was claimed as the area's first 6b pitch, whilst at Telegraph Hole two high-standard slab routes were created with *Blinding Flash* and *Flashdance*. Finally, Littlejohn tidied up an earlier indiscretion, when he freed *The Pinch* at Cradle Rock. Sidmouthian yokel Bruce Woodley (a devout pasty-eater and confirmed cider-soak) was also active in 1983, transforming Berry Head Quarry with four very impressive but rarely-repeated lines, *Burning Bridges*, *Sunset Boulevard*, *Dirt Eater* and *Desparête*. He also freed the popular *Peg's Progress* at Meadfoot Quarry.

1984 saw Nicholson's re-emergence as he grabbed the bold and compelling line of *Devonshire Cream* (after several airborne retreats), along with the technically superb *American Express* and *Dumb Blonde*, all at Anstey's Cove. At Meadfoot he freed Rainy Day to produce the fine *Clotted Cream*, while Woodley added the fierce *Mukdah's Wall* to Daddyhole Main Cliff. Despite all this pumping limestone, Dartmoor still had its enthusiasts. Pete Bull adopted the tried and tested gritstone technique of prior top-roping before donning his crash helmet on *Rough Justice* at Hay-tor. Bruce Woodley's additions of *Scrumpy Special* and *The Fair* at Chinkwell Tor were fairly short but good value, whilst Nick Hancock was sated on the more substantial lines of *Blood Lust* at Low Man and *Two Way Stretch* at Vixen Tor. In 1985, after his ascent of *The Glass Bead Game* on the North Face at Haytor, Nicholson summed up the serious side of granite climbing by observing, "I'm convinced this route is a major contribution to road safety!".

The mid-Eighties saw the publication of the area's first modern guidebook, by Littlejohn and O'Sullivan. Just prior to its publication Woodley completed his campaign at Berry Head Quarry, when he beat Nicholson to *Equipoise*. On Dartmoor, *Limestone Cowboys* Nicholson and newcomer Nick White vied for the first free ascent of Wicker at Foggintor Quarry, to give one of the Moor's shortest but best hard pitches. At Chudleigh, White emerged from Nicholson's shadow and climbed *Slyboots McCall*, *Mortality Crisis* and the fine *White Life*. Dave Cope on the other hand was responsible for the introduction of Devon's first 6c with *Into the Groove*. This used one of the first bolts to be placed on inland limestone (the first being placed by Biven on *Stalactite Variation* in 1962). The new guide revealed a glut of untapped potential in the area, especially for the modern, shorter, gymnastic style of 'voie'. Although for those who craved it, there was still plenty of scope for high adventure as well.

THE POST-GUIDE RUSH

1986 began quietly save for a clutch of routes at Chudleigh's Black Crag by Exeter-based climbers. *Gorillability* by Yorkshireman Kit Wilkinson and White's *Golden Dive* have tempted a few visits to the lost world across the valley. In May, Bristol-based Martin Crocker pointed the way to future developments with his ascent of *Just Revenge* at Anstey's Cove. At the time this was the hardest route in the Shire. Still at the seaside, Nicholson and White made interesting contributions, the former with the exciting *Lumpy Universe*, whilst White unearthed the funky *Renegade* at Long Quarry Point, a route which matches *Black Ice* for quality. Finally on limestone, the remote Torbryan Quarry was re-appraised by Andy Turner, the result being the pumpy *Mayday*. Meanwhile, a strong group of Plymouth-based climbers were cutting their teeth on the remaining lines at the Dewerstone, and producing a few excellent climbs on Dartmoor. Ken Palmer produced the committing *Full Moon* and *Limbo Dancer* at Hound Tor, but they probably receive far more ascents than his outstanding *Angel of Mercy* at Vixen Tor. This event partially eclipsed Andy Grieve's ascent of the equally bold *Sly*.

By 1989 there were more active and able climbers than before in the area – White in particular being the region's first full time climber! At Chudleigh several more hard test-pieces were established including *Seventh Seal*, *Schweinhund* and the bold *Whoremoans* from White. Robbie Warke also got a look-in here, when he frightened himself up *Orpheus* and *Harvestman*. Down at Torbay there were rumblings under the roofs at Durl Head, where the Plymouth Thug Club under the guidance of Ken Palmer and Andy Grieve put up *Star Trekking*, *Foaming at the Mouth* and *A Drop in the Ocean*. The same pair plus Nick Hancock also began to realise the potential of the inland quarries. At Torbryan the plum lines were Palmer's *Little White Lie* and *Thread Flintstone*, whilst over at Hazard Quarry Grieve produced the short but ever-so-butch *Garth*, imaginatively using a tied-off and hand-placed log to protect his ascent.

OF MICE, BOLTS AND MEN

White's energies, however, were being concentrated on the Anstey's/Long Quarry Point area. The wall right of *Osram* was a major challenge, which several doubting Thomases had pronounced unclimbable. After warming up on *Odysseus or Bust*, the finer *Up the Styx Without a Paddle* was produced using 'once only' peg placements. After careful consideration a bolt was placed in the smooth right-hand section of the wall and White pulled out all the stops to create a Devonian technical masterpiece in *Shadow Beast*. The final major route of the year was the free ascent of the neck-craning *Lynch*, a rare aid route of Littlejohn's which he pronounced would go free at E2 5b (or so the story goes!). These routes marked the beginning of the Cove's rise to fame as Devon's most popular, quality-laden venue. However, other activists continued to find routes which although not as hard still had individual merit, one example being Warke's fine *Archtemptress* at London Bridge.

By spring 1988 the grossly overhanging walls at Anstey's Cove were the scene of much abseiling, cleaning, gearing, practising and swearing etc., all of which makes modern climbing the vibrant, spontaneous thing it is. In March, White administered some 'gratuitous violence' (the original name for *Empire of the Sun*) to the wall left of Just Revenge. This has established itself as one of the mid-grade(!) classics of the area. Shortly afterwards Crocker reappeared to establish the sensational *Free the Spirit*, but resorted to drilled stainless pegs for protection. Viewed objectively, Crocker's actions would seem well-intentioned, as he wanted to avoid subsequent aspirants pumping out while facing falls onto rusting stubs of metal (as with other routes on this wall). However, it does seem obvious that in the rush for new routes, the newly-emerging ethic of no bolts on natural sea cliffs was pushed aside. Perhaps the final word on what became an unsavoury affair lies with Dave Thomas, who removed the offending ironmongery before his ascent in January 1989. Crocker then went on to produce the dynamic *The Mightier*, which along with White's *How the Mighty Fall* has proved very popular.

All this excitement stirred things up to the point where original Torbay pioneer Pat Littlejohn decided to pay a long overdue visit. Climbing with White, the *Call of the Wild* lured him up the overhanging wall beneath the first pitch of Madness, creating a typically strenuous and necky outing. White then took over for *False Gods* and returned later for *Up in Arms*. Other locals got in on the act at the Cove with Pete Bull cranking out *Nebulous Crab* and *Shooting Stars*, and Warke finding his *Supernatural Anaesthetist*. On the Blonde Bombshell wall Northumbrian, Dave Turnbull, climbed the obvious overhung groove to give *The Shroud*, while White extended an earlier Nicholson route to give *More Steam, Bigger Women*. In November two more desperates were added by White in the shape of *Big Bird* at Chudleigh and the hugely technical *La Crème*, a long term bolted project to the right of Devonshire Cream. The tail end of the year also saw the rediscovery of the Churston Quarries by White and Bull, and under a veil of secrecy they uncovered an interesting batch of routes, the best being *Supercalorific* and *No Holds Barred*.

BACK TO BASICS
Action began early in 1989 at the Old Redoubt, where Frank Ramsey and White produced *Graf Spee* and *Arc Royale* respectively on the remote Bismark Wall. The major events, however, were the long awaited second ascent of Caveman by White and Thomas, followed by *Man O'War*, a free version of the first half of Iron Butterfly. At the same time Andy Grieve stumbled upon the superb *Mental Block*, perhaps the finest gem to be unearthed in the South Hams. In early spring Bull struck back for igneous enthusiasts with some tenacious attacks on the wall right of Suspension Flake at Hound Tor. His prize was the masochistically 'techo' *Toltec Two Step*. Somewhat predictably, however, it was the Anstey's Cove area that was grabbing the limelight by summer-time. Thomas set about the mind-gnumbing(sic) crack right of Call of the Wild to give *Wildebeest*. Then he and White blitzed the Empire of the Sun wall with *Sun of Righteousness*, *Might & Main*, *Rise'n Shine* and the *Avenged*

finish to Just Revenge. However, these heavyweights were eclipsed for quality by *The Cider Soak*, White's major prize of the year. Pictures of this route and others in the national climbing press tempted large numbers of climbers to what was fast becoming the South West's prime sports climbing hotspot, many not just for the climbing but for the amazing 'Waffle Supremes' served at Babbacombe's sorely-missed 'Parlour'. Back on the rock, Thomas kept up his calorie-count with a slightly harder companion to Wildebeest in the shape of *Supermousse*.

The fun continued with the summer re-opening of the Old Redoubt, where White completed his *Earth Sea Trilogy* (the first parts of which took him to Lundy and the North Devon Coast). Thomas completed a counter-diagonal to Lip Trip called *The New Stone Age*, and Crispin Waddy stepped in to make an audacious solo of Dreadnought as well as free soloing the aid pitch on *Rainbow Bridge*. Thomas then proceeded to overshadow most of the major events in British climbing that year, when he soloed the crux pitches of Caveman, whilst incorporating them into a new route, *Terra Cotta*, a mere six months since the second ascent. Churston still had a few impressive lines, of which Bull's *Warpath* and Thomas's *A Moment Spent Talking* stand out. Meanwhile White's *Roar Like Sushi* gave the locals something to chew on while he left the area for sunnier antipodean climes.

THE GRADE CRUSADE

By Spring 1990, Thomas was making regular trips to what was becoming his own private playground, the Sanctuary Wall. He toasted his next success with a *Flaming Drambuie*, added a direct finish and promptly soloed it. Not content with this, Thomas then added *Courvoisier*, which encroached onto the leaning wall left of Free the Spirit. These exploits brought a welcome breath of fresh air to the new route scene before the biggest developments yet seen on Devonian rock. Ken Palmer established his magnum opus sport route, *Tuppence*, on the leaning Ferocity Wall, a testament to a naturally gifted climber. Whilst at the Old Redoubt, North Wales-based Steve Mayers freed the entire aid route of Iron Butterfly, renaming it *Cocoon* and grading it E8 6c (or the very odd grade of F8a – he was born and raised in Plymouth!), a feat which one local wag had deemed impossible. Mayers also made some important second ascents of the Thomas/Littlejohn Sanctuary Wall horrors.

Torbay was again the focus of activity in 1991, when Palmer sequelled Tuppence with the harder and finer *A Fisherman's Tale* to give the area its second E8. The White-wag returned from his Australian sabbatical to bolt and climb a physical line through the cave in Long Quarry's Point, *Losing My Religion*. He also stamped his imprint on the crack through the roof above Blonde Bombshell to give *Blazing Apostles*. October saw Palmer again grabbing a fine route; the obvious beckoning line of flakes right of Free the Spirit gave *Caribbean Blue*.

The Sanctuary Wall again gripped its addicts in 1992. White climbed two variations on Call of the Wild, *Kill Your Idol* and *Call of Nature*, while Crocker enthused his way up the rickety wall to its left. Palmer bounced in with trying bunny-hops on the entertaining *Gus Honeybun* right of False Gods. Hawiian Rob McCloud was also active, repeating some of the harder climbs in addition to taking an *Amoebic Plunge* up the right arête of Call to Arms. As the eleventh hour struck, teenager Mark Campbell (Devon's own 'wunderkind') forced another bolt route in the Long Quarry Point cave, *Waiting for Charlie*.

EPILOGUE
Devon now sees plenty of visitors and due to its unique mixture of crags there is something for everybody. Where else in Britain can you enjoy guano-enhanced adventure before lunch, relaxed clip-routes aprés-midi and an evening's skin-rasping, granite bouldering session? No longer a dreamy backwater, Devon has routes of character and difficulty to compare with any outcrop/sea cliff area in the country. Indeed, at the time of writing, most of the hardest climbs remain unrepeated, though not through any lack of effort! There is still scope for the odd new-route, for those with the ability and vision to realise them. After all, the first pitch of The Curse awaits .

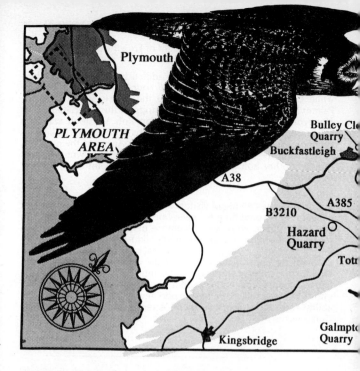

INLAND LIMESTONE

"I be aveared o'they dirty Atom bombs!
One o'these dayz uz'll get 'urtled into maternity!"

Longer than a long time ago (some people refer to it as the Neolithic era), people in Devon used to grunt at each other. This was not your usual grunting. Even now (as then) the phonetics and indeed syntax of your average Devonian are at a far remove from the clipped processes of received pronunciation, or Telephone English *az they'd 'ave it down 'ere*. For when pressed Devonians will use this diluvian-accent on the phone for *communikatin' with 'e furrineerz* (people outside their village). They also have a penchant for malapropism. For instance if you were to attend a Devonian CND rally, you might overhear the above epiphet; or in a Reg(al)-style logic on death. . . *"Our Tom iz bein' created over Execetor crematorium"*. While *up th' eel* doesn't refer to one of the many

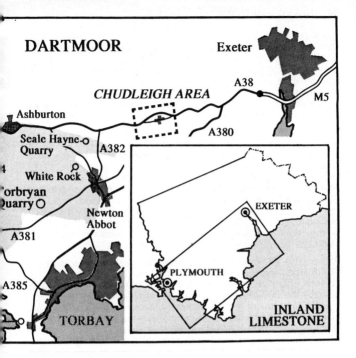

nefarious and deviant sexual practices that occur within the Shire, but to the fact that *it* (whatever *it* maybe) resides upon an elevated portion of the earth's surface, somewhat lower than a mountain.

"So where is all this leading?", I hear you asking. *Well if you be to Deb'n, then 'e be wontin' to know 'ow to interrupt what the nativz be tellin' 'e* (especially the climbers).

A typical climbing day begins with the common dilemma of *where be gwain?* (which crag shall we visit today?). A common factor dictating the choice (of crag) is the weather, a topic which Devonians love to talk about. This affectation would appear to link climbers the world over to the Great British tradition of. . . when lost for words, discuss the arbitrary ramifications of the latest meteorological phenomena. Thus if it were *blowing a Hoolie* (gale force winds), the subsequent discussion might revolve around the relative pros and cons of a wet-suited and be-flippered foray along one of the numerous sea-level traverses. However, *a hoolie-shemoolie* (a cross between high winds and a thunderflash; ie. a veritable hurricane) means one thing, and one thing only. It is the day for fearless members of the Exeter University Mountaineering Club to attempt The Parson.

Another frequently heard phrase down here is the choice expression of *mazed as a doug* (as mad as a dog), meaning a trifle unhinged. It often accompanies tales of derring-do, and can be qualified by *zawn-head*. One overzealous *bukker* was so mazed, that his on-route philosophy revolved solely around climbing in a state of great optimistic wobble. The theory being that no matter how pumped you were, how bad the gear was, or indeed how great the run-out, nothing could be as bad as the state you were already in (QED: things could only get better!).

Yer tiz, is a terse idiom oft heard in conjunction with the above scenario, its meaning encompasses a wide variety of emotions (de)ranging from the sublime – this is it we're all gunna die; to the ridiculous – thank goodness we've found the route; gear; a rest. Once the route has been brought to heel, it is common etiquette to congratulate each other with *yeah bukker yeah*, which expresses not only a sense of relief at still being alive, but incorporates a certain *joie de vivre* that can be summed up by the word *splendid*; or the Woodleyesque idiom *that was a jolly good wheeze* (which also begs the question are you game for another?).

A *Cornish Nasty* can refer to a gristle-filled pasty, or an unpleasant visitor from Kernow. However, it comes into its own when used in reference to a particularly loose or hard climb west of the Tamar (usually the former case, unheard of in the latter). Sport climbers come in for similarly rough treatment, being referred to as *Racing Snakes*. This phrase has been somewhat corrupted from its original meaning of twitchy adolescent climbers who are anorexic. The idiom has also been used with reference to anything from de-trousering, to speaking quickly and with a forked-tongue. If further modified by the addition of *what be telling uv?* (I don't believe a word of it, are you being economical with the truth?), then doubt is being cast over your latest red-point, probably because you weren't wearing wellington boots at the time.

Thus armed with the correct phraseology, you can now mingle with the natives, hopefully escaping the xenophobia that has kept inland Devon such a dreamy backwater-meadow.

CHUDLEIGH AREA

The rustic village of Chudleigh was first settled by Anglo-saxon farmers. The area was densely forested, hence the village name which stems from the Saxon *Ciedda* (a personal name) and *Leah* (which means either wood, or clearing). It lies 10 miles ╱SW of Exeter, happily by-passed by the A38 dual carriageway to Plymouth. The village inhabits a sleepy hollow at the foot of the Haldon Hills.

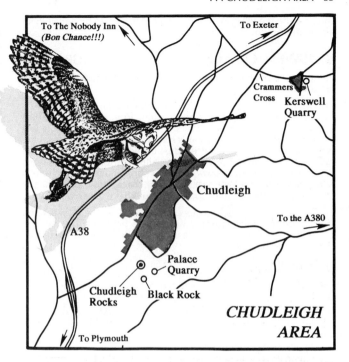

These have been a sanctuary for hermits and eccentrics down through the ages. In particular, *Lawrence Tower* still plays host to perhaps the most bizarre of these. For a small fee the brothers who inhabit the folly will give you a moody tour of the tower's confines, culminating in a atmospheric soliloquy about the Great Hall (which is approximately 20' by 20'). Due N ↑ of the village is perhaps the last surviving *Redemptoristine Convent*. In severe counterpoint to this, the village has four dens of iniquity (ie. pubs), the relative merits of which I shall leave for you to discover. However, the *Wheel Craft Centre* has a splendid tearoom.

There are two exits from the A38 to Chudleigh (N ↑ and S ↓). The access notes to each crag specify which exit to take, although if you are prepared to muddle through, then as long as the exit sign says Chudleigh, you'll find your respective destination. (On a more flippant note, the record for freewheeling from the top of Tele-graph Hill down into Chudleigh, is held by Chris Gibson and his Triumph Herald. He managed to get to the last telegraph pole on the L before the village limits. The record has yet to be equaled, let alone on-sighted.

KERSWELL QUARRY   GR 884 807

Permission to climb here should be sought from Mr Shorland, who lives at Culver House, Chudleigh.

Kerswell lies NE ↗ of Chudleigh, just off the B3344, which is the N ↑ turn-off for the village. When approaching from this direction, turn L at the first crossroads (Crammers Cross). The crossroads is just before an inn, the *Highwayman's Haunt*, and about a mile from the A38. Follow the lane until it divides, taking the LH fork. Carefully park the car on the verge opposite a walled copse. A dirt track leads across the S ↓ toe of the wood. Follow this for a few yards, until a faint track leads off LWs past a derelict shack. After about 200yds the amphitheatre becomes apparent through the dense woodland.

The Quarry comprises of a steep calcite wall on the R, separated from a further quarried wall on the L by a broad earth gully. The first route starts on the RH side of the calcite wall. The routes are described from R to L.

1   Weasel the Wizard *(WW)*   60'   E1 5a   †
A steep route on big holds throughout, which helps to compensate for the lack of gear. Start at the foot of a narrow L/R sloping slab (on the RH side of the calcite wall). Follow this for a few feet to a large hole, then trend up RWs to a deep slot. Climb up LWs to gain, then climb a L/R slanting groove. Exit this LWs where it becomes OHung. Finish direct to a BB.   (1991)

2   Songs from the Wood *(SW)*   70'   E3 6a   †
Start beneath a V-shaped OH 10yds L of *WW*. Climb up to the OH, then move L beneath it until a rounded hold can be reached above it. Pull over to gain a slanting break. Follow the calcite groove above, then step L onto a red flake. Gain the large hole above, from where more pockets lead to a BB up on the L.   (1991)

3   Woodland Bop   70'   E4 6a   †
Start further up the slope L of *SW*. Follow the obvious L/R ramp-line, passing a BR & TR, to the belay of *WW*.   (1991)

CHUDLEIGH ROCKS   GR 864 788

Approach and Access
The crag is best approached by taking the S ↓ exit for Chudleigh. Follow the signs back into Chudleigh for about 600yds (passing the Rock House Garden Centre on the R) to a R turn, which leads down past the Police Station to limited parking space where the road widens adjacent to the entrance to Palace Quarry. A footpath leads

off from a wrought-iron kissing gate and follows a wall which contours the hillside. At one point the path splits, take the upper track, which leads to a narrow neck of land where the first bits of rock appear (the North Face). Continue along the main path a little further, to be greeted with the sight of the upper portion of Gagool Buttress.

Situation and Character
Unfairly labeled as the Stoney Middleton of the South West, this vastly superior crag has been popular with both locals and itinerant *furrineerz* (no doubt on their way to the vastly inferior crags in distant Cornwall). Composed of sound, highly-weathered and pocketed Devonian limestone, Chudleigh gives good quality routes of all grades up to E6 which, for the most part, are also generously protected.

SOUTH FACE

The South Face constitutes the main crag (and obviously it's S ↓ facing). It is sheltered from the prevailing winds and, due to the rainshadow cast by Dartmoor, it is usually dry (ie. it is a good wet weather alternative, if nothing else).

To the L of the descent path is an isolated bluff of rock used by the local outdoor centre for top-roping and abseiling. There are four recorded routes on this face, **Eeny** (D), **Meeny** (D), **Miney** (D), and **Mo** (D) – (all c.1960s). A very steep path skirts the RH toe of the wall to gain the taller valley side of the buttress. The following three routes are described from R to L, as are the remaining routes on the South Face.

1   Jim's Folly   30'   S
Climb the groove on the far RH side of the wall.   (c.1960s)

2   Chainsaw Massacre *(CM)*   30'   HVS 5b
Start 10' L of Jim's Folly, beneath an OHing groove. Climb this direct to a PR & finish in the same line.   (1990)

3   One Foot in the Grave   30'   HS 4a
Climb a rib on the wall L of *CM*. Climb to & gain an obvious groove in the rib, which is followed throughout.   (c.1970s)

GAGOOL BUTTRESS
The main path continues down (R of the top-roping wall) to Gagool Buttress, the RH side of which contains the OHung mouth of Pixies' Hole, & the infamous Chudleigh Overhang.

4   Albatross   50'   E1 5b
Not a route for ancient mariners or the superstitious. Start 5yds R of the metal grill across the cave of Pixies' Hole, at the apex of an earth ramp. Climb up to an obvious knobbly conglomerate hold, then trend up LWs to a capping OH (PR). Flurry direct over this to a spacious ledge & tree belay.   (1990)

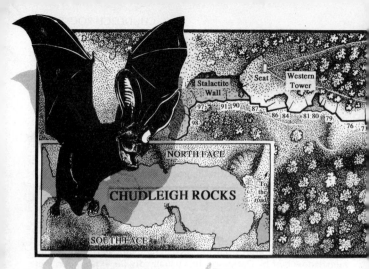

5 Farewell to Arms *(FTA)* 95' E2 5c,5b,4c

An intimidating proposition for the grade. Start at a thin OHing crack 10' L of the metal grill across the entrance to Pixies' Hole.

1 40' Climb the crack past a slanting borehole strike (on the L) & traverse LWs along a sloping shelf to a PR at its LH end. Pull LWs around the bulge to join a wide crack. Belay in the recess above.

2 25' Traverse RWs to a shallow cave & pull over the bulge into a short groove. Climb this to gain a N&PB at the base of a large flake.

3 30' (Overgrown). Layback up the flake, then climb the wall above, via a dubious flake. Finish R of a large block.   (1979)

6 Big Bird 60' E5 6b   ★★

Climb a boulder problem arête (L of the start of *FTA*) to gain the LH end of the slanting borehole strike. Thug through the bulge RWs to join *FTA* at the PR. Climb the slim groove above to another PR, then traverse R to gain & climb a hanging groove to the capping OH (PR). Launch up LWs to a good hold & a further PR, where frustrating moves lead to a standing position on the lip of the OH. Easy climbing leads to the second belay of *FTA*.   (1988)

Variation finish E4 6a From the second PR, continue up the smooth wall above to a further PR. Climb direct over the bulge above the PR to finish at Big Bird's N&PB.   (1993)

7 Seventh Seal *(SS)* 40' E5 6b   ★ †

This climbs the headwall L of Big Bird's belay. From the stance trend LWs to a blind flake *(poor wires)*. Layback the flake & make a desperate move off this (up LWs) to some poor holds & a PR. Unrelenting climbing leads direct up the wall to a sloping ledge (& a large block). Finish direct.   (1987)

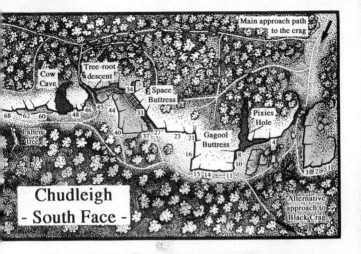

Map illustration labeled with various climbing locations and numbered routes.

Main approach path to the crag

Cow Cave

Tree-root descent

Space Buttress

Pixies Hole

34

45 46 44

31

68 62 60 48

40

37 27 23 21

16

Gagool Buttress

8
10

15 14 11

Fallen tree

4

3 2 1

Alternative approach to Black Crag

Chudleigh
- South Face -

8   Chudleigh Overhang *(CO)*   80'   VS 5a,4c   ★★
A good route *(for onlookers with a penchant for the bloody spec-tacle of the Roman Circus)*, from which many courageous leaders have bitten the dust.
1   40'   Climb the wide crack 7yds L of the grilled cave entrance. Step R at the capping OH to a large foothold, from where fierce laybacking around the OHing crack gains a slab. Traverse LWs to a large ledge & PBs.
2   40'   Step up & traverse RWs along a line of ledges (passing under the flake belay of *FTA*), to gain a short crack leading to a shelf. Climb the short steep wall above to the top.   (1960)

9   Phoenix on Fire   40'   E4 6b
Powerfully intricate. A boulder-problem start, just L of the wide crack of *CO*, leads to an OH & a PR. Brutal moves through the OH lead, past another PR, to a desperate fumble on the lip. Finish LWs to belay as for *CO*.   (1984)

10   Dripdry   80'   E4 6b,6b   ★★
Dynamically strenuous. Begin at the base of a pegged-out & highly polished crack 10' L of *CO*.
1   40'   Struggle up the polished crack to an OH & TR. Lunge up R & then LWs to a second TR, from where more testing moves lead to the large ledge & PBs of *CO*.
2   40'   Trend up RWs above the stance to the base of a vague white groove (L of the flake on *SS* & just R of pitch 2 of Gagool), passing 2PRs on the way. Climb the groove direct to another PR. Continue in the same line to the top.   (1963/82/85)

11   Logic   40'   E1 5a
Just L of the arête beyond Dripdry is a shallow groove. Climb the groove to a PR & trend up RWs (via a hidden one-finger pocket). Follow the rounded arête to the large belay ledge of *CO*.   (1965)
Variation start E1 5c/6a Known as **Dream On**. Climb the RH side of the arête (bold). The grade is dependant on the height at which you wimp-out into Logic.   (1971)

12   Gagool   90'   E1 5b,5a   ★
An excellent route that breaches the smooth face beyond the arête L of Dripdry. Start as for Logic.
1   50'   Climb the shallow groove to the PR, then traverse LWs for 10' to gain & follow a thin crack until it peters out. Trend RWs to the wide belay ledge of *CO*.
2   40'   Step up LWs onto a large block, then trend diagonally RWs to gain a hanging shallow groove. Climb the groove awkwardly to reach easier ground on the L. Follow this to the top.   (1965)

13   Gagool Direct *(GD)*   50'   E2 5c
A good fingery pitch up the centre of the wall. Start 5' to the L of Gagool, at the base of a shallow corner. Climb direct up the wall using small pockets to join & finish up the thin crack of Gagool (to gain *CO*'s belay ledge).   (1979)

14   Sly Boots McCall   60'   E4 6b   ★★
The blank face L of *GD*. Climb direct to the first of 2PRs. Step L, then attempt to gain a slim blind flake just L of the second PR. Continue in the same line to the PBs of *COPS*.   (1984)
Variation 50' E4 6a Climb to the first PR & step up R to the crack of Gagool. Reverse Gagool to the middle of its traverse, then scale the wall above direct.   (1984)

15   Combined Ops *(COPS)*   110'   E2 5b,4a   ★★
This climbs the L arête of the Gagool wall, & gives a fine sustained pitch. Start just R of the arête.
1   70'   Gain the arête by a rising LWs traverse. Follow the arête for 20' (passing a PR), then swing up L into a white scoop. Hard moves lead back RWs around the arête, to a steep slab with an obvious undercut in the bulge above. A further steep move leads to easier ground & PBs above a ledge.
2   40'   Take a diagonal line RWs (over blocks) until beneath a double bulge. Make exposed moves over these, using a hidden hold, & continue more easily to the top.   (1962)

Around the corner lies an impressive bay of rock containing the strikingly repulsive gash of Sarcophagus, flanked on either side by steep walls.

16   Combat   100'   E3 5c   ★★★
A superb route, with a real sting in the tail!
1   70'   Start 10' L of the arête of *COPS*, beneath a shallow recess. Gain the recess & make bold moves up RWs to a projecting flake on

the arête. Hand-traverse this to a juncture with *COPS*. Move up L into the white scoop, then continue LWs to a slanting niche. Climb out of the top of this with difficulty, past a TR, & continue direct to the belay of *COPS*.
2   30'   Either do pitch 2 of *COPS*; or abseil off.   (1971)

17   Tendonitis   70'   E4 6a   *
A more direct version of Combat. From the LH end of Combat's flake climb direct up a shallow groove, passing a PR, to join & finish up Combat at the slanting niche.   (1984)

18   Obstreperous   70'   E6 6c   †
A sparsely protected free version of an old A2 (of the same name), with some eliminate-style climbing tacked onto the top. Start as for Combat, but swing up L into some pegged-out pockets L of the groove of Tendonitis. Follow these then move diagonally LWs to gain a large flat hold on *BTS*. Climb the blank-looking bulge & wall directly above the flat hold, to finish at *COPS*' belay *(abseil inspection advisable)*.   (1966/91)

19   Oesophagus   100'   E1 5b,-   **
A classic jamming crack which is both strenuous & technical.
1   85'   Steep climbing gains the obvious hand-jamming crack, which is followed to a niche at 50'. Step up RWs & climb a pair of cracks to good holds which lead to the stance of *COPS*.
2   15'   Scramble off LWs to finish, or abseil off.   (1962)

20   Before the Storm *(BTS)*   70'   E3 5c
A bold & committing pitch. Start between Sarcophagus & Oesophagus. Climb directly to the crack of Oesophagus, then move up & slightly R to large flat hold in the middle of the wall. Step R into Combat to finish.   (1984)

21   Sarcophagus   110'   VS 4a,4b,-   **
This is a route you won't forget in a hurry *(especially if you have a hangover)*.
1   30'   Struggle up the limb-swallowing cracks, formed by the large obvious corner, to a cave stance.
2   50'   Technical wriggling up the chimney leads to a large OH. Traverse LWs (beneath the OH) for 10' along a smooth exposed slab which leads to a short corner & NB.
3   30'   Finish up the corner above & belay to a stout oak tree; or, continue up an earthy gully & belay at the top.   (1960)
Variation 2a 50'   VS 4a Climb the chimney to the large OH. Step R & climb a shallow chimney. Exit L by traversing along a horizontal fault to the second stance.   (1960)

22   Concerto   110'   E3 5c,-   *
Strenuous & exposed climbing through the roofs L of pitch 2 of Sarcophagus. Start as for Sarcophagus.
1   80'   After 15' of thrutching up the initial cracks move onto the L wall. This leads to a block. Traverse L for a few feet, then climb

direct to a detached-looking block above the first OH. Pull past another OH & continue via a thin crack to the second stance of Sarcophagus.
2   30'   As for Sarcophagus *(pitch 3)*.   (1966/79)

23   Into the Groove   40'   E6 6c
A ballsy &, since the ethical demise of its bolt, virtually redundant proposition. Ascend the blank-looking wall 10' L of Sarcophagus, on frugal holds, to a crisp edge (sky-hook runner!). Lunge RWs to gain & climb the slight groove to the first belay of *WE*.   (1985/91)

24   White Edge *(WE)*   120'   E1 5b,5a,5a
Start 20' L of Sarcophagus, just L of a tree stump.
1   35'   Climb a short difficult rib to a ledge. Move R onto the arête & make a hard move to reach a reasonable hold & 2PRs. Pull over the bulge, regain your composure, then climb the slab above direct to a cramped stance & N&PB.
2   65'   Traverse L below the OH to the edge of the slab, PR. Move up with difficulty to easy rock leading to the stance of *GM*.
3   20'   Climb the OHing rock directly behind the stance.   (1966)

25   White Edge – Concerto   110'   E3 5c   ★★
An excellent combination. Climb pitch 1 of *WE* to join Concerto below its first OH (optional stance). Continue up the remainder of pitch 1 of Concerto, then finish up its second pitch.   (1984)

26   Army Dreamers *(AD)*   90'   E2 5c,5b   †
Eliminate style climbing between *WE* & *GM*.
1   40'   Start up the boulder-problem rib of *WE*, then continue up the steep R\L leaning groove, past 2PRs. At the apex of the groove follow a scoop RWs (above the large OH) to the first stance of *WE*.
2   50'   Climb direct through the bulge above the belay to a vague groove. Climb this & exit RWs to finish.   (1986)

There is a large OH above the R\L leaning groove of **AD** *with 2BRs in it. These give the line of* **Uncertain Smile** *E5 6c (1994). To the left of* **WE** *&* **AD** *is the mouth of a steep rocky gully, the base of which contains a small, barred cave. The gully leads up to Space Buttress.*

27   Green Mantle *(GM)*   110'   D
A good route for beginners; a bit earthy & vegetated but great fun for all those budding Greenies out there. Start just R of the small, barred cave.
1   80'   Climb the obvious crack for 15', then traverse RWs & ascend a staircase to an environmentally sound ledge. Continue to another ledge of botanical delights & belay.
2   30'   Climb the groove L of the stance, via an awkward start, to gain the top.   (1964)
Variation 1a 80' HS 4b Start 10' R of the *GM*. Climb a short corner to a ledge. From its RH side climb the steep slab past 2PRs (in common with *AD*), to join & then finish up *GM*.   (1964)

28   Tar Baby   90'   S 4a
A prominent crack & corner rising directly from the start of *GM*.
Climb *GM* to its traverse-line, step up L & then make an awkward
mantel into the groove. Climb to a ledge & finish up the broken
corner above to gain the finish.   (1966)

*The following two routes lie above the initial rock step containing
the barred cave, at the start of the rocky gully.*

29   Brer Fox   60'   S 4a
Start off the lowest portion of the tree lying in the earthy gully.
Traverse diagonally RWs on a line of flakes & move around onto a
steepish wall. Climb this to a tree, then scramble through the spiky
flora to the top.   (1961)

30   Brer Rabbit   60'   HS 4a
Follows the groove above the start of Brer Fox. Start as for that
route, then after 8' move L to a ledge beneath the groove. Follow
this to an easy staircase & the top.   (1961)

SPACE BUTTRESS
This lies atop the rocky gully above the barred cave at the start to
GM. It is a remarkably steep piece of rock offering a clutch of
cosmic pitches. Its LH side is seemingly held in place by a classic
example of *rusting modernist environmentalism*. However, the bats
have seen the lighter side of their incarceration, and appear in
convict garb for their twilight sojourns.

31   Saturn Five *(SF)*   50'   E2 5b   ★
Strenuous. Start 10' R of the cave entrance, below a pocket/thread
15' up. Boldly boulder up to the pocket, & *blast-off* up the OHing
crack above (2PRs). Move L onto dodgy rock to finish.   (1979)

32   Major Tom *(MT)*   40'   E2 6a   ★★
A minor classic which tackles the bulge L of *SF*. Start on top of the
cage. Step up R to a short flake/crack leading to the OH (PR).
Traverse R, via a hard move, to good buckets which take you out
into space (satellite PR). *Lay one on* for the next hold up L, & set the
controls for the heart of the sun.   (1984)

*At the time of writing there is a PR & in-situ wire in the OH above
the short flake/crack on* **MT**. *This would appear to be an unclaimed
direct variation of that route.*

33   Squirrel   60'   HS 4a   ★
A L/R diagonal traverse which covers some awesome terrain for the
grade. Start on top of the cage. Step onto the wall & follow the
obvious traverse-line RWs for 15', then move around the RH arête
of the buttress & continue up to an OH. Bypass this on its RH side,
then climb direct up the wall above to finish.   (1961)

34   Ground Control *(GC)*   40'   E2 5c
A surprisingly independent line up the wall L of *MT*. From the top

of the cage trend up L for 10' to a large ledge. Make committing moves back up RWs to a PR (missing, presumed lost in space) & sharp jugs just over the OH. The remainder of the wall is climbed on generous holds to the top.   (1985)

35   Devil's Elbow   50'   VS 4b
A pokey route. Follow GC to the large ledge & continue up to a tree. Traverse RWs across the wall above the OHs to a small tree, then finish at the same point as GC.   (1965)

36   Space Odyssey   75'   E3 5c (Ha!)
An inter-stellar girdle of the Space Buttress OHs (from L to R). Climb GC to the sharp jugs just above the OH & follow the break RWs, joining MT at its second PR. Descend for a few feet, by a series of hard moves RWs, gaining the relative sanctuary of SF & a PR. Space-walk a further 10' RWs, then finish over the OH above, at its widest point.   (1985)

Further L from the barred cave entrance (at the base of the rocky gully) is a steep buttress with a striking OH at two-thirds height.

37   White Rasta   50'   E2 6a
Start on the RH side of the buttress. Climb the arête to a ledge, then continue up the arête before moving L (PR) to tackle the steep groove/bulge & the wall above.   (1987)

38   Schweinhund   50'   E4 6c   ★
Climb the wall & OH between White Rasta & the obvious roof crack of PMF passing a dubious hidden PR & a good TR that protects the crux. Only masochists need apply.   (1987)

39   Pigs Might Fly (PMF)   40'   E3 5c   ★★
. . .and you've about as much chance of flashing this route. Climb up the wall leading to the OH, then using the obvious (but devious) crack, gain the steep slab above.   (1983)

40   Christmas Corner (CC)   50'   VS 4b
Start R of the lowest part of the wall, below a large slanting groove. Climb the groove to the capping OH. Skirt this on the L, then continue easily to the top.   (1966)

41   Biko   40'   E2 5c
A one-move-wonder. Follow CC to the OH, then pull straight through this to join up with CC again.   (1984)

L of CC there is a highly polished wall, with a number of delicate delights.

42   Salome   50'   S 4a   ★
A lascivious climb, starting on easy slabs at the lowest part of the wall. Follow these LWs around the rib from CC, then climb the obvious ramp to a small ledge. Don't lose your head on the final steep section, which is harder than it looks (the crack on the R proves useful).   (c.1960s)

43   Seventh Veil   40′   VS 4c
An interesting pitch. Start at the tree stump L of Salome. Step up R to a small perch. *Divested of veils*, step L, then climb naked & alone up the steep smooth wall to the top.   (c.1960s)

44   Seventh Veil Direct   40′   E1 5a   ★
Start L of the tree stump. Boldly climb the wall with scant (that means no) protection. *Double entendres* aside, things can get a little hairy from the middle upwards!   (c.1960s)

45   Hot Ice   25′   E4 6a   ★★
A mini classic; firmly in the honorary grit mould. This energetically frightening *Russian Routlette* takes the short striking arête to the L of the Salome wall *(jitter ye not!!!)*.   (1978)

COW CAVE AREA
About 10yds L of Hot Ice is the Tree Route Descent, & just L of this is a short wall, apparently with two VSs on it! These go by the names of **Bang** & **Monty Python's Flying Circus** *(only worthwhile if you happen to be a half-pint version of Alan Ladd or Tom Cruise)*. The next route takes the thin mean crack, just R of a treacherously wide one, where the wall gains a respectable height.

46   T.N.T.   30′   HVS 5a
Climb the thin crack, via a perplexing series of off-balance moves, which leads to a bold finish.   (c.1970s)

47   Guy Fawkes Crack *(GFC)*   40′   VS 4c
This short, wide crack gives an interesting problem if off-width climbing is your main vice.   (1960)

To the L is a further speleological phenomenon in the shape of Cow Cave, the mouth of which is breached on the R by the off-set grooves of Smoke Gets in Your Eyes & on the L by the classic graunch of Loot. The Tree Root Descent provides a convenient way down from this part of the crag.

48   Smoke Gets in Your Eyes *(SGIYE)*   60′   E3 6a   ★★
Provides a frustratingly awkward but eminently rewarding experience, which follows the disjointed grooves between *GFC* & Cow Cave. Climb the first slabby groove to a bulge, then traverse LWs to gain the other groove. Move up this (2PRs) with difficulty, then exit RWs by a hard move (past another PR) to reach better holds which lead to the top.   (1964/71)

49   Smokey Joe   55′   E3 6a   ★
A variation on *SGIYE* which does away with its kinaesthetically ugly crux. From the top of the first groove step R & gain a standing position on the small glacis on the RH rib. Climb the slim groove above to join the parent route at its finishing moves.   (1984)

50   Charlie Chaplain Walks on Air   30′   E3 6b.
L of the base of *SGIYE* is a R\L fault arching over the RH side of Cow

Cave's mouth. Climb up & lurch along the fault, past a PR, to join Loot. Abseil off here, or finish as for that route. (1980)

51 Loot 80' E1 5b *

A fine, intimidating line which is virtually always dry. Start on the L wall of the cave mouth, below a hanging chimney. Squeeze up through the chimney (which can be exited LWs after a few feet). Continue up the open groove above (past a PR) to the OH, & a large TR. Follow the crack out LWs into an OHing groove (with arm-wrenching difficulty) which leads to the top. (1960)

52 The Mane Man (TMM) 80' E4 6c ** †

A free version of the formerly aided Leo (A2). Climb the squeeze of Loot then traverse RWs to the base of a white groove. Climb this to the OH (PR) & then work out across the thin seam (TR & PR) to the lip. Powerful moves up LWs lead to a jug & a problematic move to gain the top. (1965/88)

53 Thug'n'ell 70' E3 6a †

A variant finish to Loot which starts up Twang then traverses RWs into Loot after Twang's crux (this is to avoid the squeeze of Loot). Follow Loot to its TR, then turn about face to undercut-out along the RH side of the capping OH. Finish as for TMM. (1990)

54 Twang 70' HVS 5b **

A fine route up the wall, hanging slab & steep groove L of Loot. Gain the large ledge L of the start of Loot, then climb the difficult wall above (past a hidden PR) to the base of an inverted V-groove. Pull over this LWs & then attack the OHing groove above. At its apex, swing RWs on large holds to an exposed finish on widely-spaced incuts. (1968)

55 Highly Strung 70' E4 6b

Lies between Loot & Twang. Follow Twang to the base of the hanging rib. Climb this direct, past 2PRs & a TR, to finish just R of Twang (bridging out to the hanging rib on the R reduces the grade considerably). (1985)

56 Reek 60' HS 4b,- **

Technically interesting & deservedly popular.
1 35' Start as for Twang & move to the LH end of the wide ledge, then step up L to stand atop the bulge. Climb the groove, to the L of the nose, to a stance.
2 25' Climb the easy slab for a few feet, then step R & go up a short wall to the top. (1961)

57 Spearhead 60' HS 4b,- *

Worthwhile despite having little independent climbing. Climb onto the wide ledge as for Twang.
1 35' Follow Reek to the prominent nose, then move up & R across the wall & climb through the eponymous 'spearhead' to gain the stance of Reek.

2   25'   As for Reek *(pitch 2).*   (1961)

The following seven routes either start from, or are reached via, a terrace at the foot of the wide deep crack of **BOC.**

58   Leek   60'   HS 4b,-
Start at a small corner L of the initial wall of Reek.
1   40'   Climb the corner & then traverse L to a terrace. Continue on small holds & then enter the groove between Reek & *BOC.* Follow this to the stance.
2   25'   As for Reek *(pitch 2).*   (c.1960s)

59   Barn Owl Crack *(BOC)*   65'   HVD   *
A route of great character. This is the obvious wide crack L of Cow Cave. Climb to the terrace beneath the crack, & then swim up the crack itself, the narrow middle section being the most difficult. The crux can be avoided by escaping out R to the stance of Reek (as any sane person would) from the small ledge at 20'. Regain the crack 15' higher.   (1960)

60   Barn Owl Variant   60'   VS 4b
Start on the terrace. Climb the crack of *BOC* for 6' to a small ledge. Step L, then climb the wall above using a series of pockets. Take the obvious line onto the arête & climb a tower easily on its LH side to the top.   (1967)

61   Ashtree Buttress   50'   VD
From the top of Reek & *BOC,* a buttress can be seen with a tree growing from it. Climb up to & pass the tree on the R. Steep pleasant climbing remains to the top.   (c.1960s)

The highest & most impressive parts of the South Face lie to the L of **BOC** *& are host to the major classics of Inkerman Groove, Black Death, & The Spider.*

62   The Slot   60'   HVS   5a   *
A gargantuan, nay epic, struggle! Belay beneath the obvious 'slot' above the LH-end of the terrace below *BOC.* Make steep moves to enter the slot, which is followed for 20' to an OH. Exit to the R with difficulty, then climb the steep wall directly to the top.   (1960)

63   Panga   60'   E3 6a   *
A strenuous & technically demanding pitch. Start on the slab some 10' L of The Slot. Climb the obvious flake past a PR, & step up L with difficulty to gain a small foothold. Make a series of hard moves to gain a slim groove & PR, from where a last ditch lunge brings the comfort of easier ground & a PR in a groove. Either finish up LWs or lower off the PR.   (1966/79)

64   Island Racer   60'   E4 6b   †
An eliminate pitch that breaks out RWs from the initial flake of Panga, to make the most of the wall between Panga & The Slot. Finish direct over the bulge above.   (1990)

Directly beneath the wall of Panga is a shallow cave/recess which sports a generous OH. The following three routes are based in or around this, & finish on the slab above the cave.

65   Napalm   30'   VS 4c   †
A scrappy route on the RH side of the recess. Climb easily for 15' to the OH. Surmount this via the groove on the R & belay on the slab (traverse RWs then scramble off).   (1988)

66   South Face *(SF)*   40'   E4 6a   ★
A power-packed outing. Follow the line of Napalm until beneath the OH. Traverse LWs along a line of holds, past a PR, to a hanging groove in the OH. Climb this to its apex & somehow scratch over the lip to the slab above. Either lower off the ring PR on *MW*, or finish up Panga.   (1983)

67   . . .king Hell   40'   E4 6b   †
Even more powerful & problematic than *SF*. Climb direct to the first PR on *SF* from the L, then finish as for that route.   (1985)

68   Machete Wall *(MW)*   100'   E2 5c   ★★
An excellent expedition, taking the main line of the wall 10' to the L of Panga. Start just L of the OHing recess of *SF*. Climb up for 15', then mantel into a groove leading up RWs to a PR at a bulge. Climb the vague niche above (PR). Trend up LWs to a good foothold, then move up R across a slab to a large pointed block. Standing on this, step L into a groove, which is followed for 10'. Step R & continue in the same line to a PB.   (1961)

69   Mortality Crisis *(MC)*   110'   E4 6a   ★★
Good eliminate-style climbing between *MW* & *IG*. Climb to the mantel of *MW*, then step L & up to a PR. Climb the wall above to the base of a diagonal white groove (joins *PL* at this point). Follow this to its end, past 2PRs, then move up L onto the arête of *IG*. Follow this to a TR, then step R to an undercut & climb directly above it to finish.   (1985)

70   Penny Lane *(PL)*   125'   E3 6b   ★
A fine, intricate route. Start 20' L of *MW*, beneath an obvious terrace at 25'. Gain the RH end of this, then step up R into a short groove (PR) & follow a horizontal break out R. Climb the wall to a PR in the curving white groove of *MC*, then traverse RWs on thin holds to gain the slab on *MW*. Step up LWs beneath the OH to gain a thin crack on its LH side. Forceful climbing up this brings the top within g(r)asp.   (1968/79)

71   Inkerman Groove *(IG)*   110'   VS 4c   ★★★
A definite classic, which tackles the long, L-facing groove to the L of *MW*. Start as for *PL* & climb to the terrace at 25', then step up L to bypass a bulge (in common with Wogs to here), until it is possible to traverse R along the lip of the bulge to the base of the groove proper. Follow this for 30' to a small ledge, where a rising

Nick Tetley on Oesophagus (E1 5b) Photo. Pete Bull

Nick Hancock on Banzai (E2 5b) Photo. Andy Grieve

traverse RWs gains a larger ledge & then the belay.   (1960)

72   Inkerman Groove Direct *(IGD)*   100′   HVS 5a   ★★
A fine variation on the above, although the exit is a little dodgy.
Follow *PL* to the PR in the short groove, then step up LWs to an OH
at the base of the groove on *IG*. Pull over this (PR) to gain the
groove, which is climbed in its entirety to reach broken rock. Finish
easily by trending LWs.   (1971)

73   Black Death *(BD)*   100′   E4 6a   ★★★
Superb! A sustained pitch on excellent rock. It tackles the centre of
the narrow, impending wall to the L of *IG*. Follow *IGD* to gain a
standing position just above the OH, midway along *IG*'s traverse.
Climb straight up the wall for 15′ to gain a shallow groove with a PR
at its top. Trend up RWs to a bulge & pull up over this LWs, using
hidden holds. Easier climbing leads to the top.   (1966/82)

74   White Life *(WL)*   100′   E5 6b   ★★★
In the mould of the above but harder. Follow *BD* to its shallow
groove & PR, then step out L & climb steeply past a hidden PR to a
slanting break under a bulge & a further PR. Step L past this to gain
the slim groove above, PR. Finish direct to the belay of *BD*.   (1985)

75   Musical Women #2   120′   E5 6b,6b   ★★
An eliminate-style traverse, very much in keeping with the tradition
established by its namesake at High Tor.
1   70′   Climb Panga to its second PR & traverse LWs into *MW*.
Move L & reverse the crux of *PL*, to gain & climb *MC* to where it
joins *IG* at an awkward stance on a cramped sloping ledge.
2   50′   Follow *IG* for 15′ & traverse LWs beneath the bulge, to
cross *BD*. Continue LWs & finish up the remainder of *WL*.   (1987)

76   Wogs   120′   HVD   ★★
A classic for its standard & a route of great character. . . despite its
name. It climbs the obvious fault to the L of *IG*.
1   25′   Climb to the ledge at 25′ (there are a number of ways of
doing this), then belay.
2   55′   Climb up L until it is possible to step LWs through a bulge
& so gain, & follow, the long crack above to a stance on top of a
pillar.
3   40′   Climb up into a bay. Step L across this onto a slab to gain
easier ground, then climb over the wall above to finish.   (1923)
Variation 3a 45′ Climb up to a projecting ledge on the R (above the
slabby bay), then nip over the wall above to finish.   (c.1960s)

77   Sisyphus   110′   VS 4b,-
A less pleasant companion to Wogs, which is slowly rejuvenating
its flora to take on a lost world demeanour. The main part of the
route climbs the LH side of the pillar L of Wogs. Start at a rib 10′ L of
Wogs.
1   70′   Climb to the obvious traverse-line, then move L along this
for 15′. Break through the OH on the L, then continue up R to a

stance & chockstone belay level with the narrow ledge on the
second pitch of Wogs.
2   40'   Awkwardly climb the crack above to the second stance of
Wogs, from where a short delicate slab leads to the top.   (1961)

78   Central Pillar *(CP)*   110'   HVS 5a,4b
Supposedly a good route, though seemingly lost to future genera-
tions through neglect. The route wades up the flora-infested pillar,
starting 20' L of Wogs at a wide uneven crack.
1   70'   Climb the crack awkwardly for 10', then step L & go up easily
to a bulge which is split by a crack. Follow the crack to ledges above
the bulge (PR), & continue up the centre of the pillar via a thin
crackline, to the second stance of Wogs.
2   40'   Scramble up above the stance to a large chockstone in the
corner above. Traverse up RWs, using large handholds, to an OH.
Step R, then climb up a short groove to some large ledges. A short
wall leads to the top.   (1965)

79   Tantalus   115'   E1 5b,5b
With a bit of traffic this would become a worthwhile outing. Start in
the same area as *CP*.
1   50'   To the L of the start to *CP* is an OHing crack. Climb this & exit
LWs. Move up & belay at a horizontal break below an obvious fault.
2   65'   Follow the fault for 8' to a ledge. Move delicately L & up to a
PR (missing), then climb direct on small pockets to the base of a
broken groove. Climb this & exit LWs to finish. An easier alternative
is to move L across the wall to good footholds, then gain the bottom
of the broken groove.   (1966/79)

WESTERN TOWER AREA
To the L of Tantalus the ground drops away sharply to form a
vegetated basin into which a path descends. On the R is the natural
weakness of Scar. In the centre is the pillar-like buttress of The
Spider, L of which is the lower & more compact wall of Stalactite.

80   Scar   140'   VS 4a,4b,-   *
A good climb following a bold natural weakness. Start to the R of two
caves 10' up in the rock, near the earth slope on the RH side of the
grassy hollow.
1   60'   Climb direct to a small tree stump, then step L & go up a slab
to a large terrace & a belay below a corner with a tree stump in it
(shades of The Wrinkled Retainer).
2   50'   Climb to the ex-tree on gritty rock, then climb the slightly
OHing RH wall (desperately) to a tree belay.
3   30'   Use the tree to gain good holds above a smooth scoop, then
step L & climb the easier wall to finish. Harder for people of limited
physical stature.   (1960)

81   Never on Sunday *(NOS)*   120'   HS 4a,4b   **
An excellent second pitch. Start beneath the two caves L of the start
of Scar.

1   60′   Climb to the caves & then awkwardly move out of the RH one onto the slabs. Go up these to the terrace & belay.
2   60′   Climb a gritty corner for 10′ (just R of Scar), then traverse diagonally RWs to a small ledge around the arête. Finish direct up the wall above; tree belay.   (1961)
Variation 2a 60′ VS 4c Climb the groove direct to the point at which you step around the arête to the small ledge.   (c.1960s)
Variation 2b 60′ VS 5a The small ledge has been gained direct by climbing the face beneath it.   (c.1960s)

82   Leap Year Finish *(LYF)*   45′   HVS 5a   *
A good finish to *NOS* in a very exposed position. From the tree at the top of Scar traverse L across the wall, using the tree branch for the first few moves. A hard move then brings you to good holds & a PR. Climb up over a bulge, then up steep rock to finish.   (1964)

83   Stepping Out *(SO)*   120′   E3 5c   *
Desperate! This follows the OHing L arête of Scar's second pitch.
1   60′   As for *NOS*.
2   60′   Start as for Scar to the dismembered tree, then swing up LWs to gain the arête. Follow the arête, via hard moves, leading up to an overlap & PR. Finish as for *LYF*.   (1985)

To the L of Scar is Western Tower, which provides some of the most exhilarating climbing in the area. Its base has recently been cleared of trees, & it is now relatively quick-drying.

84   The Fly   150′   HVS 4b,5a,-   *
A good route, exposed & with an air of seriousness. Start 7yds L of the two caves, beneath a ledge at 8′.
1   55′   Climb to the ledge & take the crack on the R to another ledge. Continue up the groove above to a terrace & PBs.
2   60′   Walk a few feet R, then move up onto the steep wall. Go diagonally L to beneath the RH side of a perched block in the centre of the face. Climb up onto the block, PR, then traverse horizontally L from the block for 10′ & pull up to a small stance just L of the arête. Block & spike belays.
3   35′   Climb the rib to a groove which leads to the top.   (1965)

85   The Spy   130′   E3 5b,5c   *
At two-thirds height the Western Tower is split by a diagonal fault. This climb follows the fault from the perched block (on The Fly) in an excellent position. Unfortunately the first pitch is a bit of a jungle bash. Start 10′ L of The Fly, at a zigzag-shaped crack.
1   50′   (Vegetated). Climb the crack to a ledge. Move R & climb a wall with difficulty, past a PR, to another ledge. Make a hard move up a corner to reach a small bush & using this climb the slab on the L to the first stance of The Fly.
2   80′   Move up L onto a vegetated ledge & continue straight up & around the RH side of the perched block. Climb direct for another 10′ to gain & follow the L/R slanting fault-line (beneath a slight OH)

which leads to an enormous jug. Move up RWs to join the *LYF*, then make a long stride RWs onto the lip of an OH. Climb the wall easily to the top.   (1968/73)

Variation 1a 50' (5c) Finer & cleaner climbing. Follow the original to the second ledge. Step L & make a hard move onto a clean white slab, then climb direct to the stance of the Fly.   (1992)

86   The Spider *(TS)*   130'   E1 5a,5b   ★★★
One of the best climbs on the crag. The final wall is delectable. Protection is good, but hard won & a trifle sparse on the first pitch!
1   45'   Start as for The Spy to the ledge at 8'. Step L, then climb a steep wall to a ledge. From the L end of the ledge make a difficult move to gain a large foothold on the slab above. Boldly continue to the PB of The Fly.
2   85'   Climb RWs to the vegetated ledge. Move up & round the LH side of the perched block to the small stance above it & a PR. Climb straight up to break through the bulge via a rattling TR & gain some small holds on the steep slab above. Go diagonally RWs to good finishing holds to the R of a small tree; exposed.   (1965)

87   Great Western *(GW)*   140'   VS 4b,4b,5a,-   ★★
A good, although rather polished, line which is very tricky if wet! Near the L end of the tower, & just before the lower face becomes fluted, there is a shallow corner. Start here, a few feet to the L of The Fly.
1   40'   Climb the corner to the second of two ledges, PR. Traverse L using good high handholds, then mantel onto the belay ledge.
2   20'   A narrow slab leads up to the R. Climb this thinly to the PB of *TS*.
3   30'   Climb the wall above the stance to an OH (PR). Move up into the groove on the L, then climb the groove to a large stance & tree belay.
4   50'   Climb the LH arête of the Western Tower to finish.   (1961)

88   The Web   130'   E4 6a   †
An eliminate line based around *TS*.
1   45'   As for *TS*.
2   85'   Climb up to the OH (of *GW*), then move up RWs over it to a TR & *in-situ* wire. Hard moves lead up LWs to a finger ledge & then back RWs to the block of *TS*. Finish as for that route.   (1988)

89   Espionage   80'   E4 6a   †
A mini Musical Women #3! Start as for *SO*. From its PR step L to the big jug at the end of the crux of The Spy, then reverse the traverse of that route. From a good layaway on The Spy pull straight through the bulge to join *TS* on the steep slab. Traverse LWs to gain the arête & finish up this.   (1987)

90   Pig's Ear   160'   E4 4c,6b,-   †
Formerly an aid route entitled **Titan** A1. Start 20' to L of *GW*.
1   65'   Climb on flutings for 15', then make a hard move to a

traverse leading RWs to the first stance of *GW*. Climb straight up behind the stance to an OH. Move L to clear this, then go up to a stance below the large OH, PB.

2   45'   Follow the flared crackline across the OH, past several PRs, to a desperate move on the lip, then stroll up to the third stance of *GW*.

3   50'   Go over a small OH above the belay to reach an area of shattered rock to L of *GW*. Climb this to the top.   (1965/84)

The next route starts in the middle of the low wall L of Western Tower (up which it finishes). The other routes all finish on the terrace above the low wall. To get off this terrace traverse RWs (facing out) for 50', & scramble down an earthy rib, then descend a cleaned slab to regain the ground.

91   Stalactite   170'   VS 4b,4a,-
A rather rambling route, though with good climbing initially. Start about 30' to the L of *GW*.

1   55'   Climb for 10' on stalactite formations, then move R to a ledge. From the RH side of this go up to another ledge, then traverse RWs to reach a deep groove. Climb this to a grassy terrace.

2   25'   Above is a large OH. Climb a crack L of the OH to gain the slab above. Traverse R above the OH & then continue to a stance shared with *GW*.

3   90'   Climb the rib on the L to a small tree. Traverse LWs onto a slab & climb this to the top.   (1962)

92   Grim Reaper   50'   E3 5c
Originally climbed with a bolt as **Stalactite Direct**. Climb the groove 10' to the R of Stalactite, then join that route at its second ledge. Follow the vague groove above, past a TR, after which a positive attitude is needed to finish!   (1962/86)

93   Harvestman   50'   E5 6a
Follow Stalactite to the break above the first ledge (crucial runners). Climb a vague calcite flake (to stand in the break) & continue, via hard moves, up LWs to gain a standing position on the steep slab above. Boldly continue to the finishing terrace on good but widely-spaced holds.   (1987)

94   Whoremoans   50'   E6 6b   ★★ †
A real gripper. Start just L of Stalactite. Climb up to & through some overlaps below an obvious PR. Hard moves gain a vague rib above the PR, which leads to a bold finish (in common with Harvestman). Belay well back from the edge.   (1987)

95   Atropos   35'   E3 5b   ★
Walk up the slope L of Stalactite for 30' until beneath (& to the L of) an obvious cleaned streak above a break. Climb up to the break, then gain & follow the cleaned streak (bold) to the top.   (1987)

96   Orpheus   40'   E6 6a
Follow Atropos to the first break at 10'. Hand-traverse this RWs for
10', then climb up the wall above L of Whoremoans (with your
heart in your mouth). Finish just L of that route.   (1987)

97   West End   110'   HS
A route of little significance that takes the disconnected & rather
vegetated groove just L of Atropos. Continue up the appalling
forest of weed & bramble if you dare!   (1967)

98   Stuff the E5s   30'   M
Climb the middle of the obvious clean buttress L of West End. This
is also the descent from the Stalactite terrace.   (1987)

GIRDLE TRAVERSES

99   Rubble Trouble   105'   VD
A R-to-L traverse of Gagool Buttress, which gives access to rock
hitherto beyond the reach of leaders of this standard.
1   40'   Start from the belay of Albatross. Launch out along the
traverse line leading LWs across ledges to the large belay ledge of
Gagool, PBs.
2   50'   Step up L from the stance & gain a break leading LWs to the
arête. Foot-traverse this, then swing around the arête to belay on
the stance of Combined Ops.
3   15'   Step up L & finish up the easy break to the top.   (1988)

100   Eastern Girdle   195'   E1 5b,5b,-,5a
This is a traverse of the Sarcophagus area (from L to R). Start as for
White Edge.
1   60'   Follow White Edge for 30' up to the slab. Traverse RWs to
the cave stance of Sarcophagus.
2   50'   Move R to the crack of Oesophagus & climb this to the
niche. Exit diagonally RWs, then continue to bear RWs to the belay
of *COPS*.
3   45'   Move down R & follow the obvious traverse-line to the
belay of Gagool.
4   40'   As for Gagool *(pitch 2)*.   (1962)

101   The Equation   210'   E3 5b,5c,6a   ★★
A varied & taxing experience for the grade. Start as for *SGIYE*.
1   70'   Climb the initial groove of *SGIYE* to the OH, then hand-
traverse LWs along the horizontal break, past a bush, until easier
ground leads to Loot. Move L across a smooth wall to a good
foothold, then go up through the 'spearhead' to the stance of
Reek.
2   70'   Move L & climb down *BOC* for a few feet. Traverse LWs &
move around the nose of the buttress (with considerable difficulty)
into The Slot. Continue L beneath the bulge, to gain the upper
groove of Panga, P&NB.
3   70'   Move down & L past a block onto a slab, follow the overlap
LWs, then reverse the traverse of *MC* to its TR. Continue across *IG*

& then straight across the blank-looking wall to the L on hidden pockets to the second stance on Wogs. There are a further two pitches leading LWs to the top of Scar & finishing up the *LYF (but seeing as machetes are so cumbersome to carry. . .).* (1970/78)

102   South Face Girdle   305'   E1 4b,4b,-,-,5a,5b,5b
Atrocious as a whole, but with reasonable climbing in the first & last sections.
1 & 2   (80')   As for Stalactite.
3   40'   Traverse R beneath the OH & then drop down to the second stance on *GW*. Go up R to the vegetated ledge, & descend from its RH end to the terrace of Scar.
4   80'   Cross the terrace to a short narrow slab. Go up this, & traverse RWs along the obvious line for 25' to a scoop & belay.
5   50'   Cross the wall of pitch 1 of Wogs to a short rib. Mantelshelf (as for *MW*) onto a slab & traverse RWs along this to the ledge below *BOC*.
6   25'   Climb a few feet up Leek & step R to join Reek. Move R beneath the 'spearhead' & cross the steep wall into Loot.
7   30'   Finish up the latter half of Loot; or abseil off (which reduces the grade to HVS). (1962)

NORTH FACE

The North Face, especially at its RH end, is one of those places where you expect to find Doug McClure running for his life from an oversized lizard (you could say the area has character). The cliff itself is a rather sombre and featureless affair when compared to the South Face, but this does not negate the fact that there are some fine routes on solid rock. However, after rain it does have a rather damp aura, which takes several days of good weather to dispel. The cliff forms the boundary wall of the garden to Rock House, which is privately owned by the Boulton Family. **The owners thoroughly approve of climbing, but do request that climbers call at the house to sign a visitors book, so that they know who is on their property**.

From the main path, the crag is gained by descending a steep track down the R bank of the narrow neck of land (mentioned in the approach details). The North Face divides into three separate areas: the lower, less attractive LH section (The Tropics), which is the area you first come across. This is followed, after Muddy Gully, by the taller Garden Wall which lies immediately behind Rock House (the Land That Time Forgot bit); and finally the East Face forms a short wall at right-angles to Garden Wall.

THE TROPICS
The rock appears, at first, as a mossy overgrown wall some 40' in height. This wall plays host to three very scruffy routes, **Götterdammerung** (M -1966), **Valkyrie Rib** (VD – 1966) & **Tristan** (S – 1966). The

Chudleigh
- North Face -

Footpath to South Face

Narrow neck of land

Steep bank

Descent to North Face Routes

crag proper starts just R of an earthy chimney & the first routes are described in relation to this.

1   Highway '65   55'   HS 4b
An interesting pitch. Start 25' L of the chimney beneath a perched block half-way up the face. Climb to the block, then traverse R for a few feet to a PR. Move up & then step back L onto the block (PR). Continue direct to the top on good holds.   (1965)

2   Route '66   55'   HVD
Start 15' L of the chimney, below a crack. Climb up to the corner at the foot of the crack, then move up R & trend back L to a large ledge. Climb the crack using its RH side, then finish over blocks (keeping L of Ivy League).   (1966)

3   Ivy League   50'   D
The rock staircase L of the chimney forms the substance of this route. Climb up just L of the chimney, then step L onto a ledge. Continue diagonally LWs to mantelshelf onto a larger ledge (borehole TR). Climb direct to the top past a tree.   (1965)

4   Ancient Mariner   60'   HS 4b
Start as for Ivy League. Follow Ivy League for 15', then move up R & climb a delicate slab to good holds. Climb straight up to an OH, which is taken direct to finish on big jugs.   (1967)

5   Gemini II   60'   S 4a
A pleasant, open route, starting R of the chimney. Climb the L edge of the wall, only diverting to the R to avoid two small OHs at 30' & 50' respectively.   (1965)

6   Gemini I   60'   S 4a
Start 6' R of Gemini II. Climb up for 10', then make a rising traverse

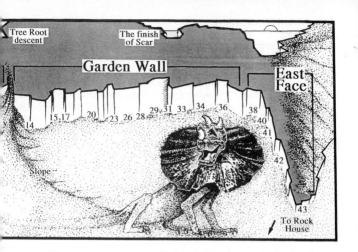

LWs (good fingerholds) along a flake. Climb direct, then mantelshelf onto a large ledge. Step R into an open groove, then climb steep rock on the R to a PR. Break through the OHs above (with difficulty) to finish. (1965)

7 Tropic of Capricorn 60′ VS 4b
A pleasant pitch, although lacking good protection. Start below some obvious borehole strikes at the LH end of the wall. Climb up slightly RWs on sloping holds for 15′ to an old wedge runner. A difficult step R followed by a mantelshelf leads to steeper climbing (using downward-sloping holds) to gain the top. (1963)

8 Tropic of Cancer 60′ VS 4c
Start 15′ R of the previous route. Climb a slight groove for 12′ to a ledge. Continue direct until beneath a bulge, then pull through this on poor holds to finish either on the L or the R. (1963)

9 Ben Gunn 60′ S 4a ★
A reasonably clean & worthwhile pitch. The start is marked by an open groove on the RH side of the face. Climb the short groove to a ledge, then move up R to a large projecting block. Step L & climb the groove to the top. (1963)

10 Long John 60′ E1 5b †
Start just R of Ben Gunn. Follow a deep crack RWs, then move L to an obvious projecting block. Step up to, then climb over a large bulge (PR) & continue direct to the top; bold but easy. (1988)

11 The Notch 60′ HS 4b
Start beneath an obvious R\L slanting corner (near a tree-covered mound). Climb over slabby rock to gain a small ledge, then continue to the larger ledge above, via a delicate move. Climb the

corner (PR), then traverse LWs with difficulty to skirt an OH (PR).
Continue steeply to the top.   (1963)

12   Two Stroke Banana   70'   HVS 5a
A steep route which is difficult to protect. Start L of & lower than
LS. Climb a shallow L/R leaning groove, then exit RWs onto a ledge.
Step up to a small crack & make a long stride LWs. Climb the steep
wall above, then step L & continue diagonally RWs over easier
terrain to reach the top.   (1967)

13   Little Subtleties *(LS)*   60'   HVD
Hidden by a mantle of prehistoric vegetation *(no doubt fuelled by
giant reptilian excreta)*, this climb starts L of the foot of the Muddy
Gully.
1   25'   Climb a slab until it steepens, then traverse L to a ledge.
Climb to another ledge & belay (PB).
2   35'   Negotiate the OH above via the obvious break. Step L,
then finish direct up the wall (climbing up the wall just L of this
pitch bumps up the grade to S 4a).   (1965)

*Muddy Gully forms the demarcation line between The Tropics &
Garden Wall. It also gives an easy way down, which can be tricky in
wet weather. The ground falls away to the R of the gully & the North
Face rises to its full height of 90'.*

GARDEN WALL
All the climbs on this wall are steep & of a consistently high
standard. The rock is sound & there are fewer downward-sloping
holds in comparison to the LH section. Unfortunately it is possible
to climb anywhere on this wall at HVS, with one exception. However, several routes (such as Nimrod) follow aesthetic & fairly
inescapable lines.

14   Sexus   90'   HS 4b,4a   *
A sadly neglected route up the extreme L edge of the face (bounding the RH side of Muddy Gully). Start below a small tree about 15'
up.
1   75'   Climb up the steep wall R of the tree to a PR, then continue
up a shallow groove on the L (past the tree) to a small OH. Skirt this
by stepping L (PR), then go back R again to climb a steep rib on
excellent holds. Stance & PBs under an OH.
2   15'   Traverse R from the stance, then pull strenuously over the
OH, to finish by a blackthorn tree.   (1964)

15   Plexus   100'   VS 4a,4b   **
A fine inescapable line; R of Sexus are two prominent cracks about
15' apart.
1   50'   Follow the LH crack for 15', then climb up the wall to the R
of the crack (passing 2PRs) to a sloping ledge below an OHing wall,
PB.
2   50'   Climb the short crack above, then traverse L beneath a
large block to a small ledge (PR). Climb straight up to a bulge & PR

15' from the top. A steep move through this leads to some ledges which are followed easily to finish.   (1964)

16   Garden Wall Eliminate   90'   VS 4c,4c
A direct line between Sexus & Plexus. Start just R of Sexus.
1   40'   Climb the rib L of Plexus to a ledge. Trend up LWs, then back RWs to the stance of Plexus.
2   50'   Move out LWs, then climb straight over a bulge (strenuous). Continue direct to, then climb over, another bulge to reach the upper wall (in common with Sexus & Plexus).   (1966)

17   Nexus   95'   S -,4a   ★★★
Probably the finest route of its grade at Chudleigh; interesting throughout & exposed on the crux. Start 15' R of Plexus below the second crack.
1   65'   Follow the crackline to a very large block on the L. Gain the top of the block, then go horizontally RWs to a small stance & PB in a corner.
2   30'   Traverse back LWs, then climb a steep wall to gain a small ledge. Continue via a difficult step up LWs to reach good holds which lead to the top.   (1964)

18   Prometheus   100'   HVS 4a,4c   ★
A steep & exposed route. Start as for Nexus.
1   50'   Climb the crack of Nexus for 10', then step L onto a slab. Climb a shallow groove to the stance of Plexus.
2   50'   Traverse RWs for 10', then climb up to a line of incut holds which trend up LWs to a small ledge (PR). Continue delicately until a large hold can be reached above an OH. Pull up over this, then step R to climb an exposed rib which leads to the top. Tree belay well back from the edge.   (1965)

19   Nemesis   90'   HVS 5a (1pt)
An artificial line that has very steep & exposed climbing. Start as for Nexus. Climb Nexus for 25' to some jammed flakes. Step L & move up to a bay beneath a large block. Climb the LH side of the block, then step onto a ledge with a loose spike. Step up (PR), then climb a shallow groove which leads to an obvious square break in an OH (hard). Make a long reach up to place a peg above the OH & use this to pull over. Move L to a small ledge, then go up the final wall to the top; exposed.   (1966)

20   Thornifixion   100'   HVS 5a,4a
An interesting climb, despite being rather scrappy. Some 20' R of the start of Nexus there is a short steep slab trending up LWs; start below this.
1   50'   Reach a ledge at 6', then climb the very delicate slab to good holds. Continue more easily to a good stance & PB just below a curious hole in the rock.
2   50'   Climb direct over an OH, then continue past the stance of Nexus to the start of a ramp running up RWs (PR). Follow this for

roughly 20', then pull awkwardly over the OH above & climb more easily to the top. (1964)

Variation 2a 50' HVS 4b Known as **The Rosy Exit**. From the PR at the start of the ramp climb the obvious line above to an OH split by a crack. Climb this & continue LWs to the top. (1967)

21 Diana 90' VS 4c

Follow a thin layback edge to the first 'hole' on Thornifixion. Step R & up into a slabby groove (PR). Follow this to a small OH which is climbed on its RH side (delicate & exposed), to gain the second 'hole' of Thornifixion. Climb the OH above, then a short slab & finally a bulge to gain the top. (1966)

R of Thornifixion there is a wide expanse of grey wall terminating in the striking cleft of Colossus. A line of ledges cross the wall about 20' above the ground, making the first pitches a mere formality. The obvious break (R of centre) is The Dial, whose first pitch is commandeered by some of the other routes.

22 Nimrod 90' HVS 5a,5a ★★

An excellent route; sustained & delicate. Start as for Thornifixion.
1 20' Climb the slab of Thornifixion, then traverse RWs to a ledge & PB.
2 70' Move up L to the base of a thin curving crack which is followed to a prominent PR. Mantelshelf onto a ledge at the foot of a ramp which runs up RWs. Climb the ramp, with the aid of a high borehole on the R, to a PR on the lip of an OH. Move R & finish up steep but easy ground. (1965)

23 Grey Wall Eliminate 90' HVS 4b,4c

A vague line between Nimrod & Scorpion. Start at a weakness L of the start of The Dial.
1 20' Move up to gain the LH side of a ledge. Step into a large scoop in the rock, then climb up to a spacious ledge (PB).
2 70' From the LH edge of the ledge climb delicately up some slabs, trending slightly LWs. Move back R & up to a depression (borehole strike). Climb over the bulge above the depression to emerge at the top of the ramp of Nimrod. Continue straight up & over the final tottery OH. (1966)

24 Scorpion 90' HVS -,4c

Not too difficult technically, but an intimidating lead which is not that well protected. Start as for The Dial.
1 20' Follow ledges which trend up LWs to the stance of Nimrod.
2 70' Climb a vague line directly above the stance to a small OH. Move R, then step up to a ledge (PR). Climb the wall above on good incuts to a long borehole strike (poor PR). Reach for holds over the lip of the bulge above & pull up onto a ledge containing a small sapling. Climb the slab above, then overcome a small OH to gain the top. (1965)

25 Orion 95' HVS -,5a
Despite a rather artificial line it provides interesting climbing. Start as for The Dial.
1   25'   Climb up the broken corners to the stance of The Dial.
2   70'   Trend LWs to a small ledge (shared with Scorpion), then go diagonally RWs to some ledges (The Dial is just on the R). Move up, then traverse back LWs under a bulge on sloping footholds & finger incuts. Make a difficult pull over the bulge & finish direct past a thorn bush.   (1965)

26 The Dial 90' S -,4a
This is the obvious L/R slanting weakness, which dominates the R flank of the grey wall. Start below this line.
1   25'   Gain the highest ledge & belay (PB).
2   65'   Climb to a large projecting ledge on the R. Move up slightly LWs on sloping holds for a few feet, then climb back diagonally RWs on better holds to a steep finish (2PRs).   (1964)
Variation 2a 65' S 4a Known as **Crescendo**. Climb the shallow groove directly above the stance of The Dial, then continue straight up keeping just L of The Dial.   (1967)

27 Cygnus 90' VS -,4c   *
A fine pitch which gives a good introduction to the more difficult routes based upon the grey wall. Start as for The Dial.
1   20'   Follow The Dial but belay on a stance a little lower & further to the R of that route.
2   70'   Climb to the projecting ledge (PR). Make a long stride LWs, then climb an open groove & the following short wall which leads to a sloping ledge (PR) below a steeper wall. Trend up LWs to easier rock which is climbed on good but widely-spaced holds. Finish just R of The Dial.   (1965)

28 Andromeda 105' HVS 4b,4c   **
An excellent route which takes a L/R diagonal line up the RH part of the grey wall, parallel to The Dial. Start 20' R of that route.
1   25'   Climb up to & over an awkward bulge in the wall, then move L to the first stance of Cygnus.
2   80'   From the RH end of the stance climb to a small ledge with a hidden borehole (slot-in peg). Move up, then continue by bearing slightly RWs to a PR just L of an OH. Traverse RWs beneath the OH to the foot of an open groove (PR). Climb up steeply on widely-spaced holds, then follow a rib on the L to the top.   (1965)
Variation 2a 80' HVS 5a Climb direct from the PR (before the traverse RWs under the OH). Continue RWs by following a natural line of weakness up to a difficult bulge; finish direct.   (1965)

29 Perseus 90' HVS 5b   *
The finest technical pitch on the North Face. Start beneath a wall 10' L of the obvious cleft (of Colossus). Climb an open corner, then traverse LWs for 6' & continue up a smooth wall to a borehole (PR). Move R for a few feet, then go up to a bay of rock containing a

borehole (slot-in peg). Bridge up to a bulge (PR), then make a difficult move L to a foothold. Go diagonally LWs to another bulge (PR), then finish up the groove of Andromeda.   (1966)

30   Perseus Direct   90′   HVS 5a
Improves the line but misses the crux move. From the initial corner of Perseus climb straight up into the bay of rock, via a difficult mantel. From the PR above the bay make another hard mantel onto a sloping ledge on the R. Climb LWs through a break in some OHs (PR) to the top.   (1970)

31   Colossus   90′   VS 4b   ★
An imposing line with some bold climbing up the great cleft, which is the most striking feature of the face. Start in a cave at the foot of the cleft. Climb up the LH corner of the fissure & continue by back-&-footing until just above a PR near the top of the cleft. Make an exposed swing round the OHing R wall, using a prominent flat handhold, then continue up the rib to another PR. Step back L, over the top of the cleft, to a large ledge & finish direct.   (1964)
Variation finish 4c Climb the slab above the swing-out R, instead of going L again.   (c.1960s)

32   The Track   245′   HVS 4b,5b,5a,4c,4a   ★
A high-level girdle of Garden Wall. An excellent route, sustained & on perfect rock. Start at the foot of Colossus.
1   90′   Climb Colossus to a tree belay near the top.
2   45′   Descend the final open groove of Andromeda to the PR beneath the OH. Traverse LWs with difficulty to join Cygnus at its PR. Move up steeply, then step L to a stance on The Dial.
3   50′   Climb The Dial for a few feet, then move out L across a delicate slab to the sapling above the crux on Scorpion. Continue L on good footholds to the top of the ramp of Nimrod. Descend this, then make a delicate traverse LWs to the stance of Nexus.
4   45′   Traverse horizontally LWs for 15′ to join Prometheus. Follow that route up & across its traverse, then continue to the top stance of Sexus.
5   15′   Follow Sexus over an OH to the top.   (1965)
Variation 2a 100′ HVS 5b A more sustained pitch which avoids any deviation in line. From the PR by the OH on Andromeda traverse horizontally LWs into The Dial, then make a long stride L to reach the PR on Scorpion. Go L again to a borehole strike (PR), & move L to the ramp of Nimrod. Continue along what remains of pitch 3 of the original route.   (1970)

33   Caveman Rock   90′   HS   4a
Journey back down through the millenia to 'The Route That Time Forgot'. Dive into the ivy R of Colossus & fend off the ensuing barrage of oversized lizards, crazy-eyed McClures & loose blocks (which are not made of polystyrene) to the top.   (1,001,964 BC)

34   Hansel   90'   HS 4a   *
Enjoyable for its grade; it follows the narrow slabby wall at the RH end of the grey wall, just R of the jungle of Caveman Rock. Start at a prominent bulge at ground level, 12' left of a corner formed by a fluted face to the R.
1   40'   Climb, using all manner of sloping footholds, towards a block set in a short steep wall at 25'. Step L onto the block, then climb easy slabs to a ledge by a tree.
2   50'   Climb a steep groove (above the ledge), to easy slabs leading to an OH which is surmounted *en-route* to the top.   (1966)

35   Gretel   85'   HS -,4a
Start R of Hansel & just L of the corner.
1   35'   Climb easily for 10' to the base of a narrow slab. Follow the LH side of the slab on sloping holds, to gain the large ledge above; stance & TB.
2   50'   Trend up LWs to a ledge below a bulging wall 6' R of Hansel. Climb this on small holds to reach & pull over onto a double-handed jug above the bulge. Continue up easy slabs, bearing RWs to the top. Tree belay well back from the edge.   (1966)

36   Yggdrasel   80'   HVS 5a
A delicate route which follows the corner formed by a slabby wall on the L & the fluted face on the R. Climb the corner to an OH. Turn this on the R, then take the slab on the L to a sloping ledge & PR. Step R, then gain a smooth groove with difficulty. Follow the remaining slab to a tree belay.   (1967)

EAST FACE
R of Yggdrasel lies the East Face, which is mainly composed of calcite flutings & is of a totally different nature to the rest of the North Face. The calcite is not always reliable as it holds together indifferent base material, however, one or two of the routes are worthwhile.

The following three routes begin beneath a tree growing out of a grass ramp R of Yggdrasel.

37   East Gully Wall *(EGW)*   70'   VS 4b
A poor route. Climb up to the tree. Continue direct for 10', then traverse LWs for 10'. Follow the natural line up the face to finish beside a tree (L of a large block).   (1966)

38   Bolero   70'   HVS 4c   *
A fine route which follows a line straight up from the start of *EGW*. Climb to the tree & continue up to a ledge in the middle of the face, then move L for a few feet. Climb up to, then hand-traverse RWs along, good holds until a steep move gains the top.   (1966)

39   Alpha One   70'   E2 5b   †
An eliminate-style route. Climb to the tree, move R onto some obvious blocks, then go LWs into the middle of the face. Climb diagonally RWs to finish L of a large block.   (1984)

40   Seguidilla   70′   VS 5a
Start 10′ R of *EGW*. Climb a steep wall (with difficulty) to a desperate exit onto a grass-ramp. Follow the shallow groove above, then move up LWs to a huge jug. Continue easily to some large flakes, then climb direct up the wall above (past a small sapling on the L) to a mantelshelf finish; tree belay.   (1968)
Variation The initial wall can be avoided by climbing Bolero to the tree, then by following the grass-ramp RWs for 10′ (which reduces the grade to HS 4b).   (c.1960s)

41   Sickle   60′   HS 4a
Not particularly worthwhile but the second pitch is in a good position. Start beneath a crack, beside a large iron spike which projects from the rock.
1   30′   Follow the crack for a few feet, then climb the wall R of this to a ledge. The smooth groove above is climbed to a larger ledge & belay.
2   30′   Move out L to avoid a large OH, then climb the loose wall above to the top.   (1965)

42   Hammer   50′   VS 4b,-
Start 15′ R of Sickle, beneath some organ-pipe-shaped flutings.
1   35′   Climb steeply to the L on rounded holds to gain a ledge.
2   15′   Finish up the wall R of the tree.   (1965)

43   Rock House Corner   70′   HVD
A bit of a misnomer, considering that this climbs the arête which overlooks Rock House. It gives a pleasant pitch, though protection is limited.   (1965)

BLACK CRAG   GR 867 786

This is the small cliff which is just visible from the approach path to Chudleigh Rocks (on the opposite side of the river). Follow the normal approach to Chudleigh Rocks, but where the path splits take the lower alternative & follow it down to the river. Cross this at a large fallen tree & climb the steep slope beyond to the base of the cliff. The routes are described from R to L.

1   Hands Off Argentina (*HOA*)   40′   HVD
The obvious black corner at the RH end of the R wall.   (1982)

2   Aggravation   40′   HVS 5b
Climb the wall just to the R of *HOA*.   (1982)

3   19th Nervous Breakdown (*19NB*)   45′   E1 5b
Start to the L of *HOA*. Climb a bulging wall to a TR, then climb a discontinuous crack to the top.   (1982)

4   Out on a Limb (*OOL*)   60′   E3 6a.
Climb the OHing arête L of *19NB*, via its LH side, to a small OH & poor PR. Step R & climb a steep groove LWs to a bulge. Pull over this awkwardly, then finish direct.   (1986)

5   Darling Nikki   60'   E4 6a   ★
Climb the wall immediately L of the start of *OOL* to a pocket. Attack
the steep wall above, past a PR, until a lunge up RWs allows the
base of a thin ragged crack to be gained. Follow this to a ledge.
Traverse LWs to a tree; lower off.   (1986)

6   Golden Dive *(GD)*   60'   E3 6a   ★★
A fine route. Start in the middle of the L wall of the buttress, below
a large pod-like pocket at 35'. Climb direct to this, then follow a
crack above it to the tree; lower off.   (1986)

7   Gorillability   60'   E3 5c   ★★
High in the grade & a minor classic. Climb the wall 10' to the L of
GD to a ledge (PR above). Step up LWs past the PR, then power
through a bulge to a fine finishing crack.   (1986)

8   Poetic Justice *(PJ)*   55'   E3 5c
Start beneath a wall which lies between Gorillability & a hanging
corner on the L. Climb this past two pockets, a TR & a loose tree
stump. Move R, then climb a crack to the top.   (1987)

9   Wind Bandits   50'   E2 5b
Climb up to the RH side of an OH, then follow the hanging corner
(L of *PJ*) in its entirety.   (1987)

PALACE QUARRY   GR 867 787

There are, to be frank, some miserable places to climb in Devon,
and this is quite possibly the most sordid. This scrappy quarry (seen
from the parking bay for Chudleigh Rocks) contains the can-
nibalised wrecks of numerous decrepit jalopies. It also has the
appearance of a bomb crater manicured by Worzel Gummidge
(and you're still interested?).

Permission to climb here has not been granted. For those who would
risk prosecution to climb in such a diabolical environment, there is
a vague path which contours the hillside LWs from Black Crag. The
descent from all the routes is L of Tremor Buttress.

TREMOR BUTTRESS
At the LH end of the quarry is a large buttress, the LH side of which
is scarred by a recent rockfall & (for the moment) topped by an
unstable-looking OH. R of the scar is a wall facing the quarry
entrance, the LH arête of which is taken by:

1   Tremor   70'   S 4a
Climb the R wall of the arête to a small OH at 40'. Step L around the
arête to a slabby groove (PR). Follow this delicately, then step R to a
foothold on the arête. Continue to a ledge, then gain a further
larger ledge & TB. Scramble to the top.   (1967)

2   Olympia   70'   VS 4b
Start 20' to the R of Tremor by some yellowish rock. Climb up LWs

to gain a water-stained niche in the centre of the face. Traverse RWs, then climb a groove to join the RH arête which is followed to the top (scramble off as for Tremor).   (1976)

3   Quiver   60'   S 4a
Climb a vague set of grooves on the RH side wall (2PRs), then scramble to the top as for Tremor.   (1969)

R of Tremor Buttress is. . . The Grim Grotto, a prominent cave about 25' above ground level. The following route starts from a grass ledge just R of The Grim Grotto's RH edge.

4   The Wild Bunch   110'   VS 4c,4c
Loose is the only adjective that jumps to mind regarding this route. Start from the grass terrace (at ground level) below & R of the 'Hole in the Wall'.
1   70'   Climb the shattered buttress, trending RWs below a series of ill-defined, short cracks to a vague niche (shot-hole TB).
2   40'   Step L, then climb up to a hard move over the final bulge. Scramble off LWs as for Tremor.   (1976)

R of The Grim Grotto is the Main Face (for what it's worth). Its dishelleved appearance belies its truly mediocre nature. All the routes begin from an insubstantial grass terrace running out RWs from beneath The Grim Grotto.

5   The Bat   120'   HVS/A1 4c,5a   (An alpine ★)
Although not quite up to its Scottish namesake's standard, the whirr of falling rock gives it a more authentic alpine aura. Start some 15yds R of The Grim Grotto, beneath a short finger-crack at the LH end of a wave-like bulge at 50'.
1   60'   Climb direct to the crack in the bulge, past an ancient PR. Use two pegs for aid to overcome the bulge, then move RWs to gain easier terrain & a T&PB.
2   60'   Follow the vague groove above the stance, then trend LWs to a shallow OH which is taken at its widest point using a peg for aid. The slab above gives reasonably solid sport all the way to a tree belay atop the wall.   (1976)

6   Zen   140'   HVS 4b,5a
This partly ascends the strident diagonal fault that cleaves the top half of the face. Start from beneath the RH end of the wave-like bulge at 50'.
1   40'   Climb up to a spike, then traverse R to awkwardly gain a ledge & PR. Continue LWs to another ledge & belay.
2   100'   After a short orange slab on the L, step up R to a ledge. Gain the R\L diagonal fault-line, then follow it LWs (staying just beneath it) for 30' to a good ledge & TR. Difficult climbing above this leads to a tree near the top (PR) just R of a short corner. Continue up the corner to finish.   (1969)

7   The Rainbow   120'   VS 4a,4b
Start as for Zen.

1   60'   Follow Zen to its first belay, then trend RWs over more vegetated ledges to a cave/recess in the central fault, PB.

2   60'   Step up L to a large TR. Climb direct for 10', then bear R & continue to some huge blocks beneath a semi-circular OH. About 10' from the apparent top, move R & climb a smooth slanting groove to some ledges & finish easily.   (1969)

The recorded routes further R have been somewhat disfigured by further quarrying, leaving the face as an essentially virgin canvas for aspirant loose-routers to do their stuff on.

8   Astral Traveller   300'   HVS 4b,4c,4b,4c,5a
A girdle of the quarry from L to R, starting L of Tremor.

1   40'   Climb the wall for a few feet, then traverse out R to the arête of Tremor & belay.

2   50'   Move down & across to the water-stained niche of Olympia, then bear RWs up a groove to belay on the RH arête.

3   70'   Cross Quiver to a prominent ledge & move R to a reverse mantel. Continue along some ledges to. . . The Grim Grotto.

4   40'   The slab R of the Grotto is followed to a horizontal traverse & a tricky move down to the niche of The Wild Bunch.

5   100'   Climb a short groove on the R, then a sloping ramp (which crosses The Bat) to join & finish up Zen.   (1976)

NEWTON ABBOT-TOTNES AREA

A region rich in thespians and alcoholic beverages (are the two not synonymous?). From the mead produced by *Buckfast Abbey* (by the world's oldest and most venerated teetotal apiarist), to *The Cider Bar* in Newton Abbot, the whole scene is supported by a cosmopolitan glut of artists, musicians and theatre students centred in and around the bohemian paradise of Dartington. If the aim of the day's sojourn is to chill-out while indulging in a little vertical brachiation, then you've just stumbled upon Shangri-la.

The area consists of the sporting arena of Torbryan Quarry, and the bastion of eccentricity; Hazard Quarry. Separating the two is *The Plains Café* in Totnes, a major chill-bin for artistes and climbers alike. There are numerous other quarries dotted about the place which would have felt more at home in the Esoterica section, were it not for the fact that they are composed of limestone.

SEALE HAYNE QUARRY   GR 826 734

Lost forever (it would seem), in a harsh tangle of briar and bindweed, are these routes established by the Seale Hayne Pioneer Club. They are recorded here for posterity and as an example of the bitter struggle between the human desire to impose form over the chaos of nature. Both the recorded routes climb a barely-discernable wall, directly opposite the path into the quarry.

1   Palmer's Folly *(P'SF)*   50'   D
This starts by a red stain produced by water running down the cliff. Climb the wall direct.   (c.1960s)

2   The Avenue   60'   M
Start about 45' R of *P'SF*. Trend LWs up the wall to finish at the same point as the last route. The loose rock at the top provides a soul-searching climax.   (c.1960s)

WHITE ROCK   GR 838 712

This buttress is pleasantly situated above the N ↑ bank of the River Lemon, roughly 1½ miles ←W of Newton Abbot. A footpath leads to the crag from Chercombe Bridge, or if approaching from the E→, from Ogwell Mill. The face was produced by quarrying, the lower half being an easy-angled slab which leads to a steeper wall.

1   West Buttress   50'   VS
There is a prominent ledge midway up the LH side of the wall. Gain this direct, then follow the shallow groove above to a rather loose finish; tree belay.   (c.1960s)

2   Central Route *(CR)*   110'   D
Start at the lowest point of the face. Follow the natural line of weakness up the wall past a large ledge. Finish up the obvious break in the steep wall above.   (c.1960s)

3   East Buttress Route 1   60'   HS
Start R of *CR*, beneath a briar-covered ledge. Climb a direct line to the top, via the ledge.   (c.1960s)

4   East Buttress Route 2   40'   VS
Climb the fault-line on the RH side of the wall.   (c.1960s)

TORBRYAN QUARRY   GR 824 665

Approach and Access
From the large roundabout on the A380 outside Newton Abbot, take the exit for the town centre and follow the road signs for the A381 to Totnes. Take the first turn R into Ipplepen, then follow the road through the village towards Torbryan. Ignore the first turning R to Torbryan and continue to the bottom of a steep hill. There is a parking space on the L (opposite a farm house), beside a junction marked "Wellbarn Cross". The quarry entrance is 20yds back up the hill on the R. For those approaching from the S ↓, take the A38 to the Totnes exit, then follow the A381 from Totnes to Ipplepen, and follow the rest of the description above.

Teignbridge Parks Authority wish it to be known that they are not against climbing at this venue. However, they are only willing to allow a small number of climbers to visit the crag at any one time. Thus, if there are three teams already up and running at the crag, find another venue (because if you don't you'll be responsible for getting the place banned). After all it's not like this is the only place to climb in Devon.

Situation and Character

A deservedly popular sport venue, being both steep and liberally supplied with calcite flutings and *in-situ* gear. The odd hold is not above suspicion, but this tends to add a little spice, rather than detract from the climbing. The quarry faces ←W, so it doesn't catch the sun until the afternoon (in the summer), and due to the OHing nature of the wall it can be climbed on even during steady rain.

There is a splendid *Danish Bakery* in Ipplepen which makes some of the stickiest sweets on the planet (a definite rival to those continental bakeries that British climbers are so besotted with). However, the pubs in Ipplepen aren't worth a second glance when compared to *The Old Church House Inn*, which is nestled between a gaggle of quaint cottages in the village of Torbryan.

The six routes that follow all begin from a large flat access ledge which is situated up on the LH side of the quarried wall.

1   Peggy Potato *(PP)*   40'   6b+ (E3 5c)
A poor route. Start at the extreme LH side of the access ledge, beside a large flake half-buried in the ground. Climb to a BR, then gain & climb a L/R slanting groove (BR). Step up RWs (BR) to gain a large ledge with a BB above it.   (1987)

2   Pebbles   45'   6c (E3 6b)   ★
Start just R of *PP*, below the LH end of a ledge at 15'. Climb direct to the ledge, then pull over a slight bulge on the L to the first of 3BRs leading slightly LWs up the wall above. Climb this to gain the large ledge & BB of *PP*.   (1989)

3   Wages of Fear *(WF)*   45'   7a (E4 6a)   ★
Start 10' R of *PP*, below the RH end of the ledge at 15'. Follow a vague groove up LWs (past a BR), to hard moves to gain the ledge (BR above). Trend up LWs in line with a white streak to another BR. Finish direct to the BB of *PP*.   (1988)

4   Vicious Delicious *(VD)*   50'   7b (E5 6b)   ★★
A tad scary as well as technically sustained. Follow *WF* to the ledge & second BR. Step up RWs, then climb direct to another BR (bold). A thin series of layaway holds lead up a steep shallow groove to a blind slap for a jug. Large holds lead up LWs to another BR, from where some sketchy moves up RWs gain a BB.   (1993)

5   Little White Lie *(LWL)*   50'   7b (E5 6b)   ★★
A technically deceitful delight. Start 2yds L of the major groove-line of *Mayday*. Climb diagonally LWs via a thin crackline (4BRs), until

Torbryan Quarry

beneath a slight bulge (just R of the groove on *VD*). Hard moves over the bulge lead to a good ledge, then step up L (past a BR) to finish as for *VD*.   (1987)

Variation. 7b (E5 6b). Start 4yds L of Mayday, below 2BRs in line with the bulge. Climb direct past the 2BRs, via hard moves which lead to the parent route. Finish up this.   (1991)

6   Mayday   50'   6c (E3 5c)   ★★★
The route of the quarry (for its grade). Start from the extreme RH end of the flat access ledge. Gain & climb the dominant groove-line (5BRs), which divides the *LWL* wall from the central face. Continue via the LH side of the capping OH, then finish up a short wall to gain a BB; lower off.   (1986)

7   Threadbare   70'   7c+ (E6 6b/c)   ★★
An eliminate line with some fine, sustained climbing & a height-dependant crux. Start 5yds R of Mayday. Climb the RH side of a blank wall (BR) then traverse LWs from the second (BR) to gain the base of a hanging groove. Follow this to a shallow OH at its apex (BR), then step out L & continue up the wall R of Mayday (PR & 2BRs). Finish via hard moves up a slight groove, then hand-traverse the top of the wall LWs to a BB.   (1991)

8   Thread Flintstone *(TF)*   70'   7b (E5 6a)   ★★★
The route of the quarry. It takes the bulge & shallow groove 5' R of Threadbare, & is marked by 6BRs. Desperate moves up to, then over the bulge lead to a small ledge at the base of the shallow groove. Climb this, then step up RWs before climbing direct to another bulge. Finish via the desperate short groove above to gain a BB above a thank-god jug; lower off.   (1987)

9   Bam Bam   80'   7b (E5 6b)
Start 5' R of *TF* below the LH side of a shallow arch. Climb a short crack (BR), then lunge up RWs for a good edge (BR). Trend up RWs across a wall (BR) to the middle of the diagonal break of *BOD*. Pull over the slight bulge above, then climb direct up the wall (BR) to join *LBA* at a PR (missing). Climb up RWs to gain & follow the blunt rib (BR), then continue up the headwall to a BB just below the top of the crag.   (1991)

10   Barney Rubble *(BYR)*   75'   7a+ (E5 6a)   ★
Start 3yds R of Bam Bam, on the RH side of the shallow arch. Climb the slim groove (formed by the arch) past 2PRs. Hard moves lead up LWs to a BR. Continue diagonally LWs to join the end of the diagonal break on *BOD* (TR). Follow *BOD* to another TR, then step up RWs (TR) & climb over a desperate bulge (2PRs). Continue direct to the BB of Bam Bam.   (1989)

11   Boogie on Down *(BOD)*   70'   E4 6a   ★
Start 4yds up the rake from *BYR*. Awkwardly gain the ledge below the RH end of an obvious R\L diagonal break. Follow this to its end (TR), then climb the shallow groove above to a further 2TRs below a

bulge. Hard moves lead up LWs through this. Either finish direct, or trend up RWs to the BB of Bam Bam.   (1987)

12   Look Back in Anger *(LBA)*   70'   E4 6b   ★
Follow *BOD* to the diagonal break. Where the break widens, climb direct up a thin crack (PR) to another PR (missing). Make an ingenious traverse RWs around the rib onto the ramp of Famine & climb this to the top.   (1987)

13   Famine   60'   E2 5c
The route follows the vague wide groove & its blunt LH rib, which bounds the RH side of the main wall. Start from an obvious tree on a small ledge at the top of the grassy rake. Traverse LWs to gain & climb the groove until forced onto the LH rib (bold). Follow this until it is possible to step back R & climb the wall above by the easiest line to a BB.   (1980)

14   Blight Delight *(BD)*   60'   E2 5c   ★
A fine steep pitch up the wall to the R of Famine. Start just to the L of the tree belay. Follow Famine to a short vertical crack with 2TRs. Climb past these to a further TR, then trend up RWs to a PR just below a thin ledge. Finish direct.   (1987)

15   Spud   50'   E3 5c
Totally inconsequential *(included only because Jon slipped me a fiver to get his name in the guide more often)*. Climb the white streak between *BD* & Wilma.   (1991)

16   Wilma   50'   E3 6a
Climb direct up the wall behind the tree belay of *BD*. Gain the first of 2PRs, then boldly scratch up the remainder of the wall to join *BD*. Finish as for that route.   (1988)

17   Death of King Edward   30'   HVS 5a
Climb the short crack R of the tree belay of *BD*.   (1987)

18   Raph Skrøtöm's Septic Toenail   20'   HVS 5a
This climbs the isolated buttress 30yds further R.   (1988)

GIRDLE TRAVERSES
The quarry contains two fine counter-diagonal traverses, which make the most of the pumpy climbing to be had.

19   Yabba Dabba Doo! *(YDD)*   140'   E5 6a,5c   ★
A L-to-R traverse of the quarry with plenty of good climbing & *in-situ* protection.
1   80'   Start as for *WF* to its second BR, & traverse RWs to pass the fourth BR on *LWL*. Continue RWs into the main groove of Mayday. Step across Threadbare to take a hanging belay in *TF*.
2   80'   Climb up RWs to the PR on *LBA* (missing), then descend to the obvious footledges on the rib. Pull around into the vague wide groove of Famine, & follow this for a few moves (PR). Traverse RWs into *BD* (PR), & finish up this route.   (1988)

20 Crosstown Traffic 100' E4 6a ★
The R-to-L equivalent of *YDD*, & a good pump as well. Start as for
BOD. From the end of the diagonal break step L into *TF*. Traverse
across Threadbare into Mayday, & then lunge LWs to the large
ledge atop *LWL*. Finish as for that route. (1988)

HAZARD QUARRY GR 755 592

Approach and Access
From Totnes follow the B3210 towards Avonwick for about 3 miles.
The turn-off for the quarry is marked "Hazard Farm". It is advisable
to obtain the farmer's permission to climb here, as well indulge his
curiosity. A further short drive along the lane leads to a parking
place, just past a disused lime kiln.

Situation and Character
Referred to in the previous guide as esoteric, the quarry has now
stepped up a league and become mostly eccentric. However, this is
not meant to be taken as a disparaging remark, for there is a wealth
of fine, interesting and peculiar climbing to be had. The rock is not
above suspicion in some areas, being a mix of solid limestone and
indifferent shale. However, the starred routes are well-gardened
and solid.

The crag itself is a quarried face that rises dramatically from rolling,

verdant pasture. It is S↓ facing, and being cut into the hillside, amply protected from both strong winds and gusty showers. The face is about 300yds long, and over 100' high. A large horizontal roof caps the highest wall, which is stained by black streaks. This is bound on the R by the grossly OHing prow of Garth (and further R by the OHing bay of Samurai), and on the L by the blunt rib of Dumnonia. There are slabby walls to either side of the main area, and a short OHing wall on the R at right-angles to the main face.

The L end of the LH slabby wall is taken by **Meadow Fly**, 120' VS 4c (1979), which climbs up and L to an OH. It then finishes up an arête on the L.

1   Green Ranger   115'   HVS 4b,4c
Start roughly in the centre of the slabby wall.
1   50'   Climb up to the obvious cracks. Step R, then climb straight past a small oak tree (on the L), before traversing back L to belay.
2   65'   Bold. Continue up behind the tree on small holds to gain a sloping ledge. Move up L to reach a superb TR, then climb the groove awkwardly to exit by a large tree.   (1979)

Two routes climb the obvious cracks & caves to the R of Green Ranger. The LH line is taken by **Twilight**, *100' VS 4c   (1979), &the RH crack is* **Pastoral**, *100' VS 4c (1979).*

2   Boss Hogg   130'   E1 5a
Start 10' L of the blunt rib of Dumnonia. Climb easily to a borehole

TR above the first shale band, then traverse LWs for a few feet. Continue diagonally LWs to a large TR, then finish via the easiest line up the remainder of the wall.   (1987)

3   Dumnonia   120'   HVS 5a,4b
Start beneath a vague groove at the base of the blunt rib, which leads up to the LH end of a huge capping OH (atop the black-streaked wall).
1   70'   Climb past a loose block at 15', then move R to good runners in a crack. Move back L, then step up to the first shale band. Climb boldly to the large tree in the groove.
2   50'   Climb the groove behind the tree, & then the wall above, until it is possible to move R onto the edge. Step onto the slab & jungle-bash to finish.   (1978)

4   Absent Friends   120'   E2 5b,5c
An eliminate-style first pitch leads to a good second pitch through the bulge R of the tree belay of Dumnonia.
1   70'   Climb directly to the crack at 15' which is 5' to the R of the start of Dumnonia. Continue direct, keeping just R of Dumnonia, to its tree belay. Bold & very eliminate.
2   50'   Step out R, then climb awkwardly to a ragged crack in the bulge. Pull over this, via some hard moves, to gain & then finish up the slab above.   (1988)

5   The Boltin' Hazard *(TBH)*   70'   E5 6a
Halfway along the base of the main black-streaked wall is a cave/niche. The route starts some 20' to the L, beneath an obvious BR. Climb up just R of the BR passing an upside-down PR on the way. Hard moves up to & past the BR lead to good holds in some boreholes. Continue up RWs to a BB.   (1987)

6   A Poke in the Hole *(PH)*   70'   E3 5c   ★
Climb to the top of the cave/niche to a partially hidden PR. Hard moves lead up RWs, & then back L to a good borehole layaway & poor PR. Traverse up RWs to another borehole & PR, then trend up LWs to the BB of *TBH*.   (1987)

7   The Black Streak   70'   E4 6a
Climb the wall stained by a dark-coloured diagonal stripe (running the full height of the wall), past a PR at 20'. Hard moves up LWs over a bulge, lead to a naturally rising traverse-line to gain a BB (in common with *TBH*).   (1987)

8   Spear & Jackson *(SJ)*   40'   E1 5b
The slabby white groove on the RH side of the face leads to some prominent boreholes at 20'. Hard bridging up the groove above gains easier ground & a TB. Abseil off; or do the. . .   (1987)

9   Hazardous Traverse   120'   E3 5b,5c
1   40'   As for *SJ* to its TB.
2   80'   Move up L to a PR, then traverse LWs just below the PR

(past various boreholes) until the edge of a black rib is reached (*Friends*). Step up LWs around the rib to a PR on *PH*, then continue to the BB of *TBH*. Step down LWs via hard moves to some more boreholes which are followed to a white rib. Step down around this to gain the tree belay of Dumnonia.   (1987)

10   Therapeutic Structures   50'   7c+ (E6 6c)   †
A bold & powerful undertaking. To the L of the wildly OHing prow of Garth is a steep white, curving rib with 2BRs. Climb direct past both BRs. Finish airily up RWs to the BB of Garth.   (1989)

11   Garth   50'   7b (E5 6a)   ★★★
The route of the quarry. A flat-out, look at my pectorals, hairy chested celebration of the pump. Climb direct to the base of the fin that sticks out into the middle of nowhere. Invert & pass a TR to gain the flying rib & a natural TR (which is hard to place). Thug up to another TR, then wilt across RWs onto a cramped slab & the final TR. Stride out LWs & finish direct to a BB.   (1987)

12   Scone-on. . . (the Cream Tea Slayer)   60'   E2 5c   ★
Start as for Garth! After 10', traverse RWs to the base of a hanging groove & climb this, past 2TRs (the second is *in-situ*). From the second TR step out L to follow a wafer-thin flake out past a BR to the arête of the prow of Garth (hard & exposed): or, wimp-out & squirm into a cleft above the BR, which is much easier than it looks. Finish as for Garth.   (1988)

13   Banzai   70'   E2 5b
Start at a cave R of the base of Garth. Climb up the slanting chimney above the cave to gain the top of an obvious large nose of rock. Traverse RWs via a rising line of holds until beneath a curious keyhole flake (TR) in the lip of the bulge. Swing up RWs past this, & scamper up the wall to a TB. Abseil off.   (1987)

14   Le Hazard   70'   7a+ (E4 6b)   ★★
Powerful stuff with a whiff of Peak-style tactics! Start at the lip of a large low-level roof, beneath a crack with a PR at the base of it. *Stick-clip* the PR, & hand-over-hand up the rope until abreast of the PR. Climb the crack to a BR out R. Traverse RWs past this to an overlap & another BR. Lunge up for the break (tricky), & finish as for Banzai. Abseil off.   (1988)

15   Samurai   70'   E3 5c   ★★
A fine, although committing route which climbs the RH side of the low-level OH & prow R of Garth. Start at the base of some deep cracks which are R of an elder tree. Climb the cracks until it is possible to traverse LWs on good undercut jams. Step down to a small hold by a borehole, from where difficult moves lead up past a PR & around the arête to gain the keyhole flake (TR). Follow Banzai to its TB. Abseil off.   (1979)

16   Underwhelmed   70′   E3 5c
The obvious line above & parallel to Samurai. Start as for Samurai & climb straight up for 30′ to a large TR. Traverse LWs to gain an undercut lip of rock, then pull up into a short corner (PR). Traverse LWs to gain a slab, then finish diagonally LWs to gain the TB of Banzai. Abseil off.   (1988)

17   Grooverider   70′   E2 5b   ★★
Start 10′ R of Samurai, below the LH end of a ledge just above head-height. Gain this, then climb a vague groove direct past a BR to another ledge. Climb up RWs to gain the LH side of a sharply-defined groove (PR), then swing gymnastically into it on jugs & move up to another PR. From the top of the groove traverse RWs (PR) for 5′ to a TB.   (1988)

18   Tapes of Wrath   110′   E3 5b,5c
Start 10′ to the R of Grooverider, beneath an orange cleft.
1   60′   Climb the cleft for 15′ to a spike, then step up L past the BR on Grooverider to gain a decaying ledge. Foot-traverse this LWs to the sanctuary of a solid niche, then step down L to a cave (TBs).
2   50′   Follow the rising traverse-line of a wide break (3TRs) which leads LWs to the edge of the buttress. Climb a short groove, then traverse LWs to the TB of Banzai.   (1988)

19   Croix de Guerre *(CG)*   60′   E3 5c   ★★
A fine route up a solid grey wall behind a clump of elder trees R of Grooverider. Climb direct to a BR at 25′. Step up L through a bulge, then continue past 2TRs to a further BR. Climb direct through the bulge above to the TB of Grooverider.   (1988)

20   Haphazard   70′   HS 4b
Climb the middle of a slabby wall (some 10yds R of *CG*), then finish just L of an OH. There are other routes hereabouts, but none of these are worth recording.   (1979)

21   Loose Grit   50′   E1 5b
Start below a clean steep crack at the RH end of the Haphazard wall. Near the top of the crack step out L onto a ledge, then go back up RWs to finish at a tree. Abseil off.   (1987)

At the RH end of the quarry is a low, unquarried, rust-coloured wall: The Dawn Wall. The routes are described from R to L.

22   Squonk   45′   E1 5a
Start 15′ L of where the wall peters out, by a curious cross-shaped recess topped by a crack. Climb the crack to a small ledge & continue slightly LWs to a vegetated finish.   (1986)

23   Ikhnaton   50′   E2 5b
Climb the wall L of Squonk direct, past a TR, then move slightly LWs on frail holds to a small ledge. Finish direct.   (1986)

24   Itsacon   50′   E1 5b
Follow the shallow scoop L of Ikhnaton into a crack (TR). Climb this
to a ledge, & continue direct to the top.   (1986)

BULLEY CLEAVE QUARRY   GR 742 667

Opposite the Black Rock Hotel (on the outskirts of Buckfastleigh) is
a quarry containing a bottled-gas works. Although not open to the
general public, the current owner (Roger Bowley) is willing to allow
small bands of dedicated "loose-rock" athletes to climb here (at
irregular intervals). There is a remarkable amount of rock, however
it would take a good deal of work and traffic before it was in any fit
state to climb.

The Quarry forms an amphitheatre 150′ in height. Its S ↓ wall is
formed by a long fin of rock with steep rock to either side. This is
The Pier, some parts of which are less than 2yds wide at the top.
Roughly 15yds from the end of the summit of The Pier (where it
degenerates into thick bushes) there is a small clearing containing
an aluminium stake belay. This is the final belay for the first two
routes described.

Descent is via a ←W retreat along the top of the exposed and
crumbling ridge of The Pier, from where a faint track leads down
RWs through the trees. Follow this to a path, which leads back
down into the amphitheatre.

1   Junior Leader *(JL)*   185′   VD   †
There is a prominent arête on the wall overlooking the workshops,
start beneath this.
1   25′   Climb up L of the arête to a ledge & tree belay. This pitch is
shaded from the omnipresent threat of rockfall by a small OH.
2   120′   Follow the RH side of the arête to a large flake at 45′.
Stand on this, then move R & climb direct (on good holds) to a
grassy ledge & a poor belay.
3   40′   Traverse RWs along the obvious line, then move up to the
aluminium stake belay.   (1985)

2   Me Thane   200′   S 4a,-   †
Start beneath a R\L trending depression, 30yds R of the arête of *JL*.
1   80′   Follow the depression up LWs for 50′ to a rib. Trend back
RWs (steep) to a sapling, then traverse RWs to some bushes on a
large ledge.
2   120′   Traverse back LWs to the sapling, then climb up to an
unstable-looking rib composed of cracked blocks. Climb the wall
just R of this, then trend LWs easily to a ledge & bush. Traverse RWs
for 30′ to the aluminium stake belay.   (1985)

*R of the start of Me Thane is an area of rockfall beneath some
shattered OHs. R again (of this area) a fault-line trends up & RWs
across the lower third of the wall. Start beneath the fault-line.*

3   Molyslip   200'   S 4a,-   †
The slippery black ore of the fault provides the main technical difficulty.
1   80'   Follow the fault for 30', then move steeply up RWs to regain the fault & continue up it to a ledge (bush belay).
2   120'   Climb LWs (easily) over ledges to a long sloping ledge. Walk along this to its second bush, then climb the short steep wall above. Trend RWs to finish on loose rock.   (1985)

GALMPTON QUARRY   GR 877 561

This grotty quarry is recorded here for posterity's sake only. Thankfully the owners, the local shipwrights, have seen fit to ban climbing. They could not have done you a better service. The rock is rather featureless, while its quality is not above suspicion (when it can be found beneath the copious layers of tumescent flora), and the protection is. . . well to be honest, it's non-existent. All the climbs are on the main face, which is bound on the L by an unclimbed rib, and on the R by a corner that would give David Bellamy ecstatic apoplexy.

1   Port Tack   90'   VS 4b
Start on the LH side of the face, just R of a bramble-filled gully. Climb a wall to an oak sapling at 20'. Make a gently rising traverse RWs, followed by a long LWs saunter (about 10' from the top) to gain the finish.   (1966)

2   Main Mast   90'   S
A line with minimalist appeal; it has nothing to offer. Climb the centre of the face on sloping holds to a ledge, then follow a shallow groove leading to a *clarty* exit.   (1966)

3   The Final Taxi *(TFT)*   110'   E1 4c   †
. . .leaves around 10' L of a large tree on the RH side of the main-face, *my advice to you is to be on it*. Trend diagonally LWs on clean rock to a small bush two-thirds the way up the wall (the only runner, *it could do with some 'Baby-bio' if you're in the vicinity*). Continue direct for a further 25', then move RWs to finish on the edge of the face.   (1984)

4   Up the Creek   60'   S
Climb the obvious dark band of rock (R of *TFT*).   (1984)

5   Ropeway   60'   S
Start behind the large tree R of *TFT*. Climb an open scoop, then trend LWs up the wall to finish.   (1966)

6   Slipway   60'   S
Start 20' R of the large tree. Take a parallel line to Ropeway to finish at the same point as that route.   (1966)

PLYMOUTH AREA

Plymouth is flush with a nautical history spanning the millenia. King Athelstan probably had a flotilla of hide-bound coracles based here, and the city also played host to Francis Drake and his fateful game of *boule* on the Hoe. Pirates, naval ratings of every description and round-the-world yachtsman have plagued the local women (and men) ever since, right up to the city's present day standing as the re-fitting centre for the Royal Navy (much to Rosyth's chagrin).

There are four developed cliffs within the city limits of Plymouth. They offer a variety of *ersatz* climbing to the impoverished urbanite. Hexton, Hooe Lake and Radford quarries share a rather fine location close to Hooe Lake (which is a large salt-water enclosure), whilst Richmond Walk occupies a banned location (to climbers at least) at the Stonehouse end of Union Street. Plymouth's saving grace is that it does possess some extensively fine bouldering which is dealt with elsewhere.

RADFORD QUARRY   GR 505 531

Cars should be parked at the end of Hooe Lake by the dam bridge. The entrance to the Quarry lies just beyond a chain-link fence adjacent to the car park. Follow the quarry track into the amphitheatre, where the main slab becomes apparent. There is literally nothing on the slab (that goes for protection as well), but the following offerings provide the best of the climbing.

1   Left Edge   100'   HS 4b
Start 10' R of the L arête. With anally-retentive precision follow that line to a PB in a short groove just below the top.   (1972)

2   Loner   100'   VD
Climb direct up to, then gain a L/R diagonal gangway (R of Left Edge). Step back LWs & climb direct to a ledge. Continue up to an earthy ledge before ending up at the PB of Left Edge.   (1970)

3   Gangway   100'   HVD
Start below the middle of the diagonal gangway. Take the easiest line up to a bulge, then traverse LWs to gain the gangway (old bolt stub). Continue RWs up to an earthy ledge, then step up L to a larger ledge. Climb up a corner to a pocket, before traversing LWs to the PB of Left Edge.   (1969)

4   Mac's Route *(MR)*   100'   VS 4b
Follow Gangway to the bulge, passing the remains of a bolt. Climb over the bulge & traverse RWs across a black streak. Continue direct to an earthy ledge, then climb over a shallow overlap to a

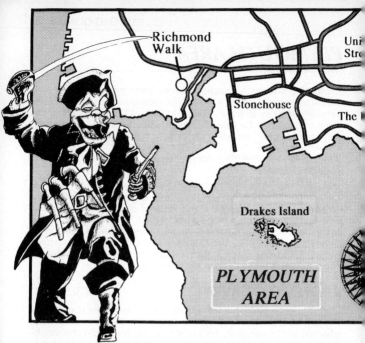

pocket followed by a ledge (PB). Either abseil off, or climb friable
rock on the R to top-out.   (1972)
Variation Climb direct up the slab to join *MR* just R of the black
streak. Climb over the bulge using a small pocket.   (c.1970s)

5 Central Route *(CR)* 110′ HVS 5a
Start 10′ R of *MR*, below a slight bulge (L of a black streak). Climb
direct to the bulge (flattened bolt). Step up LWs to gain a small
ledge, then go directly up to a long ledge. Climb diagonally RWs
for 30′ to a PB.   (1972)

6 Strictly Private 115′ HVS 5a
Follow *CR* to the flattened bolt, step R to some undercuts & continue direct up the bald slab to finish.   (1977)

7 Rockets 110′ VS 4c,4b
Begin 20′ L of Cleavage at the base of a thin crack.
1 70′ Climb direct to a depression below a vegetated ledge.
Continue delicately up to a second depression, above which there
is a ledge (PBs).
2 40′ Move up L to a further depression; finish direct.   (1970)

8 The Long Slide *(TLS)* 110′ HVS 5c
Climb the slab direct, about 10′ L of the obvious crack.   (1977)

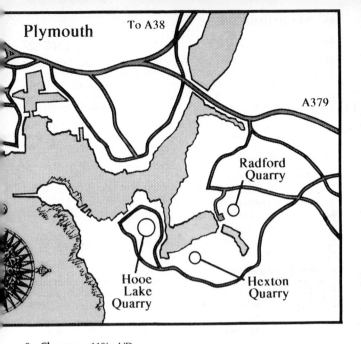

Plymouth
To A38
A379
Radford Quarry
Hooe Lake Quarry
Hexton Quarry

9 Cleavage 110′ VD
Follow the obvious crackline up to a large ledge & PR, then continue direct to the top; finish up a corner. (1969)

10 The Lonely Hold 115′ HVS 5a
A parallel line to *TLS*. Start 10′ R of the obvious crackline. Follow an overlap LWs to the crack, then finish up Cleavage. (1977)

11 Lunatic 120′ S 4a
1 70′ Follow the corner bounding the RH side of the slab, to a pocket & a PB above.
2 50′ Move up to the overlap, then traverse LWs beneath it to finish as for Cleavage. (1972)

Many traverse-lines have been done, the best being the line at 40′ which passes beneath the bulge:

12 Tremulous Traverse 150′ VS 4b,4c,-
1 60′ Follow Left Edge until level with the bulge below the gangway. Traverse RWs beneath the bulge to the remains of a bolt on *MR*. Continue RWs to belay by the flattened bolt on *CR*.
2 70′ Delicately traverse RWs to a pocket, & continue R to join Cleavage. Climb up to its PR & belay.
3 20′ Climb Cleavage, or abseil off. (1972)

HEXTON QUARRY   GR 502 527

The quarry is council-owned. From the car park (next to Radford Quarry), follow the footpath across the dam toward the sewage works. Skirt the smell RWs to where the path steepens, then continue up the hill (ignoring the LH fork in the path) to a stile on the R at the top of the hill. Walk across a heath to the top of the quarry.

There are a number of short cobweb-encrusted routes on the smooth slab at the back of the quarry, opposite the houses. The most effective entry is to abseil from trees on the quarry rim. The routes are described from R to L.

1   Suburbia   65'   VS 4c
Climb the slab just L of the RH bounding corner.   (1983)

2   Ringworld Engineer   65'   VS 4c
Follow the vague weakness on the RH side of the slab.   (c.1970s)

3   Hot Fun   70'   HVS 4c
Climb directly up the middle of the slab to a thin overlap. Follow this for 10', then step L & finish direct.   (1979)

4   Slippin' and a Sliding   65'   HVS 5c
Follow Hot Fun to the overlap, then move L & climb to a thin crack. Trend back RWs to climb the blank slab above, which leads to better holds & the top.   (1983)

5   Charlie Don't Surf   65'   VS 4c
"...he just sits in the jungle getting stronger". Climb the slab direct, via the obvious pocket.   (1983)

6   Depression   60'   HVS 5a
Climb the depression on the LH side of the face.   (1983)

HOOE LAKE QUARRY   GR 496 528

The owner's disposition towards climbing in the Quarry is none-too-favourable.

This is an immense quarry which has unfortunately been overrun by vegetation. The cliff is ←W of Hooe Lake, and is approached by following road signs for Turnchapel. After descending the hill between Hooe and Turnchapel, turn R into Barton Road (just after the 'Gulf' garage) which runs along the ←W shore of Hooe Lake. Pull into a layby on the R after 400yds (just past a lime kiln fenced-off by blue metal bars).

The path to the quarry leads past the lime kiln & through a gate bearing the legend "Danger, disused quarry", to appear beneath the start of the Left Wing. The quarry can be conveniently divided into four sections: (1) The Left Wing consists of steep slab-angled grey rock and is heavily vegetated. The upper third is loose but at a lower angle. (2) The Central area lies to the R of the Left Wing (into which it merges), and is very loose even by Devonian standards. (3) Continuing RWs past a fence which blocks the path, you come to the Right Wing, most of which faces N ↑. The Right Wing is much steeper than the Left Wing and has many more features in the way of gullies and ribs. (4) Finally, there is the Turnchapel Face.

THE LEFT WING

There are three huts at the foot of the face (each in various stages of dilapidation) which serve as useful identification features. The first hut has two walls standing; only the foundations are left of the second; while the third is more or less intact. Above the first & second huts is a large tree covered ledge about 50′ up the face. This is The Forest. In fact the ledge is not continuous, as a narrow rib of rock divides it in two. This rib is a feature of Party Line. The quickest way down is to abseil. There is an overgrown path down from the top of the Left Wing round to the L. If this path is used, care should be taken to avoid damage to the fences & other obstacles.

1 Decembrist 70′ HVS 5a †
Start just L of the first hut. Climb up to a sloping ledge at 15′. Continue with difficulty up the slabby rock above to the foot of a thin crack. Climb up to the R, using the crack as a side hold, until a ledge beneath a small OH is gained. Step L & climb the groove above to a large hawthorn bush at the top. This pitch is poorly protected throughout.   (1965)

2 Octobrist 80′ VS 4c †
A line just L of The Forest. Start at the LH end of the first hut.
1 40′ Move up the light-coloured rock angling R up to a ledge. Climb the slight groove with difficulty (PR), then move R onto the end of The Forest. Tree belay.
2 40′ Traverse L for 5′ & climb up to a ledge beneath OHs (top ledge of Decembrist), PR. Move up R beneath the OH & scramble LWs to finish.   (1965)

3 Party Line 90′ S 4b †
The easiest line so far recorded. An enjoyable climb, but the top is even more vegetated than the start. Start just R of the second hut.
1 40′ Climb up (trending LWs), to finish by a move R beneath a slight OH to gain The Forest.
2 50′ Step L onto the slab above the OH. Climb this to broken ground, then move RWs to the LH limit of the sound rock above. Climb a short wall, then scramble LWs to the top.   (1965)

4 Jacobin 90′ VS 4b
The first route on the cliff. Start R of the second hut.
1 40′ Trend up LWs to a sloping ledge at 15′. Climb slabby rock above to a small ledge (PR), & move up RWs to gain the RH end of The Forest.
2 50′ Climb up for 20′ to a ledge (TR). Step out L to a large

foothold, then move up delicately over a slight bulge onto the lip of the slab above. Make a tricky move to the R to gain a small bush. Scramble over earth & ivy to the top.   (1965)

5   Bolshevik   90'   S 4a   †
A direct line up slabs R of The Forest. Start about 30' R of the second hut.
1   60'   Climb easy ground for a few feet, L of a slight groove, to a small ledge above which the rock steepens. Move slightly R (PR), then move up & R, & continue direct. A final steep step leads to a grass ledge & small tree belay 8' higher.
2   30'   Move 5' R from the belay. Climb steeply up & then back L to large blocks. Climb over these, & continue LWs over indifferent ground to the top.   (1965)

6   Bachillinus   100'   HS 4b   †
Start just L of the third hut.
1   60'   An unprotected pitch. Climb diagonally up LWs to a ledge at 40'. Move back R into a shallow groove, & climb this until beneath a shrub-covered ledge. Traverse RWs beneath this ledge to a sapling belay.
2   40'   Climb up, R of the main ledge, then move L & climb a broken rib L of a slabby depression.   (1965)

7   Hammer   100'   S 4a
Start behind the RH corner of the third hut, to the R of a depression in the cliff.
1   45'   Follow a line diagonally up to the L (passing a number of borehole strikes & a small cave) to gain a tree belay on a small ledge.
2   55'   Climb diagonally up to the R until broken rock is reached. Then climb straight up to the top.   (1965)

8   Sickle   100'   HVS 5a,4a   †
Start some 15' R of the third hut, beneath two borehole strikes.
1   45'   Using the borehole strikes climb up to a small ledge on the L; small bollard runner above. Climb up RWs beneath a small OH until below a small cave mouth some way above. Surmount the OH at this point, then climb up to the cave. Traverse RWs to a grassy ledge & tree belay.
2   55'   Climb slightly LWs up the corner above (L of a slab), then continue over broken rock to join & finish up Hammer.   (1965)

9   Trotsky   100'   VS 4c,-
The first pitch gives some of the best climbing on the Left Wing. Roughly 50' R of the third hut there is a projecting block (at 70'), which is above a pinkish slab. Start beneath the block.
1   60'   Climb a slight depression on the L, then move R & up to a small L-shaped OH, PR. Turn this on the L to a ledge. Traverse RWs for a few feet above the OH, then move up to a hole in the rock. Move out L & climb up the pink slab, turning the block on the R. Flake belay with stance on the block.

2   40'   Move L & go direct, before angling RWs (beneath loose blocks) to the top.   (1965)

Nothing, as yet, has been climbed in the central section. Some 200yds further round to the R is:

THE RIGHT WING
The Right Wing begins on the other side of a retaining fence, opposite an isolated pinnacle. The initial buttress has an impressively smooth front face (Broken Gate Buttress), which is as yet unclimbed. The first route lies between two sets of gates.

10   Kulak Groove *(KG)*   90'   HVS 5a,-   ★
A route of great character. Start about 10' L of the RH gate, beneath a prominent groove that becomes a crack at the top. There is an ivy-covered OH at 20', which bounds the groove's RH side.
1   80'   Climb up to a small flake, PR. Traverse out L with difficulty, then move up & R to a small bush. Climb the groove & then a slightly OHing crack to a tree belay a few feet from the top.
2   10'   Continue easily to the top.   (1965)

The following three routes (R of the fence), lie within the boundary of a caravan park. The owner's disposition towards climbing is unknown.

11   Sunday Express *(SE)*   90'   HS ?,4a,-   †
An amusing & enjoyable climb up the undercut rib 40' R of the obvious line of *KG*. Unfortunately the workmen's hut that was originally used to begin this pitch has disappeared. To compound this, the start is currently very overgrown.
1   40'   Climb up onto the roof of the hut (which no longer exists), & make a bold move onto the rib above the OH. Move L & climb the rib to the shoulder. Move R to a ledge & PB.
2   40'   Move back L & climb the rib until it is possible to step L above an OH. Continue to a tree belay just below the top.
3   10'   Continue easily to the top.   (1965)

12   Noebbles Buttress   100'   HVS 5a,-   †
This route is on the face of a buttress between *SE* on the L, & a prominent L/R slanting groove on the R.
1   55'   Climb up the OHing niche at the base of the buttress, & pull out of this LWs to gain the wall & slab above. Climb diagonally RWs up the vegetated slab, then move L into a short groove which leads to a broad ledge & belay.
2   45'   Wander up over loose rock to finish.   (1966)

TURNCHAPEL FACE
This is the face R of the Right Wing's RH arête. The route lies towards the RH end of this wall, & is in plain site of the landowner's house.

13   Genesis   70'   VS 4b   †
Start beneath an OH to the R of (& below) the large slab in the

centre of the face. Climb the groove in the LH corner to a sloping ledge beneath a bulge. Surmount this bulge on the R, then move delicately L across the slab beneath the large OH to a sapling. Climb the wall beyond for 20', then make a difficult mantel over a bulge, & traverse 10' R & up to the top.   (1966)

RICHMOND WALK   GR 459 543

The long limestone bluff overlooking Stonehouse Creek happens to be very accessible (10mins walk) from the city centre, but surprisingly quiet. That could have something to do with the fact that you are not allowed to climb here. This is unfortunate because there is a lot of climbing to be had. Many routes were done during the 1960s, and subsequent developments left the crag plastered-in routes, between routes, between routes. The rock is generally clean and sound, though in places the final 10' are dubious. A raised pathway divides the face into two distinct sections:

THE LEFT WING
It would be viable to climb on this face as it lies behind a huge retaining fence of a warehouse. However, it has become somewhat overgrown (through neglect), & the base is an almost impenetrable tangle of briar. The routes are described from R to L.

L of the raised walkway is a smooth grey wall followed by a corner.

1   Last Wall of the Castle   60'   VS 4b
A slightly improbable line up the steep grey slab. Start 20' R of the corner, & climb to a ledge above a slight OH on the R. Mantel onto a small ledge (PR), where another mantel leads to a move R. Climb the more broken rock above to the top.   (1970)

2   Armadillo   50'   HS 4b
The corner crack is laybacked on huge holds to a ledge. Continue with difficulty round the RH side of a slight OH. Step L (precariously) at the top to finish.   (1970)

3   Sahib Ibizi *(SI)*   65'   VS 4b
Start 10yds L of the corner. Climb up steeply on large sloping holds to a niche. Follow a slab out RWs to an OH (PR), then pull up over this on a good hold & stand up. Step into a blocky corner, then exit L at the top.   (1970)

4   Titus Groan   60'   HVS 5b   ★ †
A strenuous route up the impending pink wall. Start beneath a grey scoop, just L of the *SI* niche. Climb this by handjams (on the L), & step R beneath a steep crack. Follow this painfully to an awkward move onto a small hanging block. Hand-traverse across the OHing wall to some jammed blocks on the arête, then move up LWs to a sloping ledge. Finish LWs.   (1970)

5   White Rabbit   55′   VS 4c
Follows a line through the OHs further L. Start on the rocky platform at the LH end of the face. Climb to the foot of a steep corner on the L of a yellow & pink wall. Follow the corner to an OH, which is overcome by jams up on the R. Pull over onto a ledge, then make exposed moves up RWs to finish.   (1969)

THE RIGHT WING
The RH section is about 60′ high, & split at half-height by a prominent line of OHs. A R-to-L traverse follows this line (400′ HVD). The lower slabs give some fine problems of all standards. L of the long OH there is a groove:

6   Traffic Jam   60′   VS 4b
Climb the wall L of the groove; finish diagonally RWs.   (1980)

7   Traffic Lights   60′   VS 5a
Climb the blunt arête R of the groove.   (1980)

To the R, & above the long OH, is a smooth wall. At the RH end of this wall is another groove:

8   Mayflower   60′   HVS 5b
Follow the groove (loose rock); finish LWs at the top.   (1980)

9   Drake's Circus   60′   E1 5b
The rounded arête is climbed to a slight OH, where a move R gains a gap in the ivy & the top.   (1980)

10   Brec to the Vag   60′   E1 5b
Climb up to a crack in the OH. Jam this to a PR over the lip, then finish direct.   (1981)

The RH end of the face is defined by a slabby arête, topped-off by a wall. This gives the line of:

11   Brewery Arête   60′   VS 5a
Follow the arête in its entirety.   (1969)

12   Cash Investment   60′   HVS 5b
Climb the wall between the arête & an OHing groove.   (1980)

13   Diamond Lil   60′   VS 5a
Climb the OHing groove, then exit RWs to gain & follow a ramp leading back L to the top.   (1969)

14   Night Club   60′   E2 5c
Climb the wall R of the last route.   (1980)

SEA CLIFF LIMESTONE

> *Full fathom five thy father lies;*
> *Of his bones are coral made;*
> *Those are pearls that were his eyes;*
> *Nothing of him that doth fade*
> *But doth suffer a sea-change*
> *Into something rich and strange. . .*
>
> Ariel's Song – The Tempest

Regaling you with tales of beaches made of ice-cream, a sun which never sets, crystal clear water and probably the best routes in the world *(as they'd have it at Carlsberg)*, would not only be insulting your intelligence, it would also be selling the area short. Suffice it to say that The Armada, Napoleon and Hitler all made a bee-line for Torbay's fair shore-line. Well they headed in this general direction, but were dissuaded from landing by xenophobic local climbers like Drake, Nelson and Captain Mainwaring. Even T.S.Eliot was moved to verse:

> The sea is the land's edge also, the 'limestone' into which it reaches, the beaches where it tosses its hints of earlier and other creation: It tosses up our losses, the torn seine, the shattered lobster pot, the broken oar and the gear of foreign dead 'climbers'.
>
> (The Dry Salvages)

The area is a veritable pastische of climbing styles, type, character, nature, quality. . . to the extent that Monsieur Roget *(of dinosaur book fame)* gave up the ghost when he came to finding words that could equal Torbay, vis-à-vis climbing. The reason for such diversity revolves solely around the panoply of limestone rock-types that are on offer. Every buttress has a completely different feel. At Telegraph Hole you can be crimping the tail of a crinoid, while edging on the match-stick head of one of its distant cousins, roughly 6' removed on the family slab. The wave-like sweep of the Ferocity Wall at Anstey's Cove is in stark contrast to the grossly overhanging, and thinly bedded, horizontal breaks of the Old Redoubt. Then again the Dovedalesque rock of the Exile Buttress bears no relation to the composite rubble of The Wake Wall (the former directly atop the latter). They do say that a change is as good as a rest. If that is the case then you'll be able to climb all day, without fear of ever running out of steam. And with variety being the spice of life, you had better like Tindaloo.

However, this tale of near perfect bliss does need tempering some-

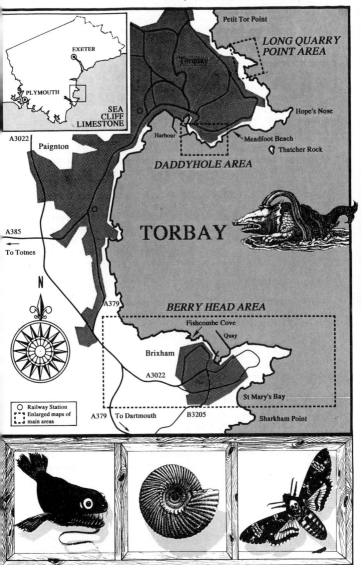

what, if only to bring it back from the brink of complete fabrication. Therefore. . . an acquired taste for loose rock can come in very handy on some of the less (and not-so-less) frequented routes. For in many respects, the surmounting of unstable terrain has been taken to quite exquisite lengths. Sanctuary Wall readily jumps to mind as such an example, while the Old Redoubt gives off an aura of great wobbliness despite being perfectly sound. Then there are cases of whole buttresses ignobly slipping off for a quick dip in the briny (check-out Daddyhole, or the ex-quarry pinnacle at Long Quarry Point). However, these considerations pale into obscurity when compared with. . . FULMAR VOMIT!!!

Intrinsically linked with climbing on the limestone of Torbay, is the ubiquitous aroma of guano, and unfortunately that of the vomit produced by the common or garden *fulmarus vulgaris*[1]. So powerful is the subliminal image of the said nefarious emmision, that it has permeated many cultural idioms: "There's no fulmar vomit on me"; "As happy as a pig in fulmar vomit"; "If you fell in a puddle of fulmar vomit you'd still come up smelling of fulmar vomit (and most certainly not roses)". I wouldn't go so far as to recommend the use of a full-biff chemical warfare suit, but it is in your best interests to keep a weather-eye on where the birds are nesting, and give them a generously wide berth.

SOME SEA CLIFF CLIMBING TIPS

Do not trust *in-situ* **gear.** There are an inordinate number of *in-situ* pegs and threads, as well as a few wires on the sea cliffs around Torbay. They are all in various stages of corrosion. Wherever possible back these up with some of your own hand-placed gear.

Many of the newer routes actually begin at the HWM. It is a good idea to uncoil the rope into a rope bag, so that you are ready to belay as soon as you get to the stance. Always belay securely, as large swells and the apocryphal Seventh Wave have a nasty habit of turning up at the most inconvenient of moments.

Invest in a Tide Time-table booklet for the area (usually 40p). It will save a lot of wasted time, energy and frustration.

It is a good idea to keep your *broddler* close to hand (or even pirate-fashion) on most of the traditional routes, for the impromptu gardening of vital holds, as well as the recovery of expensive wires.

Stay away from nesting sea-birds, especially fulmars.

---

[1] Pavlov proved, beyond any shadow of doubt, that the involuntary ducking-tic afflicting the majority of sea cliff climbers, could be faithfully reproduced in a controlled environment. Releasing a tiny amount of the infamous substance into a homeostasis chamber containing a climbing-pig (a rotund oaf, paid a guinea for his trouble), Pavlov candidly remarked that "the subject impulsively attempted to scale the walls, while bobbing and weaving in a state of wild-eyed terror".

LONG QUARRY POINT AREA (LQP)

Inhabiting the stretch of coastline N ↑ of Torquay, are an odd assortment of buttresses, crags and sea-level traverses. They encompass the much vaunted sport climbing arena of Anstey's Cove, the realm of insecurity known as Sanctuary Wall, and an unsung wealth of peculiar climbing constituting **LQP** itself. The satellite crags of Babbacombe and Petit Tor are also dealt with here (park above Oddicombe beach to reach Petit Tor).

When in Torquay follow the road signs for Babbacombe. These will eventually lead to a DIY Superstore, that has the attendant attraction of free parking. Having parked your motor, locate and follow the public footpath (beware the omnipresent and pungently-objective dangers of canine excrement) up onto Walls Hill Downs.

Tearooms and shops (selling comestibles and kitsch souvenirs by the plastic bucketful) abound in Babbacombe, which is a five-minute walk N ↑ across Walls Hill Downs.

PETIT TOR POINT   GR 927 663

Apart from having the distinction of being Torbay's most N ↑ limestone outcrop it is also the most under-developed. It is easily seen from either **LQP** or the Babbacombe Crags and exerts an almost sirenesque influence on all but the most devout anti-new router.

A quick boulder-hop and some easy traversing at the N ↑ end of Oddicombe Beach lands you in a quarried basin (the Devil's Armchair) with no real climbing appeal. However, the N ↑ ridge of the basin forms the S ↓ edge of a narrow cliff with a seawashed, wave-cut platform at its base. The platform is exposed from mid/low tide. Beware; the tide comes in exceedingly fast, so keep an eye on it. The sea-level traverses to gain the foot of the cliff (one from either side) are in fact far harder than the climbing there at present, so it is best to abseil from trees at the N ↑ end of the cliff.

1   Cunard Line *(CL)*   200′   HS 4a,4b
The natural rising L/R traverse line of the cliff, which starts at a scoop just above the wave-cut platform, beside a steep rib which forms the LH boundary of the crag.
1   120′   Climb up until steep moves R around the rib gain a ledge on the large slab beyond. Follow a discontinuous ledge system RWs, then belay beneath the slabby upper wall (PBs).
2   80′   Climb up to a scoop above the stance, then traverse RWs along a ramp. Step up a few feet, then trend RWs again for some 40′, until the top is gained.   (1979)

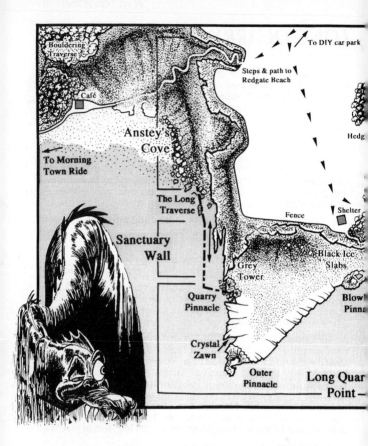

2 Deadline 110′ VS 4c,4b
Start at a faint weakness in the steep initial wall, about 20′ to the L of
a low cave.
1   40′   Climb the weakness to an obvious horizontal fault. Follow
this LWs to a shared stance with *CL*.
2   70′   Gain a R\L slanting weakness & follow it for 15′ to some
crystalline pockets & a PR. Climb direct to the ledge above (PR), &
continue for a further body-length before traversing LWs to a large
foothold (PR). Move up to an OH, then move L to gain a short rib
which leads to the top.   (1971)

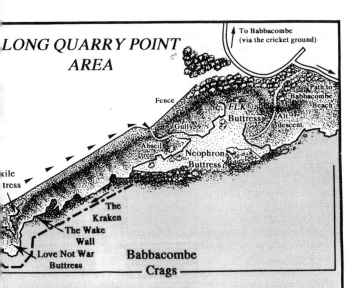

LONG QUARRY POINT AREA

To Babbacombe (via the cricket ground)

Fence

ELK Buttress

Path to Babbacombe Beach

Alt descent

Gully

Abseil Tree

Neophron Buttress

xile tress

The Kraken

The Wake Wall

Love Not War Buttress

Babbacombe
——— **Crags** ———

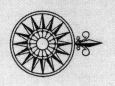

*Five leagues and more the beast did
   scourvage;
a great head prowed and gristening;
drippling fangs and wreakaged wake,
a portent of its ravening...*

BABBACOMBE CRAGS   GR 933 654

Approach and Access
From the DIY car park in Babbacombe (mentioned in the **LQP** Area
notes), walk up onto Walls Hill Downs and head for a distinctive
white shelter. The separate crag notes take over from this point.

Situation and Character
The area is comprised of a chaotic scattering of craglets, wooded
dells and pungent grottoes extending from Babbacombe Beach, to
the descent path which leads down into **LQP**. The area is more of a
summer/autumn venue, although calm days during the winter and
spring can give the crags more of an atmospheric feel.

WITHY POINT ROCKS

These Rocks form the E→ delineation of Babbacombe Beach. From the white shelter on the far side of Walls Hill Downs, turn ↖NW & follow a footpath which leads (after 550yds) to some bushes by the retaining fence. The bushes hide some steps which descend to a metalled road that hairpins down to Babbacombe Beach. The initial (squarish) buttress juts out into the sea beyond the beach-head jetty. There is a further square-cut buttress set into the hillside above a rocky cove (uncovered at low tide), which lies directly behind the initial buttress.

The first route makes an exploratory excursion along the HWM of the N ↑ face of the buttress jutting into the sea.

1   Quick Dip   60'   HVS 5a
A low tide traverse of the HWM along the wall facing Babbacombe Beach (from R to L).   (1990)

The following two routes tackle the squarish/recessed buttress in the hillside behind the Quick Dip buttress. There is a huge cave in its RH side, with a long seawashed wall set at right-angles to the cave. The wall & the cave meet to form the chimney of:

2   Siddaw Bwurda *(SB)*   80'   VD
A lack-lustre digression up the dripping confines of the chimney *(which would appear to be the seagull equivalent of a public convenience).* Forty pungent feet of climbing up the fissure lead to a decrepit PR. Above lies an OH, after which a traverse RWs gains a slab & the top.   (1969)

3   Kermit's Evening Special   75'   E2 5b   †
Start 20' L of *SB*. Climb up a wall to the L of a large ledge, then move up to an obvious break. Traverse LWs along this for 25' until a hard move gains the top.   (1986)

GASKINGS ROCK AREA

A leafy seaside dell which provides a clutch of fine routes. About 400yds ↖NW of the white shelter (& 100yds before the bushes that hide the descent steps leading to Babbacombe Beach), nip over the fence where it forms an oblique corner, & scramble down to the mouth of a grassy gully. R of the gully is a sheltered hollow containing a tree. Either; (1) abseil to the base of the crag from here (to gain the base of Neophron); or (2) continue to scramble to the base of the gully (via a rope handrail) to end up between the Neophron & Quantum of Solace Buttresses. All the routes are described from R to L.

*The RH section is dominated by a wooded slope, part way which is the camouflaged buttress of **FLK**. There are three prominent grooves on the buttress, the furthest R being taken by:*

4   All That Fall *(ATF)*   105'   HVS 5a,5b   ★
A direct & exposed (although well protected) route up the RH side

of the buttress. Start below an earthy bay at 50'.
1   55'   Climb a wall for 10', then trend RWs across a smooth slab to the base of a hanging right-angled groove. A determined series of moves up this leads to a PB in another bay up & R of the earthy bay.
2   50'   Pull over the OH, past a PR, into an open groove. Follow this to finish up the wall, exiting R at the top.   (1969)

5   Fake's Last Krapp *(FLK)*   120'   HVS/A1
An exposed route taking a shallow groove R of *ATF.*
1   50'   Follow the cleanest line to a stance & PBs in an earthy bay.
2   70'   Move up into another bay on the R. Use a peg to place another in an irregular crack on the L. In the same crack use another peg & three *wires* for aid, then pull into the groove on finger-jams. Move up R to a thread, step back into the groove (PR) & climb it to a rib which leads to easy ground; tree belay.   (1968)

6   Krapp's Last Fake *(KLF)*   90'   VS -,5a   ★
1   50'   As for *FLK.*
2   40'   Gain the ledge up to the L of the stance (PR), where graceless moves lead into an excellent corner. Follow this to a step L over a rib to finish.   (1968)

Some 10yds L of **KLF** *is a grey wall, with a central crackline.*

7   Quantum of Solace   60'   S 4a
A reasonable route on sound rock, although in dire need of a clean. Start 10' R of the crack. Climb to some ledges, then step L into the crack. Follow this to the top.   (1967)

L of the descent gully is a bulging, mottled white wall. Its LH section is dominated by the corner of Iconoclast. A boomerang-shaped series of grooves to its R forms the line of:

8   Neophron   120'   E3 4a,5c   ★★
Fine, sustained climbing. Start behind the largest tree (of the clump) at the base of the wall.
1   30'   Thrash up the vegetated wall for a few feet, then traverse RWs for 10'. Climb the wall above (past a PR) to a ledge. Move up R then back L to a PB 15' below & R of the base of the first groove.
2   90'   Make a rising traverse LWs to an area of crystalline rock. Step up R to a PR, then awkwardly gain a white shelf (poor PR). A scary traverse RWs on conglomerate rock gains the base of the first groove, which leads (via a short wall) to the second, the apex of which has a jug & minute spike (runner). Gain the final groove & follow the crack in its RH wall to the top.   (1969/79)

9   Iconoclast   110'   E2 -,5b   ★★
A feast of interesting features gives this dramatic corner a unique feel. Start L of Neophron, beneath a short corner leading to the base of the larger corner above.
1   30'   The short corner leads awkwardly (& lethally if damp) to a

stance & spike belay at the base of the corner.
2   80'   Pass a bulge in the corner (at 30') with difficulty, to gain the
capping OH. Traverse RWs under this for 10' to gain a jug, then
climb a short wall to exit LWs over a grassy cornice.   (1969)

10   The Cabinet of Doctor Caligari   110'   E5 -,6a   ★ †
An intimidating line with some fragile rock, which weaves up the L
wall of Iconoclast's corner.
1   30'   As for Iconoclast.
2   80'   Trend up diagonally LWs (from the base of Iconoclast's
corner), via a thin crack, to some ledges. Follow a steep groove,
passing a tied-off PR, to reach a poor sloping ledge with a good jug
above it. Using layaways up on the R make a long reach to better
holds on the lip of a bulge (TR). Continue direct to a small cave,
then gain & follow a hanging arête (TR) to finish direct over the
grim grassy cornice.   (1994)

11   Fear of Flying (FOF)   190'   E3 5c,5c   †
Since the large rock fall described in the previous guide this route
has remained unrepeated. Therefore approach with caution. Start
roughly 50yds L of Iconoclast, beneath a louring red-coloured wall.
1   100'   Traverse in from the L along muddy ledges, heading for a
shallow groove with a prominent PR & a sling at its apex. From the
PR traverse RWs with difficulty to another PR, then move up to
excellent holds above a bulge. Continue RWs to a big flake, which
has to be negotiated with care before descending to a stance & PB.
2   90'   Climb diagonally RWs (past a PR) to reach some big holds
on steep bulging rock. Climb up LWs to a pocket beneath an OH,
then make a long reach R & continue to traverse RWs (sustained) to
a rest at a deep crack. Continue to a deep slanting slot, then move
down & across the LH wall of Iconoclast. Follow this up & across its
traverse to join & finish up Neophron.   (1976)

*The following Scandinavian beastie is a sea-level traverse linking
Gaskings Rock to* **LQP**. *It is also used to approach The Wake. Start at
low tide on seawashed boulders L of* **FOF**.

12   The Kraken   700'   VII+   ★★
If climbed clean (ie. no jiggery-pokery with a rope, or recourse to
the out-of-bounds & bitterly cold waters inhabited by this monster)
this presents a feat befitting the attentions of any budding Beowolf.
1   360'   Initially easy climbing, or boulder-hopping, leads to a
smooth corner. Cross the top of this (4b), & continue past several
inlets to the base of a large OHing cliff (pallbearers for The Wake
depart here).
2   60'   Step onto an OHing wall from a huge boulder leaning
against the cliff, & climb up L for 10' to better holds. Follow a
slightly descending LWs traverse around an arête onto a slab
(taxing 5b).
3   80'   Continue LWs to a constricted corner (optional stance)
flanked on the L by another steep wall at right angles to the corner.

Climb the wall using hidden pockets, & then diagonally descend on a flake-line leading to desperate moves to gain & pass the L-bounding arête (6a). Continue LWs to the end of some ledges & belay.

4 60' Traverse the HWM LWs to an OHing nose, which is negotiated by some more arduous climbing (5b), then gain a quarried platform beneath the slab of Love Not War.

5 70' From the far side of this, excellent rock (about 20' above the HWM) leads to a small ledge above a cave (4b). A crack up to the L is descended LWs to gain slabbier rock (4c), then belay.

6 70' Continue to traverse LWs (with moves of 4c), to a smooth-looking wall beneath the plateau of **LQP**. Finnish by wandering along the base of this for a further 60' before topping-out to the quarry floor above.   (1969)

13 The Wake 160' E2 5b,5b,4c   *
An inauspicious, although apt location for a funeral (especially that of a Beowolf found wanting). A fierce adventure route; not recommended for the faint-hearted. Follow pitch 1 of The Kraken (2hrs either side of low tide – with a calm sea) to the base of a large OHing wall. A steep groove trends up LWs above a large boulder beneath the LH side of the wall. . .

1 30' *(Kyrie elieson)*. A merciless pitch. Step off the boulder to gain a large flat flake after 10'. Move up to a L/R slanting groove which is followed to a spacious stance on the L.

2 70' *(Lacrimosa)*. Take the open groove above the RH end of the stance to gain some sloping ledges. Step R to the conspicuous (& often weeping) L/R diagonal crack. Earnestly follow this to a rest where it expires, & pull over a bulge to good holds in a steep groove leading to another spacious ledge & spike belay.

3 60' *(Libera me)*. Climb the corner behind the stance. After 30' a steep scramble gains a tree belay.   (1976)

EXILE BUTTRESS
The crag is approached by following a vague path through a hedge roughly 50yds N ↑ of the white shelter. After a further 40yds the path ends atop a grassy shoulder. Descend a steep rocky slope on the R (facing seaward), then walk along the base of an ivy-covered wall to a flat grassy ledge above the buttress proper. A quick abseil gains the base of the buttress. On the R is the clean white groove of *HRB*, & to the L is the prominent scoop of The Exile. The routes in this area are described from R to L.

14 Harlem Rude Boy *(HRB)* 70' E4 6a   **
The RH side of the buttress is dominated by a clean-cut white groove. Start at the base of this. Climb onto a L/R sloping ramp, then pull up LWs over a bulge to gain the groove proper. Follow this (TR) to boldly gain a second TR in a pod above a bulge. Step onto the RH wall & climb this to the next bulge & a PR. The groove above leads to a TB.   (1993)

15   Me & My Magnum *(MMM)*   70'   E5 6b   ★★
This route takes the centre of the bulging wall L of *HRB*. Start beneath a TR 12' up the LH side of the wall. From this, head up R to a pocket (PR), from which a long move gains a jug. A blind slap up R is rewarded with a layaway & TR. Climb the steep wall above direct to a TR & PR. Continue in the same line, past a PR, to finish up the wall (PR) on pockets & hidden edges just R of a slight groove (T&NB).   (1993)

16   The Exile   70'   E2 5b
This used to be an ill-frequented & solitary route on an isolated buttress, until it was joined by a posse of contemporary routes. Start beneath the large depression at 20' & just L of *MMM*. Master the bulging wall beneath the depression, then climb up RWs from the hollow to a larger scoop. Follow the RH edge to a jug & PR. Finish as for *MMM*.   (1971)

17   Rave to the Grave   70'   E3 5c   †
Start 12yds L of The Exile (& 3yds R of *YKS*), beneath a blunt arête. Climb the arête (strenuously) via a series of large sloping holds to gain a short deep crack. Continue direct up wall above to an OH (PR). Pull over this on the L & continue up RWs to a T&PR (the belay of *YKS*). Climb the shattered wall above, then scramble through some bushes to a tree belay.   (1994)

18   You Know the Score. . . *(YKS)*   100'   E5 6b,6b   ★ †
A powerful start leads to fine, open wall climbing. Start 15yds down to the L of The Exile, beneath a bald R\L leaning groove.
1   70'   Boulder up the groove past a TR & 2PRs to a deep pocket & a hard-to-place #1 *Friend*. Climb the wall above via a large undercut to a flat hold & PR. Continue direct to the OH above (PR) & pull through this to the base of a short smooth slab. Traverse RWs to the arête & a T&PB.
2   30'   Traverse RWs to a PR, then climb direct to the capping OH (PR). Blind moves over this lead to a nasty loose exit & a tree belay well back from the edge.   (1993)

19   Hardcore   60'   E5 6b   ★★
Improbable wall climbing on immaculate holds. Start just L of *YKS*, beneath a line of holds trending up RWs to 2PRs (poor). Claw up the wall above to a sharp jug (PR), & continue direct by scaling the LH side of a white pillar to a PB.   (1993)

LOVE NOT WAR SLAB
The best way to reach this area is by descending the footpath that lies behind the white shelter (leading to **LQP**). About three quarters of the way down there is an overgrown traverse-line that begins at a wide crack. Scramble up this to a narrow grassy ledge, at the end of which there is a small cave, from here the descent becomes more discernable. There is a quarried platform just above the HWM & rising from the RH side of this is a vegetated rib:

20   Love Not War *(LNW)*   255'   HVD   ★
This route enjoys a fine situation, & has the added attraction of uniquely-weathered holds on the upper pitches (if you can be bothered to dig them out). Start at the foot of the rib.
1   50'   Follow the loose & exposed rib, or the open corner on its L, to a large ledge & PBs.
2   25'   Climb the wall L of a vegetated area to another ledge with high TBs.
3   60'   Trend diagonally LWs along the obvious line, then move back R to a narrow stance.
4   120' (Only 30' of which could be called rock climbing). Take a L/R diagonal line for 15' overlooking the sea, then move up to a terrace. Aim for the ash tree above (the belay), scrambling over shrubs to reach it.   (1967)
Variation 4a 100' HS 4a The original & less pleasant finish. From the third stance, move up about 6' & exit from the face by traversing LWs over loose vegetated rock. Scramble up through a small ash tree to good TBs on the L.   (1967)

Up L of the quarried platform is a steep wooded slope, with an impressive (although fairly vegetated) dark grey slab rising above the tree-tops:

21   Snoopy   150'   VS -,4b,4b
This scales the dark grey slab, starting by the sycamore tree.
1   70'   Climb easily for 40' to a PR, then traverse RWs across a smooth slab to a good stance & PBs.
2   40'   Traverse back L above the slab (for 15') to arrive awkwardly at a foothold & PR. Move up to a borehole (slot-in peg), & continue direct to a sloping stance at another borehole (PBs).
3   40'   Move up to a groove & continue up RWs for 5' to a PR. Traverse LWs around a bulge & follow a groove (beware the loose rock) until the angle eases. Belay on pegs.   (1969)

R of the quarried platform (looking seaward) there is a wall above a shallow cave at sea level (mentioned in The Kraken). The following route climbs the wall above the cave.

22   Sea Slater   60'   HS 4b
Traverse out from the quarried platform to gain the crack above the cave, then move R at the top to finish.   (1986)

LONG QUARRY POINT   GR 937 651

Approach and Access
From the DIY car park in Babbacombe (mentioned in the **LQP** Area notes) walk up onto Walls Hill Downs, then stroll over to the white shelter by the retaining fence. Behind the shelter is a gap between the retaining fence and some hawthorn bushes. Squeeze through this and follow the steep descent path to the quarry floor below.

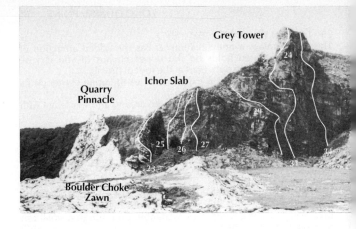

Situation and Character
LQP is an extraordinary sight. Perpendicular walls of quarried limestone descend to a broad, grassy (almost machined) plain which
stretches out into the bay. The Quarry faces due E→ which makes
for a bleak winter venue if it is at all windy. During the summer the
sun remains in the quarry until noon, after which it becomes a
shady retreat from the heat of the day. The rock is generally sound,
even the omnipresent concretions have stood up well to the traffic.

**The routes around the seaward rim of the Quarry are described first,
followed by the routes on the high landward walls and slabs.** The first
feature to be encountered is the Blow-hole Pinnacle, connected to
the Outer Pinnacle by a long, low sea wall (good for traversing). A
series of shorter walls lead to Boulder Choke Zawn, which guards
the entrance to the base of Quarry Pinnacle. R of Quarry Pinnacle is
the first landward buttress; the smooth grey Ichor Slab, which lies
below the LH toe of the menacing bulk of The Grey Tower. R again
is the black wall of Shadow Beast, followed by the inset slab of
Basking Shark and the main sweep of The Slabs.

BLOW-HOLE PINNACLE
This lies directly across from the descent path. There are two
approaches to the routes. Either descend the seaward face of the
pinnacle, or slither down the gash L of the blow-hole.

1   Waterline   30′   6c+ (E3 6a)   ★
When looking seaward from the back of the hole, the line takes a
rising L/R series of sloping ledges (BR), to some good undercuts
(BR). A desperate finish over the lip of the OH, leads to a BB up on
the ridge.   (1991)

2   Losing My Religion (LMR)   80′   7b+ (E6 6b)   ★★★
A sensational route (9BRs). A big boulder inhabits the bottom of the

Long Quarry Point

blow-hole. At mid/low tide it is possible to gain this, then boulder-hop to a niche (BB) at the base of a steep rib (which rises up to meet the roof of the hole). Climb the RH side of the rib to gain a hanging wall. Traverse LWs to meet the multi-tangential facets making up the maze-like crux. Attain the sloping ramp beyond & head for a beckoning TR. Climb the wall above direct to a BB on the ridge. At mid/high tide it is possible to traverse LWs to the second BR & continue from there.   (1991)

3   Waiting for Charlie *(WFC)*   60'   7c (E6 6b)   ★★
Using the seaward approach, descend a slab LWs to a BB at the base of the hanging outer arête of the cave. Climb the underside of the OHing arête (past 4BRs & a TR), to join *LMR* at its TR. Follow *LMR* to finish.   (1992)

At the time of writing there is an unfinished bolted project on the LH wall of the cave.

OUTER PINNACLE
This pinnacle has a long, hidden seaward face. It also forms the most seaward extent of the quarry floor.

4   Jumping Jack Flash *(JJF)*   100'   VS -,4c
Start L of the pinnacle (facing seaward).
1   60'   Traverse in about 15' above the HWM, then continue diagonally LWs to a band of OHs. Step down & across to a cave with TBs.
2   40'   Climb a crack on the L until it is possible to move into the corner, PR. Climb this on layaways to gain steeper white rock, where an escape L is possible. (The original finish continued over the OH – HVS 5a).   (1968)
Variation 1a 40' Begin on the other side of the pinnacle. Slide down a slot in the rock about 15' from the sea, then climb diagonally RWs into the cave (interesting).   (1969)

5   High & Dry   90'   E1 -,5a/b
A steep & nasty crux on suspect rock. Start as for *JJF*.
1   40'   Follow the traverse of *JJF* to a stance on a slab beneath a
rounded ramp running up LWs (20' before the cave belay of *JJF*).
2   50'   Climb the ramp to a delicate move LWs to gain a good
foothold. Trend up LWs into a corner (past a PR), then step up RWs
with difficulty by using some undercuts. Finish via a hard move LWs
to good jugs.   (1968)

CRYSTAL ZAWN
Essentially the preserve of the deep-water soloist. This is a compact, hidden wall which can be found by standing on the 'Cove'
side of the Outer Pinnacle. Where the Pinnacle starts to rise from
the quarry floor a slab of Verdonesque rock drops away into the sea
(this provides some of the finest climbing in the area & can be
scaled anywhere at S 4a or below). Crystal Zawn bounds the RH
side of the slab (looking seaward). The routes are described from R
to L.

6   Midget Gem   20'   E2 5c
Descend the slab to the HWM, then step across a fissure onto the
wall. Climb this on crisp pockets to a thin crack snaking through
the overlap. Gamely follow this to the top.   (1987)

7   Crystal Pockets *(CP)*   25'   E1 5b   ★★
Follow Midget Gem, then traverse the HWM LWs to the middle of
the wall. Trend up LWs to a line of large pockets which lead
through a bulge. Follow these to the top.   (1987)

8   Honour Bright   20'   E1 5b   ★
Gain the start by descending easy rock on the far side of the wall.
Traverse RWs along the HWM to gain the base of a steep corner.
Climb this to an interesting exit.   (1989)
Variations This route can also be gained by continuing the traverse
of *CP* (E2). Alternatively, if the R arête of the corner is followed by
this approach the grade is E3 6a.   (1989)

BOULDER CHOKE ZAWN
This is a bay of rock at sea-level about 100yds from the Ichor slab.
Its most striking features are the OHing seaward arête taken by
AOA, & the OHing diagonal crackline of Et Tu Brutus (at mid/low
tide the zawn can also provide an alternative approach to Sanctuary
Wall). The routes are described from R to L.

9   Arapiles, Oh Arapiles *(AOA)*   40'   25 (7a/E4 6b)   ★★
From atop the arête descend the glacis to the L (looking seaward) to
a quarried bay peppered with old iron spikes. Tie these off with a
rope to set up a belay at the HWM. From this point climb diagonally
LWs (bold), toward the arête to gain the first of four Arapiles-style
bolts (either use a keyhole hanger, or sling with *wires*). Follow the
BRs up the seaward face of the arête. Finish direct past the last BR.
BB well back from the edge.   (1992)

10   Have a Good Flight   45'   25 (7a+/E4 6b)   *
Follow *AOA* to the arête, where tenacious moves out onto the L wall lead to a BR & an extrapolated crux to the top via a short groove.   (1992)

11   Et Tu Brutus *(ETB)*   65'   6b+,7a (E4 5c,6a)   **
Descend into the zawn & belay below the start of a calcite shelf which runs horizontally RWs to the arête (10' above the HWM).
1   25'   Boulder up RWs to gain the shelf, then boldly hand-traverse RWs (past a BR) to gain a good N&BB where the shelf peters out near the arête.
2   40'   Step up & foot-traverse LWs along the shelf to the first of 4BRs. Follow the ensuing crackline tenaciously, to finish up the wall above the final BR.   (1992)

12   Red Centre   30'   21 (6b/E2 5c)   *
Belay below a hanging fang of rock which is just beneath a wide R\L diagonal crack (L of *ETB*). Gain the fang (BR) & mantel onto the bottom edge of the wide crack. Continue direct up the wall above (past 2BRs) to the summit.   (1992)
Variation Gain the start of the wide crack & follow it to the top; HVS. The corner to the R has also been climbed at VS.   (1992)

QUARRY PINNACLE
The routes are gained by descending into Boulder Choke Zawn & navigating a passage RWs (looking seaward) through the maze of rocks to a bay of sea-washed boulders which are exposed at mid/low tide. Since a rock fall this is now two separate pinnacles, divided by the conspicuous corner of *SC*. Again the routes are described from R to L.

13   Flambé   45'   VS 4c
On the zawnward face of the RH pinnacle are two OHing cracks. Flambé is the RH of the two. Steep hand-jamming up the crack leads on to the slab, then follow the thinner continuation crack pleasantly to the top.   (1978)

14   Crêpes Suzettes   50'   HVS 4c   *
Start beneath the LH OHing crack. Climb this forcefully, then move L into a scoop. Leave the scoop by tenuous moves, following the thin crack above to the top.   (1978)

15   Sea Slip   55'   S 4a
The obvious curving groove on the seaward face of the RH pinnacle. Start among the boulders at the foot of the groove. Climb a short OHing crack, then step LWs to gain the base of the groove. Follow this until it ends, then finish up a short wall. Starting up the cracked slab further L reduces the grade to VD.   (1978)

16   Ship's Biscuit   65'   E2 5b
The thin crack between Sea Slip & *SC*. Trend LWs to a foothold, then step L to climb the slab above direct to the top.   (1988)

17   Storm Child *(SC)*   50'   S 4b
Start below the corner which divides the pinnacle into two. Step up onto the L wall, before trending RWs up a crack which leads into the corner. Follow this to the top.   (1978)

18   Afterglow   80'   E1 5a
Climb the centre of the slab L of *SC* below & L of a groove in the upper face. Climb the obvious line *(there isn't one but you can pretend)*, trending slightly R to the base of the groove. Traverse LWs for 10' then go up diagonally RWs to finish.   (1983)

19   South Seas   80'   E1 5b
Climb direct up the slab for 60' on small holds (keeping just R of the arête), then trend RWs to a recess & continue up the face above to finish L of Afterglow.   (1988)

The next three routes all start from some ledges directly under the OHing Sanctuary Wall side of the LH pinnacle.

20   Slipperman   70'   E2 6a
Below the lip of the OH in the centre of the wall are two red patches & a PR; start below these. Move RWs on big jugs in a L/R slanting crack. Continue RWs to a square hold, then pull awkwardly onto the slab & follow the L arête of the slab to the summit (in common with South Seas).   (1988)

21   Supernatural Anaesthetist   70'   E4 6a   ★ †
Follow Slipperman to the end of its L/R slanting crack, then follow a break LWs until beneath a PR. Hard moves past this lead to a large hold & easier climbing up the summit slabs.   (1988)

22   Lamia   40'   E2 5c
Start below the notch formed by the LH side of the pinnacle where it rises from the quarry floor. Climb straight up the white wall to a crack leading LWs. Follow this to big holds on the slabby L wall of the pinnacle, then move L to finish.   (1988)

THE RIDGE
This forms the LH rim of the quarry (& the RH edge of Sanctuary Wall). Combining The Long Traverse with The Ridge & Grey Tower forms a taxing & atmospheric expedition.

23   The Ridge   70'   VD
Gain the ridge from the R & follow its crest to bushes above the Sanctuary Wall. A path wanders up R & then LWs through thorn-scrub to the top; or the base of Grey Tower.   (1964)

24   Grey Tower   60'   HS 4b
An exposed pitch up the white rib forming the upper LH edge of The Grey Tower. Approach via The Ridge & belay (peg in a borehole) beneath the rib. Climb the rib to a grey slab (PR), & follow its RH edge to the top.   (1964)

ICHOR SLAB
R of The Ridge is a smooth, dark grey slab which gives three worthwhile routes:

25   Ikon   60'   E3 5c   *
A bold undertaking. Start 15' L of the obvious central weakness of Ichor beneath a thin crack. Climb the crack to the overlap, pull over this & continue until footholds on the R can be reached. Finish direct up the short wall above.   (1979)

26   Ichor   70'   E2 5c   *
The obvious central weakness of the slab. Follow a line of holds for 25' to a PR, then make a taxing move up LWs to gain a thin crack. Sustained climbing up the crack leads to a flat handhold. Head towards, then follow a slanting grassy crack before moving R to a ledge at the top.   (1968)

27   The Big 'Y' *(BY)*   70'   E2 5c   *
Start beneath the RH arête of the slab (down to the R of Ichor). Climb this until a rising traverse LWs can be made to clip the PR of Ichor. Move up to, then traverse RWs along an undercut flake to a PR. Finish up the thin crack above.   (1983)

28   Complete the Asterisk   70'   E4 6a
An eliminate-style route between Ichor & *BY*. Start just L of *BY*. Climb to a tied-off PR at 12', then join & continue up *BY* to its PR at the undercut flake. Pull over the bulge above (PR) to gain a thin crack up on the L. Follow this to finish.   (1988)

THE GREY TOWER
A must for any enthusiast of gripping esoterica. ". . .Offer(s) good sport to those prepared to give it a go", was how it was sold in the last guide. Blade pegs & a hammer are *de rigueur* for most *voies*.

29   Cross Route *(CR)*   150'   S 4a,4a,4a
A veritable smörgåsbord of scrappy trivia. Start a few feet R of a large flake & about 20' L of The Magus.
1   40'   Scramble to a shallow groove & follow it to where it steepens. Bear R for a few feet, then move back L & climb the LH wall of a corner to a stance & PBs.
2   70'   Climb onto a calcite ledge, then traverse RWs for several feet to a small sloping ledge. Climb the block & wall above to a slab, then traverse LWs to a ledge below a large crack.
3   40'   Cross the slab by a rising traverse LWs, on small footholds, to the top (Grey Tower is an appropriate finish).   (1969)

30   Suicide   140'   HVS -,5a-
". . .is painless", however this route proves to be anything but. A woefully contrived, & utterly meaningless variation on *CR*.
1   25'   Start as for *CR* but continue traversing diagonally RWs to gain the calcite ledge on pitch 2 of *CR*. Belay at some dilapidated PRs equipped with a heavily corroded krab.

2   85'   Step R to another antique PR, then climb direct on poor rock to a black slab. Traverse LWs to a bigger slab & belay.
3   30'   Climb up until beneath an OH (above the slab) to gain easier ground & a scramble to the top to belay.   (1986)

31   The Magus   310'   HVS 4a,5a,4b,4c,4c,4a
An arduous & involved expedition, *but not as long-winded or as disappointing as the book*. It appears contrived but on the whole it follows a natural line. Locate a chipped arrow near the centre of the buttress below a very big borehole strike which forms a man-made shallow groove 50' up.
1   50'   Climb more or less direct (slot-in peg in a borehole) to a good stance at the base of the borehole strike/groove.
2   60'   Move down R for 15', then step R with difficulty to some ledges. Climb diagonally RWs for 20' (past 2PRs) until a hard move gains a brief respite on a good ledge. Climb direct to another ledge & good iron spike belay.
3   60'   Move up L awkwardly onto a larger ledge, PR. Traverse LWs along the slab (past a PR), then step down where it becomes a steep ramp. Continue LWs, then move up to PBs in an obvious slanting corner crack.
4   60'   Move up to an earthy niche & step R onto a block (PR). Climb steeply to a ledge (PR), then step R & gain a large terrace with difficulty (PB).
5   20'   Move to the LH end of the terrace & climb steeply on doubtful rock to a bush ridden slope. Scramble up for 5' to a PB in a borehole at the foot of Grey Tower.
6   60'   Climb Grey Tower to the top.   (1969)

32   Steppenwolf   260'   HVS 4c,4c,4c,5a,5a   ★
A route with presence, albeit spartan & cold *(traits that Hesse would have approved of)*. It takes a direct line up the shallow rib that bounds the open groove of Gilded Turd. Another chipped arrow marks the start, which is up the slope from the start of The Magus.
1   80'   Climb the rib for 25', then step L to a borehole (PR). Continue L for a few feet & climb up to a small ledge, from where the OHing L rib can be gained. Climb this (PR), until a line of undercuts leads R to another PR. Continue to a stance & PB above.
2   50'   Climb up to reach a rib L of a layback crack (PR) from where a short traverse LWs gains a large doubtful flake. Climb over this LWs, then continue direct to a cave stance.
3   40'   The OHing rib L of the cave is gained by an awkward move & followed until a step R gains a stance & PB.
4   50'   Move up R to a sloping ledge & climb a short wall to the top of a chimney. Strenuous moves to the R lead to a stance.
5   40'   Climb the OHing crack above to reach a sloping ledge. Continue up a short groove to finish.   (1970)
Variation 3a 70' E2 5b Move up & RWs until beneath the headwall. Trend up LWs, then make some difficult moves to gain a good

hold. Stand on this (using a dubious peg as a handhold), then climb direct up the steep wall above until the angle eases. Step L to a slab which leads to the top.   (1974)

33   Gilgamesh   280'   HVS 4b,4b,4b,4c,4a
Start beneath a vague buttress to the L of Gilded Turd (& just R of Steppenwolf), marked by a chipped arrow & the letter "G". Pegs & a hammer are essential.
1   70'   Climb up (trending LWs) to a series of overlapping slabs. Move back slightly R to an OHung corner leading to a stance (PB -in common with Steppenwolf).
2   70'   Move up easily for few a feet, then climb a corner leading to a large cave stance.
3   50'   Traverse RWs for 20', then move up & continue RWs to a corner below a red wall (TBs).
4   40'   Traverse LWs across the red wall to a spike, then climb up strenuously to a large ledge.
5   50'   Take the obvious line out LWs, over doubtful blocks, to finish on the summit of the Grey Tower.   (1969)

34   Gilded Turd   210'   HVS 4c,4c,4a
A route which requires a cool head (despite being low in the grade) due to the sloping nature of the holds & sparse gear. The start, marked by yet another chipped arrow, is about halfway up the scree beneath a vague white triangle of rock.
1   90'   Climb to a PR at the apex of the white triangle, traverse RWs for a few feet, then trend diagonally LWs to a glacis (PR on L). Climb the steeper wall above to good holds, then trend up LWs to a short corner. Follow this to a good stance & PB.
2   70'   Traverse LWs for 10', then climb direct for 25' to a horizontal crack (PR). Step up awkwardly & climb a vague groove on the R with difficulty (PR) to another glacis. Move R, then continue up LWs to a spacious stance & PB.
3   50'   Traverse LWs to a shattered rib which gives pleasantly exposed climbing to the top.   (1969)

35   Girdle Turd   320'   VS 4a,4b,4b,4c,4a
A L-to-R traverse of the obvious horizontal fault at about two-thirds height. Start at a crack formed by a large flake near CR.
1   80'   Climb the crack to a rib which leads to a small OH. Traverse LWs under this until it is possible to pull into an OH-capped groove. At the top exit L & go up to a TB in the fault.
2   40'   Follow the fault RWs to the third stance of The Magus.
3   80'   Climb The Magus for a few feet, then traverse RWs on undercuts to a small ledge on an arête. Around this is the cave stance of Gilgamesh. Follow this route for 20' to a stance below a chimney.
4   40'   Climb the chimney to a chockstone, then step R onto a block. A grass ledge provides a stance (TB in the corner above).
5   80'   The harrowing gangway on the R leads awkwardly to an

iron spike which is used to gain a ledge on the R. Follow this RWs until it peters out, then step down & move R to a loose groove which leads to the top. (1969)

THE SHADOW BEAST WALL

At the top of the scree slope R of The Grey Tower there is a dark black & red-streaked, dome-shaped wall. The routes tend to be on the bold side. However, the rock is excellent & protection (when reached) is sound. The first route described follows the curving corner on the LH side of the wall.

36 Osram 80′ HVS 5a   ★
Climb the corner for 15′, then step L to a ledge. Step back up R into the corner & follow it (past a bulge) until beneath broken rock. Step out R onto a slab, which is followed to a BB. (Either top-out by scrambling off LWs, or climb the following route). (1967)

37 The Odyssey 185′ HVS 5a,5a
A worthwhile continuation to Osram which traverses the upper band of rock from L to R.
1 110′ Climb the thin crack L of the belay to gain the obvious traverse-line. Follow this RWs on good holds for 60′ (past several PRs & BRs), until the line peters out at a PR. Continue RWs (thin) to a smooth niche & PB.
2 75′ Climb diagonally LWs for 10′ to a smooth rounded groove containing a PR. Follow the groove (delicate) to finish easily up vegetated slabs. (1969)

38 Ulysses 170′ E3 6a,5b
A bold pitch. Start 5′ R of Osram, beside a blunt rib (forming the LH side of the *USP* groove).
1 90′ Climb the blunt rib past a PR, then step up L onto a white

scar with a PR at its apex. Pull over a slight bulge to gain the start a of L/R rising ramp. Follow the ramp (bold) to another large white scar (PR). Step L, then climb the steep slab above which eases in both angle & difficulty. Scramble to the BB above.
2   80′   Step L & climb the thin crack of The Odyssey before traversing LWs to a PR. Move delicately up to good holds beneath a conspicuous short corner (PR). Exit RWs from the top of this (PR) & climb direct to finish up rather suspect rock.   (1969)

39   Odysseus or Bust *(OOB)*   90′   E4 6a   ★
An easier version of *USP*. Follow Ulysses to its second PR, then follow a lower ramp-line RWs to a ledge. Hard moves lead up & RWs to a PR at a bulge. Climb the bulge direct to a ledge & PR (in common with Ulysses). Step up R to gain & follow a shallow groove that leads to a BB.   (1987)

40   Up the Styx, Without a Paddle *(USP)*   100′   E5 6b   ★★
This climb follows the line of the impending groove down & R of *OOB*. Boulder up the wall to a BR. Perplexing moves past this lead to a brief respite at a good hold before more hard moves lead to a PR. Launch up the thin flake holds trending up LWs, to join & finish up *OOB*.   (1987)

41   Shadow Beast *(SB)*   100′   E6 6c   ★★★
Devilishly technical with a touch of bold climbing. Climb the centre of the black wall R of *USP* to a pocket. Make a rising traverse LWs to a BR, then climb up RWs towards 2PRs. Step up R & head for the distant BR above. Boulder up past this to a hard step L onto a big knobble. Scratch RWs up the vague shallow groove above (BR) to a further hard move to gain the base of a thin crack (PR). Follow the crack to a slab which leads to a BB.   (1987)

42   Thesaurus *(SB)*   70′   E4 6c
A slippery companion pitch to either *USP* or *SB*. Fathom a way up the bald steep slab (just R of the BB) to a BR. Faith-&-friction past this to easier ground (BR). Continue directly (past another 2BRs) to a perplexing finish to gain the BB (lower off).   (1987)

43   Hart of Darkness *(HOD)*   110′   E5 6b   ★
Start 25′ R of *SB*, beneath a stepped crackline on the RH side of the black wall. Climb the crack for 60′, to a PR beneath a shallow OH. Pull over this to a pocket at the base of a thin crackline. Hard moves up this lead, past a PR, to an exposed finish. Easier climbing leads to a PB at the base of the upper band of rock.   (1987)

44   The Minor Tour   70′   E4 6a
A good pitch to tack on to *HOD* (seeing as it begins from *HOD*'s belay). Climb a rusty brown streak above the belay to a TR, then move up (first RWs, then back L) to a PR & TR at the LH end of a small overlap. Continue direct to another PR, then foot-traverse LWs along a thin break to hard moves which lead to the BB of Thesaurus (lower off).   (1987)

THE SLABS
R of the Shadow Beast Wall is an inset slab (stained black), which is the substance of Basking Shark, while R again is the impressive sweep of the Black Ice slab.

45 Basking Shark *(BS)*   120'   E5 6b/c   ★★
Scramble up to a PB at the base of the inset slab. Move up to a PR at 10', then make a tasty rockover before continuing up L to bigger holds. Proceed to the overlap which is negotiated via a short groove (PR above). Climb up to another PR & small foot-ledge. Step L & ascend with difficulty to good holds. Climb the steeper rock above (with interest) to a niche & PB in common with The Odyssey. (Abseil off, or finish up The Odyssey).   (1990)

46 Normal Hero *(NH)*   80'   E3 5c
An alternative start to *GTT*. Start some 20yds R of *BS*, at the base of a L/R traverse-line which rises across a steep wall. Follow this, past a TR, & continue to an obvious block. Move up 5', then traverse RWs along a vegetated break for a further 20' to good holds beneath a bottomless corner. Climb this to the stance at the end of pitch 1 of *GTT*.   (1973)

47 Carbon Paper   50'   E4 6a   ★ †
A fine climb which has produced a number of copies. Climb the wall above the start of *RTD*, past a variety of *in-situ* gear, to the vegetated break of *NH* & finish as for that route.   (1990)

48 Ruby in the Dust *(RTD)*   180'   VS 4b,4c   ★
(It gets the star for botanical interest). The conspicuous rake of vegetation that rises across the slabs from L to R. The protection does not grow on trees. Start where the rake begins.
1   100'   Follow the rake, sometimes using it for the feet, until it rounds a slight rib to gain an easier-angled (& more vegetated) area of rock which leads to a narrow grass stance & PB.
2   80'   Continue RWs for 40', via a gently rising line, to a bulge below the edge of a smooth slab (PR). Make a difficult high step RWs (PR above), then continue more easily RWs to finish on the RH side of The Slabs.   (1973)

49 Renegade   170'   E4 6a,6a   ★★★
A magnificent excursion straight up the guts of the wall. Start some 20' to the R of *RTD* below a vague line of "slopers" leading to *RTD*'s rake.
1   80'   Climb the wall (bold) to a PR just above the rake of *RTD*. Step out L beneath the PR & follow a line of pockets to the base of a thin crack (PR) which leads to a shallow groove. Bold climbing up the groove gains a B&PB, where the wall becomes a slab.
2   90'   Discontinuous thin cracks lead up RWs to a good footledge & some poor wires. Boldly gain the ledge up to the L (good #2½ *Friend*), then boulder up RWs to a dangerously-poor PR. Either go up then R, or traverse RWs beneath the PR (more advisable), to gain

a line of holds leading past a PR to another PR. Hard moves, up L past the last PR, gain the 'bitter oasis' of a bald slab. Quit this (thankfully) via exposed moves up a thin flake up on the L. Trend RWs to a broad ledge & BB.   (1986)

50   Black Ice   170'   E3 5c,5c   ★★★
A *tour de force* of its era. You may need your gardening gloves during the summer though. Start about 50' R of Renegade, beneath some graffiti.
1   90'   Hard moves through the graffiti lead boldly to a horizontal break, PR (missing). Climb direct, via hard moves, to the base of a white scoop. Step up (bold) to reach the rising traverse of *RTD*. Move slightly RWs, then climb the 'crozzly' wall above (for a few feet), before heading LWs to a PR & better holds. Bearing slightly RWs, climb a line of thin cracks with some difficulty to gain a ledge above a bulge; PB.
2   80'   Move R & climb to a narrow ledge (PR). Continue to a horizontal crack which is followed LWs to the final steep wall. Move up to a crack on the L where a few steep cranks gain easier ground & the BB of Renegade.   (1973)
Variation 1a 90' E3 5c Start below a thin crack which runs down LWs from the white scoop to the top of a shattered block, just L of a tree (at the base of wall). Follow this line, to join & finish up the parent route.   (1979)

51   Grip Type Thynne *(GTT)*   300'   E1 5b,5a,4c,5a   ★
A long-winded expedition with a smattering of vegetation. It takes a natural, oblique R\L line across the slabs. Start about 15' up a grassy rake & about 20' R of Black Ice.
1   130'   Follow the slab diagonally LWs past a PR, then move up with difficulty into the white scoop of Black Ice. Follow this route past the 'crozzly' wall to easier-angled rock. Traverse diagonally LWs past the belay of Renegade to a grassy ledge; spike & PB.
2   30'   Step up before traversing RWs for 10', then move delicately up to good holds. Go diagonally LWs to a broad band of grass, & traverse this RWs to a good PB (L of a wide curving crack).
3   80'   Pull up into, then follow the wide curving crack to gain a clean grey slab. Traverse LWs across this, then climb diagonally LWs over more vegetation to a large grassy stance.
4   60'   Above & to the L of the stance is a wide groove/ramp; follow this to an exposed final wall. Climb the wall, & step R to good holds leading RWs to the top.   (1968)
Variation 4a 120' VS 4b Known as **Jaywalk**. A serious pitch offering an alternative finish to *GTT*. Make an exposed, vegetated traverse LWs for 45', then move into a smooth scoop (PR, the belay of The Odyssey). Move up R into a groove, then climb the obvious line leading diagonally LWs to a white ledge where the slabs are less steep (PR). After 5' of slab climbing trend diagonally LWs over grassy rock to the top .   (1969)

52 Captain Buttwash *(CB)*   170'   E3 6a,5b

A tempting line which somehow fails to live up to expectations; starting as for *GTT*, "at a large foothold 3' up"(sic).

1 90'   Climb up, using several sloping cracks, to reach the base of a very blank section of wall. Use small holds which lead to a PR, then move past this with difficulty to gain the sloping ledge above. Surmount the flake on the R & climb the wall above on horizontal breaks. Belay as for *RTD*.

2 80'   Climb direct over the bulge (PR) to a horizontal break & another PR. Climb up the middle of the blank slab above (past 2PRs), then finish up a groove.   (1990)

53 Band of Rusty Gold *(BRG)*   280'   HVS -,-,4b,4c,5a

A devious route, that remains un-recommended. On the R of the slabs is a short quarried wall, near the top of which is a red scar.

1 80'   Take the easiest line to below the red scar. Traverse RWs, then continue direct to a PB on a broad ledge.

2 30'   Traverse LWs along vegetated ledges, past the next slab line, to a PB under a steep wall.

3 90'   Climb the wall to gain a slab, & follow this LWs to below a white scoop. Climb the wall above to a small stance (PB).

4 30'   Traverse RWs to a high step to gain the smooth slab above. Move up past a PR, then traverse 10' R to a ledge. Gain the ledge above & a PB (escape is possible from here).

5 50'   Traverse LWs for about 30' to a difficult move up into an easy groove. Climb this to a PB. Scramble off.   (1973)

54 Coup de Grâce *(CDG)*   210'   VS -,5a,4c   ★

The original route of the slabs, & still worthwhile. Start beneath the highest point of a quarried wall, some 30yds R of Black Ice.

1 80'   Climb the wall to a large grass ledge. Move L to a PB beneath a slab running up to the L.

2 90'   Climb up a flake to a PR at hand level, then make a thin traverse LWs to good holds. Move easily up a slab bearing L, until the flake crack thins & curves over (PR). Make a high step up to gain the smooth slab above (in common with *BRG*), then follow *BRG* to its belay.

3 40'   Step back to the lower ledge, then move up LWs until beneath a bulge. Overcome this, & the perched flakes above it, to make exposed moves LWs beneath the final OH. Finish easily by scrambling up RWs to gain the top.   (1967)

55 Magic Carpet Ride *(MCR)*   160'   VS -,4c

Takes the smooth slab R of *CDG*. It is rather vegetated but pitch 2 gives sustained & quite serious climbing. Start about 15' in from the R edge of the quarried wall by a chipped arrow.

1 75'   Climb to a thin crack, then continue LWs up a ramp. Follow a vague groove (past grassy rock) to a stance & PB.

2 85'   Gain the grassy ledge (PR). Step up delicately LWs to good holds. Continue LWs for 10', then follow a line of thin cracks past a

prominent PR. Finish up either *CDG* or *RTD*.   (1969)

GIRDLE TRAVERSES

56   Transference   310'   E1 -,5a,5b,5a
A low level traverse of the slabs, rising from R\L. Start at the RH side
of the quarried wall.
1   100'   Cross the quarried wall at about half-height to a stance &
PB below & R of a large prominent flake.
2   60'   Climb up, then traverse LWs to gain a flake. Traverse LWs
along the top of this (crossing over pitch 1 of *CB* in the process) &
belay on joining *RTD*.
3   80'   Climb the wall above for 10', then traverse LWs with difficulty past a PR (in common with *GTT*), then follow the rest of *GTT*
to its first stance.
4   70'   Move to the LH end of the ledge, then climb down & step L
into a niche. Move up LWs, then traverse LWs into the large corner
fault & either climb this (certain death) or scramble down the grass
to regain the ground.   (1973)

57   Safari   555'   HVS -,4c,4c,5a,4c,4a,5a/b   ★★
A high-level traverse of the slabs from R to L. A taxing expedition
that is both sustained & nerve-wracking *(you may well have to send
out the odd gun-bearer on the more intimidating pitches)*. After
pitch 4 it may be preferable to finish up *GTT*. Start as for *MCR*.
1   75'   As for *MCR*.
2   70'   Follow the traverse-line of *MCR*, but at the end of that
route's traverse continue LWs for a further 20' (PR) until steep
climbing on good holds leads to the second stance of *CDG*.
3   70'   Traverse LWs for 15' (PR), then step down & reverse the
"high step R" of *CDG* to a PR. Continue horizontally LWs for 30'
(2PRs), then step down & traverse LWs to a large white ledge, PB.
4   60'   L of the ledge is a sharp flake, which should be treated with
respect. Go along this until it peters out, where thin moves LWs
lead to better holds on the smooth ramp on pitch 2 of *GTT*. Go LWs
up the ramp to a stance on a grassy ledge.
5   80'   Climb pitch 3 of *GTT* to its large grassy stance, then either
finish up pitch 4 of *GTT* or:
6   50'   Traverse horizontally LWs as for Jaywalk to take a stance in
the smooth scoop, PB.
7   150'   This pitch combines parts of The Odyssey & Ulysses.
Move down L for 5', then make thin moves horizontally LWs to gain
good holds on the obvious traverse-line, PR. Follow this easily for
60', then continue delicately for a further 20' to another PR. Step up
with difficulty to the foot of a conspicuous short corner (& a further
PR). Climb this, then exit RWs past a PR. Continue direct, taking
care with the rock.   (1969)

SANCTUARY WALL   GR 937 651

Approach and Access
Approach from **LQP** by; (a) descending into Boulder Choke Zawn
and skirting the base of the Quarry Pinnacle at mid/low tide; (b)
abseil from an old iron spike on the RH side of the Quarry Pinnacle
if the tide is high.

Alternatively follow The Long Traverse from Anstey's Cove for a
more atmospheric (and the most popular) passage. The routes are
described from L to R (as if approaching via this traverse).

Situation and Character
This is the large wall running along the headland from **LQP** towards
Anstey's Cove. It is acutely OHing and provides some of the most
spectacular and nerve-wracking climbing in Devon. The main
feature of the cliff is a huge central fault which begins as a wide
OHing crack and becomes an open, vegetated corner higher up.
The fault itself gives a poor route (Cinqtus) and a much finer one up
its RH edge (Sacrosanct).

Many of the routes on this cliff rely heavily on *in-situ* gear, most of
which is in various stages of decay. A lot of the older pegs have
been replaced with stainless steel pegs, and the majority of modern
routes are also equipped with these. However, you would be wise
to back up any peg with another runner if at all possible (and that
goes for all sea-cliffs and most of the inland crags of Britain).

1   Madness   250'   E5 5c,5c,6a   ★★★
The obvious soaring traverse-line across Sanctuary Wall gives
strenuous, intimidating, & wildly-exposed climbing. From the
promontory forming the outer edge of the Sanctuary, climb a slab
to easy ground, then continue scrambling to reach a belay near the
start of the line.
1   60'   A chilling hand-traverse RWs along a sloping shelf gains an
obvious groove. Continue RWs along the shelf to a hanging stance
at a corner (the upper groove of *CTW*).
2   80'   Move around the RH arête of the corner, then traverse
RWs to where the ledge ends at some suspect incuts. Swing down
R & continue at a slightly lower level to a long OHing ledge. Move
up from the RH end of this to an obvious hold, then pull up around
the rib on the R. Descend until a good crack on the R is reached,
then climb this to the stance of Sacrosanct.
3   110'   Move R & up as for Sacrosanct to a small ledge (optional
stance). Launch out across the faultline (which becomes difficult &
strenuous), following it to join pitch 2 of Incubus at a bulge. There
are a number of finishes: Either; (1) climb LWs to the top as for
Incubus; (2) pass the bulge on the R as for *CTA*; or (3) reverse pitch
1 of Incubus to end up in **LQP**).   (1983)

2 Brittle Road to Freedom *(BRF)*   180′   HXS 5c,5c 5c
A route which laughs in the face of the modern grading system. It is
a unique combination of pitches guaranteeing a wild trip through
all states of delirium. Start at the extreme L end of Sanctuary Wall
proper, at a TR & multiple *Friend* belay directly beneath the OHing
groove-line of *CTW*.
1   70′   The Asteroid Belt. From the belay continue LWs along the
obvious decaying shelf to an awkward niche. Bridge up out of this
on gradually improving rock to some ledges. Move L & belay as for
the first pitch of Madness.
2   60′   As for Madness *(pitch 1)*.
3   50′   Finish directly up the corner above the hanging belay (in
common with *CTW*).   (1988)

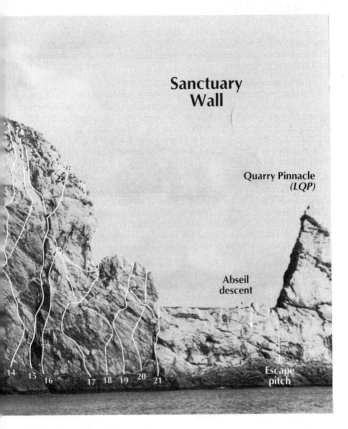

Sanctuary
Wall

Quarry Pinnacle
(LQP)

Abseil
descent

Escape
pitch

14 15 16 17 18 19 20 21

3   Balls of a Child   70'   E7 6b   †
This is the stuff that nightmares are made of. Belay as for *BRF*.
Scramble up LWs above the Asteroid Belt for 12' to a PR. Climb
straight up the hair-raising wall to a jug rail at 10' (2 poor PRs).
Trend up LWs (past 2PRs) to reach over a bulge to gain a big sloper
& stacked PR. Continue diagonally LWs to gain the ramp of Madness. Climb direct up the headwall to a good PR & a cemented jug
on the R. Finish up the L/R leaning groove.   (1992)

4   Kill Your Idol *(KYI)*   80'   E6 6b   ★★★
A sustained & provocative pitch at the upper limits of its grade.
Belay as for *BRF*. From the third PR of *CTW*, launch out L to gain a
seemingly detached square block (PR). Continue up LWs, then
diagonally RWs (past 2PRs) to gain the ramp on Madness. Step L to

the base of an incipient crack. Climb the crack (PR), then step L to the base of a slim groove. Climb this (passing 2PRs) to the top; PBs & abseil point directly above the exit. Two ropes are needed to reach the reef below.   (1992)

5   Call of the Wild *(CTW)*   80'   E6 6b   ***
The awesome hanging groove above the middle of the OHung wall (to the L of the central fault) is gained by bold, fierce climbing. Scramble to a stance directly beneath the groove (as for *BRF*). Climb up steeply (past 2PRs) to a big loose flake & tied-off PR. Climb up & RWs following a slight ramp to reach the base of the upper groove. Climb this on steadily improving buckets to the top. Belay as for *KYI*.   (1988)

6   Call of Nature   80'   E6 6b   ***
A more sustained version of *CTW*. Climb that route to its third PR, then climb up RWs to a good spike in the crack (in common with *CTW*). Step out R around the edge of the groove, then climb the crack to cross over Madness (R of the RH arête of the *CTW* groove). Climb the wall above past a PR in a thin crack. Continue direct to the top. PB in the bluff of rock above.   (1992)

7   Wildebeest   90'   E6 6b   **
The aggressive & mind-gnumbing crack 40' R of *CTW*. Hard & dynamic. Climb the crack past a PR, an obvious wire placement & a further 2PRs to gain the easier upper wall & cracks. These lead to a good ledge & possible belay. Alternatively, there is a block & ring PB some distance up the loose slope.   (1989)

8   Supermousse   90'   E6 6b   **
Start 10' R again of Wildebeest, at the base of a similarly OHing crack. Climb it before the bogeyman gets you.   (1989)

Some 10' R of Supermousse is a wide & OHing crack which becomes a huge fault-line higher up (effectively dividing Sanctuary Wall into two). The following two routes are based around the fault.

9   Cinqtus   180'   HVS 5b,4a,-
Climb easily to a stance in a small corner about 30' above the HWM & 15' R of the fault, PBs.
1   40'   Climb up to, & then LWs to a flake (PR). Make a long reach up to a horizontal crack (PRs), then traverse LWs along this to cross the top of the wide crack. Pull up to a ledge & continue to traverse LWs to a large stance. T&PBs.
2   70'   Climb the corner above (difficult near the top), then traverse LWs to a wide ledge.
3   70'   Easy climbing & some scrambling leads up over the rock above, trending LWs (the corner has been climbed all the way to the top, but is very loose & vegetated).   (1968)

10   Sacrosanct   120'   HVS 4c,5a   **
A strenuous & exposed climb taking the crackline in the RH edge of

the central fault. Belay as for Cinqtus.
1   40'   Follow Cinqtus to the flake & PR, then traverse LWs to the
wide crack. Climb this to a ledge, then traverse L to a large stance
(in common with Cinqtus).
2   80'   Traverse RWs across a slab & then climb its RH edge to an
exposed ledge (optional stance). Climb the OHing crack above to
reach easier ground & the top. Either belay to a tree (a long way off
to the R), or whack in some pegs.   (1969)

11   Flaming Drambuie   80'   E5 6b   ★★
A highly intoxicating experience. From the initial belay of Sacrosanct climb direct to the base of a steep hanging groove (PR).
Powerful moves are required to gain entry to this, which leads to
unrelenting climbing to reach the optional stance of Sacrosanct.
Pull over a bulge (up R of the scoop) into a scoop (PR), then make a
hard move R to a jug & PR. Swing wildly RWs to more good holds,
then make a long reach to gain a juggy break. Finish direct; belay
well back from the edge.   (1990)
Variation start Originally the route began as for Courvoisier (before
the two routes were rationalised).   (1990)
Variation finish From the PR in the scoop above Sacrosanct's
optional stance, pull forcefully up LWs over the bulge, then finish
airily up the arête & slab above.   (1990)

12   Courvoisier   80'   E6 6b/c   ★★
Gain the highest ledge up R of the base of Sacrosanct, & start
beside a small bush growing beneath a groove running up RWs.
From the base of the groove climb direct, past a good flake, to a jug
(good sideways #4 Rock). More flakes lead to a pocket on the L.
Move up to a large flake (in-situ wire), then climb direct to gain the
break of Madness. Traverse RWs to a steep hanging groove & climb
it (passing a multitude of PRs), then exit LWs onto the final wall.
Climb this direct to finish.   (1990)

13   Free the Spirit (FTS)   100'   E6 6a   ★★★
Bold & improbable climbing up a superb wall. Start from some
ledges, beneath a slight L/R leaning groove (7yds L of the major
groove line of CTA). Climb the groove to its termination at a
tied-off PR. Step up R, then sprint diagonally LWs across a daunting
wall to gain the base of a thin, incipient crack, TR & PR. Follow this
to a bulge, then step up LWs to gain the ramp-line of Madness.
Climb up to the lip of the bulge above (PR) from where a short wall
leads thankfully to the top.   (1988)

14   Caribbean Blue   100'   E6 6a   ★★★
A stunning route which starts 5' L of CTA at a faint diagonal brown
streak. Climb along the thin diagonal break in line with the streak
(PR), then follow holds leading up LWs to another PR. Continue in
the same line to a juncture with FTS. Climb directly up the wall
above (past 2PRs, a TR & an in-situ wire) to gain a steep groove, &
then the ramp of Madness. Finish direct over a bulge. Either belay

here, or top-out & belay well back.   (1991)

15   Call to Arms *(CTA)*   130'   E4 5c,5c   ★★★
A route of grotesque steepness, following a superb line (spoilt only
by the addition of the PRs on *AP*). The first weakness R of Sacrosanct is an open groove which OHs sharply. Start beneath this.
1   80'   Climb the groove to reach a small stance in a larger groove
coming in horizontally from the R (Incubus).
2   50'   Climb up the groove above the stance, via bridging, to gain
the base of a large OH. Swing out RWs to bypass this (difficult),
then trend RWs above to belay at an iron spike.   (1980)

16   Amoebic Plunge *(AP)*   80'   E6 6b   †
The blatant arête forming the RH arête of the *CTA* groove (6PRs).
Start at the foot of the arête & follow it, via pumpy face-climbing, to
a dynamic move from 'crimps' to an obvious jug. Continue up a
crack which leads to the belay of Incubus. Either finish up Incubus,
or reverse that route to get off.   (1992)

17   Up in Arms *(UIA)*   70'   E4 6b
Start 4yds R of *CTA*. Climb a line of large flake holds leading up LWs
to a PR at 20'. Head up LWs on large holds to a hard move up L, PR
on the R. Climb direct for a few feet, before trending RWs to the TR
on *ID*. Continue direct (via a big jug on the R) to finish at the start of
Incubus (ie. in **LQP**).   (1988)

18   Incubus Direct *(ID)*   140'   E3 5c,5a
A strenuous pitch, with very poor protection. It climbs the sharply
OHing wall below the start of Incubus. Begin about 20' to the R of
CTA, at a disjointed crack (marked by a small arrow).
1   70'   At 15' make a committing move to reach holds above a
large rattly block to gain the relative security of a decent PR. Trend
up LWs to a projecting ledge & natural TR, then climb the smooth
slanting groove LWs to the stance of Incubus.
2   70'   Climb the groove above the stance to the OH. Pull up
around the LH side of the OH & move up a corner for a few feet,
until the sounder wall on the L can be climbed to finish.   (1970)

19   False Gods *(FG)*   60'   E4 6a   ★★
Start 5' R of the start of *ID*, below & R of a PR at 15'. Follow a line of
good flakes to the PR & continue direct on good holds to another
PR (in common with *ID*). Climb the wall above direct to gain a break
& hidden PR. Step R to the base of an OHing flake/groove, which is
followed to a sloping shelf. Exit up the obvious groove on the L (5' R
of *UIA*).   (1988)

20   Gus Honeybun *(GH)*   60'   E5 6b   ★★
*A dynamic little number, whose bunny-hopping namesake would
be of great assistance.* Start 15' R of *FG*, beneath two diagonal
faultlines. Climb directly up the wall on small incuts to 2PRs. A long
blind dyno for a hidden jug up on the R, & then another hop, leads
to a break & PR. Pumpy climbing over the bulge above gains a

further break & another PR. Finish on good holds.   (1992)

21   Morpheus   35'   E2 5b
Climb the crackline 10' R of the start of *GH*, then trend RWs at the
top to avoid some loose flakes.   (1988)

22   Opium Eater   70'   E4 5c
A strenuous route with some loose rock. Follow Morpheus to
where it is possible to gain & follow a line of flakes across the
impending wall on the L. Finish as for *FG*.   (1988)

*To the R of Morpheus lies a long low wall culminating in the
remains of* **LQP**'s *ex-Quarry Pinnacle. The hanging groove in the
low wall just L of the pinnacle gives an escape pitch from the
Sanctuary Wall (protected by a PR – HVS 5a), should it become
cut-off by the tide. A couple of variations have been done L of this.*

23   Incubus   100'   HVS   5b,5a   ★★★
An excellent route which follows the impressive R\L slanting
groove at the RH end of the Sanctuary Wall. Start from the quarry
platform of **LQP**, by a notch at the foot of The Ridge.
1   30'   Make a freaky step-down through the notch, then traverse
LWs across an intimidating wall (hidden small incut holds) to gain &
follow a rising line of weakness to a stance on the slabby L wall of
the groove (PB).
2   70'   As for *ID* to the top. Descend the ridge either by climbing,
or abseil off an old iron spike.   (1968)

24   One Step Beyond   100'   E4 5c   †
An intimidating R\L traverse of the RH side of Sanctuary Wall. Start
as for Incubus. Follow pitch 1 of that route, then continue LWs to
join Caribbean Blue. Down climb for 8', then traverse up diagonally
LWs to reach the optional stance of Madness (*pitch 3*). Finish up
Sacrosanct.   (1994)

ANSTEY'S COVE   GR 935 650

Approach and Access
From the car park adjacent to the DIY store in Babbacombe (mentioned in the **LQP** Area notes), walk slightly RWs across Walls Hill
Downs to a retaining fence. Below this is a flight of concrete steps
(sign-posted "To Redgate Beach"). Descend these to be confronted by the aggresively OHung Empire Wall on the L, and a short
vertical wall hidden behind a clump of trees on the R. The first five
routes described climb the short wall behind the trees.

Situation and Character
This is *the* venue to visit for those travelling S ↓ for the first time.
The crag is S-facing, sheltered from the wind and composed of a
very hard and compact limestone. It is generally OHing and for the
most part amply protected with *in-situ* gear and bolt or fence-post

Anstey's Cove

belays. Added to all this, Redgate Beach is within spitting distance of the routes (well more of a hefty gobette), and has the attendant attraction of a café, pedaloes for hire or guided boat tours around the bay during the summer.

1 Crooked Man   80′   HS 4a
A curving line which separates the ivy on the L from the sounder wall to the R. The rock is rather poor. Climb the short wall to gain a ramp, which is followed RWs to below a steep corner. Climb this & the earthy ramp above to the top.   (1968)

A worthless route climbs the scrappy rock twixt Crooked Man & Charlie, known as **One Way Street** *E1 5b (1987); it finishes as for Charlie.*

2 Charlie   50′   E3 5c   ★
Climb the pocketed wall behind the clump of trees to a PR at 20′. Step L to a niche, & follow a wide crack up RWs. Just before another larger niche, veer up a thin crack on the L (past a TR) to gain the top.   (1987)

3 Small Change *(SC)*   40′   E1 5c   ★
A fine steep pitch taking a R\L diagonal crack across the wall. Start L of a deep zigzag crack. Climb bearing L to an obvious flat hold, then move up into a niche. Climb up the face on the LH side of the

Anstey's Cove

Sanctuary Wall   Long Quarry Point

niche, to reach large doubtful holds & the top.   (1975)

4   Big Bills   50'   E2 5c
An eliminate route which crosses *SC*. Start as for Charlie, then head
up RWs to join *SC*. Continue direct up the wall to a jug below a
small OH, step L & finish up the wall above (TR).   (1987)

5   Little John   35'   S
Start about 20' L of the steps, at a zigzag crack below an obvious
V-groove. Climb the crack to a steep scoop. Step up & R, then
move L into the niche at the top. Strenuous.   (1969)

EMPIRE WALL
Returning back across the path; the Empire Wall forms the leering
LH flank of the Mitre Buttress. The following two routes lie at the
extreme LH end of the wall (adjacent to the concrete steps). The
first salient feature is the jamming crack of Tiny Tim, 10' R of a
chossy corner.

6   Big Jim   35'   E1 5b
Boulder up the wall L of the crack of Tiny Tim to gain a jug at 15' (be
careful not to use the rotten rock behind you). Climb the wall
above RWs to the top.   (1984)

Anstey's Cove
– Empire Wall –

7   Tiny Tim   35′   HVS
The L/R slanting crack. Climb the crack with increasing difficulty, until better jams & jugs lead more easily to the top.   (1969)

8   Timeless Skies *(TS)*   45′   E2 5c
Start below a tube-like pocket just R of Tiny Tim. Gain the pocket, then move up RWs on smaller pockets to a PR. Continue slightly RWs, past a TR, to the top.   (1987)

9   White Winds   50′   E3 6a
Climb up the conglomerate rock wall R of *TS* to a dodgy PR. Continue to a second PR, from where a series of powerful moves gains the finish of *TS*.   (1987)

The following eight routes are described in relation to a large fallen flake at the foot of **HM***.*

10   Sirens of Titan *(SOT)*   60′   E3/4 6a
Dangerous! Climb the wall above the LH end of the deceased flake via some pockets (PR), to gain the hanging groove up L. Hard moves up the groove, on unstable rock, lead to a bulge & another PR. Finish up the wall above, past a TR.   (1987)

11   Crook Bruce *(CB)*   60′   E4 6a   ★
Follow *SOT* to its first PR, then gain the base of a short ragged crack. Follow the short crack to a pumpy & committing traverse RWs, which leads to a diagonal groove & *in-situ* belay.   (1977)

12   Avante-garde   65′   E5 6b   ★
Follow *CB* to the end of the short ragged crack, then continue straight up the wall above (passing a P&TR) to the top.   (1991)

13   Heathen Man *(HM)*   60′   7b (E5 6b)   ★
Stiff for the grade & sharp on the skin. From the RH end of the flat flake climb (awkwardly) up the RH side of a conglomerate pancake of rock, then make hard moves up RWs to gain some pockets. Follow these to a jug beneath a bulge, & finish direct via some one-finger pockets (5BRs) to the belay of *CB*.   (1988)

14   Sun of Righteousness *(SOR)*   60′   7b+ (E6 6b)   ★
Violent for the first 20′. Step off from the RH corner of the fallen flake & follow the line of 3BRs leading diagonally RWs from the start of *HM*. From the third BR trend back up LWs to join & then finish up *HM*.   (1989)

15   Rise'n'Shine *(RS)*   90′   7b+ (E6 6b)   ★★
A L/R rising traverse of the Empire Wall. Follow *SOR* to its third BR. Traverse RWs to gain *ETS* at its fourth BR & continue hand-traversing RWs to gain the RH arête of the wall. Climb this past two further BRs to gain the top.   (1989)
Variation 7b+ Known as **Rye'n'Shy**. Finish up *ETS*.   (1989)

16   Oozy in My Pocket   65′   7b (E6 6b)   ★ †
Start 15′ R of the dead flake, beneath a PR at 15′. Climb past the PR

to a juggy pocket (PR & TR above), then swing up R on crimps to a long move LWs to gain a decent hold. Follow *SOR* to the RH end of a horizontal break, then climb the wall above before trending LWs to the belay of *CB*.   (1992)

17 Empire of the Sun *(ETS)*   70'   7b (E6 6a)   ★★★
One of the nouvelle classics of the South West. Start 20' R of the recumbent flake, beneath a groove & a prominent break 25' up the wall. Climb the groove (bold) to gain a short wide horizontal break (BR). Hard moves gain the pocket above (BR), then swing up LWs to a jug. Continue up past a horizontal crack (BR) to gain a diagonal break leading RWs to a slight bulge (BR). Exit RWs over the bulge, then trend up RWs to a BB.   (1988)
Variation start 7b (E6 6b) Climb the wall R of the original start (2BRs), joining *ETS* at the break (unfortunately both starts are prone to seepage early in the season).   (1993)

18 Just Revenge *(JR)*   90'   7c+ (E6 6b+)   ★★★
A magnificent addition, which free-climbs the aid route **Just One More** A2. Start 10' L of the R arête. Climb up to & then swing up RWs past a BR (at 15') to gain a slanting break (BR). A powerful move leads to the next break, where a step L yields another BR. A long reach on small holds (in a short slanting crack) is followed by a lunge for a pocket (BR). Gain the ledge above (BR), then climb the crisp wall above to another BR, before tackling the remainder of the wall to the belay of *ETS*.   (1969/86)

19 Avenged   75'   7c+ (E6 6b+)   ★★★
A worthwhile variant of *JR*. Follow *JR* to its fifth BR, & immediately head up L past a further BR to join *ETS* at its final bulge, BR. Continue as for that route.   (1989)

At the time of writing, a line of BRs exists between **ETS** *&* **JR** *-this is an incompleted project.*

20 Might & Main *(MM)*   90'   7a (E5 6a)   ★
Bold in parts & not without its share of interesting rock. Climb the obvious arête R of the *JR* to a niche. Step L around the arête & follow the LH side of this in its entirety (6BRs), finishing RWs up the final part of the arête (as for *RS*).   (1989)

MITRE BUTTRESS
The seaward wall of the buttress is in the shape of a quarried OHing scoop, which from a distance resembles the head gear of a pontificating ecclesiarch. The face is criss-crossed by a number of short gymnastic routes as well as the longer classic of The Mitre, which starts R of *MM* below a polished flake/crack:

21 The Mitre   90'   E3 6b   ★★
An exciting pitch on good rock with the first 20' giving the hardest climbing by far. Start 10' R of the arête of *MM*. Climb direct to a BR, & make some hard slaps up L to gain a sloping ledge at 20'. Pull

through the bulge above to gain & follow the wall R of the arête (BR), which leads to an uncomfortable scoop. Step L to a spike, then swing up on good holds to a sloping ramp (BR). Climb diagonally LWs across the vertical wall, past an L-shaped pocket, to gain a ledge & the top.   (1968/79)

22   Mitre Direct   70'   E4 6a
Climb the arête of *MM* to the niche & pull through the bulge as for The Mitre. Climb the wall just R of The Mitre to gain its upper scoop on its RH side. Negotiate the bulge above (BR), then climb direct up the ensuing wall. Either follow the ramp up RWs or traverse RWs to a BB (on *HMF*).   (1986)

23   How the Mighty Fall (*HMF*)   60'   7a+ (E5 6a)   ★★
An excellent pitch up the leaning wall R of The Mitre, which has more than its fair share of slopers. Start at the base of The Mitre. Make a rising traverse RWs (BR) to gain a standing position on a sloping ledge to the R. Step up L (BR) to a squat niche & exit direct (past a BR) to a steep shelf & BR. Step up L to another steep shelf (BR), then layback a blunt rib to the final BR. Scratch directly up the wall to a BB (no wimping out RWs).   (1988)

24   Waffle Supremacy (*WS*)   55'   7b+ (E6 6b)   ★
A route of myopic subtlety, squeezed in-between *HMF* & The Mitre. Start below the RH end of the sloping shelf at 15'. Gain the ledge & trend up LWs to a slight groove & BR. Climb the groove direct (past another BR) to good holds on a block (BR). Trend up RWs across the scooped headwall (BR), to finish at a BB below the edge of the buttress.   (1990)

25   The Mightier (*TM*)   50'   7c+ (E6 6c)   ★★
A powerful problem over the bulging wall R of *HMF*. Start as for *WS*. From the RH end of the sloping shelf step R to a BR. Gain a thin flake leading up LWs (BR), then make a blind move for a jug on a sloping ledge (BR). Frustrating moves lead (direct) to the final BR, the top, & the BB of *WS*. The route originally traversed RWs to the arête at the third BR, before trending LWs to the fourth BR – reducing the grade to an easier 7b+ (E6 6b).   (1988)

26   The Mightiest   40'   E4 6b
A scrappy problem up the arête to the R of *TM*. Climb up to a niche at the start of the arête, then stretch up L for a good hold (BR). Boulder up LWs past this, then climb easier ground (the L edge of a slab) to the belay of *WS*.   (1991)

27   The Cope   90'   S
The retaining slab on the RH side of the Mitre Buttress. Start beneath the slab at a shallow R-facing groove. Follow the groove & continue up the L edge of the slab until the angle eases. Easy scrambling leads to the top.   (1968)

To the R of The Cope is a recessed & V-shaped wall of good, rough rock containing:

28 Time Bandits *(TBS)* 60' 6c+ (E3 6b)
Start at a BB below the V-shaped wall (L of an obvious corner).
Boulder up the wall past a BR, then climb direct to the next BR at
the base of a stepped groove. Follow this to the bulge (BR) which is
taken direct to another BR. Finish direct to a BB.   (1988)

29 End of an Era *(EAE)* 60' E1 5b
Climb the crack contained by the obvious corner direct (past 4BRs)
to either top-out, via loose rock, to a fence-post belay; or make a
dash LWs to the BB of *TB*.   (1988)

30 Epoc 60' VS 4b
Start 5' to the R of *EAE*. Climb the cracked wall to a small ledge,
then go diagonally RWs to a terrace & PB. Either escape LWs up a
groove to the top, or abseil off.   (1968)

31 Era 60' VS 4c   ★
A fine pitch starting 10' R of Epoc at a L/R diagonal crack. Climb the
crack to the top of a pedestal. Continue directly up the wall above
to the PB on the terrace.   (1968)

32 Time Passages *(TP)* 60' HVS 5a
Start a few feet R of Era, beneath the centre of the pedestal. Climb
to the top of the pedestal & trend up RWs to an *in-situ* TR & short
crack. Finish direct up the wall to the terrace & PB.   (1987)

FEROCITY WALL
Lying to the R of Mitre Buttress & the V-shaped wall is the showpiece of Devon sport climbing. Beginning at the magnificent arête
of *DC*, a dazzling array of routes criss-cross a fossilised wave of
OHing rock which runs down the slope towards the sea.

33 Devonshire Cream *(DC)* 50' E5 6a   ★★★
A bold & seriously stunning pitch. Start by the toe of the arête. Pull
up RWs onto a short balancy wall, then follow this to where the
arête begins to steepen. Committing moves up the arête (& RH
wall) lead past a BR to gain a sloping ledge (BR). Climb the arête
above (on its LH side) which leads to a BB.   (1984)

34 Sole Fusion 55' 7a+ (E5 6a)   ★★
In the same mould as *DC*. Follow that route to its first BR, then
make a wild traverse out RWs to the obvious protruding block (BR).
Climb the wall above to a BB 5' R of *DC*.   (1987)

35 Cream Topping 55' 7b (E6 6a)
Another bold undertaking. From the second BR on *DC*, step out R
& launch up the L/R slanting groove to a BR. Climb the shallow
groove above to the BB of *DC*.   (1987)

36 La Crême 50' 7c+ (E6 6c)   ★★★
Sustained & technically demanding climbing up the immaculate
flared shallow groove 15' R of *DC*. Climb the initial flake/crack to

Anstey's Cove
– Ferocity Wall –

gain the oblique groove. Follow this past a couple of slight bulges, to powerful moves which lead up RWs to gain the protruding block; finish direct (4BRs & BB).   (1988)

37   Project
The project on the R looks radical, this is just plain un-feasible. It follows the line of the twin black streaks R of La Crême.

38   Project
This hopes to follow a line of BRs up RWs from the start of the initial flake/crack of La Crême, while the finish has been sketched-out LWs across incomprehensible terrain. Probably hard even by Peak standards.

39   Ferocity   50'   A2
Start 10' to the R of La Créme, beneath the LH end of a ledge at 15'. Attempted as a free climb but as yet the potential first free ascensionists have been found wanting.   (1969)

40   Tuppence   50'   8a+ (E7 6c)   ★★★ †
Start 20' R of La Crême, beneath a thin vertical crack & the first of 6BRs. Steel fingers & an extrasensory perception for problem-solving should land you at the BB.   (1990)

41   A Fisherman's Tale *(AFT)*   50'   8b (E8 6c)   ★★★ †
In the mould of Tuppence but harder & finer climbing. Start 15' R of Tuppence, below a slight OHing groove at 15'. Desperate moves up this lead to the diagonal fault. Pull over the OH, then head up RWs to an undercut. Finish direct (5BRs & BB).   (1991)

42   Poppy   55'   8b (E8 6c)   ★★★ †
A connection of parts, with a dash of fresh climbing. Start up *TCS* & hand-traverse the lip of the OH LWs, to join & finish up *AFT* (5BRs). Allow slack rope when passing the third BR (a tight rope reduces the grade dramatically).   (1994)

43   The Cider Soak *(TCS)*   50'   8a (E7 6b)   ★★★
Excellent climbing up the OHing, L-facing groove 15' to the R of *AFT*. Start beneath a BR at 15'. Climb to this, & trend up LWs to gain the diagonal faultline (BR). Pull up RWs to gain the groove (BR), & follow this to the next break (BR). Climb the airy groove above to a BB.   (1989)

44   Project
Another unfinished project which climbs the bald face between *TCS* & The Lynch via very thin crimps.

45   The Lynch   50'   7b+ (E6 6b)   ★★★
Powerful climbing up the obvious R-facing groove & crackline 10' to the R of *TCS*. A magnificent route if you can jam; a total nightmare if you can't. Boulder up to the first BR, & pull over the bulge to another BR. Climb the groove to the top (past 3BRs), then exit LWs to a BB.   (1969/87)

46   Rawhide   55'   7a (E4 6b)
The subsidiary groove 8' R of The Lynch. Gain the base of the groove (BR) & climb it to an OH (BR – beware the loose flake). Pull through the OH to gain the upper groove (BR & TR) leading to the BB of The Lynch.   (1987)

To the R of Rawhide is a vegetated rib. This separates the Ferocity Wall from the St Gregory slab:

47   Mars   170'   HS -,-,4a
A route which connects the Ferocity Wall & the St Gregory slab to the Upper Tier. Start L of the vegetated rib.
1   60'   Move RWs onto the rib & climb it to a smooth brown slab, which is climbed direct to a PB in a reddish corner.
2   50'   Step L & climb a smooth slab direct to a loose corner at the RH end of an OHing wall (the Upper Tier).
3   60'   Climb the exposed corner on small holds to an OH. Turn this on the L (PR), then finish up a loose gully.   (1969)

UPPER TIER
This is the OHing wall atop the Ferocity Wall. Either do one of the routes on the lower wall or abseil off the fence-posts above the tier to get to the start of:

48   The Creaming Dream *(CD)*   30'   7a (E4 6a)   ★
Start from a BB at the LH end of the tier. Powerful moves lead diagonally RWs past the first BR, then continue in the same vein to another BR below a bulge. Climb straight through this (BR) to finish up LWs.   (1987)

49   Peak 8b   30'   7a+ (E4 6b)
Start from a BB on the RH side of the wall. Trend up LWs by undercutting a thin calcite flake (past a BR) to gain the base of a short steep groove (BR). Step up L to the second BR of *CD*. Continue LWs over a bulge (L of *CD*) to gain a further BR before finishing direct.   (1989)

50   Cry Creamdom *(CC)*   30'   6b+ (E3 5c)
From the BB of Peak 8b step up R to a BR. Continue direct (past 2BRs), to finish up a slim white pillar of rock.   (1989)

51   Tasty Snappers *(TS)*   40'   E2 5c
Start 50' R of *CC*, beneath a wall orientated at right-angles to the Upper Tier & L of the final pitch of Mars. Climb the centre of the wall to a thin crack at 20'. Follow this (past a PR & TR), then finish up the loose gully on the L.   (1989)

MOONSHOT AREA
The next feature R of Ferocity Wall is a large quarried basin which has a long white slab in its LH side. There are two old iron spikes plainly visible near the top of the slab. On the opposite side of the basin there is a steep wall with a pod-shaped cave at half-height (the line of Moonshot).

52   St Gregory the Wonder Worker (SGW)   180′   S -,4b   ★
A pleasant climb on clean rock taking the centre of the long white
slab & the steeper rib above.
1   110′   Climb the slab easily to the second iron spike, & belay.
2   70′   Traverse LWs along the smooth slab for 10′ to gain a large
ledge (TS starts just down L of here). Step up RWs & climb the rib to
a traverse RWs around the nose on the obvious line a few feet from
the top. Beware the loose rock on the finish above the end of the
traverse.   (1967)

53   St Mongo   180′   HVS -,5a
1   110′   As for SGW.
2   70′   Step L from the belay, then go up RWs to a footledge in the
centre of the buttress. Move up to & past a slight OH (good nut
placement) to a balancy finish.   (1993)

54   Hell's Teeth   180′   HVS -,5a
Start beneath a line of grooves & scoops 10′ R of SGW.
1   110′   Climb the line of discontinuous grooves to reach a belay
at a borehole strike (Friends) beneath a black wall.
2   70′   Step L & climb up the LH edge of the black wall to a ring PR.
Step up onto a slab, then trend RWs up a series of clean scoops to a
fence-post belay.   (1986)
Variation 2a 70′ VS 4b From the borehole belay climb diagonally
RWs for 50′, & continue up LWs to the foot of a thin slab & an iron
spike. Climb the slab to the top.   (1986)

*At the back of the quarried basin there is an obvious ramp running
L/R over the top of the LH end of the Moonshot Wall:*

55   Little Wonder (LW)   80′   VD
Start at the foot of the ramp. Follow the ramp RWs & finish up a
steep wall (PR) where the ramp becomes narrow & exposed. (1969)

56   Weeble   90′   E1 5a
Start below the ramp of LW & belay beside a prominent black wall.
Move across onto the black wall to gain a ledge up on the R. Climb
on widely-spaced holds to an overlap, then step up R to a flake.
Awkward moves lead onto the slabs above, from where a groove
leads to the top (or escape up the rib on the L).   (1981)

57   Nebulous Crab (NC)   60′   E3 6b
The slight nose R of Weeble. Gain the top of a pedestal (PR) at the
base of the prominent black wall. Tricky moves up RWs lead to the
nose (PR). A manic mantel for a hidden hold, leads to the slabs
above. Finish as for Weeble.   (1988)

58   Starless & Bible Black (SBB)   70′   E4 6a
Start 15′ down to the R of NC, & 10′ L of the obvious crack of
Moonshot. Climb to a PR at 15′ (some loose rock). Hand-traverse
the diagonal crack LWs to another PR. Climb direct to a BR in the
wall above, where hard moves over the bulge lead to easier ground

& a niche. Climb directly out of this & up the wall above on slightly
shaky holds.   (1989)

59 White Dwarf *(WD)* 70' E4 6b   †
('ard 6b mate, & impossible for dwarves). Start as for *SBB*, but
continue direct up the wall above the first PR to a second PR. Move
LWs up to a BR & climb a line of thin holds to gain a pocket & TR at
the end of the *LU* traverse. Finish as for that route.   (1993)

60 Shooting Stars 80' E4 6a
Follow *WD* to the second PR, then bold climbing leads directly up
the wall (past the crux of *LU*) to gain a third PR. Continue direct
until interesting moves over the bulge above lead to easier ground
& the top. Tree belay a long way back from the edge.   (1988)

61 The Lumpy Universe *(LU)* 90' E2 5c   ★★
The best route on the wall. Start at the foot of the obvious crack of
Moonshot. Climb the crack to the cave at 15', then exit diagonally
LWs along a faint seam to gain a large pocket & TR after 15'. Climb
straight past a PR in a groove, then continue direct up the wall
above a slab (PR) to the top.   (1986)

62 Moonshot 70' E1 5b   ★
A worthwhile route which climbs out of the prominent cave in the
smooth wall (forming the RH side of the quarried basin). Scramble
up to a PB below the cave. Follow an obvious flake/crackline to the
cave. Step up L, then traverse back RWs across the top of the cave
(keeping low) to good holds by a small bush. Move up & slightly L,
then go straight up the slabby wall to the top. Tree belay well back
from the edge.   (1968)

63 Melange 70' E1 5b
Circuitous & eliminate in nature. Follow Moonshot until just below
its cave, then gain a line of flakes leading up the RH side of the cave
to join Moonshot at the bush.   (1987)

64 Sod the Cosmos, Sniff the Coke 65' E2 5b
A more independent line up the rock to the R of Moonshot. Start
up that route to the ledge below the cave (TR up to the R). Climb
RWs along a scoop (PR) & reach up R to a good flake. Follow this to
a patch of broken rock. Carefully climb to a red niche. Pull up RWs
on good holds to gain & finish up the sharp arête.   (1989)

*The following route links the Cocytus Area to the Moonshot Wall; it
begins about 50' down & to the R of the gully which leads up into
the quarried basin.*

65 St Jude 160' S -,4a
A poor route. Start near a shallow corner which is virtually in the
centre of a wall of clean crystalline rock.
1 80' Climb the wall following the line of a thin crack (stained
black), then take a stance below the edge of the quarried basin.
2 80' Move out R & climb the exposed RH edge of the basin (on

Anstey's Cove
– Cocytus Area –

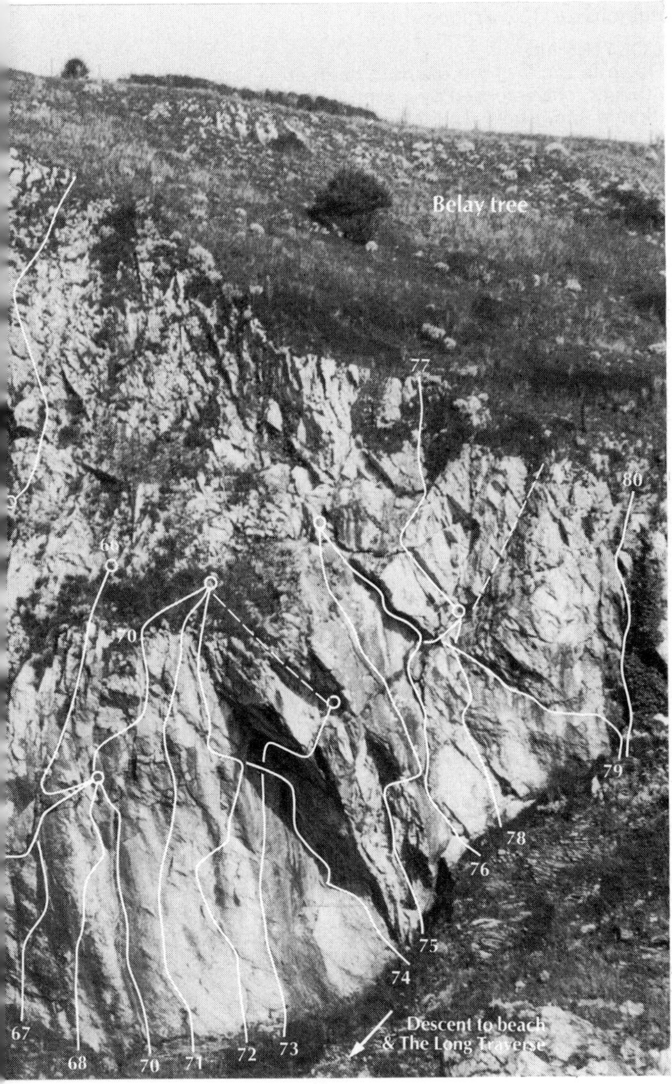
Belay tree
77
80
66
70
79
78
76
75
74
67
68
70
71
72
73
Descent to beach
& The Long Traverse

dubious rock), to a rubbly finish.   (1969)

COCYTUS AREA
Down to the R of the quarried basin are a series of steep walls &
grooves, characterised by a central amber-coloured wall (taken by
Blonde Bombshell). To the L of this wall is the groove of Cocytus &
L again is the short wall of American Express. On the R of the
buttress is the prominent corner of The Shroud, which is overlooked by the huge slanting roof taken by Blazing Apostles.

66 Aornis 80' S
The next feature R of St Jude is a curved groove topped by a huge
hanging flake (the black wall climbed by *AE* is just on the R).
1   40'   Climb the groove to a large perched flake. Step R, then go
up to a ledge. BB on the R.
2   40'   Move back LWs, then follow some cracks to easy rock.
Bear R to a PB. To finish from here either scramble diagonally LWs
into the quarried basin or follow pitch 2 of St Jude.   (1968)

67   Dumb Blonde   40'   E3 6a   ★
Start below the LH of two weaknesses in the wall between Aornis &
Cocytus. A hard problem start leads to a poor runner placement at
the base of a slight groove. Sustained moves lead up & then LWs to
join Aornis on the RH side of the hanging flake.   (1984)

68   American Express *(AE)*   40'   7a+ (E4 6a)   ★★★
A mini classic. Climb the wall via a vague groove to a pocket (BR).
Continue direct up the wall above (BR) to a dynamic move for a jug
(BR). Finish LWs up a short OHing groove to a BB.   (1984)

69   Torbay or not Torbay   40'   7b (E4 6b)
Eliminate climbing up the arête between *AE* & Cocytus. Start just L
of the arête & follow it to the top, past 3BRs.   (1985)

70   Cocytus   70'   E3 6a,5b   ★★
A compelling line up the strikingly-smooth groove which bounds
the LH side of the amber wall.
1   40'   Climb the groove (marred by the remains of two BRs
replacing the original PRs – it is now protected by two very poor
pegs), to gain a sloping ledge on the L (BB).
2   30'   Climb the short wall behind the stance & traverse RWs
across a slab to pull round a bulge into a groove. Finish out LWs by
an exposed layback, to a BB on the R.   (1968)

71   More Steam, Bigger Women !!!   70'   7b (E5 6b)   ★★★
(Supersedes **Torquey** E4 6b). A fine route. Start 5' R of Cocytus,
below a slim groove topped with a BR. Bold climbing up the slim
groove leads to the first BR. Desperate moves past this gain a
second BR, then step R slightly & climb direct to the bulge (BR).
Long moves on jugs lead past another BR to even longer moves
gaining the sanctuary of a niche. Step R (BR) & climb a crack to a
grassy ledge & BB.   (1985/88)

72 Blonde Bombshell *(BBS)*   70'   E5 6b   ★★
Excellent climbing up the centre of the amber wall. Start 15' R of
Cocytus, beneath a BR at 15'. Climb up the wall (past the BR) to gain
a short crack, from where hard moves lead up RWs into a red
scoop. Step up RWs around the arête, then head up LWs to gain an
OHung ledge. Climb the OHing wall above, via a layaway, to reach
better holds leading to a grassy ledge & BB.   (1983)

73 Blazing Apostles *(BA)*   70'   7b+ (E6 6b)   ★★
This climbs the arête, slab & huge OH R of *BBS*. Boulder up the wall
just L of the arête (BR), & continue up the arête to a third BR. Hard
moves lead up then diagonally RWs across a slab (BR), to gain the
groove of The Shroud. Climb up several feet to gain a wide break
out across the OH. Follow this (past 3BRs) to a niche beyond the lip
(BB). Either continue up the slab on the L, past a BR (5c); or reverse
to the second BR in the OH & strip the route.   (1991)

74 The Shroud   50'   E5 6b
The obvious dominant corner-line fails to live up to expectations.
Start below the OHing arête of *BA*. Gain the RH side of a large
alcove at 15', then cross this to its LH corner. Fearsome high-steps
& bridging to get established in the corner (PR), lead to a slab (BR).
Continue up the corner to join & finish up *BBS*.   (1988)

75 Groove & Slab *(GS)*   80'   E1 5b
The groove in the arête (which forms the OH of *BA*). Climb for 10'
to a ledge & ancient PR, then pull up into the groove. Climb this,
then hand-traverse a shelf leading RWs to a small ledge on the arête
of Acheron. Climb the slab direct to a horizontal crack, above
which is a sharp-edged crack forming the rest of the route. Climb
this & the slab above to a B&PB.   (1976)

76 Acheron   80'   HVS 5a   ★
A fine route taking the slanting corner above & to the R of *GS*. Start
by scrambling up a short chossy corner to a chockstone belay R of
the smooth initial corner. Climb the corner to a sloping ledge
beneath an OH. Continue up the smooth R\L leaning corner, then
move up & L to a B&PB.   (1968)

77 Lethe   95'   VS 4c,4b
An exposed, but inferior variant of Acheron.
1 45' Follow Acheron to the OH, then traverse RWs to a small
stance & PB.
2 50' Climb the OHing groove above. Swing L on reaching the
capping OH, then continue direct until it is possible to step L at
some bushes to gain the grass slope above; iron spike belay well
back from the edge.   (1968)
Variation 2a 30' VS 4b Step R into the bottom of a corner, which is
climbed direct to the top (exposed).   (1981)

78 Deadly Assassin   50'   E3 6a
The line of PRs & TRs to the R of Acheron. Start 5' R of Acheron,

boulder up to a PR. Climb up slightly LWs to gain & climb past a TR (& crucial wire) to pull up onto the steep slab above. Climb the groove above to the iron spike belay of Lethe. (1990)

79   Agent Orange   70'   E3 6a
Some good climbing which proves even tastier for the second. Start just L of Gut Bucket. Climb for 10' to a PR, then launch out LWs across a constricted slab to another PR. Hard moves past this lead to a good hold & some poor wires. Keep traversing L to join & finish up Acheron. (1988)

80   Gut Bucket   40'   S
Climb the chimney at the RH end of the wall. (1968)

Below the Cocytus Area, a faint path descends to the boulder beach. This leads to the start of The Long Traverse; the most popular approach to Sanctuary Wall.

81   Walking on Sunshine   60'   VS 4b
Start beneath the curving white arête at the beginning of The Long Traverse. Climb the RH side of the arête to where the rock turns to shale (stake belay). Scramble off RWs. (1988)

SEA-LEVEL TRAVERSES
Anstey's Cove provides the starting point for two contrasting sea-level traverses; one along each of the headlands which protrude into the bay from either side of the Cove.

82   The Long Traverse   350'   III/VIII-(tide dependant)   ★★
A magnificent adventure, which has been accomplished at all states of tide, time & tempest. Start from the boulder beach below the Cocytus area. Traverse RWs on good holds throughout to gain the reef beneath Sanctuary Wall. Continue beneath the base of of the wall (desperate at high tide), then skirt the base of the Quarry Pinnacle to reach **LQP** (it's reversible as well). (1962)

On the opposite side of the cove are a low line of cliffs running out past the S ↓ headland, these give:

83   Morning Town Ride   6800'   VI-
An entertaining excursion if begun at high tide. There are long sections of sustained climbing & several harder parts. The route is described in stages rather than pitches.
1   1100'   Scramble across some boulders, then traverse to the first point. This can either be negotiated by traversing along the HWM or overcome via the needle's eye-like formation.
2   1200'   Another bay similar to the first.
3   700'   From a platform move down to the HWM for 20'. The R wall of a large cave is then traversed with difficulty (40' HVS sustained) just above the sea. Continue easily to the next point.
4   3800'   The huge cove. Continuous climbing to a small beach halfway (escape possible up an iron ladder). Hope's Nose is reached by further sustained traversing. An OHing wall near the

end is overcome by; (a) swimming, (b) a stomach-traverse above an OH, or (c) escape onto a grassy slope, then descend a loose chimney beyond the wall. (1968)

DADDYHOLE AREA

This is where it all started, in more ways than one. Just over the way is *Kents Cavern*, which is thought to have been the oldest habitation of Homo Britannicus (it's well worth a visit on a rest day). And many of the early hard routes were established at Daddyhole, along with the superlative Gates of Eden.

Refreshment can be requisitioned from an ice-cream van in the car park atop Daddyhole Plain during the summer, or via a swift drive down to *Macari's* beside the harbour in town. This Italian-style establishment stands head and shoulders above the other cafés of the area, in that it provides a splendid view across the bay of Naples, as well as that of Torbay *(if the wall paper is still hanging by the time you get there)*.

Locating Daddyhole Plain can be a tortuous affair (even when you know where it is). The easiest approach is to drive into the centre of Torquay heading for the harbour. Circumnavigate this, passing a clocktower / roundabout and drive up past the Imperial Hotel, following signs for Daddyhole Plain (via Daddyhole Road). These lead up to a car park with extensive views across the bay toward Berry Head Quarry. The Cliffs are below and to either side of the car park.

MEADFOOT QUARRY GR 928 628

Approach and Access

From the car park on Daddyhole Plain, follow a set of steps descending E→ towards a wooded path that leads out on to a scrubby shoulder of rock opposite Daddyhole Main Cliff. Descend the path on the ridge to gain the quarry basin. The seaward rim is defined by a squat pinnacle (the start of Plimsoll Line Cliff), and in the background is a wave-cut platform and the isosceles block of Triangle Point.

Situation and Character

The crag is a pleasant and popular cliff thanks to easy access, a sunny SE↘ aspect, and the fact that the climbs are not too serious by Devonian standards. On the L side of the face are a couple of easy-angled slabs of a climb anywhere nature, bounded on the R by the elegant Diamond Rib. R of this is the slab of Mayday, then the

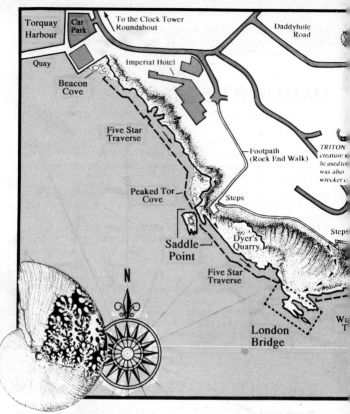

steeper Coal Face routes, to the R of which and high on the cliff is a large tree (on Nest Egg and Tree Root).

1 Central Slabs 80′ VD
Start beneath the inset slab just L of *DR*.
1 50′ Climb the slab to an iron spike, then trend RWs to belay.
2 30′ Step back L & climb a steep slab, then force an exit through some prickly bushes to gain the top.   (1966)

2 Diamond Rib *(DR)* 80′ HS 4b   ★
A fine delicate pitch. Start beneath an obvious rib. Follow this with increasing interest until a small block is reached near the top. Step R, then finish direct.   (1967)

3 Mayday 90′ VD
Start beneath a clean slab R of *DR*.

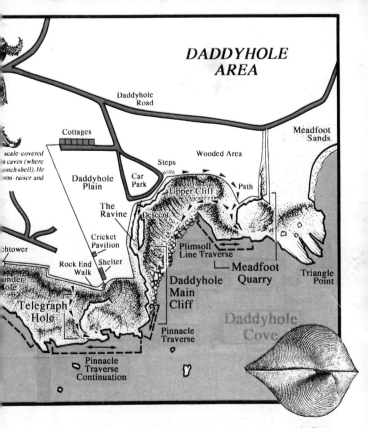

1 70' Climb easily up the slab before moving into a shallow groove. Climb the corner above, then step R & trend up LWs to a stance on more broken rock.

2 20' Climb bearing LWs up the final wall. (1967)

COAL FACE
This is a dark steep slab/wall roughly in the centre of the quarried face.

4 **Nervous Laughter** 100' E1 5b †
Follow *TTL* for 20', then step L & climb up to & over an OH. Continue up a steep slab to a further (slight) OH, from where broken rock leads to the top. (1986)

5 **Third Time Lucky** *(TTL)* 100' HVS 5a *
A fine route up the steep face 7yds up R of Mayday (& just L of

Descent
path

Meadfoot Quarry

Demeter). Climb the wall directly to the bottom of a shallow groove, which is followed to a poor ledge below a thin edge. Use this to reach the slabs above, which lead to a ledge with an iron spike at its RH end. Finish direct over a loose OH.   (1981)

6   Demeter 100' E1 5b
Start at a line of grooves R of the Mayday slab. Climb the grooves for 25' & step R to a PR, then step L & up to a shallow groove. Continue up to a sloping ledge just R of another shallow groove, then climb a steep wall to an obvious OH. Better holds lead across a groove to an iron spike, above which the R wall leads more easily to the top. Tree belay.   (1979)

7   Median 100' HVS 5a,5a   *
Start as for Demeter.
1   70'   Climb to the PR, then mantelshelf onto a ledge in the centre of a black wall. Trend slightly LWs, making use of a crack, until it is possible to gain a cramped stance.
2   30'   Climb a groove to an OH, then traverse RWs (PR) to reach easier ground & the top.   (1970)

8   Grand Slam 100' E2 5b
Start about 5yds R of Median on the highest ledge (PB). Climb direct up the wall, past a PR (missing) in crystalline rock on the R, to gain a narrow ledge. Difficult moves, via a brittle crack, lead up L into Median. Follow this route to some cracks which trend LWs. Climb these to join & finish up *TTL*.   (1980)

9   Revolver 110' E1 5b
A reasonable route which climbs the centre of the Coal Face.
1   80'   Climb a steep wall until a step R is made to a shallow ramp, then follow this to a good hold on top of a block. Climb with difficulty to gain a prominent PR on the Girdle, & continue straight up to a stance beneath an OH.
2   30'   Step down to a rising traverse RWs to gain the top.   (1976)

10   Rubber Soul *(RS)* 100' HVS 5a,4a
Start from some ledges beneath a projecting square block on the RH side of the Coal Face.
1   80'   Climb onto the block & move up to a small ledge (PR). Follow the broad rib above with little in the way of gear, then move R to belay at a tree (on Nest Egg).
2   20'   Step L & make an exposed traverse LWs above the dark wall of the Coal Face, to finish on good holds.   (1967)

11   Nest Egg 100' S   *
An enjoyable route on excellent rock. Start R of *RS*, directly beneath a tree on a ledge at 80'.
1   80'   Climb straight up to a small ledge at 30', then continue up the shallow grooves above to gain a tree below a groove.
2   20'   Climb the groove, then finish R of the OH.   (1967)

12 Tree Root   100'   VD
Start at the foot of a fault running up LWs to the tree belay on Nest Egg. Follow the fault without undue difficulty to the tree (optional stance). Climb the groove behind the tree, then move L at the OH & finish up the wall above.   (1967)

13 Pegs' Progress   75'   E2/3 5c   ★
A steep route up the LH of the two thin cracks in the gently OHing wall R of Tree Root. Take care with the gear; several punters have decked off this route. Start just R of Tree Root below a niche (on the Girdle). Climb up to the niche, then step L & up to a good hold, after which a strenuous move gains another jug high on the L. Climb the crack above, then move L to more generous holds before climbing steeply RWs to finish.   (1969/83)
Variation From the top of the crack finish up the obvious L/R slanting crack, which is way streno mate.   (1983)

14 Clotted Cream   70'   E4 6a   ★★
A powerful addition, which free-climbs the aid route **Rainyday** A1. A bellyflop finale seems to be the only way of topping-out. Just L of the arête bounding the RH side of the cliff is a groove which leads up LWs to the base of a thin crack (the substance of the route). Climb the groove until the crack is reached, then follow this to its peristaltic climax.   (1969/84)

15 Hermeda   60'   VS 4b
An interesting route taking the grooved arête which bounds the RH side of the cliff. Move into the corner from the R, then climb to an obvious pointed block. Climb to an OH (skirt this RWs), then gain a crack leading to an easy slab & the top.   (1968)

16 Malingerer   60'   VD
Start up & R of Hermeda. Gain the LH end of a ledge at 10', then follow the groove above the middle of the ledge. Finish direct up the easy slabs to gain the top.   (c.1960s)

GIRDLE TRAVERSE

17 The Meadfoot Girdle   260'   E2 4b,5b.4a,5c   ★
A rising L-to-R traverse of the crag which has sustained climbing & a good line. Start as for DR.
1   80'   Follow DR for 60' to the small block, then traverse RWs into Mayday & descend this for 5' to a stance (PB).
2   80'   Move RWs around a rib, then climb diagonally RWs (past a PR) to a small ledge on the Coal Face. Step up RWs past a prominent PR, then traverse RWs into Nest Egg which is followed to its tree belay.
3   30'   Traverse RWs beneath an impending wall (on the obvious line) to gain a niche.
4   70'   Climb to a diagonal crack above the niche, then hand-traverse it to gain the groove of Hermeda. Follow Hermeda around an OH to gain & finish up some easy slabs.   (1969/79)

The squat pinnacle on the rim of the quarried basin gives a pleasant micro-route on its seaward face, **Gulliver** *25' D (1966). While on the far side of the wave-cut platform, the landward corner of Triangle Point is taken by* **Pig's Ear** *40' S 4a (c.1960s).*

PLIMSOLL LINE CLIFF

Between Meadfoot & the boulder beach (which leads to Daddyhole Cove) is a slabby cliff giving an excellent low grade traverse, which is possible in either direction & at most states of the tide. The routes are described from R to L.

18   Plimsoll Line *(PL)*   200'   IV-   *

Descend an obvious ramp leading down to the sea from the quarry basin (L of the squat pinnacle – looking seaward). Follow the HWM, with the occasional deviation above or below it, to the far L arête. Gain some height before traversing LWs across a slab which leads down onto the boulder beach.   (1967)

Variation The traverse can be reversed by starting from the boulder beach in Daddyhole Cove. It can also be extended to encompass Triangle Point.   (1980)

19   Vista   60'   HVD

Some 5yds L (facing seawards) of the start of *PL* is a faulted cleft beside a gaggle of large boulders. Scramble down the cleft for 25' & belay. Climb easily across a slab to reach a R\L slanting crackline in a steeper slab. Follow this to join *PL*, then continue direct up a steep wall (on good holds) to finish on the ridge.   (1981)

20   Splash Down   60'   HS 4a

Start about a third of the way along the traverse of *PL*. Climb directly to an obvious pale scoop & continue up the steep black wall above, via a diagonal line from the L.   (1983)

21   Back Brain Stimulator *(BBS)*   60'   VD

Start about two-thirds of the way along *PL*'s traverse, just R of a small niche. Climb a wall, then a slab, trending RWs to a large flake (& possible stance in a high sea). Climb up LWs to finish via a L/R slanting slabby groove.   (1983)

22   Prime Time   60'   VD

Start 5yds L of *BBS*, at an obvious diagonal crack. Follow the crack for 40' to a small OH. Exit up the obvious groove on the R, then scramble to a tree belay well back from the edge.   (1983)

DADDYHOLE MAIN CLIFF   GR 926 627

Approach and Access

Follow the approach path as for Meadfoot Quarry for 100yds, then turn R to follow a track through the trees to the spur forming the E→ side of Daddyhole Cove. From here a narrow path contours the RH slope (facing seaward) to the boulder beach in the cove. Cross the boulders to the foot of the cliff, the base of which is well above the HWM.

There are three ways off the cliff top: (1) Scramble down the seaward slope and reverse Pinnacle Traverse; (2) abseil 150' back to the base from a tree midway between the finishes of Triton and Pearl; (3) follow a track up RWs along the cliff top and then up LWs through the thorn-scrub and trees to regain Daddyhole Plain (this can also be used as an alternative approach).

Situation and Character

This is one of the more underrated crags of Torbay, with generally sound rock and many striking lines. Three obvious corners dominate the cliff. The smooth LH one is taken by Last Exit to Torquay; Triton takes the dark, slanting corner in the centre, while the more broken corner high on the R gives the second pitch of The Pearl. Either side of Last Exit to Torquay are the fine arêtes of Gargantua on the L and Zuma on the R.

Locate a huge detached boulder at the base of the LH end of the crag. The first route begins behind this in a boulder-filled cleft.

1 Pinnacle Traverse *(PT)*   60'   HVS 5a
This skirts around the L bounding arête of the cliff & continues toward Telegraph Hole (it is also part of descent (1) from the cliff top). Climb a smooth groove leading up LWs from the boulder-filled cleft, then step up to gain a traverse-line of huge jugs leading LWs to the arête. From the arête follow a crack running up diagonally LWs (PR), towards a ramp-line which leads to a saddle beyond the pinnacle (using the PR for aid reduces the grade considerably to VS 4a).   (1967)

2 Pinnacle Traverse Continuation   500'   VI-
This extends *PT* to the headland just beyond the finish of The Watchtower, passing Telegraph Hole on the way. It is possible in either direction, & although discontinuous, it offers some good climbing if the best line is taken.   (1968)

The following four routes are described from R to L. They are approached by traversing LWs (along the HWM) from the boulder-filled cleft at the base of **PT***, to gain a reef whose top lies just above the HWM (ie. best approached at mid/low tide).*

3 Caliban   90'   HVS 4c
From the RH end of the reef climb direct up the wall to join *PT* at its PR, then step LWs past this to a niche (optional stance). Move up to an OH & make a strenuous traverse up RWs to a small ledge. Step L, then follow a red groove to the top.   (1969)

4 Aqua Marina *(AM)*   80'   E1 5b   ★ †
A fine pitch on excellent rock. From the LH end of the reef follow a R\L leaning ramp to a shallow OH topped by a hanging groove. Gain the groove (natural TR) & climb it to a juncture with *PT*. Step L

Daddyhole
– Main Cliff –

& tackle the bulge above to gain a sinuous crack, then climb a broken wall to finish. (1990)

5 Stingray 80' E3 5c/6a ★★ †
A break leads down LWs from the base of the initial ramp of *AM*. Follow this to gain pockets, then climb up to a shallow OH. Pull over this using a large undercut & follow good (but hidden) jugs up LWs to a long reach for a thin crack. Climb the orange runnel above to gain *PT* & finish as for *AM*. (1990)

6 Troy Tempest 80' E4 6a/b †
The crisp wall L of Stingray. Approach via *PT*, then descend a gully to gain the LH side of the wall. Foot-traverse the lip of a shallow OH (RWs), to gain a slight depression. Climb diagonally LWs to gain *PT* & finish up a smooth wall L of *AM*. (1990)

All the following routes on the Main Cliff are described from L to R.
The next climb tackles the golden brown wall above the boulder-filled cleft (ie. the start of PT).

7 Tobacco Road (TRD) 80′ VS 4b ★
Good jug-hauling up the nicotine-stained wall (low in the grade).
Climb the initial groove of PT, then move LWs up the wall until
beneath an OH. Traverse LWs delicately to the arête, then climb
with care to the top. (1967)

8 Rocketman 100′ E3/4 5c,5b
A spectacularly dodgy route through the OHs above TRD.
1 60′ Climb to the large OH of TRD, then traverse RWs (by
vicious fist-jamming) across a hanging wall to a horizontal spike.
Move R along a sloping ledge to a PB.
2 40′ Step down & traverse RWs to join Pantagruel at a PR. Step

back LWs to gain a short groove. Boldly pull over the capping OH to a large detached flake, before being 'beamed-up' to an escape LWs via a less daunting scramble.   (1979)

9   Return to Earth   90′   E3 6a   †
Sound advice. Start at the base of Pantagruel, below a R\L diagonal flake-line. Follow the flake to join Rocketman at its steep fist-jamming traverse. Follow this RWs into a niche (just before the spike). Climb direct over the OH above & either belay immediately, or scramble up easier ground to the top.   (1993)

10   Pantagruel   125′   E4 6a,4b   ★★
A character-building lead, especially in its upper reaches. Start on boulders below an OHing corner to the R of *TRD*.
1   100′   Climb straight over the initial bulge into the corner, then follow this very strenuously past a PR. A difficult exit RWs leads to less steep rock (PR). Traverse RWs to a small ledge (poor PR), then step up & continue RWs with difficulty to reach a corner/crack & restricted stance.
2   25′   Climb the corner to the top.   (1967/77)

11   Readymix   140′   HVS 4c,5a
A strenuous route on curious rock, which follows the obvious crack L of the arête of Gargantua. Start as for Pantagruel.
1   80′   Make a rising traverse RWs below a large OH, then move RWs over a bulge (PR) into a corner. Climb steep rock on the R for 15′ to gain a restricted stance.
2   60′   Climb up to a bulge, then follow the awkward corner crack above until the angle eases. Step L & finish up Pantagruel.   (1967)

12   Gargantua   140′   E1 4c,5b,5a   ★★
Exposed & intimidating climbing on the rib/arête between Readymix & the large corner of *LET*. Start at a bank of shale below the corner of Readymix.
1   30′   Scramble up the shale for a few feet, then climb RWs to a flake crack which leads to a small ledge (NB).
2   60′   Climb into the open groove above, then move up L with difficulty (past a PR) to a good rest. Surmount the bulge above direct, then continue up a steep wall until a step R gains the arête again. Follow this to a niche.
3   50′   Traverse RWs below a tiered set of OHs, via a line of small holds, then step up & move back L above the first OH on much better holds. Move up into an OHing groove, then exit LWs to scramble over easier rock to finish.   (1967)

13   Gates of Eden *(GE)*   130′   HS -,4b,4a   ★★★
The classic of Daddyhole, which gives exposed & exhilarating climbing in impressive surroundings. Beneath the corner of *LET* is a huge leaning block, the LH side of which forms a wide chimney.
1   60′   Climb the chimney for a few feet, then ascend the LH wall to a ledge. The flake crack above leads into a corner which is

climbed for 10' to a stance (PB).
2 35' Climb the corner until it begins to steepen, then traverse LWs between two OHs to step up into a niche on the arête (PB).
3 35' Step down LWs out of the niche to gain the base of a broad corner crack. Climb this to the top.   (1967)

14 Last Exit to Torquay *(LET)* 120'   HVS -,5b   ★★
A tempting line on perfect rock. Start as for *GE*.
1 60' As for *GE*.
2 60' Climb the corner to the first OH, from where some difficult bridging (PR, missing through over abuse) leads to better holds. Continue to another OH which is overcome via holds on the R wall. Finish easily up what remains of the corner.·   (1967)

15 Suicide Blonde 140'   E6 -,6b   ★★★ †
A bold proposition up the middle of the thin wall R of *LET*. Tenacious stamina & a cool head are de rigueur *(rather than peroxide & pills)*.
1 60' As for *GE*.
2 80' Gain & follow a thin crack running up R of the belay (passing 2PRs) to a line of good holds leading up RWs, then back L to a L/R trending groove. Follow the groove (for 5') to some flakes in the overlap that caps it, then pull over onto the LH wall to reach a PR. Step up RWs & attack the vague groove above to attain a pocket & PR. Continue to another PR, where thin moves & a long reach lead directly to a jug *(& a resurgence of the will to live)*. Finish up the wall above.   (1993)

16 Zuma 140'   E4 -,6a   ★★
A fine line based upon the arête R of *LET*.
1 60' As for *GE*.
2 80' Climb *LET* for a few feet, then step R into a shallow L/R trending groove (poor·PR). Follow the groove to the projecting block on the arête. Step out R to a good rest, then climb the slabbier RH side of the arête for 10'. Regain the LH side of the arête (where it becomes smooth & OHing), then move up to some pockets on the L. Trend back RWs on the arête.   (1977)

17 Triton 165'   VS 4a,5a   ★
The big central corner gives interesting & well protected climbing on solid rock. Start as for *GE*.
1 90' Follow *GE* to the top of the flake/crack, then continue up the edge of a large flake on the R until some steep moves lead to ledges & a PB near the corner.
2 75' Attain the base of the corner. Follow this until a hard move gains better holds on the L wall & the top.   (1967)

18 Beast of Eden 140'   E5 4a,6a   ★
Formerly the aid route **East of Eden** A1. The meat of this excellent cut goes straight up the guts of the wall between *Zuma* & *Triton*. Start as for *Triton*.

1   80'   Follow Triton to the top of the large flake & belay.
2   60'   Climb over poor rock to the base of a steep wall. A number of thin cracks cleave the wall. Climb the most continuous LH one in its entirety, passing 3PRs.   (1971/85)

19   Porno For Pyro's   150'   E5 4a,6b   ★ †
A powerful addition that is both short & sharp. It takes the RH of the three cracks in the headwall.
1   90'   Follow Triton to its belay near the corner (or abseil in from the trees at the top).
2   60'   Climb the wall above the belay to the base of a L/R leaning ramp. Follow this for 10', then trend up LWs to the thin crack (3PRs). Follow the crack strenuously, then dyno for a sharp jug above the third PR. Continue up a vague groove to finish.   (1993)

20   Neptune   150'   VS 4c
The slabby wall to the R of Triton. Start at a narrowing chimney on the opposite side of the block to *GE*. Climb the chimney to a ledge at 30' (optional stance), then climb the crack above to gain a rib. Traverse LWs into the centre of the wall, then climb this until it is possible to reach a horizontal crack which leads back RWs to the rib. Follow the rib to an unstable finish.   (1967)

21   The Bead   150'   VS 4c
The RH rib of the Triton corner. Start as for Neptune. Follow Neptune to the ledge at 30' (optional stance). Climb the crack which leads up RWs to gain the rib at a good ledge. Step R & climb a pink slab to good holds, then continue bearing RWs up various slabs & walls to a loose finish.   (1967)

22   Fandangle   180'   HVS 4b,5b   ★
Excellent climbing in the upper part compensates for a vegetated, but still pleasant first pitch. Start by scrambling up a loose shale-rake beneath the RH part of the crag. Belay beneath an OH with a very prominent flake forming its RH side.
1   110'   Climb up to & past the OH by using the flake, then continue straight up for 30' (past a PR) to a groove with a layback-crack in it. Follow the crack until it peters out, then climb a slab to a good NB at a large flake.
2   70'   Double ramps run diagonally up the OHing wall on the R. Move along the lower ramp until some small incuts enable the higher one to be gained (PR). Use the thin crack above to make hard moves onto a sloping ledge on the R, then continue easily to finish as for The Pearl.   (1967)

23   The Pearl   190'   HS 4a,-   ★
A good varied route taking the RH of the three great corners. Start as for Fandangle.
1   120'   Climb to a PR, then make a rising traverse RWs (2PRs) to reach a gully, which leads to a good stance.
2   70'   Climb the corner above to the top, with a diversion LWs at

20' to avoid a bulge.   (1967)

24   Mukdah's Wall   200'   E4 4a,5c   †
A fine line up the OHing white wall R of the final pitch of The Pearl.
Beware; a recent rockfall has altered the start of pitch 2.
1   120'   As for Pearl.
2   80'   Climb up to the red flake above the stance, then continue
up the blunt arête (on its RH side). Step back LWs along ledges,
then follow a crack system to within a few moves of the top. Finish
direct, rather than climb the deceptive LH crack.   (1984)

GIRDLE TRAVERSE

25   Snakecharmer   355'   E4 5c,5a,6a,4c,5b   ★
A rising L-to-R traverse of the main cliff, having sustained difficulties & a lot of fine climbing. Start as for *TRD*.
1   100'   Climb to the first OHs (down & R of the large OH taken by
Rocketman) & traverse RWs, using a flake crack, into a smooth
groove (PR). Break through this onto slabbier rock & traverse RWs,
rising gently, to join Pantagruel (PR). Continue horizontally RWs
below the line of Pantagruel, to join Readymix which is descended
for a few feet to its stance.
2   35'   Follow the obvious line RWs (PR) to the arête of Gargantua,
then traverse easily to the PB of *LET*.
3   80'   Climb up the corner for 10', then step R to a short groove &
a poor PR. Move down RWs to better holds leading to the arête, &
climb this for 20' to some large blocks, where runners can be fixed
to protect the second. Continue horizontally RWs to the stance &
huge TB of Triton.
4   70'   Step up, then traverse a slabby wall to gain the arête.
5   70'   As for Fandangle *(pitch 2)*.   (1976/78)

THE RAVINE
This area lies below & R of the car park atop Daddyhole plain. It is
reached by descending the messy chimney found at the extreme
RH end of the car park (looking seaward). The routes ascend the
excavated walls to the R.

26   Ash Tip Slab *(ATS)*   50'   S 4a
Start below a slab at the LH end of the ragged wall, L of a small
sycamore tree by the base of the large fallen ash tree. Climb the
slab past some small flakes & diagonal cracks to some vegetation.
Move R & up to a TR & tree belay. Abseil off.   (1988)

27   Bin Bag   50'   HS 4a
Start R of *ATS*. Climb up to a large shattered scoop, then move up &
slightly L (past a TR) to the belay of *ATS*. . .   (1988)

28   Waste Disposal *(WD)*   50'   HVS 5a
Start 5yds R of Bin Bag below a TR at 12'. Climb past the TR to reach
a second TR, then move up RWs to another TR. Continue straight
up over a slight bulge to a PB. Abseil off.   (1988)

29   Hunt the Dump *(HTD)*   50′   E1 5b   ★
Start 15′ R of *WD*. Take a direct line past a PR & 4TRs to gain an OH.
Pull over this to a PB. Abseil off.   (1988)

30   Tin Can Alley   50′   HVS 5a
Start 10′ R of *HTD* & immediately L of a large triangular OH 6′ off the
ground. Pull onto the wall (PR up & R), then follow a flake/crack
(past another PR) to a sapling & TR. Continue up a crack, trending
RWs to a PB. Abseil off.   (1988)

31   Keep Britain Tidy *(KBT)*   50′   VS 4b
Start at a corner/groove R of the triangular OH. Follow the groove,
past a PR & 2TRs, to a TB. Abseil off.   (1988)

32   Football Graveyard   50′   E1 5c
Start R of a thin crack (R of *KBT*). Climb the thin crack direct, & step
R to some pockets on a rib. Stand on the flat hold above, & traverse
diagonally RWs to an overlap with a flake/crack on the R. Follow
this, then bush-bash to the top.   (1989)

DADDYHOLE UPPER CLIFF
The descent used for the Ravine could also be one way of gaining
access to this ill-frequented clifflet, which lies directly underneath
the outer rim of the car park. The other descent is by a ramp at the
E→ (Meadfoot) end of the car park. Both approaches are best
attempted when armed with a pair of secateurs.

33   End Crack   45′   VD
A pleasant route on the wall R of the descent chimney. Climb the
crack & corner behind a tree to a small ledge. Step up RWs, then
back up LWs to climb the slab & groove above.   (1969)

34   Imperial Wall   60′   HVS 5a
The fine arête to the R of End Crack. Start at a detached flake just L
of the arête. Climb direct up a wall (difficult) to reach the crack
system above. Follow this to finish R of a tree.   (1977)

35   Romeo & Juliet *(R&J)*   70′   VD
A scrappy route. Climb an obvious chimney R of the large OH
which caps the LH side of the crag.   (1968)

36   Ramshackle   65′   S 4a
A worthwhile climb which follows a zigzag crack system some 20′ R
of *R&J*. Climb a narrow slab to some large wedged flakes. Continue
up the crack to a ledge. Climb the wide crack above, then finish
diagonally RWs.   (1969)

37   Sabre Tooth *(ST)*   60′   HS 4a
An interesting route which starts beneath a large horizontal fang of
rock half-way up the cliff (& R of Ramshackle). Climb a reddish
brown slab, then gain a sitting position on the fang. Step R & follow
the L/R slanting line to the top.   (1969)

38   Brass Bound Crack *(BBC)*   55'   HVS 5a
The obvious crack in the R wall of a groove some 10yds R of *ST*.
Climb the groove, via its RH fork, to gain the crack. Move up to a
rest, then continue up an OHing groove to finish.   (1969)

39   Eubulus Williams   45'   VS 4c
Start 5yds R of *BBC* beneath a R\L slanting groove. Climb straight up
for 15', then move LWs (via a layback) into the groove. Follow this
easily to gain the top.   (1969)

TELEGRAPH HOLE (PARSON'S HOLE)   GR 926 627

Approach and Access
Follow the path from the RH end of the Daddyhole Plain car park
(looking seaward) under an arch onto Rock End Walk. Some 30yds
past the arch a faint path leads down LWs through some bushes
toward the sea. This brings you dramatically to the rim of the Hole.
Continue to descend the path to a man-made wall. Climb over this
to gain a rocky rib which is followed to the quarry floor.

Situation and Character
This SE-facing and secluded little cwm is a veritable sun-trap during
the winter and dries very quickly after rain. It probably offers the
best slab climbing in the area. The main part of the cliff consists of
an impressive slab, bounded on the L by the corner of Nardly
Stoad's Climb and on the R by the stepped corner of Discuss the
Thoughts of Chairman Mao. R of the latter is an unattractive face,
notable for its many downward-sloping ledges and a central niche
with a tree in it (the stance of Mighty Atom). All the routes on the
crag are described from L to R.

THE SEA WALLS
From the foot of the descent path a white glacis leads down to a
small bay just above the sea (Pinnacle Traverse Continuation leaves
Telegraph Hole at this point).

1   Saline   40'   S 4a
The striking white corner at the extreme LH end of the bay (directly
above the sea). Climb the corner to an awkward finish & belay well
back from the edge.   (1984)

2   Praline   40'   VS 5a
R of Saline, & L of two RWs curving cracks, there is a vague groove.
Climb the groove, via a boulder-problem start, which leads to some
more hard climbing before exiting LWs.   (1984)

3   Aquiline   60'   HVS 5a
Follow the two RWs curving cracks to reach some stepped OHs.
Pull direct through these, then climb up the slabby wall above.
Belay to the wall just L of the descent path.   (1984)

Telegraph Hole

4   Telescopic Arms   35'   E1 5b   †
Hidden in the sea-wall between Saline & Stratagem is an alcove.
Climb the slabby RH side of the alcove, until hard moves up LWs
gain holds on the lip of an OH. Pull through the OH to a spike belay
atop the wall.   (1984)

*Directly below 'the' telegraph pole on the seaward rim of the quarry
is an OHing bay of highly stratified rock. Either abseil or down-
climb the easy groove at the RH end of the wall (looking seaward).*

5   Megatarts   50'   VS 4c
Start at an OHung niche above the HWM on the LH side of the wall.
Climb through the OH to gain a short corner above the niche.
Follow this, then climb the stratified wall to finish.   (1984)

6   Stratagem   50'   VS 4c
From the OHung niche at the start of Megatarts traverse RWs to
climb through a break in the low OH. Step R, then climb straight up
the wall above to finish.   (1978)

7   Stratatarts   60'   HVS 4c
Start as for Megatarts, then follow the most accommodating break
RWs. Finish via the RH edge of the wall.   (1984)

THE MAIN FACE
This begins R of the descent path, with the first in a quintet of
Carrolesque trips up a vegetated buttress L of an impressive slab.

8   Mad Hatter   50'   D
Start about 10' R of the descent path. Follow a rib for 45', then
traverse RWs to avoid the wall at the top.   (c.1960s)

9   Mock Turtle   50'   M
The shallow grassy groove R of Mad Hatter.   (c.1960s)

10   Nardly Stoad's Climb (NSC)   70'   S
Start just L of a small corner which is 10' L of a large tree at the base
of the impressive slab. Steep rock leads to the base of a corner,
where bridging gains a small ledge. Continue up the steeper rock
above to finish by a small tree.   (1967)

11   White Queen   75'   S
The upper reaches of this route give pleasant & delicate slab pad-
ding. Climb NSC to the base of a corner, where a small rib just L of
the corner is climbed until a short traverse LWs can be made. Climb
the slab above, then finish LWs.   (1969)

12   Slithy Tove   70'   HVD
Climb a small corner just R of NSC, then the rib above. This leads to
within 10' of the top. Step L & finish up NSC.   (1967)

13   Bird Scarer (BS)   90'   E2 5c   ★
A bold line up the L edge of the main slab. Start behind the large
tree. Climb to a ledge & follow a vague groove to a PR, then step L

& climb up to reach another PR. Move up to a further PR, then step L & continue steeply to the top. (1983)

14   Let Your Fingers do the Walking   130'   E4 6a   ★ †
From the first PR on *BS* (at 25') traverse diagonally RWs, via a short crack, to 2PRs. Step RWs around a rib to another PR (on Crinoid), then continue diagonally RWs until beneath an impending wall. Climb this direct, past an obvious PR, to finish up the slab above with care-free abandon. (1988)

15   Blinding Flash (*BF*)   100'   E4 6a   ★★
Good climbing with excellent lob-potential. Start 5yds up the slope from the large tree. Climb straight up for 40' to a short crack. Make a series of thin moves to a PR up on the L, then step up to climb the steep slab above, bearing RWs to better holds & the top. (1983)

16   Flash Dance (*FD*)   90'   E3 5c   ★★★
Splendid, although slightly bold climbing up the natural line of weakness on the slab. Start beneath the RH side of the slab, near an alcove-like depression at the base of the slab. Climb up the wall to a PR at 20', then continue direct to the RH side of a shallow ramp (small wires / *RPs*) leading up LWs. Boldly stride out LWs to gain this & the 2PRs at its end. Climb the slight bulge above, past a projecting PR, to reach a large handhold above a further PR. Move up to a narrow white ledge & the top. (1983)

17   Crinoid   90'   E1 5b   ★★★
A superb route which follows an elegant line up the R edge of the slab. Climb the first 20' of *FD* to the PR. Step up above this to a good hold, then traverse RWs to gain & follow the rib (bold, despite 2PRs). About 15' from the top a thin diagonal fault leads out LWs. Foot-traverse along this, then finish as for *FD*. (1967)

18   Midas Touch (*MT*)   70'   HVS 5a   ★
A pleasant route that follows a shallow R\L trending scoop R of Crinoid. Start 15' up the slope from the alcove-like depression at the foot of *FD*. Climb bearing L for 30', then go direct up the wall (delicate) until beneath a steep wall. Follow the base of this LWs to where it becomes vertical, then climb straight up the wall above (on small holds) to the top. (1967)

19   Liaison with Lenin   70'   HVS 5a
Start at the base of the corner-line formed by the two main faces. Climb the L wall of the corner to a ramp running up LWs. Follow this to its end, where a break in the steep wall above enables the upper slab to be reached. Make a rising traverse LWs along the most obvious line to reach the top. (1980)
Variation (known as **Total Control** E1 5b). An inferior version which starts further L, & gains the flake below the ramp. Climb the ramp for a few feet, then pull through the bulge & finish just R of the parent route. (1983)

20   Buzby   230'   E2 5c,5c   ★★
A traverse of the main slabs, providing fine sustained climbing.
Start just R of the descent path.
1   150'   Climb a short rib to the start of a rising traverse-line at
two-thirds height. having gained a sloping ledge on the main slab
(beyond the groove of *NSC*), climb RWs to a good foothold in a
crack. Step R to a projecting PR (on *FD*), then make hard moves
straight up to a good hold & PR. Traverse RWs to belay at a large
flake on *MT*.
2   80'   Climb down RWs for 10', then traverse RWs to a ledge level
with the belay. Climb a short ramp on the L, then pull up over a
bulge to another bulge. Take this direct & then traverse diagonally
RWs to the top.   (1981)

21   Discuss the Thoughts of Chairman Mao *(DTC)*   80'   VS 4b
The corner-line formed by the two main faces joining at right-
angles. Follow the corner to a bulge, then bridge over to the ledge
above. Continue up the corner, over the next bulge, then climb out
RWs to finish.   (1967)

22   Jericho   80'   VS 4a
Don't hum too loudly. Start 10' R of *DTC*. Move up to a step R onto
a projecting ledge, then continue to an iron spike. Trend LWs up
slabby rock (keeping the OHing reddish wall to the R). At a break in
the red wall move up steeply to stand on a loose-looking block on
the R. Continue to a PR, where awkward moves gain easier ground
& *terra firmer*.   (1983)

23   Swing Low   80'   S
This follows a boomerang-shaped line up the wall which begins R
of Jericho & then crosses over that route. Start below the tree in a
niche. Climb direct until just beneath the niche, then gain & follow
the obvious R\L trending weakness (OHung by a reddish wall) to
join & then finish up the corner of *DTC*.   (1967)

24   Mighty Atom *(MA)*   85'   E1 4a,5b
A fine cap-feather-of-a-route for the ardent *connosewer* of
esoterica. Start by a shallow black groove, beneath (& some way to
the R of) the tree in the niche.
1   40' Climb over some ledges, past an iron spike, to a tree belay in
the niche below a steep corner.
2   45'   Climb the corner by laybacking, then exit strenuously RWs
onto a sloping ledge. Move up to the summit stone wall, which is
by-passed by an exposed traverse LWs.   (1967)

25   Mighty Cheese   130'   S -,-
This one goes out to the rubble-posse. It involves rambling peregri-
nations up the unsound buttress R of *MA*.
1   80'   Start about 30' to the R of the most forward part of the
buttress, below a projecting block. Climb to this (PR), & overcome
it to the L. Scramble over some shifting blocks, then belay by some

even more unsound blocks.
2 50' Ignoring the sound corner above (!?!), traverse LWs towards *MA*. Climb the corner R of this until it ends, then scramble off LWs (underneath the wall) to finish.   (1967)

LONDON BRIDGE   GR 923 627

Follow Rock End Walk (as for Telegraph Hole), then continue along the path to pass beneath a watchtower. After descending several flights of steps, the path begins to rise gradually via two sets of steps. Step off the main path 10yds past the second set of steps and descend a faint track towards the sea.

The crag takes the form of a natural arch composed of sound rock. There are a number of climbs on the OHing landward (N ↑) face of the arch, as well as routes on the short walls facing the arch.

THE SEA WALLS
To the R (facing seaward) of the land-bridge which joins the arch to the mainland there is a steep grassy bank which is the descent to:

1 Arch Temptress *(AT)* 60' E1 5b   **★★**
Scramble down the grassy bank to a sharp fin of rock beside the arch, 15' above the HWM. The route follows the striking line of flakes which run underneath the landward-side of the bridge & continue up the wall beyond.   (1987)

The next route on the landward sea-wall is reached by an abseil down the L side of the bridge off a stake in a rocky knoll several yards away from the edge. Belay in a small corner on the RH side of the wall (at low tide). A hanging, knotted rope was used to protect the following two routes.

2 Chicken Head *(CH)* 45' E4 6b   ★ †
Traverse LWs along the ledge, past a white groove, to a line of vertical edges which lead up the blank wall R of the *AT* flake. Desperate wall climbing leads to the obvious chicken-head at 30'. Finish direct up the wall above.   (1987)

3 Dance on Dinkies. . . 35' E3 6a   †
From the belay ledge on the HWM, traverse LWs until beneath the white groove. Climb this until it fades into the wall above, then carefully exit RWs to gain the top.   (1987)

4 Duckless in Torbay 35' S
Climb the obvious corner above the belay ledge.   (1987)

5 Torbay's Fowl Community 35' S
Climb the crack R of the corner, then step R onto the arête. Follow this easily to finish.   (1987)

6 Beak Roamer 35' HVS 4c
Artificial & fairly serious. Step R from the belay & layback onto the

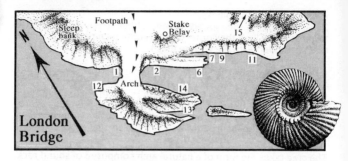

London
Bridge

arête which is followed with interest to the top.   (1987)

The following three routes climb the steep face separated from the
CH *wall by a deep chimney. Abseil from an iron stake & take a*
hanging belay about 10' R of the chimney & 5' above the HWM. The
first route partially ascends the chimney.

7   Widespread & Hipless *(W&H)*   40'   VS 4c
Traverse LWs (slightly higher than the stance) on small holds, until
it is possible to bridge out LWs onto a small ledge on the L arête of
the chimney. From here bridge up the cleft (runners in R wall), then
step out onto the R wall to finish.   (1987)

8   Ducks Might Fly   40'   E3 6a
An eliminate. Climb the thin crack between *W&H* & the prominent
crackline of *LDB*. Finish direct up a grey wall.   (1987)

9   Last Duck to Bombay *(LDB)*   40'   E1 5b
Climb straight up from the stance to gain the start of the obvious
crackline. Follow this with difficulty to a ledge & PR. Finish direct
via some loose rock.   (1987)

The next two routes can be reached either by traversing 20' R from
the previous stance or by abseiling further R & belaying just above
the HWM.

10   Crispy Duck, No Noodles *(CDN)*   30'   VS 4c
Follow a line of black pockets RWs to the top.   (1987)

11   Something Ducky   30'   VS 4c
Climb the orange wall & slight bulge R of *CDN* (on good incuts) to
gain a short crack, which leads to the top.   (1987)

THE ARCH
The following routes lie across the bridge, on either the OHing wall
or the seaward face of the arch.

12   Atheist   40'   E3 5c   ★★
The route follows the OHing RH corner of the arch when looking

seaward. Abseil to a hanging belay at the HWM, some 10′ R of the corner. Traverse LWs at the level of the belay, then climb the corner strenuously to the top.   (1987)

13   Undertow   40′   HVS 4c
Start on a detached slab which pokes out into the sea on the far LH side of the arch (facing seaward). Cross the small inlet behind the slab to gain the slabby main face. Climb up around the R arête to a ramp. Follow this to a loose finish.   (1987)

14   Jehovah Kill   80′   E5 5a,6b   *(de-geared)*   †
A once bolted route; yet to be reclimbed in its present state. It climbs a L/R diagonal line on the OHing landward face of the arch. Start as for Undertow, at low tide.
1   25′   Hand-traverse the HWM, around the arête, to the OHing landward face. Take a stance in a niche at the start of a L/R diagonal line of flakes.
2   55′   Follow the steep flakes which lead up RWs to the base of an OHing groove. Hard moves up this, via some excruciating contortions, gain the capping OH. Step out RWs past a PR, to gain a flaky corner & then the bridge.   (1992)

Further E→ of London Bridge is a rocky scoop that runs down to the sea. This leads to the start of:

15   The Watchtower   700′   VII-   ★★★
A real belter. There are plenty of thrills, spills & spume to be had on this crabwise foray toward Telegraph Hole. It is possible at all states of the tide, unless a high sea is running. The traverse extends to the sloping quarried platform on the E→ headland (which opens up the possibility of linking it to the Pinnacle Traverses).
1 & 2   Roughly 250′ of climbing, just above the HWM (moves of 4b – & an abundance of optional stances) leads to a TB at the mouth of a deep zawn known as Thunder Hole.
3   Climb the highest of the flake/cracks leading up into Thunder Hole, until they end at a flat-topped spike. Fix a sling & pendulum across the zawn to holds on the opposite wall. Climb up to a PR, & flick the tape off to avoid rope drag. The second now pendulums from lower down using a tight rope (via the PR), & he/she uses either jumars or 'batpersons' up the rope for a few feet (Thunder Hole was originally crossed by a quick doggy-paddle. If the above politically gender-correct antics are deemed 'unsound' then swimmimg is still a viable option).
4   Traverse horizontally RWs for 25′. Move up to an OH (good TR high up) & continue RWs with difficulty (past a PR) to good holds on the edge of the wall. Down-climb to a good belay (5b, a stunning pitch).
5   Move R & climb a groove for 10′, before bearing RWs across a slabby wall to a break which leads easily RWs to a tree belay near the top of the cliff (5a).
6   Step around the corner & descend a groove to sea-level.

Traverse on good holds to smoother rock, then climb steeply to some ledges (4a). Continue traversing to a long ledge with a TB on its RH end.
7   Superb. Traverse horizontally RWs for 30' to a series of overlaps (6a), then climb (trending RWs) to a horizontal break which leads to a sloping quarried platform.   (1968/72/91)
Variation 7a Step up to a good foothold, then climb direct up a wall on small holds (5c) to easier ground (serious). Continue direct to belay at some bushes, from where a forested scramble regains Rock End Walk.   (1968)

16   Jekyll & Hyde   80'   HVS 4c
A useful escape pitch. About 15' before the TB on the edge of Thunder Hole, there is a line of projecting cracks & flakes . Follow these to a chockstone. Step R, then follow a shallow groove (take care with the rock near the top). Scramble up the rambling scrub slopes to finish; tree belay.   (1968)

SADDLE POINT   GR 922 628

This lies further along Rock End Walk from London Bridge (from where it is easily seen). Follow the gradually rising path, to descend a final set of steps to a concreted path (overlooking Peaked Tor Cove). To the L is a sign (located beside a retaining wall) advertising the fact that the Council is not wholly in favour of climbing in the Borough. Scale the wall, without recourse to the sign, then drop down onto a vague path which leads almost immediately to the top of the seaward slab of Mass Murderer, and then the base of Dyers Quarry.

Despite first appearances there are some surprisingly good climbs to do (no one seems foolhardy enough to 'trubble' with the rubble of Dyer's Quarry). The routes lie either side of a large decaying corner (still unclimbed) opposite Saddle Rock. To gain the routes either abseil down the steep slab of Mass Murderer (the rope can be used to belay below the loose finishes) to ledges above the HWM; or traverse in from Peaked Tor Cove to the ←W, or the quarry floor to the E→. The routes are described from R to L.

1   Mass Murderer (MM)   60'   E4 6a (de-geared)   †
A notorious route because it was probably the first bolted route (for free climbing) in the Torbay area. From a ledge above the HWM climb the narrow slab R of the wide corner/crack, past several PRs (missing) to a very loose finish.   (1980/85)

2   Date with the Devil (DWD)   60'   E1 5b   ★
The striking arête L of the wide corner/crack. Climb the corner for a couple of feet, then swing up L through the bulge to gain the arête proper. Follow this direct (past a PR) to a loose finish. Prearrange the belay rope before climbing.   (1984)

Dave Pegg on How the Mighty Fall (F7a+) Photo. Nick White

Kit Wilkinson on Cocytus (E3 6a) Photo. Pete Bull

3   Devil's Alternative *(DA)*   65'   E3 5c

A testy pitch up the centre of the steep slab L of *DWD*. From the belay of *MM* traverse LWs for 15' to gain a ledge beneath a bulge, then belay. Climb up RWs to the bulge & tackle this by pulling up LWs to stand on the steep slab above (PR). Climb the wall above between a thin crack & a vague flake (*RPs* essential!) to a L/R slanting ramp-line leading to the top.   (1984)

4   Blue Monday   70'   E2 5b

Start L of *DA* at the foot of some cracks running up the L edge of the crag. Climb the crackline which leads to a difficult traverse diagonally RWs to follow the finer continuation jamming crack. The standard loose finish awaits.   (1984)

The easiest approach to the next route is to leave the car in the public car park by the harbour (loadsa-money) & descend the steps, leading into Beacon Cove, beside the large building E→ of the harbour. Alternatively make the walk from Daddyhole car park to the centre of town!

5   Five Star Traverse I & II   1000'   V+

A traverse of the low cliff under the Imperial Hotel. It provides a pleasant frolic above the sea & is a good introduction to the more serious coasteering of the area. Traverse the low-angled slabs, for about 300', to a small zawn. Skirt this (at 4c) to a second zawn of similar difficulty. Carry on past the private beach of Peaked Tor Cove (keeping a weather-eye open for unbridled 'Garbonzas') & continue at 4b to the smooth-looking LH wall of the defile created by Saddle Rock. Fine climbing across this wall (5a) leads to the rocky basin of Dyers Quarry. The traverse can be extended by following the low sea walls to London Bridge.   (1967/68)

Variation The traverse is also a great challenge at high tide. The highlight proves to be the negotiation of the beautiful white wall running out of Peaked Tor Cove (at a sustained 6a/b).

BERRY HEAD AREA

₁Deep. . . deeper (and further still) into the arcane mists of time, the spectre of fear forged its lair. ₂From the fires of horror it pulled forth the crucible of terror and began to pour the molten gore of decayed polypi into huge slabs, which it cemented together with foreboding. ₃Coiled within its sepulchre, it slumbered the sleep of the nightmare regions, and waited. . .

Berry Head *(The Book of Dread) Chapter I*

There are no initiations into the mysteries of the Great Cave at The Old Redoubt. It has a fascination which battens onto climbers and

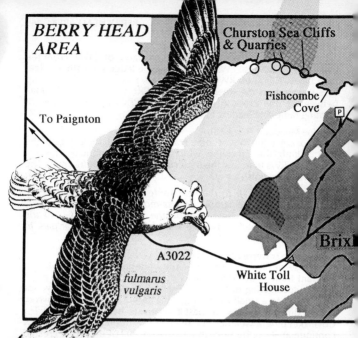

BERRY HEAD AREA

Churston Sea Cliffs & Quarries

Fishcombe Cove

To Paignton

Brix[

A3022

fulmarus vulgaris

White Toll House

goes to work upon their souls; the growing regrets, the longing to escape, the powerless disgust, the surrender, the hate. . . *the horror*[2]. It ceases to be a grainy photograph for a youth to pore gloriously over, and becomes a place of darkness. A place that has to be revisited again, and again. . . and again.

However, you'll find that there is more to the Berry Head Area than The Old Redoubt, though that crag is one of the more stunning adventure climbing arenas (even on a global scale). While the audacious few (you know, the scared people) are warp-factoring out across the huge cavern, the rest of us are all catching the sun at the base of the Coastguard Cliffs. Tidal approaches don't figure in the equation when soaking up the atmospheric delights of Berry Head Quarry; or when deciding which sport-route to dabble on at Churston. Even the itinerant hunter of esoterica can fossick to their heart's content in and around the Cradle Rock and Durl Head buttresses.

Sadly the café scene is not as well endowed as it could be. The

[2] *As the well known philosopher Sophisticuffs used to say "Cuius testiculos habes, habeas cardia et cerebellum" – when you've got them by the short and curlies, their hearts and minds will follow.*

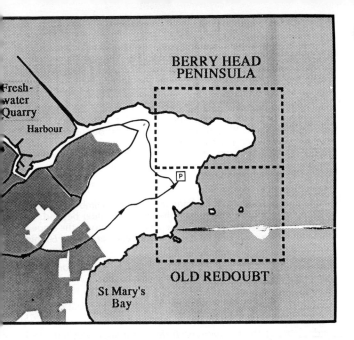

tea-shop in the Northern Redoubt gets full marks for being on tap, but its culinary fare leaves a lot to be desired. However, a tour of the *Golden Hind II* in Brixham harbour, and some time spent ferreting through *Ye Olde Shell Shoppe* will while away the hours of a rest day.

The area encompasses the entire S↓ headland of Torbay, and the coastline stretching off to the ↙SW. The best way to get there is to take the bypass around Torquay and Paignton (A380) leading to the A3022 and Brixham, from where the various access notes to each crag take over.

CHURSTON (Sea Cliffs & Quarries)   GR 915 572

Approach and Access
Follow the A3022 toward Brixham, passing a white weather-board clad toll house (on the R) just inside the town limits. Take the first turn on the L, sign-posted for Fishcombe Cove, and follow the road for half-a-mile. Immediately after a short one-way section, the car park appears down on the L. A footpath leaves the bottom LH

corner of the car park, leading past a holiday chalet complex to a wooded hillside. Follow the path down RWs through the woods to arrive at the shingle-covered beach of Fishcombe Cove. The crags lie on the far side of the Cove's grassy shoulder.

Situation and Character
The cliffs and quarries are N-facing, but generally sheltered from the prevailing weather. For the majority of the time it's cold but dry during the winter. It's also an excellent retreat during the heat of the summer, when places like Anstey's can become oppressively hot. Although quarried, the rock has a natural feel, providing a variety of protection and holds, the most prolific in each category being TRs and calcite flakes.

THE SEA CLIFFS
These are approached by crossing the Cove and climbing the steep path on its opposite side to gain the grassy shoulder beyond. The crags can be seen from here, and a faint path contours the slope to their foot. The cliffs behind the boulder-beach are about 60' high and abound in cracks and corners.

On approaching the cliff the first major feature is a big corner. The following route starts beneath this:

1   Gremlin   50'   VS 4b
Climb the corner which steepens towards the top. Exit direct via some tricky moves.   (1975)

Midway along the boulder-beach there is a large perched block. Scramble up past this (& the tree above) to gain the base of a calcite corner on the R:

2   Merlin Rocket *(MR)*   60'   HVS 5a
A strenuous crack, with good protection. Climb the corner to a niche. Step up R to an OHing crack leading to a large spike in a second niche. Follow the crack to top-out through hawthorn scrub. Tree belay well back.   (1967)

3   Hornet   60'   VS 4c
Start just L of a corner to the R of *MR*. Use the obvious flake to gain the base of the steep corner, then climb it on good holds to a loose finish. There is no option but to abseil from bushes back down the line.   (1975)

The sea-washed walls further R are shorter, but sound. They begin at a large block. A narrow cleft behind the block gains the first bay which contains Enterprise. Beyond this are a tangle of blocks, cracks & chimneys too short to record, & a wide crack at the RH end of the bay, which gives easy access to the top of the cliff.

4   Enterprise   50'   S 4a
Fine climbing up the clean, curving crackline in the first bay. The last few feet are the most taxing.   (1967)

5 Surprise 50' E1 5b
Climb the disjointed crackline R of Enterprise.   (1988)

THE QUARRIES
These lie beyond the Sea Cliffs. Follow the path from the summit of the grassy shoulder to the top of the point where a black chain-link fence is encountered (the boundary of a golf course). After a 100yds or so, a faint path cuts down through the bush to break out onto the rim of the first quarry. The most prominent feature is Bloodhound Buttress, which erupts from the tangle of indigenous flora in the centre of the quarried basin. Hidden behind an arboreal curtain, down and to the L, are two black pocketed walls at right-angles to each other. These form an intimate gallery space for some *en plein air* masterpieces:

6 Born Toulouse *(BT)* 40' E4 6b   ⋆
Climb the artistically pocketed crackline snaking up the LH side of the first black wall. A boulder-problem start *(which would have left Lautrec stumped on the reach front)* leads, past 2TRs & PR, to a slim groove & a TB around a convenient tree.   (1988)

7 The Impressionist 40' E5 6b   †
A bold undertaking involving a considerable amount of sketching. Climb the thin crackline 20' R of *BT* to some finger-ledges leading LWs to a PR. Climb the slim groove above, continuing diagonally LWs to the belay.   (1988)

50 yds to the R of The Impressionist is another French master, masquerading as a pocketed wall:

8 Monet For Old Rope *(MFOR)* 40' E2 5c   †
Climb the LH side of the pocketed wall (3TRs), then surmount the bulge above direct to a ledge & BB.   (1988)

9 Freudian Gymslip *(FG)* 40' E1 5b   †
Some 5yds R of *MFOR* is a thin crack which is just L of a much wider crack, *(further analysis would prove embarrasing)*. Climb the thin crack direct to a ledge at 25'. Step L & climb the arête (PR) which finishes at the ledge & BB of *MFOR*.   (1988)

10 Beware the Sphinx 40' VS 4b   †
Climb the wide crack (R of *FG*), leading to a groove/corner above. Follow this to gain the BB of *MFOR*.   (1988)

There is a large block-like stack on the seaward rim of the quarry, providing a number of fine micro-routes. However, the best lies on the seaward face:

11 Great Dane 25' S 4a   ⋆
Climb the striking central crackline of the seaward face, gained by traversing along the HWM of the stack from its LH side (when looking seaward).   (1988)

Further R of the black pocketed walls is the Bloodhound Buttress.

The first route climbs the wall R of the far L arête:

12   Barking Mad *(BM)*   60'   E2 5b   †
You'd have to be to climb it. An awful route; escapable, unsustained & with poor rock. Climb the wall directly below the arête, just L of some cracks, to a shale break. Attempt (in vain) to find independent climbing R of the easy arête (3PRs). Scramble through unyielding shrubbery to top-out.   (1989)

13   The Gambler   60'   E3 6a   *
The striking crackline in the headwall (of the LH part of the buttress) is gained by starting up the cracks R of *BM*. There is a fiendish crux toward the top of the crack.   (1989)

14   Bloodhound   100'   E2 4c,5c   *
Worthwhile. Scramble up from the R to gain a stance on a large ledge below a crack R of the R arête.
1   50'   Climb the crack strenuously to gain a narrow ledge, which leads LWs into a large cave.
2   50'   Move L along the ledge for 10' until beneath a steep slab (PR). Stand up on two flat holds to sniff out a series of hard moves, bearing slightly R to the start of a thin vertical crack (PR). Another hard move leads to better holds & a BB (abseil off).   (1969)

15   Trism   80'   E4 6a   ** †
Start L of the arête of Bloodhound. Climb the wall boldly to the cave at half-height. Pull over the RH side of the cave into a niche on the arête (TR). Undercut up LWs (2TRs) to a hard series of moves past a BR, then gain an exposed rib. Follow this to a BB on the summit (abseil off).   (1989)

16   Junebug   70'   E4 6b   * †
Follow Bloodhound to the top of the crack, then step up R onto a ledge. Climb diagonally LWs, past a PR, to gain the arête (TR). Trend back up RWs to a PR, then climb the centre of the orange lichen-covered wall to a BB on the summit.   (1989)

17   The Corner   60'   E3 5c
Roughly 15yds to the R of Junebug is a striking corner, which is reminiscent of numerous other striking corner-lines. Climb the corner until it peters out, from where a strenuous hand-traverse RWs (2PRs) leads to a BB.   (1989)

18   Roar Like Sushi *(RLS)*   60'   7c+ (E6 6c)   ** †
Fine climbing up the middle of the blank wall R of The Corner. Climb up to the RH side of a break at 15', then step L to gain & climb a pocketed wall past 2PRs. Fierce moves lead up R (BR), then back LWs (BR) to a slight groove (hard-to-clip BR). Desperate moves up this gain the BB.   (1990)

19   Warpath   70'   7a+ (E5 6b)   *
The arête to the R of *RLS* is climbed mostly on its LH side. A line composed of 2PRs & 2TRs show the way. Excellent climbing, but a

tad nasty at the top.   (1989)

The following route climbs the L wall of the striking arête 100yds to the R of Bloodhound.

20 A Moment Spent Talking *(MST)*   50'   E5 6b/c   †
Follow the line of *in-situ* gear, leading up R & then back L from the arête, to a shale ledge (a pre-arranged rope from the oak tree above is needed for the belay).   (1989)

21 Arêtez Vous   40'   E4 6b   ★★ †
There is another isolated arête about 60yds to the R of *MST*. Climb the undercut arête (desperately) past a BR. Proceed up past a PR to the top. Scramble through brambles to belay on trees well back from the edge.   (1990)

Further along the coast (towards Paignton) are two more quarries, reached by a pleasant path from the first quarry. The second quarry is fairly large but loose & featureless, having no routes at present. The third contains a large isolated block with a dark slab facing seaward. This gives:

22 Slipshod   50'   VS 4b
Climb the L rib of the dark slab for 20', before trending diagonally RWs to the top (descend the vegetated slope behind).   (1969)

The following routes lie on the impressive prow-shaped wall above & to the R of the dark slab of Slipshod.

23 Salmon Run *(SR)*   40'   E2 6a
Start on the LH side of the wall. Climb up to a TR & PR before leaping up to a thin break (TR). Trend up LWs to a ragged crack & follow this (PR) to an awkward mantel to finish.   (1988)

24 Satanic Traversities *(ST)*   50'   E3 6a   †
Follow *SR* to its second TR, & traverse RWs along the obvious line of jugs to a TR. Continue to traverse RWs to the belay of Supercalorific. (Starting from slightly higher up the slope reduces the grade to 5c).   (1988)

25 The Invisible Man   50'   E3 6a   ★★ †
Intricate face climbing. Start just R of *SR*. Trend diagonally RWs (past a BR) to an obvious projecting block & a further BR. Climb direct to the traverse-line of *ST* & follow that route to the belay of Supercalorific.   (1990)

26 No Holds Barred *(NHB)*   50'   7a+ (E5 6b)   ★★★
Improbable & sustained wall climbing which follows the line of *in-situ* gear 15' R of *SR*. A TR, 2BRs & PR show the way. Trend up RWs past the PR to gain a ragged crack which leads to the belay of Supercalorific.   (1988)

27 Supercalorific   60'   E3 5c   ★★
Start 10' R of *NHB*, beneath an obvious line of calcite flakes. Climb

direct past a TR to gain the flakes, then follow these (past a further 2TRs) to a PR. Step up LWs to a PR at a bulge & pull over this LWs. Climb a short wall to the belay.   (1988)

28   Walking Tall   65'   E3 5b
Follow the line of TRs 10' R of Supercalorific, interlinked by calcite 'drips' & flakes, to a bold finish.   (1988)

29   Cream Tea Special   70'   HVS 4c
The dramatic R arête of the wall. Start at the base of the arête on a red shelf of rock. Climb up the arête using holds on its LH side, passing a TR & poor PR at half-height. Finish direct (past a PR) to a grassy exit & a tree belay well back.   (1988)

The arête of the wall hides the steep white groove of:

30   Bearing Down *(BD)*   70'   E5 6b   ★ †
Bridge up the groove to a poor PR. Step L, then move up for a few feet before stepping back R to regain the groove. Hard moves past a poor PR gain an uncompromising position beneath a distant PR. Clip this & breathe a huge sigh of relief, before making hard moves past it. Finish up RWs to a P&BB.   (1988)

*50 yds R of **BD** is a short wall containing the thin crack of **RS** on its RH side. The scruffy walls between the two routes abut to form the oblique groove/corner of:*

31   Raph's Route *(RR)*   40'   VD
Climb the slabby groove to a shelf adorned with a tree. Trend up LWs to a good TR, then follow the groove back R to finish. Tree belay well back from the edge.   (1988)

32   Spurting Wildly   40'   HS 4a
Follow *RR* to the shelf. Step R, past the tree, to a groove & climb it (PR) to a LWs finish.   (1988)

33   There She Blows   40'   7b (E4 6b/c)   ★ †
A fierce technical problem which tackles the wall L of *RS*. Climb the wall direct, past 2PRs & a BR, to gain the top.   (1990)

34   Ramming Speed *(RS)*   30'   E1 5b
Climb the thin crack (PR) to finish LWs at the top.   (1988)

FRESHWATER QUARRY   GR 923 567

Up to 140' high and with plenty of scope for new-routers, this quarry would give several worthwhile additions were it not for the fact that climbing here is forbidden. The following two routes have been included for the sake of completeness only.

To reach Freshwater Quarry from Brixham, follow signs for the harbour and circumnavigate this to where the road hairpins LWs up a steep hill. Signs for a car park appear on the R. Follow these down to the sea and the crag.

1   Animals are People *(AAP)*   110'   S 4a,4b   ★
A fine line up the big corner opposite the entrance to the car park proper. Scramble up into a cave (TB).
1   60'   Gain a ledge & walk to a huge spike at its RH end. Climb the wall above, past an OH, to an earth-floored stance (P&NB).
2   50'   Climb for 20' to another large ledge, & continue up the corner (past an OH), to the top.   (1968)

2   Dulux   140'   S
The only recorded details of this route are somewhat sketchy. It starts somewhere R of *AAP*, & in two 70' pitches it meanders from ledge to ledge, through a few bulges & around the odd OH to a lamp post belay *(possibly a shaggy dog story?)*.   (1964)

The following route is a sea-level traverse linking Brixham to Berry Head (hence the name). Begin just beyond the breakwater forming the E→ extent of Brixham harbour:

3   Brixham to Berry Head Traverse   2,400'   IV
A high tide start adds little in the way of excitement to this perfunctory linking of Brixham to Berry Head. However, it is an excellent way of upping the days footage.   (1969)

BERRY HEAD PENINSULA   GR 946 566

Approach and Access
Berry Head is the S ↓ extremity of Torbay. The best approach from the N ↑ is via the A3022, following signs for Brixham. Just inside the town limit sign there is an old white toll house, turn R here down Monksbridge Road, following signs for Berry Head. The signs lead all the way to the car park next to the Southern Redoubt, a Napoleonic edifice, built to dominate and defend the whole bay from French invasion. The area is extensive, so access notes accompany each cliff.

The agreed climbing ban affects three buttresses within this section; Upper Ranger, Lower Ranger, and Oz Wall (as well as Barnacle Traverse Continuation). The ban extends from 15th March to 31st July. The symbol (R) denotes this restriction.

Situation and Character
Being a headland, the crags face variously N ↑,S ↓ and E→, so virtually any climactic condition can be dealt with from a climbing point of view. The areas themselves are incredibly diverse, ranging from the small friendly Coastguard and Red Wall craglets to the atmospheric arena of Berry Head Quarry.

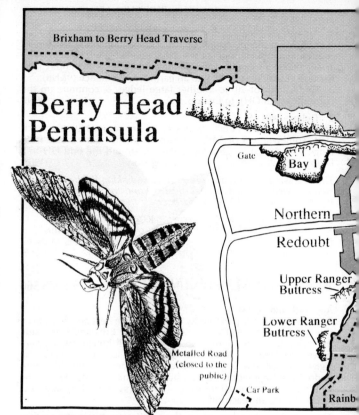

Berry Head Peninsula

Brixham to Berry Head Traverse

Gate

Bay 1

Northern

Redoubt

Upper Ranger
Buttress

Lower Ranger
Buttress

Metalled Road
(closed to the
public)

Car Park

Rainb

BERRY HEAD QUARRY

The Quarry is N-facing and can be a rather unsavoury experience in the depths of winter, due to the rock staying damp as a result of the ubiquitous lichen. However, during the summer it provides an excellent alternative to the banned Old Redoubt.

From the car park follow a road which leads past the Northern Redoubt (containing the Café and Coastguard Station), to a locked gate atop a rough metalled road leading down into the quarry. This is split into two bays, beyond which lies the Main Quarry Wall. Bay 1 (on the R beneath the descent road) is reached by following a narrow defile past a gate into the amphitheatre. Bay 2 is to the L of the narrow defile, and is defined by the rickety arête of Salt, followed by a long wall with some (as yet) untapped potential. This

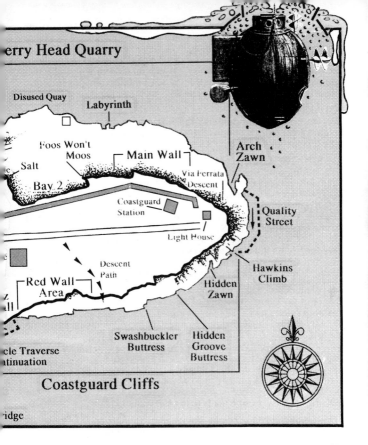

wall is bound on the L by the protruding edge of Foos Won't Moos, before the bulk of the Main Wall becomes evident. It is advisable to have a selection of pegs and a hammer for some of the climbs. The routes are described from R to L.

QUARRY BAY 1
The first route climbs a slab which lies to the R of two pools on the far side of the first quarried bay (below the descent road).

1 Caius 65′ E1 5b
R of the two stagnant pools is a dark reddish slab, with a wide fissure in its bottom LH third. Climb the fissure, then the slab above to some vegetation. Climb the steeper wall above to belay on a large ledge. Scramble off LWs.   (1984)

2 Semi-detached   30'   HVS 4c
Justifiably named; *as well as the usual rack of car-jacks, a couple of
acrow props wouldn't go amiss*. On the far side of where the two
pools meet there is a pile of boulders. Climb the obvious tottering
flake in the blunt arête above these.   (1984)

QUARRY BAY 2
Before entering the defile to the first quarry there is a long vegetated arête (which bounds the RH edge of the vast rambling bay to
the L).

3 Salt   200'   HS -,-,-
A tottering pile; described in the previous guide as ". . .an esoteric
gem left to rediscovery" *(sic(k)!)*. It follows the profoundly loose &
vegetated arête to the fort walls. Start 10' R of the arête, at the base
of an open corner.
1 60'   Gain a ledge beneath the corner, which is climbed past
some loose rock on the R, to a block belay on the arête.
2 70'   Climb the arête for a few feet, before mantelshelving onto
a ledge on the R. Follow the LH side of the arête for 50' to a belay.
3 70'   Climb straight up the arête, until beneath a knife-edge of
rock. Climb this & belay on top of the fort wall.   (1970)

4 Winterlude   220'   VS 4c,-,-,-
More of the same. Start 20' L of Salt, beneath the RH side of a short
smooth calcite wall.
1 50'   Climb the wall direct to a square block on the lip of a wide
ledge.
2 50'   Trend up LWs over large unstable blocks, to a stance & PBs
on the arête of Salt.
3 60'   Continue up the arête to a grassy ledge below the final
knife-edge of rock on Salt.
4 60'   Traverse RWs (some loose rock) to follow a break in an
OHing lip. Easy ground leads to the fort wall.   (1970)

*The following route climbs the cleaner, though equally loose, L-
bounding arête of the large rambling bay (ie. some 150yds L of Salt):*

5 Foos Won't Moos *(FWM)*   180'   S
If appearances are anything to go by then this is a far worthier route
than its counterpart, Salt. Even then it is questionable that it should
be deemed 'worth climbing'. Start near the bottom of the long
grassy ramp which bounds the RH side of the Main Quarry Wall.
1 20'   Climb a short corner 20' to the L of the arête.
2 70'   Start directly above a slab & go diagonally RWs to some
jammed blocks on the arête. Climb the arête to a large boulder-
strewn ledge & belay.
3 40'   Climb over some broken rock (on what might be loosely
described as the arête), then move RWs to belay.
4 50'   Traverse RWs to "tuck round the knob" as it was
euphemistically put in the 1971 guidebook.   (1970)

Opposite **FWM** *on the seaward rim of the quarry there is a pinnacle which contains a blow-hole & the ill-frequented gem of:*

6   Labyrinth   60'   VS 4c   ★★
A fascinating, although tortuous affair. Nip over the wall on the LH side of the pinnacle (marked by a red figure 10) & skirt the base of the pinnacle to the HWM, then belay. A hard LWs traverse gains the obvious cleft, where primitive caving skills lead toward a divine guiding light & a painless rebirth.   (1971)

MAIN QUARRY WALL
Opposite the pinnacle and L of *FWM* there is a partially obscured, compact orange/pink wall which lies directly below a large sloping grass ramp. The next route starts some 50' to the L of this wall.

7   Dirt Eater   150'   E4 6a   ★ †
Fine climbing up a clean reddish face (split by a thin crack) at the beginning of the quarried wall proper. Climb the crack, moving R then back L (PR) to gain a ledge. From its LH end climb up to join *YR*, which is followed to its stance. Move R & climb the square white groove above. Traverse RWs for 10' to a TR, then climb the wall above to a ledge. Traverse back LWs to finish up some cracks in the arête.   (1983)

8   Yellow Rurties *(YR)*   170'   HVS 4c,5a   ★
Start on a small grassy mound some 9yds to the L of Dirt Eater, just R of a much larger mound.
1   110'   Follow a thin crack to a couple of pod-like pockets, then head towards a slight borehole at 25' (slot-in peg). Move up into a wide shallow groove on the R & climb to a large TR. Continue for 15' to a PR in a borehole, then gain the ledges above. Traverse RWs until 5' beyond a large flat foothold (PR), then climb up RWs to a stance.
2   60'   Traverse LWs to climb a wide crack, then exit this RWs to some ledges. Move up to a good hold, then trend RWs to the final corner which leads to the top.   (1970)

9   Dust Devil   170'   E1 4c,5a,5b
Start from the apex of the larger mound L of *YR*, directly below the clean blank corner of *BGB*.
1   70'   Climb a broken wall (TRs) to a stance & TB at the foot of the blank corner.
2   50'   Traverse horizontally RWs to the edge of a hanging buttress, then move up for a few feet before teetering RWs across a delicate slab. Climb a corner to another good stance (PBs).
3   50'   Climb the steep wall L of the stance, then make some hard moves over a bulge into a short chimney. Climb this & finish LWs up the obvious line.   (1970/78)

10   Desparête   150'   E3 5c   ★★ †
A fine route up the magnificently exposed R arête of the blank corner. Follow Dust Devil until beneath the arête. Move up onto

Berry Head Quarry

the RH side of the edge, then cross an OHing red wall diagonally LWs to hinge around the arête on a hidden pocket (TR). Climb up to a ledge, then follow the most obvious line to the top.   (1984)

11 Burning Bridges *(BGB)*   150'   E3 5c   ★★ †
Very bold climbing up the magnificent, large blank corner high in the centre of the face (a wire-brushing would not go amiss). Start beneath the corner & climb the wall direct to it (as for Dust Devil). Follow the corner in its entirety, past a borehole TR in the lip of a shallow overlap at half-height.   (1983)

12 Sunset Boulevard *(SB)*   150'   E4 6a   ★★★
This is the impressive thin crack in the wall L of BGB. Start 15' to the L of *BGB*. Climb a crystalline wall to trend RWs into a corner (slot-in peg in a borehole). Move up to a nut slot, then make a rising traverse LWs until the crack system can be reached. Follow this up LWs to a large ledge. Traverse to its LH end, where easy climbing leads up LWs to a steep L/R exit crack (pre-place a rope to belay, unless the pitch is split).   (1983)

13 Home Brew   170'   HVS 4b,4c,4b
A yeasty concoction which mainly follows the RH of two parallel cracks in the centre of the face 20' to the L of *SB* (pegs useful). Start 4yds L of a vegetated cave, below the line of the LH crack.

1 50' Climb up (in line with the crack) for 25', then traverse RWs to some ledges & a cave stance.

2 60' Step out R from the cave, then climb direct to a stance below an OH (PBs).

3 60' Climb the OH on its RH side, then traverse LWs along a ledge system to gain a larger ledge. Trend RWs up the wall above to gain the top. (1970)

Variation 1a 50' VS 4b Gain a large fin of rock from the L (directly beneath the cave stance). Step up to a horizontal break, then climb over a bulge & up to the cave (overgrown). (1971)

14 Paranoid 160' E1 5b,5b ★★

A fine route which follows a thin sinuous crack in the light-coloured wall 30' to the L of Homebrew. Slings required for TRs. Start below a cave 20' up the wall.

1 100' Climb direct to a cave, then skirt the R edge of this to gain the crack above & follow this until it peters out. Gain & then follow a thin crack (slanting R\L) to a good hold & continue to a poor TR. Move up R with difficulty to gain a small stance below a V-groove.

2 60' Climb the V-groove to an OH, then traverse RWs on poor holds to a small ledge (PR above). Step L into a steep open groove which leads to the top. (1970)

15   Boo-bah Plost *(BBP)*   160'   HVS 4b,5a
The original route of the quarry, & in dire need of traffic. It takes the groove bounding the RH side of the dramatic, slender pillar of Equipoise.
1   60'   Climb the groove, then step up R to a ledge. Climb past some recesses, then move R to gain a large sloping ledge (PBs).
2   100'   Climb a subsidiary calcite groove on the R for 30', then move back L into the main groove (PR). After 20' step out R & climb steeply to some ledges. From a ledge about 20' from the top, move out LWs to gain & climb the final corner (PR).   (1970)

16   Equipoise   150'   E4 6a   ★★★ †
The stunning white pillar in the centre of the quarry. Start below the LH rib of the pillar. Climb up & slightly RWs, past two pockets (TRs), then climb the clean wall above on good edges (slot-in peg in a borehole) to a prominent ring PR. Move R & climb the arête for 30' (runners in *BBP*), until it is possible to move back L (PR) & up to another PR. Move up to yet another PR, from where balancy moves lead to a ledge. Climb the steep crack above which leads to the top (pre-place a belay rope).   (1985)

17   Beggar's Banquet *(B'SB)*   140'   E2 5a,5b   ★
An exposed, serious yet worthwhile undertaking up the long open groove L of the white pillar.
1   90'   Follow Equipoise to the pockets & TRs at 15', then head up LWs to a small ledge (PRs). Climb to a borehole TR, then step L to climb up into a short corner. Abandon this LWs after a few feet to continue past a hollow block to a stance.
2   50'   Climb diagonally RWs to some exposed ledges (PR), then move up LWs with difficulty to some more ledges. Climb direct to the top on steeper rock.   (1970)

18   Graunching Gilbert *(GG)*   150'   HVS 4c,-
Start 25' L of *B'SB* (pegs useful).
1   90'   Climb bearing slightly R to a shallow OH with undercuts in its lip. Trend RWs under this & up to a slight V-groove, which is climbed on small holds. Above is a niche with a borehole in its back wall which can be used for a peg belay.
2   60'   Finish easily over ledges to the top.   (1970)

19   Arncliffe   150'   VS 4b,4c,4a
Not recommended for people of a nervous disposition (if at all). About 50' L of *B'SB* are some small caves. Start 10' L of these, at a niche topped by a honeycombed roof.
1   50'   Climb the back of the niche & pull straight over the OH to a small ledge. Continue to a cramped stance & PBs.
2   50'   Move diagonally LWs, then back R to the foot of a groove (in line with the stance below). Gain the groove (PR) & climb it to a cave & TB on the L.
3   50'   Pull straight out of the cave on huge holds, then move R to gain easier climbing & the top.   (1970)

*The main wall of the quarry loses height at this point & drops down
to meet the ground. In a subsidiary bay up to the L is the crack
system of:*

20 Malteaser   100′   HVS 5a
Climb the shallow cracks & flakes in the wall. Traverse RWs at 85′ to
gain & finish up the wide crack in the red headwall.   (1983)

GIRDLE TRAVERSE

21 Opus Dei   510′   E2 4b,4c,4c,5b,4c (1pt),5a,5a   ★
A good, sustained girdle crossing the face from L to R at two-thirds
height. The climbing is reasonable apart from one hard section.
Start as for *GG*.
1   40′   Climb diagonally RWs to a cramped stance on an arête
below a shallow corner (PBs).
2   70′   Move into the corner, then traverse RWs along the obvious
line (PR) to meet *B'SB* just below its stance; gain this & belay.
3   50′   Climb up for 10′, then step R to a small ledge which is
followed until it ends (PR). Step down & traverse the exposed face
of the Equipoise pillar to gain *BBP*. Climb the RH crack to a block on
the R, then belay.
4   90′   Traverse RWs, then descend slightly to join Paranoid at a
groove below an OH. Hard moves RWs lead to a small ledge (PR
above), from where the continuation traverse leads RWs to a crack
(PR). Step across a sandy band of rock to a comfortable stance (PBs).
5   110′   Traverse RWs to the groove of Homebrew, then continue
awkwardly to a small ledge beside an impressive wall. Abseil from a
PR on the R, then pendulum to a small stance on Dust Devil (below
the smooth corner of *BGB*).
6   50′   As for Dust Devil; ie. step up onto the rib & climb RWs
(PR), to a corner. Stance & PBs 10′ higher.
7   100′   Move up above the belay to gain the rib on the R. Traverse
RWs under an OH, then descend a short slab to the final corner of
YR. Climb this for 10′, then step across onto an exposed buttress on
the R. A horizontal break leads to a vertical crack & the 'terminal'
grass slopes. Epic!   (1971)

ARCH ZAWN
At the E→ end of the quarry is a natural arch of rock jutting into the
sea. This defines the N↑ side of a square cut zawn. A lower sea
cliff, which forms the traverse of Quality Street, runs S↓ of the
arch. Two iron spikes mark the descent to the routes in the zawn
(or alternatively, the start of Quality Street). Boulders in the bed of
the zawn are uncovered at low tide and may be reached by a
descending traverse from the seaward end of the platform forming
the base of the arch. The RH wall of the face forming the landward
side of the zawn, gives two interesting routes. These are
approached by descending to the white wave-cut platform beneath
Arncliffe.

22   Sunkiss   30'   E2 5c
The striking landward arête of the buttress must be treated with caution, as the gear is a 'tad' low when it comes to attempting the crux. *You have been warned!*   (1983)

23   All Because. . .   45'   E1 5b
Climb the more amenable seaward arête, via a thin crack. Approach by a LWs traverse of the HWM from a gully which leads down LWs from the foot of Sunkiss.   (1983)

To the L of Sunkiss (looking seaward) there is a slight pinnacle on the seaward rim of the wave-cut platform.

24   Crunchie   60'   HS 4a
Step down R (from the Sunkiss side of the pinnacle) to the HWM & traverse RWs to an open corner. Follow this to the top.   (1983)

The following three routes are approached by scrambling down to the platform in the zawn:

25   Seaworm   90'   HS 4b,4a
A climb of questionable character. Start at the obvious slimy corner towards the L side of the face.
1   50'   Climb the corner to a bulge at 20', then move RWs over this to gain a small pedestal. Move R & climb a crack to a spacious ledge & large TBs.
2   30'   Climb up R to a ledge composed of calcite blocks. Follow this LWs, then finish up a guano-encrusted tunnel.   (1970)

26   Stag Party   90'   S 4a
Start at a crack 20' to the R of the initial corner of Seaworm. Step R into the crack & climb it to an OH. Move R, then climb a widening crack to gain some ledges & an optional stance in a cave (with TBs). Step L onto a pillar & climb steeply to another cave. Climb the final OH direct.   (1970)

27   Rastus   95'   HVS 4c,4c
Either start at low tide, below a crack 10' R of Stag Party; or traverse in from Seaworm. Climb up for 10', then move R & swing into a cave. Climb the slab R of the cave, then pull up LWs into a crack, which is followed to some ledges. Step LWs to an OHing corner (above a recess) & climb this to the top.   (1971)

On the opposite side of the zawn is a black wall & corner rising dramatically from the sea. The following three routes are approached by abseiling down the corner to take a hanging belay (Friends & wires) 10' above the HWM, & 5' beneath a TR.

28   Man in Black   50'   E2 5c   **★★**
Traverse RWs from the belay to gain the fearsome corner-line. Desperately bridge, jam, pull & push your way to a slightly OHing exit over the final shield of rock.   (1983)

29 Gothic 50' E4 6a   ★ †
A dark passage, via the centre of the black wall. Climb past a TR
above the belay to a L/R diagonal crack (PR). Trend up LWs to a
poor PR, then continue up LWs slightly to another PR. Climb up by
trending RWs, then finish direct.   (1993)

30 Breathless 55' E5 6b   ★ †
Traverse horizontally LWs from the belay to a large pocket (PR).
Head up LWs to a TR & continue in the same line to a further PR
(bold). Step up RWs to the final PR & finish direct.   (1993)

*The low cliff running S ↓ from Arch Zawn is traversed by QS. There
is also a vertical route at the start of QS:*

31 Milky Bar Kid 50' E1 5b
A fine route which climbs the OHing white wall above the first
pitch of QS. Start from the large ledge at the end of pitch 1 of QS.
Climb up RWs into a cave. Pull over the OH on the L, then go up
slightly RWs to finish via the obvious slanting break.   (1983)

32 Quality Street *(QS)* 230' V+   ★★
A sea-level traverse connecting Arch Zawn to the Eastern Shelf of
the Coastguard Cliffs. Possible at any state of the tide, but not
during high seas, *when only mad seals & Devonian coasteers play
out in the midday squalls.* Start beside a chimney formed by the S ↓
side of Arch Zawn.
1   40'   Cross the chimney about 5' above the HWM & traverse
LWs to a large ledge. Climb up to a cave & belay.
2   40'   Traverse horizontally LWs for 15', then climb diagonally
LWs across a gritty wall (moves of 4a) to a small ledge & TB.
3   60'   Continue more or less horizontally LWs to a TB at the far
end of a long ledge.
4   70'   Traverse LWs for 20' to the foot of a light-coloured slab &
climb this, via a thin crack slanting L/R (moves of 4a), to belay
beside a large flake.
5   20'   Move R & climb a crack to a large terrace & belay.   (1968)

COASTGUARD CLIFFS

These are the cliffs to the S ↓ and ←W of Arch Zawn. The quickest
and easiest approach from the car park is to use the descent path
100yds past the café in the Northern Redoubt. This leads down to
the start of the Western Shelf, beyond which lies the Eastern Shelf.
The Eastern Shelf can also be approached by (a) traversing the
grassy ledges leading S ↓ from the end of Berry Head Quarry
(above QS); or (b) by a *Via Ferrata* descent which lies to the L of the
lighthouse (looking seaward) marked on the plan for Berry Head
Peninsula. The climbing is on various steep, clean walls and small
zawns cut into the shelf of a high wave-cut platform which extends
towards the Old Redoubt (or on the buttresses and somewhat
vegetated slabs above the shelf).

WESTERN SHELF
Halfway down the descent path there is a short wall on the L (20'
high), extending for approximately 100yds. It contains many lineless routes that are not worth recording, except for a mid-height
traverse of the wall (**Memories** 200' HVS 5a). To reach the first clutch
of routes from the foot of the descent, turn E→ or L (looking
seaward) and walk along the raised wave-cut platform. After a
sea-filled crevasse the platform begins to rise to about 60' above
sea-level, heralding the start of a buttress characterised by the
central and bottomless corner of Swashbuckler.

1   Sirocco   60'   S 4a
Pleasant climbing up the ←W side (or R looking seaward) of the
buttress. Start at the base of a crack in the seaward face (just R of
the L edge). Climb the steep crack on good holds, then continue
delicately in the same line to the top.   (1979)

2   Broadside   90'   S -,4a
Start to the ←W of the buttress, atop a short chimney.
1   40'   Descend the chimney & traverse RWs about 15' above the
HWM (around a rib) & belay on the far side of the next small bay.
2   50'   Step back L to a ledge, then move delicately up & L around
a rib. Continue past a block (TR) to the top.   (1979)

3   Squall   100'   S 4a
The blunt arête 15' L of the corner of Swashbuckler. Follow Broadside, then belay beneath the arête. Straightforward climbing up the
arête leads to a deep hole on its RH side. Continue up the RH side
of the arête, via some thin cracks which lead to a ledge. Continue
up the break above to gain the top.   (1979)

4   Swashbuckler   100'   S 4a,4a   ★
The impressive central corner gives surprisingly easy climbing.
Start on the E→ side of the buttress at lowish tide.
1   40'   Make a descending LWs traverse to the face of the buttress, then cross this to a hanging stance at the base of the central
corner.
2   60'   Climb the corner direct on good holds.   (1968)

5   Blood & Sand   100'   E3 5c   ★ †
Between Swashbuckler & *DFJ* there is a slim pillar. Approach as for
Swashbuckler & belay at its hanging stance. Traverse RWs to a TR in
a chimney, then follow an obvious crack until it peters out. Move
RWs to an arête. Climb this for several feet, then boldly swing out
RWs until a hard move gains an obvious jug (PR). Continue direct to
finish.   (1988)

6   Douglas Fairbanks Jnr.   *(DFJ)*   90'   HVS 4c
The OHing groove immediately R of pitch 2 of Swashbuckler.
Approach via that route & belay below the line. Follow the steep
groove past semi-detached blocks to an OH. Step L to a ledge on
the arête & finish by a rising traverse RWs.   (1983)

7   Piracy   50'   S 4a
Around the arête (E→ of *DFJ*) is a large crack. Take a stance at the HWM beneath the crack & follow it to the top.   (1992)

8   Jim Jam   50'   S 4a
Start some 20' to the E→ of Piracy & belay below a pair of cracks (just above the HWM). Using both cracks, climb until it is possible to swing L & gain a layback to finish.   (1979)

Further E→ of the Swashbuckler buttress is a similar cliff that offers up several gems. The routes are approached from the E→ side (or LH side looking seaward) of the buttress, beginning at a ledge 20' above the HWM. The furthest route to the L is described first & is approached by a sea-level traverse.

9   Hidden Groove *(HG)*   110'   HS 4a,4b   ★
An interesting excursion. Start on the ledge.
1   60'   Descend an awkward crack to a ledge level with the HWM (awash at high tide). Skirt around a rib on the L, then go up an adjacent groove for 15'. Make a slightly descending traverse LWs across the front of the buttress to the 'hidden' groove at the far end of the face.
2   50'   Climb the groove direct to the top.   (1979)

10   Cloudburst   90'   VS 4a,4c
1   50'   Descend the awkward crack (as for *HG*) for a few feet until a traverse LWs leads across a steep wall to an arête. Step across the groove beyond this, then make a horizontal traverse LWs to a suspended groove in the middle of the face.
2   40'   Climb the groove, then step L at an OH to a ledge. Continue up a discontinuous zigzag crack, then make difficult moves up the steep wall above to finish.   (1979)

11   Calcite Diamond   80'   E1 5b   ★★
A real pearl, which boldly climbs the arête R of Cloudburst. Approach as for Cloudburst & (after skirting the rib) move up to a NB (a steady solo to this point). Step L & go straight up the arête to a good high handhold. Stand on this to make a series of tenuous moves up & across the wall, until easier climbing on the arête leads to the summit.   (1980)

EASTERN SHELF
The Eastern Shelf begins at a rocky shoulder which lies beyond the *HG* buttress. The shelf extends to the finishing terrace of the Quality Street *(QS)* traverse. It encompasses a small zawn (the first feature E→ of the rocky shoulder), and a quarried bay that is bound on its RH side by the red wall of Blind Pew. Above the red wall is the finishing terrace of *QS*, and the steep grey slab of Flying Fifteen.

The routes in the small zawn beyond the rocky shoulder are described from R to L.

12   Placebo   35'   VS 4c
Abseil down the landward side of the zawn, & establish a belay at the HWM. Make a rising traverse LWs to reach some good but ragged cracks, which are followed to the top.   (1984)

13   Tied Line   50'   E1 5b
Approach as for Placebo. Traverse LWs just above the HWM for 25', then make a difficult pull LWs through a bulge to the base of a crack, which is followed to finish.   (1984)

14   Ray Zazorn   40'   VS 5a
Approach by scrambling down from the rocky shoulder to gain the LH end of the wall (beyond the finish of Tied Line). Descend to the HWM & step out R onto the wall, via hard moves, to a good hold & a crack leading to the top.   (1984)

Just beyond the small zawn there is a large rib of rock which descends toward the sea. The following four routes are either based around the rib, or climb the back wall of a quarried bay to its R.

15   Thursday Rib *(TR)*   80'   S
Climb the R flank of the rib until the rock steepens. Trend up LWs to a scoop on the edge of the rib, then continue to a large ledge (& belay). Scramble off LWs.   (1961)

16   Thursday Corner   80'   HVD
Climb the corner just R of *TR*, trending LWs onto the arête when the corner becomes too vegetated.   (c.1960s)

17   Schizophrenia   150'   HS 4b,4a
The steep grey slab in the centre of the back wall of the bay.
1   70'   Climb the RH side of the slab, stepping R to pass a bulge. PB below a steep wall.
2   80'   Climb the steep wall & either continue up loose rock, or traverse RWs to the final corner of *GW*.   (1967)

18   Fine, Little Hands   70'   HVS 5a   †
Start at the LH end of a red crystalline wall beyond the grey slab of Schizophrenia. Climb direct up the L edge of the crystalline wall to a slightly OHing nose of rock (just R of the grey slab). Step up R onto a slab, where delicate climbing leads up RWs to the belay ledge of *FF*.   (1992)

19   Little Heart *(LH)*   70'   E1 5a/b   †
Climb the red crystalline wall to a small step in an overlap. Surmount this (via the step), then traverse RWs for a few feet & climb straight up a slab to a grassy ramp. Follow this to the belay ledge of *FF*.   (1992)

The sloping floor of the quarry meets the sea via a small shallow inlet formed by a narrow spit of rock. The landward wave-sculpted wall of the inlet provides the introductory climbing (at low tide) to the next four routes, beginning with:

20   Crystal Corner *(CC)*   60'   D
1   30'   Traverse the wave-sculpted wall RWs (at low tide), to a corner formed by a smooth red wall. Climb the corner to regain the quarry floor.
2   30'   Continue up the corner formed by a glacis & the red wall, to finish on the terrace of *QS*.   (1961)

21   Captain Flint   90'   E1 5a   †
The arête & wall L of pitch 2 of *HC*. Follow *HC* to its stance on the far side of the arête. Step LWs & climb the arête on small holds to where it begins to steepen. Step up RWs & finish up the sheer wall above (L of the finish to *HC*).   (1988)

22   Hawkin's Climb *(HC)*   90'   HS -,4a,-   ★★
Fine open slab climbing, hidden behind the R arête of the red wall.
1   30'   Follow *CC* to the corner, then traverse RWs along the HWM on barnacle-encrusted holds to reach the arête. Step up R around the arête to some small ledges & belay.
2   60'   Gain & follow the thin L/R slanting crack which runs up the slab to a large flake. Traverse RWs to a crack leading to the finishing terrace of *QS*.   (1961)

23   Rum Truffle   100'   HVS -,5a   †
1   50'   Follow *HC* to the arête & continue RWs for another 20' (reversing part of *QS*) to reach a long ledge just above the HWM; TB at its LH end.
2   50'   Climb down RWs for 10', then follow an arête to a break (on *QS*) & a good TR. Climb the bulge above, then finish by boldly attacking a slab & an arête which lead to the RH end of the finishing terrace of *QS*.   (1988)

The E→ side of the quarried bay is bounded by a smooth red wall which is topped by the finishing terrace of **QS** *(easily gained via a steep glacis). The following route starts 5' R of where the glacis meets the top half of the red wall (ie. above pitch 1 of* **CC***):*

24   Blind Pew   45'   E4 6a
A nasty piece of work. Boulder out (diagonally RWs) over the yawning void above *CC*, to a bulge after 15' (*sky hook* runner in pocket). Pull through the bulge RWs, then climb a vague groove in the slab above. Finish on the terrace of *QS*.   (1984)

The next three routes climb a steep grey slab above the concluding terrace of **QS** *(gained via the glacis). The LH side of the slab is defined by a vegetated crystal-cake fault:*

25   Gugu Wack *(GW)*   130'   HVS 4c,-
Unless re-cleaned this is a worthless route which is difficult to protect. Start beneath the crystal-cake fault.
1   70'   Climb easily to where the fault steepens, then move up with difficulty onto the slab above which leads to the PBs of *FF*.
2   60'   Above & slightly L of the stance is a solid corner in an area

of loose rock. Climb this to the top.   (1969)

26   Sun's Rays   70'   E1 5a
Start 5' R of the crystal-cake fault. Climb a line of steps, trending L/R, to meet the L end of the *FF* traverse. Step back L to a small ledge & climb direct up the wall. Belay as for *FF*.   (1992)

27   Flying Fifteen *(FF)*   70'   HVS 5a   ★
A fine bold pitch. Start 10' R of the crystal-cake fault. Climb the wall for 15', then move up RWs to a ledge (poor PR). Traverse LWs for 10', then climb direct to a sloping ledge & PB.   (1968)

RED WALL AREA
This lies at the ←W end of the sea-level terraces. The best approach is to take the descent path 100yds past the café in the Northern Redoubt, as for the Coast Guard Cliffs (Western Shelf). Evening Buttress is just R of the descent path (looking seaward). The routes are described from R to L.

28   Evening Arête *(EA)*   90'   VD
The first feature of the buttress is the RH arête, capped by a prominent nose. Follow the arête easily for 60' to gain the nose (TR). Climb a steep wall R of this to the top.   (1967)

29   Evening Buttress   60'   VD
L of *EA* is a slanting crack running up the face of the buttress. Climb the centre of the wall (trending RWs), then move LWs over an overlap to a ledge. Either finish here, or climb the rock above as another pitch.   (1961)

Around the corner to the L is the bay of **CC**, *containing the sheer wall of* **KQ**. *The first route here climbs the RH side of the wall facing* **KQ**.

30   Photo Thirty-six *(P36)*   40'   E4 6a   †
A short, exacting problem with marginal protection. Start on the RH side of a rust-coloured wall, atop a pedestal at 12'. Climb a short line of pockets (R of the scooped central crackline) to gain a rounded break. Move R & finish via a long reach & a scramble to a grassy ledge (huge TB).   (1988)

31   Three Dozen Valium *(TDV)*   60'   E5 6a   ★ †
A serious climb up the red wall opposite *KQ*. Start 15' L of *P36*, below a huge flake. Climb up the RH edge of the flake to gain an intermittent crack (TR). Follow this past a PR, then continue slightly LWs over a bulge. Climb up the wall above to the top. Belay as for *P36*.   (1988)

32   Raw Umber   60'   E4 5c   †
Another serious route. Climb the LH edge of the huge flake to a ledge. Ascend the pocketed wall above (L of the *TDV*), passing a poor TR to gain a horizontal break. Climb the wall above via a large quartz pocket, then join & finish up *TDV*.   (1994)

Nick White on Suicide Blonde (E6 6b) Photo. Charlie Woodburn

Nick Hancock on Rainbow Bridge (VIII+) Photo. Andy Grieve

33   Izitso   100'   HVS 5a   *
Climb the centre of a slab (L of the *TDV* flake) to a crack, then
follow this to a suspect block. Move up LWs on good holds to a
ledge (optional stance). Gain the wall on the R & continue RWs
until it is possible to step up to some good ledges. Continue direct
to a good edge, then climb more easily to the huge TB atop *P36*.
Scramble off RWs.   (1981)

34   Captain's Corner (*CC*)   115'   VS 4c
Worth doing for the first half only. It takes the large, blind corner to
the L of Izitso. Climb the corner with increasing interest to a large
terrace. Finish up the loose, broken corner above.   (1961)

35   Killer Queen (*KQ*)   70'   E5 6b   **
A bold proposition (despite appearances), which climbs the centre
of the smooth red wall L of *CC*. A problematic start leads to a break
(PR above). Pull over a bulge on pockets (PR), then climb the wall
(2PRs -poor) to a short crack. Trend diagonally LWs, & finish up the
arête. Belay in a grassy alcove on the R.   (1987)

36   Captain Scarlet (*CS*)   50'   E2 5b   †
. . .*indestructible*. Climb the obvious arête bounding the LH side of
the *KQ* wall, passing some unstable-looking conglomerate knob-
bles on route to a ledge. Climb the looser continuation arête
above. Belay as for *KQ*.   (1987)

37   Ruddy Corner   80'   HVD
Climb the unappealing corner L of *CS*. A short wall & flake lead to
the red corner. Gingerly tiptoe up this on suspect rock to a ledge.
Move up & R on poorer rock, from where less stressful stuff leads
to the top.   (1967)

38   Red Crack   70'   HS 4a
Pleasant enough *(to warrant climbing)*. Follow a thin crack R of a
wider one which splits the centre of the red wall (L of the *KQ* wall).
After 40' follow the obvious traverse-line LWs to reach a shallow
corner, which is climbed to a belay (scramble off).   (1961)
Variation VS 4b It is possible to climb direct up the wall from the
start of the traverse. Using a quartz-lined pocket, surmount an
overlap to gain the slab above. Trend LWs to finish.   (c.1960s)

39   Ruddigore   60'   HS 4a
Climb the shallow groove L of Red Crack.   (1967)

40   Blood   50'   E1 5b   *
An excellent pitch. Start below the LH side of the red wall. Climb
easily for 10', then step R to climb straight up the wall above (TR) to
gain the half-way ledge. Step L & move up via some pockets to gain
a flat hold. Mantel onto this, then finish direct.   (1969)

41   Veins   50'   E2 5c
Start as for Blood. Climb straight up the wall to a large ledge on the
L. Continue direct, keeping L of Blood.   (1988)

There are three striking corner lines to the L of the red wall. The first is:

42   Red Monk   50'   VS 4b
A poor route. The red corner-line just L of Veins hasn't been the same since the demise of its capping OH.   (1967)

43   Oh Brother!   50'   E2 5c   ★ †
From the foot of Red Monk's corner trend out LWs to gain & climb the hanging arête (PR). The final section of the arête provides some excellent climbing.   (1994)

44   Chastity Corner *(CYC)*   50'   HS 4a   ★
The central corner is much better. Make a strenuous move to enter it, then climb up on good jams & layaways to finish on a ledge; block belays well back from the edge.   (1967)

45   Binky   60'   HS 4b   ★
Good climbing up the RH edge of the wall L of *CYC*. Start at a thin crack. Trend slightly RWs, & climb direct on small holds to reach a ledge on the rib overlooking *CYC*. Finish easily up the short wall above (block belays well back from the edge).   (1968)

46   Abbot's Wall   50'   S 4a
The centre of the wall L of Binky. Climb the wall direct, then finish up the main corner R of the thinner final crack of *AW*.   (c.1960s)

47   Abbot's Way *(AW)*   50'   HVS 5a   ★★
A steep route up the LH & finest of the three corners. Climb the main OHing corner for 30', then step out onto the slightly OHing L wall to gain a thin crack. Follow this to the top.   (1961)

*A short LWs traverse around the corner from **AW** leads to the start of a sea-washed ledge system & the base of an arête.*

48   Cod   60'   HVS 4c
Climb the arête & the wall above to a large ledge. Make some bold moves up & RWs to reach some good holds, then continue up over steep rock to finish.   (1981)

49   Oggie   60'   HVD
Start 10' L of Cod (& just R of a long low OH) at a series of small rough holds which are followed to a prominent nose at 20'. Gain a ledge crossing the wall at half-height, then move RWs to a small bay which leads to easier ground & the top.   (1968)

50   Hot Lips   60'   E1 5c,5a
Strenuous & problematic. It climbs through the low OH to the L of Oggie. Start 10' from its LH end, below a step in the OH.
1   30'   Climb to a good runner under the OH, & make a hard move to reach holds on the lip. Pull over onto the slab, then climb up to a belay beneath an OHing crack.
2   30'   Climb the strenuous crack to the top.   (1977)

*Where the low OH finishes on the L, there is an easy-angled wall
leading to a cave (at 30') & a juggy groove. This provides an easy way
up & down this section of the cliff.*

51   Neanderthal   50'   HVD
L of the easy descent is a corner formed by a prominent OH & a
wall to its R. Climb an open crack in the wall for 20', then pull out
LWs under a nose & climb the wall above to finish.   (1968)

52   Pathos   60'   HVS 5b
Start below the prominent OH. Launch out over the roof & climb
the steep wall above to a large ledge. Finish direct.   (1979)

The sea-washed ledges end here, at the beginning of **BT**.

53   Barnacle Traverse   (BT)   300'   III (at low tide)
From the prominent OH of Pathos, step down & traverse LWs
below the HWM until it is possible to step up & reach a ledge.
Continue to traverse across a steep wall to the foot of a shallow
corner flanked on the L by a large sea cave. Climb the corner,
moving R at the top.   (1967)

54   Relay   90'   HS 4a
Start as for *BT*. After two ribs have been negotiated there is a low
OH below a steep pink slab. Climb a thin crack past a steep move at
20', then move R to a niche below a corner (optional stance). Climb
the corner (by facing R) past loose rock.   (1979)

55   Barnacle Traverse Continuation   (BTC)   300'   VI-   **(R)**
Extends the traverse to the large platform at the foot of Lower
Ranger Buttress. Some excellent climbing (especially along the
base of Oz Wall), with a 5a OH to finish.   (1968)

OZ WALL
This is a compact wall composed of superbly weathered limestone
which is covered in *gouttes d'eau (pockets created by drops of
water)* and the odd tufa *(a tufa is like a stalactite, but attached to the
rock for its entire length)*. When approaching from the top of the
Red Wall Area, gain the top of the crag and follow the cliff-edge
←W, to a broad white ledge opposite Oz Wall (which is traversed at
low-level by the last part of *BTC*).

The RH end of Oz Wall enters a large alcove, which contains a blunt
pinnacle. To gain the base of the routes, descend the seaward edge
of the pinnacle, and traverse LWs to a broken ledge system (the
main stance) below the first route. Oz Wall can also be gained from
the path leading down into Lower Ranger Buttress (LRB). If
approaching via this path there is a large, square white boulder on
the quarry rim, which can be used as an anchor for an abseil
approach to the final five routes on the wall. The routes are described from R to L.

56 Wizard 60′ E1/2 5b **(R)**   †
Above the stance are two parallel cracks. Climb the RH one in its
entirety, finishing up a groove to an *in-situ* belay.   (1989)

57 Oz Court 60′ E2 5b **(R)**   ★ †
Climb the LH crack to gain & cross a ramp-line (which trends L/R).
Tackle the bulge above the ramp-line via a crack (TR) & continue in
the same line to the Wizard belay.   (1989)

58 Assana 70′ HVS 5a **(R)**   †
Traverse LWs across a steep slab to gain the base of a ramp-line
(trending L/R). Follow this RWs (past a TR) across Oz Court, then
head back up L to the Wizard belay.   (1989)

59 New Paths 70′ E4 6b **(R)**   ★★ †
Follow Assana to the ramp. Step up L to gain & climb a black tufa.
Step L to another tufa below an incipient crack (PR). Follow the
crack over a bulge, then trend RWs to the Wizard belay.   (1989)

60 Boulder Dash *(BD)* 80′ HVS 5a **(R)**   †
Traverse LWs at a lower level than Assana, passing well beneath the
two lines of tufa, to gain the edge of a slab after 50′. Follow this
back up RWs to finish.   (1989)

*The following five routes can be reached by abseiling down the wall
from a square white boulder, mentioned in the approach notes.
This negates the need to do the first pitch over & over again.*

61 Down With His Pants *(DWP)* 115′ VS 4c,4c **(R)**   †
1 35′ From the main stance follow an OHung diagonal break
down LWs, to a stance below a steep groove in the large OH.
2 80′ Gain the groove up on the R (PR), then follow it up RWs to
join & finish up *BD*.   (1989)

62 Pommie Granite *(PG)* 105′ E4 4c,6b **(R)**   ★ †
1 35′ As for *DWP*.
2 70′ Up L of the stance is a viciously OHung crack. Follow this
direct (PR), then climb the wall to gain a slab. Step L to a TR & follow
the groove above to a bulge (PR). Surmount this & finish via a
hanging flake.   (1989)

63 Follow the Yellow Gouttes-d'eau 140′ VS 5a,4b **(R)**   ★★ †
1 50′ As for *DWP* to its stance, then continue to follow the break
LWs to another ledge (TB).
2 90′ Climb the goutte-encrusted slab & continue RWs along the
obvious line to a belay.   (1989)

64 Over the Rainbow 120′ E3 5a,5b **(R)**   ★ †
1 50′ As for *DWP* to its stance, then continue to follow the break
LWs to another ledge (TB).
2 70′ Follow the crack in the wall above the stance to an OH
(PR). Climb this direct, then finish over the next bulge (PR) via the
hanging flake on *PG*.   (1989)

65   Hanging Rib   120'   HVS 5a,5b   **(R)**   †
1   50'   1   As for *DWP* to its stance, then continue to follow the break LWs to another ledge (TB).
2   70'   Trend out LWs from the belay to gain & follow the hanging rib, past 2TRs. After the last TR, trend back RWs to finish.   (1989)

UPPER & LOWER RANGER BUTTRESSES (URB & LRB)
These walls inhabit the thorn scrub slopes below the S ↓ wall of the Northern Redoubt. The least brutal approach is to take the fishermen's path which descends the slope to the R (looking seaward) of the telescope behind the café in the Northern Redoubt. URB has some barely worthwhile routes (up to 40'), hidden behind a dry stone wall just ←W of the fort wall. The LRB routes are just over 100' and climb a rambling wall in a quarried basin above the large platform at the end of *BTC*.

66   Laugharne   30'   HS   **(R)**   †
Start at the far LH side of the cliff, in a hidden bay beyond the dry stone wall. Climb the loose wall to the top.   (1991)

67   Cruise of a Lifetime *(CL)*   30'   HVS 5a   **(R)**   †
Start beneath an OH to the R of Laugharne. After an awkward start, trend up RWs to break through the OH on the R.   (1991)

68   Ancient Eyes *(AE)*   30'   E1 5b   **(R)**   †
Follow the blatant crack to the R of *CL*, which peters out at a ledge. Climb the continuation crack to finish.   (1991)

69   Bus Stop   25'   S   **(R)**   †
Climb the broken corner to the R of *AE*.   (1991)

70   Asante Sana   25'   VD   **(R)**   †
Ascend the ledges further R of Bus Stop.   (1991)

71   Jewel   30'   HS   **(R)**   †
Climb up a few feet L of an arête (hiding a hidden bay).   (1991)

72   Silver Cufflinks *(SC)*   25'   VD   **(R)**   †
Take the arête/rib direct.   (1991)

73   Katalyn   20'   VS   **(R)**   †
Start R of the arête of *SC*, & L of the steeper wall to its R. Climb to a small ledge, then climb direct to the top.   (1991)

74   Leavitt   35'   HVS 5a   **(R)**   †
Start just R of Katalyn, beneath a curving crack. Follow this, then stay L of the central crack to finish.   (1991)

75   The Ultimate Postcard   35'   HVS 5a   **(R)**   †
Start in the centre of the steep face, which is climbed direct via the obvious crack.   (1991)

76   Meditations   30'   HS   **(R)**   †
Climb the RH edge of the wall next the dry stone wall.   (1991)

The lower part of URB has a number of shorter pitches which are not worth recording (Thank God – Ed). The quarried basin containing LRB is characterised by more than its fair share of loose rock. There are also three arêtes between the foot of the descent path & the ←W edge of the slab (across from which is the final wall of Rainbow Bridge). The central arête has a prominent nose at 70'.

77   Clapier-dans-fils   100'   S   **(R)**   †
Start in the middle of the broken rock to the L of the first arête. Take a direct line to the top, finishing in the middle of the red wall at an imaginary belay.   (1991)

78   Mulinos   120'   VS   **(R)**   †
Climb the first arête, surmounting a small OH at 20'. Follow the arête to broken ground. Finish up the L edge of the summit OH to a blackthorn bush belay.   (1991)

79   Tulang Kecil *(TK)*   100'   HS   **(R)**   †
Start below a prominent nose R of Mulinos. Scramble to a level ramp at 50'. Climb the groove below & R of the nose, then traverse LWs beneath it. Climb direct to the summit OH & belay.   (1991)

80   Oje   120'   E2 5b   **(R)**   †
Scramble up slabs R of *TK* to gain the ramp at 50'. Pull over a small OH to a narrow ledge at the base of a short smooth wall. Delicate moves up this lead to a finger slot & some broken rock above. Scramble up to the summit OH, which is surmounted R of a V-shaped conglomerate knobble.   (1991)

81   Legin   110'   HVS 5a   **(R)**   †
L of the central arête are some cracks in the upper red wall. Start beneath these at the base of a large flake. Climb this, then the slabs above it to the ramp at 50'. Follow the cracks, then scramble over loose rock to belay R of the summit OH.   (1991)

82   Casablanca   90'   E1 5b   **(R)**   †
Start beneath the central arête. Bold climbing up a red slab leads to the base of an arête at 50'. Gain the arête from a ledge on the R, then follow it to the belay of Legin.   (1991)

83   Carreg   50'   VS   **(R)**   †
Start 20' R of Casablanca, atop a grass bank below a small flake. Climb past the flake to a ledge where the upper section steepens. Take the wall above direct on small holds.   (1991)

84   Dzirnavas   50'   HVS 5a   **(R)**   †
Start 10' R of Carreg, below a black streak. Staying R of the black streak, gain the ledge below the steep wall. Finish up a crack a few feet L of the third arête.   (1991)

85   Sai Qot   60'   S   **(R)**   †
Gain & follow the third arête to the top.   (1991)

86   Balta Maja   60′   HS   **(R)**   †
A featureless line a few feet R of Sai Qot, finishing up a steep
section to the R of the third arête.   (1991)

THE OLD REDOUBT   GR 942 561

Approach and Access
Follow the approach details for Berry Head Peninsula to the
National Trust car park beside the Southern Redoubt. A footpath
from the seaward end of the car park leads down a steep grassy
slope towards the sea, with the tottering Ultimate Trundle buttress
up to the R. The path stops above a yawning 60′ drop into the sea
(*which has been ticked*). Eschewing the airborne form of approach,
the sane punter will descend the rocky scoop to the R (facing
seaward). This leads to the start of the technically easy, but fearsomely exposed, traverse to gain a non-tidal platform at the mouth
of The Great Cave. They now have a video camera installed in the
Old Redoubt. At the end of the climbing ban and for a small fee,
the Ranger will make a copy of your ascent of Moonraker!

**It is important that the agreed climbing ban is strictly adhered to. It
extends from 15th March to 31st July, and encompasses the stretch of
coastline from the Rainbow Bridge Cliffs to Bismark Wall (Cod Rock is
also included in this ban). The symbol (R) next to a route denotes this
restriction. Failure to comply will leave your wallet £1,000 lighter**.

Situation and Character
From a British perspective, this is probably the premier cliff of the
guidebook. To say it overshadows the other crags is pointless, as its
shadow is plain to see. . . stretching plain out-of-sight across the
leaden waters of the English Channel. However, this is hardly a
grade-ist venue. Intrepid VS leaders can expect as great, or considerably more of an adrenalin rush as your average E6 jug-jockey
from this veritable maritime alp. Viewed from The Great Cave
platform, the limestone architecture above the huge roof swims in
and out of reality in a fashion that would have pleased Gaudi, while
the gothic-like corbelling of roof upon roof would probably have
appalled Corbusier. Despite appearances, the rock is extremely
sound and abounds in thank-god holds (*which is quite fortuitous
considering. . .*). Although The Great Cave platform is non-tidal,
the approach to Moonraker and Caveman etc. can only be done at
mid/low tide.

RAINBOW BRIDGE CLIFF
An extensive low cliff line of immaculate rock extends from the RH
end of The Great Cave platform, to the most ←W extent of the
Coastguard Cliffs (Lower Ranger Buttress). Apart from the traverse
of Rainbow Bridge the cliff also sports a number of vertical routes.

The Old Redoubt

Descent to Bismark Wall

The Blue Grotto

The Green Grotto

Bismark Wall

Great Ca...

1 Rainbow Bridge *(RB)*   810′   VIII+   **(R)**   ★★★
An exceptionally fine route. The climbing is on perfect rock well
above the HWM, making it a girdle traverse above water, rather
than a sea-level traverse. Only a strong party will manage this
daunting expedition in one push; several eascape routes exist for
the weary. A judicious point of aid reduces the grade to a more
amenable grade VII+, while lightweight soloists can miss out pitch
6 to give a superbly sustained VI+. Start from the RH end of The
Great Cave platform.
1   70′   Traverse RWs along an intermittent OHung ledge (15′
above the HWM), & belay near its RH end.
2   70′   (5b) Descend a crack to follow a line of pockets & scoops
leading across a very smooth wall (10′ above the HWM). Pass a
small & very tired TR, to gain a stance at the foot of a chimney.
3   45′   (5a) Traverse across some slabs to a PR under an OH. Swing
around a rib, then continue horizontally RWs (strenuous) before
moving down slightly to good holds which lead to a sloping ledge.
4   35′   (5a) Continue traversing at the level of the belay.
5   40′   (5a) Move R to a PR, & descend to a traverse leading to
better holds & a remarkable crystal cave (The Hall of Mirrors).
6   90′   (6a/b) Traverse RWs onto the wall, then climb up to a TR.
Move down RWs to some small ledges (PR). Climb a steep wall,
trending R to a shallow groove containing several PRs. Clip these,
then reverse to the start of the shallow groove. Follow a line of
holds leading horizontally RWs to the base of the hanging groove
15′ to the R. Climb the groove, & continue to traverse RWs to a

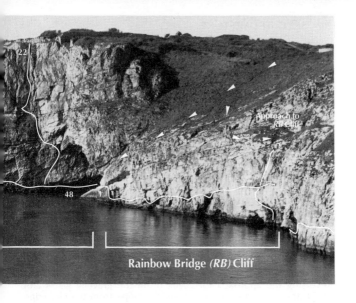

Rainbow Bridge *(RB)* Cliff

stance at the base of a gully.

7   50'   (5b) Traverse horizontally RWs across a line of pockets in the steep wall (sustained), to an obvious stance atop the constriction in the chimney which bounds the RH side of the wall.

8   50'   (5a) Descend the chimney to some ledges. Move R & down, then swing along a shelf to a good stance in a corner.

9   80'   (5b) Step down & traverse horizontally about 10' above the HWM. Exacting moves on sloping holds lead to an old TR. Either continue traversing with difficulty at the same level, or climb down to better holds below the HWM, to reach a small zawn.

10   70'   (5b) Cross the zawn & climb direct to an OH. Traverse RWs to a projecting nose, then move down & R with difficulty, continuing steeply to a stance & small flake belay.

11   60'   (4a) Straightforward climbing, past an obvious easy exit, leads to a belay on the edge of the Terminal Zawn.

12   100'   (5b) A real belter! Traverse RWs along the obvious line (well steep!) to a small cave. Climb RWs to an OH, & pull up to a traverse RWs that gains easier-angled rock. Continue RWs to a groove leading to a good stance.

13   50'   (4c) Climb straight up to a ledge, move L & pull over an OH to a short wall, which leads to the top.   (1973/89)

Variation 6a 90' (5c with 1pt) Continue the PRs in the shallow groove & tension into the mid-section of the groove which the free version gains the base of.   (1974)

Variation 12a 90' (5b) Shorter & slightly easier than the usual finish. Traverse RWs strenuously to the small cave, then climb up to gain the obvious crack cleaving the wall of the zawn. Follow this to the top.   (c.1970s)

The next four routes lie between pitches 6 & 7 of **RB**. *From mid-way down The Great Cave approach path, contour the slope LWs for 125yds (looking seaward), to a gravelly slope atop a buttress which juts out from the main cliff line. There is a large crystalline TR near the cliff edge (atop the chimney stance at the end of pitch 7 on* **RB**). *The routes are described from R to L.*

2   Out of the Cauldron *(OTC)*   50'   HVS 5a   **(R)**
Abseil to ledges at the foot of the chimney. Climb the chimney for several feet until it is possible to gain the R wall beneath a small OH. Move R beneath this, then finish direct.   (1988)

3   Witches Tit *(WT)*   40'   E4 6a/b   **(R)**   ★
An easier version of *ITF*, with the attendant attraction of a more amenable approach. Start by the crystalline TB of *OTC*. Step out L to gain & reverse the pocketed horizontal fault (pitch 7 on *RB*), until beneath a TR. Climb the dark brown wall (past the TR) to another TR & a desperate finish up the final groove.   (1992)

4   Into the Fire *(ITF)*   85'   E6 6b   **(R)**   ★★ †
Reversing the approach for 20yds (from the gravelly glacis atop *OTC*), there is a *in-situ* TB 7yds up the slope from the cliff edge. Abseil direct from this to gain a *in-situ* TB at the HWM (in a small niche on the RH rib of a large alcove at sea-level). Follow the L edge of the rib to where it merges with the RH edge of an OH. Follow the fiendish pocketed crack above this (past a TR) to join *RB*. Traverse RWs for 10', then finish up *WT*.   (1991)

5   Look, Before You Leap *60'*   E1 5b   **(R)**   ★ †
Descend LWs from the abseil TB of *ITF*, then swing into the large alcove at sea-level (L of *ITF*'s rib). Climb the LH back wall of the alcove to the OH, then traverse LWs (using undercuts) to a small TR in a pocket at the lip of the OH. Climb the wall above to finish via an easy scramble to gain the top.   (1991)

The following route climbs the shattered pillar up & R of the descent path to The Great Cave (looking seaward).

6   The Ultimate Trundle *(UT)*   70'   VD   **(R)**
Start in the centre of the pillar. Climb up (bearing RWs) to reach the prominent crack running up the RH side of the pillar. Follow this easily to the top.   (1967)

THE GREAT CAVE
The end of the descent path leads into a rocky scoop. All the routes up to the Blue Grotto area are described from R to L. The following four routes climb the rock above the traverse to The Great Cave platform. Directly above the rocky scoop is a groove cutting dramatically up R\L, this is:

7 Sandshoe Shuffle 70′ E1 5b **(R)** ★
An excellent introduction to this intimidating arena. Climb the groove until it disappears, then continue up the wall to finish on a grass terrace. Walk off RWs along the terraces. (1989)

8 Sloop 100′ E1 5b **(R)**
A redundant pitch due to the ascent of Yardarm. However, it enables the same situations to be enjoyed at an easier standard. Belay above the first move of the easy traverse to the cave platform. Pull up into a niche, then make a slightly rising traverse LWs for 30′ to gain some small ledges beneath a slight rib. Climb direct for 15′ to a TR, then trend RWs to a projecting ledge. Continue easily to a grass terrace below *UT*. (1970)

9 Yardarm 140′ E3 5b **(R)** ★★
A strenuous & sensationally exposed pitch which tackles the L arête of the sharply OHing wall to the L of Sloop. Attention to rope-handling is a dire necessity if terminal rope drag is to be avoided. Start as for Sloop. Follow that route to its TR, then move L & down (from the TR) into an exposed bay. Climb diagonally LWs out of the bay to gain a hanging groove, which is followed briefly before stepping LWs to a small OH. Pull around the RH side of the OH & continue direct to a crack leading to a good belay. Walk off RWs along the grassy terraces below *UT*. (1977)

10 Warspite 120′ E5 6a,5b **(R)** ★ †
Start 20′ L of Yardarm, at the end of a smooth pink slab above a narrow ledge below an unlikely-looking OH.
1 60′ Climb up RWs from the belay, taking the initial OH on the R. Move L to where a long reach over the middle OH leads to a jug & poor PR. Move L to another poor PR & pull up into a red niche. Climb up LWs from the niche to stand on some projecting flakes. Pull up LWs around a hanging arête & power up the steep wall above the TR of Sloop & belay.
2 60′ Follow Yardarm to finish. (1989)

Down to the L of Warspite is a large wave-cut platform. Above this looms the awesome OH of Cocoon (formerly **Iron Butterfly** *A3). Beneath the R edge of this is a blank wall. The next route weaves a path up this.*

11 Lost Identity 150′ E6 6a,5b **(R)** ★ †
Start some 10′ to the L of the R arête. Climb up to the bulge (at 15′) & pull over this to gain & blindly climb the blank-looking wall (past a number of PRs) to join & finish up *MOW*. (1991)

12 Man O'War *(MOW)* 150′ E6 6a,5b **(R)** ★★
A once proud galleon which is now totally out-gunned by the following steel-clad pupa. It free-climbs the first half of Iron Butterfly, before making a heart stopping excursion to the arête.
1 90′ Start 25′ L of the R arête, beneath a niche at 15′. Gain & climb out of the niche to the base of some incipient cracks running

Rope showing the line of *GOG*

The Old Redoubt
– Great Cave (right-hand) –

Escape ramp

Video camera

Approach traverse

← Approach to
Magical Mystery Tour

up to the immense OH. Climb these past several PRs, to a projecting block at the lip of a bulge 10' below the roof (PR). Boldly follow the shallow horizontal overlap RWs towards the arête. Powerfully bar-ndoor up RWs around this in a literally breathtaking position. Further steep climbing up a bald groove leads to the TR of Sloop (belay).
2   60'   Finish as for Yardarm.   (1989)

13   Cocoon   110'   E8 6c   **(R)**   ★★★ †
Perhaps the most stunning pitch *(not to see the light of day)* in the South West. It free-climbs the aid route Iron Butterfly in its entirety. Start as for *MOW*, to the projecting block at the bulge. Continue direct to the massive OH, then follow the crack snaking out towards daylight. Upon attaining the lip, a further 25' of bold climbing is left between you & the security of the belay, which is reached by trending up RWs (following a line of decaying aid bolts) to join Yardarm. Either abseil off, or finish up Yardarm.   (1971/90)

14   Depth Charge *(DC)*   260'   E5 5b,6a,6a,5a,5b   **(R)**   ★★★
"Monstrously brilliant! A new breed in space-walking. . ." which climbs the black OHing groove suspended above the RH side of the huge OH of The Great Cave itself. Take care with the PRs, as they are now in a diabolical state.
1   45'   Follow *MOW* to the base of the thin cracks, then make a rising traverse LWs to a poor stance in a corner under the OH.
2   35'   Climb out LWs under the OH (manky PRs) to gain the base of the black groove. Follow this for a few feet before traversing down LWs to a stance.
3   45'   Move back R & climb the groove to a good rest (PR). Continue to make committing moves up the groove on calcite knobs, then exit LWs at the top to a stance atop a flake (PBs).
4   45'   Move up L to a small cave. Continue up a groove on the L to a much larger cave & belay (in common with Barbican); an escape RWs can be effected at this point.
5   90'   Above the cave is a rounded grey chimney. Gain & climb this to a foot-ledge leading LWs into a shallow corner. Follow this to an OH, then move RWs into a wide crack which gives strenuous climbing to gain the slabbier rock above. A wide crack across a slab leads to some shallow cracks & the top.   (1979)

15   Lip Trip   320'   E5 5b,6a,6a,5b,5b   **(R)**   ★★★
A major expedition through very hostile terrain *(take your pith helmet)*, which also pays lip-service to protection.
1 & 2   (80')   As for *DC*.
3   90'   Traverse LWs at the height of the belay to a poor PR. Trend up LWs to gain a hanging wall sandwiched between the OHs. Continue traversing (via cramped posturing) to pass an awkwardly-placed bush (Savage goes through the capping OH at this point). After another 15' the hanging corner on pitch 1 of Dreadnought is reached (optional stance). Follow the remainder of Dreadnought to its hanging stance & PBs.

4   80'   Climb the hanging groove on the L. Move RWs at the capping OH to gain a small ledge at the foot of a shallow groove. Climb this to gain & climb another shallow groove, which leads to the LH side of an oblong OH. Traverse RWs beneath this to gain a short groove, which leads to a stance.

5   70'   Move L & surmount the OH to gain and climb an awkward crack. Continue direct via the finish of *DC*.   (1980)

16   The Curse   270'   A4/HVS   **(R)**   ★★★
A real blast from the past, when the whack & dangle brigade were truly bold (most of the *in-situ* gear wouldn't even hold a tea cup these days). The line cuts across the full width of the roof of The Great Cave. Start roughly halfway into the cave & gain a greasy platform just below the roof. Belay 15' from a big blow-hole.

1   90'   (A4) Climb a mudrock wall to reach a prominent crack going diagonally across the flat ceiling to the centre of the cave mouth. Follow this for 40'. Just before it forks change to a parallel crack on the L, which leads out of the cave to a small stance (BB). Either abseil off into the sea & doggy-paddle ashore, or:

2   65'   (A3) Climb diagonally RWs for 12' to a good TR in a corner. Keeping below the poorer red rock, move out RWs over a doubtful block (& past two aid bolts) until the angle relents to vertical (5' from a grotty corner). Belay on a cramped stance in the corner.

3   55'   (A2/3) Move diagonally LWs (on grey rock where possible), to break through L of a prominent square-cut OH. Climb the wall directly for 15', then traverse LWs to the scoop which is the stance above pitch 3 of Barbican.

4   60'   Scramble off RWs across the vegetated slabs which lead to the top.   (1971)

Variation 1a 80' (A2) An inferior RH start, beginning some 20' to the L of *MOW*, which leads to the second stance.   (c.1970s)

The approach to the following routes is restricted by the tide. Mid/low tide is the only time that the traverse ledges are exposed. During neap tides this approach is barely passable, so you can either use the higher traverse (supposedly VS, but more like sustained 5b/c), or abseil from a handy metal pole atop the platform where Moonraker finishes.

17   Caveman   375'   E6 5c,6b,6a,6a,5b,5b   **(R)**   ★★★
An awe-inspiring line through the massive OHs above The Great Cave. It is probably the finest hard adventure route in creation. From the cave platform, circumnavigate the dank interior of The Great Cave to a small stance in a corner beneath a large roof, some 20' to the R of the PB cluster at the start of Moonraker.

1   60'   Trend up RWs between two bands of OHs to a niche (often damp), then step up RWs onto the wall above. Follow the horizontal strata RWs into a shallow corner & belay (15' L of the original belay which shared a stance with The Curse).

2   30'   Climb diagonally RWs to the start of the huge OHs (PR), then trend up RWs on flakes (in-situ nut). A hard move along a horizontal crack gains a niche stance, at the inner end of the prominent red flakes which hang down from the flat roof of the cave (poor PBs).

3   45'   Awkward climbing across the first hanging flake gains an obvious hand-traverse crack leading out to the lip. Pull up RWs & make a difficult move R to an in-situ nut at a hole, step down RWs and then traverse the lip for 15' to a PB (in common with DC).

4,5 & 6   (240')   As for Lip Trip (pitches 3,4 & 5).   (1982)

18   The New Stone-age   275'   E6 5c,6b,6a,6b,5c   (R)   ★★★ †
A fine counter-diagonal to Lip Trip, which inadvertently free-climbed a forgotten A2, **Black Pig**. Start as for Caveman.

1 2 & 3 (135') As for Caveman.

4   60'   Traverse RWs past the black groove of DC, then swing R on to the steep stratified wall to its R. Follow the strongest natural line up RWs until beneath a bulge (small TR & PR). Grunt through this & head up RWs to the base of a groove (PR). Climb this to a good stance (PB).

5   80'   Exposed climbing up the rib L of the stance leads to easier ground. Trend steadily up RWs to gain a large in-situ TB. Scramble off RWs.   (1989)

19   Terra Cotta   310'   E6 5c,6b,6b,5c,5b   (R)   ★★★ †
A direct variation on Caveman. A determined assault; made even more remarkable by the fact its first ascent was climbed solo.

1 & 2   (90')   As for Caveman.

3   70'   Follow Caveman out to the end of the red flakes. Instead of traversing RWs pull straight up, then step up LWs onto the sand-wiched wall on pitch 3 of Lip Trip. A good flake stretches out through the capping OH, launch out along this to the lip (good hand-jam). Before confidence wanes, lunge for better holds up on the L, then break through onto the upper wall. Continue with comparative ease to the PB on Caveman.

4   80'   Climb a thin bulging crack (directly above the stance) to where it peters out near the base of the shallow groove on pitch 4 of Lip Trip. Climb the groove to a good stance.

5   70'   As for Lip Trip (pitch 5).   (1989)

20   Savage   270'   E6 5c,6b,5b,5b   (R)   ★★★ †
The daunting OH to the L of pitch 2 on Caveman.

1   40'   Follow Caveman until 20' before its belay in the corner. Make a stance at a PB beneath the start of a shallow rib which trends up RWs to the large flat ceiling.

2   80'   Climb the shallow rib to gain the first of two horizontal bands of strata running out RWs. Traverse along the upper one until forced onto the lower (PR). Follow this until it ends (PR). Desperate moves gain a flake crack leading up RWs out of a hang-ing groove. Follow this to the lip (PR) from where steep juggy

The Old Redoubt
– Great Cave (left-hand) –

climbing lands you just L of the bush on pitch 3 of Lip Trip. Climb
directly through the crack in the OH above, then continue up a
short wall to the PB at the end of pitch 1 on Deadnought.
3 & 4   (150')   As for Lip Trip *(pitches 4 & 5)*.   (1992)

21 The Earthsea Trilogy #3   260'   E6 5c,6a/b,6b,6a   **(R)**   ★★★
A well-stacked trip through the steep rock L of Savage & the tiered
OHs above Dreadnought.
1   40'   As for Savage.
2   60'   Follow the shallow rib of Savage to the capping overlap.
Gain the lip of this & hand-traverse it LWs until beneath a TR in a
horizontal crack in the OH above. Pull up to the TR & make some
barndoor moves LWs around the lip of the OH into a groove (TR).
Follow this to a hanging stance at the base of the hanging corner on
pitch 1 of Dreadnought (N&TB).

3   60'   Follow the corner to the capping OH, then traverse LWs to gain a thin horizontal flake in the OH. Follow this out over the OH to a series of powerful moves to gain & pass a square block in the bulge above (PR). Move up to another bulge (TR), then pass an overlap beyond this to gain a thin break (PR). Climb the slim groove above the PR to hard moves which lead direct to a thin overlap. Trend up LWs above this to a ledge (PBs).

4   100'   Traverse LWs to a white scoop leading up to a faint break in a long OH. Pull over this & move up L to a line of flat holds leading RWs (past a TR) to a ledge. Climb a short groove to a steep blank wall (high PR). Hard moves up this lead to a line of holds heading RWs to a narrow ledge. Step up R, then go direct to the top on excellent holds.   (1989)

22   Moonraker   230'   HVS 5a,4c,4c   **(R)**   ★★★
Probably the best HVS in the country; giving steep exposed climbing on a magnificent & inescapable line. It follows the major crack system in the highest part of the cliff. Approach as for Caveman, then traverse for another 20' to a PB cluster just above the HWM. A short way up & to the R is the lower part of the obvious crack system.
1   70'   Make a rising traverse RWs to reach the discontinuous crack, & climb this steeply to a large chockstone in a corner. Climb diagonally LWs for 25' to reach ledges at the foot of the crack in the main corner-line.
2   60'   Climb the steep crack to a small cave at 40'. Traverse LWs, then move up to a P&TB atop a pedestal which is below & L of a leaning groove.
3   100'   Move up RWs to climb the leaning groove (exposed), using holds on the R wall to pass a bulge. Above this, move LWs on some ledges to gain a clean corner crack which leads to the top. Belay to the metal pole, well back from the edge.   (1967)

23   Dreadnought   240'   E3 5c,5b,5a   **(R)**   ★★★
The classic of the Old Redoubt & one of the finest in the South West. It traverses RWs across the LH lip of The Great Cave to gain the prominent hanging groove in the wall above.
1   100'   Follow Moonraker to the chockstone, then step out R to a PR. Make a rising traverse RWs on a band of steep rock to a hanging corner, which leads to a large capping OH. Traverse RWs under the OH with increasing difficulty (usually greasy) to a PR. A further 10' traverse RWs gains a small stance & PB (the pitch can be split by using Moonraker's belay).
2   65'   Step out LWs to gain the base of a hanging groove, which is climbed to its capping OH. Move out L & step up to a deep slot. Continue up LWs to gain a large scooped ledge, then climb the short wall on the R to a deep cave (huge TB through its LH side).
3   75'   Step L out of the cave & climb steeply to a shallow groove on the R which leads to a ledge & TR. The steep wall above is climbed to an OH. Pull over the middle of this on well-spaced holds, & continue on good holds to the top.   (1969/77)

24   Barbican   300'   E3 4c,5c,5b,5a/b   **(R)**   ★★
Sadly overshadowed, this route was in fact the first to breach the fearsome walls above The Great Cave. It is recorded here in full as a tribute. A formidable route – long, sustained & very strenuous – taking the traverse-line above the lip of The Great Cave, then a conspicuous chimney fault on the RH end of the wall. It is possible to escape after pitch 3 by climbing a belt of slabs on the R out of the cave stance. Prussik loops should be carried as a fall would usually leave the climber hanging free.
1   70'   As for Moonraker.
2   80'   Go back to the chockstone. Step up & use an aid peg *(done free now)* on the R to start a slightly rising traverse RWs on very

steep rock to a corner, which leads more easily to a big OH. Continue R with difficulty to a PR, which is used for aid *(often still the case!)*. Better holds lead up R to a tiny ledge (PBs).
3   60'   Step R & reach up to a high aid peg *(now used as a runner only)*. Steep moves gain a small cave, then climb the groove on the L to a much larger cave, PBs.
4   90'   Above the cave is a rounded grey chimney. Reach it from the R & climb to the obvious footledge leading L into a shallow corner (PR). Climb to the roof & swing R into the wide crack (PR), which is climbed to a wobbly spike. Move L & follow a wide crack which trends LWs across the vegetated slab to gain grassy cracks leading to the top   (1967/77)

25   Crocodile   110'   E2 5a,5b   (R)
Recorded before as an eliminate line between the upper reaches of Barbican & Dreadnought. The route provides a good oppurtunity to sample the steep & exposed climbing above The Great Cave, without having to climb through its ferocious mêlée of OHs. Scramble down the vegetated slab (past the video camera) to gain the cave stance beneath Barbican's final pitch, effectively reversing that route's escape pitch.
1   40'   Using a horizontal break for the hands, traverse LWs into a groove (PR). Climb direct on widely spaced holds to the RH end of an OH, from where a short corner leads to a stance & PB (in common with Caveman).
2   70' As for Lip Trip *(pitch 5).*   (1971)

26   The Hood   220'   E3 5c,5c,5b   (R)   ★★
The impressive wide crack in the wall between Dreadnought & Moonraker. Start as for Caveman.
1   80'   As for Caveman until established on the wall R of the damp niche. Climb diagonally LWs on excellent holds to join Moonraker & follow this to its stance.
2   40'   Move up & climb diagonally RWs across the steep wall (poor PR), to gain the wide crack. Climb strenuously to a stance where the crack widens to a chimney.
3   100'   Overcome the bramble bush in the chimney, then traverse LWs to an OH. Pull over this & climb the steep groove above to a junction with Moonraker. Climb the shallower groove R of the Moonraker corner to the top.   (1969/77)

27   The Quaker   225'   E3 5b,4c,6a   (R)   ★
A wandering line which provides some steep & exciting climbing. Belay as for Moonraker.
1   65'   Starting 5' L of the belay, climb straight up a gently OHing wall for 20', then bear L to a line of weakness leading to easier rock. Continue to a stance & PB on the shale band.
2   60'   A vague crack splits the wall above. Follow it to a deep hole, then bear R to join pitch 2 of Moonraker above the crack. Swing R & belay in the chimney of The Hood.

3   100'   Move out R to gain a white scoop leading up to a faint break in a long OH. Pull over this & move up L to a line of flat holds leading RWs (past a TR) to a ledge. Climb a short groove to a steep blank wall (high PR). Hard moves up this lead to a line of holds heading RWs to a narrow ledge. Step up R, then go direct to the top on excellent holds.   (1972/79)

28   Lunar Sea   190'   E3 5b,5c   **(R)**   ★
In its upper reaches this tackles the centre of the slim pillar between Moonraker & *GOG*. Start as for The Quaker.
1   110'   Follow The Quaker to the shale band, then trend up LWs over easy-angled rock to the pedestal stance of Moonraker (P&TB).
2   80'   Climb the centre of the bulge directly above the stance to gain a thin crack. Follow the crack past several T&PRs to finish direct up the centre of the slim pillar.   (1989)

29   Goddess of Gloom *(GOG)*   190'   HVS 5a,5a,5a   **(R)**   ★★
The thinner crack system to the L of Moonraker. Start beneath an obvious slanting corner 12yds further L of the PB cluster (at the HWM) of Moonraker.
1   50'   Climb easily to an OH, then move up RWs before pulling up LWs to gain the base of the corner above. Climb this to its capping OH. Traverse RWs, then move up to a small stance on the first shale band (PBs).
2   60'   Climb the wall L of a vegetated crack, then bear R (across the top of the crack) & climb to the P&TB of Moonraker. (An easier variation, 4b, is to climb the vegetated crack and then to bear right to the stance).
3   80'   From the LH side of the stance, steep moves lead up into a groove (L of a slim pillar) which is followed to a cave. Step R to a small ledge, then make some difficult moves up LWs to a thin crack leading to better holds in the final grassy groove.   (1968)

30   Pikadon   200'   HVS 4c,4c,5a   **(R)**   ★
This takes the second crackline (with two caves in its upper reaches) to the L of Moonraker. Start at the HWM belay of *GOG*.
1   60'   Climb (bearing LWs) up the steep wall L of *GOG*'s corner to an OH. Trend R towards the corner on a rising ledge, then traverse delicately LWs across a wall before moving up to a stance & PB on the shale band.
2   70'   Traverse LWs for 10', then move up over some bulges to a small ledge (PR). Climb the short steep wall on the R, then step R to gain a shallow groove. Follow this to a good stance & PB.
3   70'   Step R & climb past the first cave to a good TR in the OH above the second cave. Climb the smooth corner above (with difficulty) to a stance on the L. Scramble off.   (1967)

31   Melinda   180'   HVS 4c,5a,4c   **(R)**
The third major crackline to the L of Moonraker. Start beneath a rounded OHing rib 40' L of the corner of *GOG*.
1   50'   Climb the wall for 15', then pull up L to swing into balance

on the wall above. Climb direct for 20', then belay at a short crack.
2   70'   Climb to a PR (on Pikadon) & traverse LWs for 15' to a thin
curving crack at the LH end of a bulge. Move diagonally RWs to
another crack & follow this to a ledge (PB on the R).
3   60'   Move back L & climb a deep groove to a cave. Step R, then
follow another groove to grass ledges & belay. Scramble up steep
grass to finish.   (1970)

*The next two routes are high level traverses of The Great Cave area,
at or above the layer of the upper shaly band.*

32   The Seventh Circle *(SC)*   355'   E2 5a,-,5b,5a,-   **(R)**
Descend the grassy slope S ↓ of the metal pole at the finish of
Moonraker, then traverse back along grass ledges to meet the edge
of the face about 60' below the cliff top.
1   60'   Tentatively traverse out RWs onto the wall to a PR.
Descend the finishing crack of Melinda to gain a stance on the R (as
for Melinda).
2   50'   Continue easily along the obvious line (crossing *GOG*) to
the second stance of Moonraker (P&TB).
3   70'   Reverse the traverse at the top of pitch 2 of Moonraker,
then swing into the chimney of The Hood. Step out R & descend to
an exposed ledge, which is followed RWs until it peters out (PR
above). Make steep moves to a large scoop, then climb the wall on
its R (as for Dreadnought) to a cave stance & large TB.
4   75'   Move R (PR) & climb to some flat loose ledges. Continue
RWs to join the top pitch of Barbican, which is reversed (along the
footledge & down the awkward chimney) to the big cave.
5   100'   Finish easily up the belt of slabs on the R.   (1969)

33   The High Traverse   140'   HVS 4b,4b,5a   **(R)**
An exposed route with some fine climbing. Approach as for *SC*, but
belay 30' higher & further R (just below the finish of Pikadon).
1   60'   Move down & R to follow a horizontal break RWs to the
cave on *GOG*. Step up RWs, then continue to traverse RWs with
more difficulty, to belay beneath the final corner of Moonraker.
2   40'   Continue horizontally RWs for 30' above the lip of a large
OH, then move up to the cave stance & TB of Dreadnought.
3   40'   Climb the steep wall above (as for Dreadnought), before
going diagonally RWs to join & finish up Barbican.   (1969)

*The following eight routes lie on the cliffs running S ↓ from The
Great Cave. In view of the fact that you (may) need to climb up to
half of The Magical Mystery Tour (see page 216) before starting your
chosen route, it would be wise to start these routes as soon the tidal
ledges are exposed (as it can get very dark, & very lonely very
quickly over there).*

34   Auk   145'   E2 -,5b,5b   **(R)**   †
Start just over 100' to the L of *GOG*, at the start of a wide corner/
crack.

1   45'   Climb the crack to gain a large sloping ramp. Belay at its RH end.
2   50'   Move slightly RWs & pull up onto the loose wall above. Follow a vague groove to a PB at the base of a loose groove.
3   50'   Climb the wall R of the groove (bounded on the R by Melinda), then traverse back LWs into the top of the loose groove. Scrabble up this to finish.   (1989)

35   False Alarms *(FA)*   180'   E3 5c,5a   **(R)**   ★
A strenuous & spectacular line through the huge OHs 130' to the L of *GOG*. Start at low tide on a shallow-angled ledge below an enormous OH.
1   130'   Move R to an OHung crack & climb it to some ledges. Trend L to a vague groove, & follow this to the bottom LH corner of the first OH. Layback up to gain undercut holds leading RWs to a short groove. Climb this to gain a line of improving holds leading horizontally RWs across the lip of the OH to the arête. Continue R for a few feet to a stance at a short crack.
2   50'   Climb the crack to a ledge on the R, then make an awkward move to gain a shallow groove. Follow this, exiting LWs to finish up a steep grass slope.   (1980/81)

36   King Crab   105'   HVS 5a,4a   **(R)**
Start roughly 20' to the L of *FA*, below the LH side of a massive OH at 80'. Belay 20' above the HWM in a bay beneath a smaller & much lower OH, just beyond an arête.
1   80'   Climb up to the RH end of the first OH. Pull over this & climb a stratified wall for 15'. Move R, then pull strenuously onto a white guano-covered ledge. Climb up LWs, then follow a layback crack splitting the final OH; exposed stance & PB on the L.
2   25'   Climb the short wall above to a grass slope.   (1970)

37   Anti-matter *(AM)*   230'   VS 4c,4c,4a   **(R)**
Start 10' to the L of King Crab, at the base of a curving groove.
1   40'   Climb the groove, then exit LWs onto a steep wall which is climbed to a white guano covered ledge.
2   90'   Traverse LWs until a short groove breaks through the overlap. Climb this, then step L to a good stance & PB.
3   100'   Move back R & up a prominent groove to the top.   (1980)

38   Uncul-patter   120'   E1 4c,5a   **(R)**
A direct variation on *AM*, starting as for that route.
1   40'   As for *AM*.
2   80'   Pull over the OH above, then continue up a crack. Move L & climb straight up the wall (bold) to a loose finish.   (1980)

39   Lost Arrow *(LA)*   130'   HS   **(R)**
Roughly 100' further L of *AM* is a prominent OHing prow of rock jutting out over the sea. Belay in the small zawn just before this.
1   40'   Climb the wall to the blatant horizontal break leading RWs to the first shale band (PB).

2   45'   Follow the shale bands up LWs to a corner. Pass this LWs & climb a brown wall for a few feet to a small stance (PB).
3   45'   Climb the wall above by trending RWs to a recess. Step out L onto a grassy slope which is climbed easily to finish.   (1968)

40   The Long Goodbye *(LGB)*   220'   E1 4c,5a,5a   **(R)**
An exposed route on a remote part of the Old Redoubt, which starts by climbing the steep wall just to the L of *LA*.
1   60'   Climb the wall direct to reach a small stance (TBs).
2   80'   Move slightly L & climb a groove until it becomes discontinuous after an OH, then traverse RWs along the obvious line to a small ledge, PB.
3   80'   Continue traversing along the same line to a large detached flake, then climb up to a PR. Enter the awkward corner above to gain a ledge, then climb the vegetated wall above to a grassy slope. Belay on a bluff of rock well back from the edge.   (1981)

41   Moving Target   130'   VS 4c,4c   **(R)**
1   60'   As for *LGB*.
2   70'   Step L to the groove of *LGB* & follow it to where it becomes disjointed. The remaining grooves, which lead to the top, are surprisingly sound.   (1973)

THE BISMARK WALL
Roughly 400yds S ↓ of The Great Cave is a rocky promontory jutting out into the sea. This forms the LH side of the Blue Grotto (the final obstacle of The Magical Mystery Tour), and also provides a good vantage point from which to view the Bismark Wall. The best approach for the next four routes is to walk across the Southern Redoubt to its SE↘ wall and follow a path leading down to the rocky promontory. Two-thirds of the way down the slope, there is an outcrop of rock with a belay stake whacked into it. Set up an abseil from this to gain the base of the wall. The routes are described from R to L.

42   Dog's Bolx   100'   E3 5b   **(R)**   †
There is an obvious ragged crack going up the RH side of a steep wall, which lies R of the rib bounding the RH side of the Bismark Wall. Start just R of the crack. Climb the intimidating wall blindly on big buckets & steadily improving gear, to join Bismark at the end of its RWs traverse. Pleasant climbing LWs gains a hand-rail-like break, which is followed LWs for 15' to an obvious exit up a slight groove/corner.   (1992)

43   Git a Rat Up Ya   100'   E4 5c   **(R)**   †
Worthwhile. Start just R of the rib that bounds the RH side of the wall (taken by Bismark). Belay just above the HWM. Climb the steep wall on good holds, to join Bismark at the start of its RWs traverse. Bold moves up the wall above gain the horizontal hand-rail of Dog's Bolx. Finish as for that route.   (1992)

44   Bismark   120'   E2 5b   **(R)**
Start from a stance on the extreme RH side of the wall (10' above the

HWM). Climb up LWs for 25', then trend RWs up the steep wall to gain a traverse-line leading RWs beneath some OHs. Follow this for 25' until it is possible to gain a small ledge. Continue up a short loose wall which leads to the top.   (1980)

45   Arc Royale *(AR)*   100'   E4 6a   **(R)**   *
Start just R of the vague central crackline at a spike & *in-situ* TB just above the HWM. Trend up RWs for 25' until beneath a bulge with some obvious pockets above it. Gain these, & continue up RWs until a long reach up L to a jug gains the base of an OH (PR). Step L, then continue direct via powerful moves, to awkwardly gain a standing position above the OH. Step up L via a spiky foothold to finish up a wall & slight groove.   (1989)

46   Graf Spee   100'   E4 6b   **(R)**   **
Belay as for *AR*. Climb the vague central crackline to an OH. Extend through this to a good finger slot on the lip, then pull up to a *in-situ* TR. Climb up RWs to finish as for *AR*.   (1989)

GIRDLE AND SEA-LEVEL TRAVERSES

47   Gulliver's Travels   470'   VIII- or HXS(adistic)   **(R)**   †
A character-building L-to-R girdle of the LH section of the Old Redoubt *(only to be attempted by 'Grand Masters of Rubble')*. It contains a good deal of bold, committing, loose & varied climbing. Start below the rocky promontory, on the LH side of the entrance to the Blue Grotto.
1   60'   (6a) Climb up to gain the obvious decaying traverse-line. Follow this RWs across the mouth of the grotto (past 2PRs) to belay in a small cave on the Bismark Wall (very nasty to second!).
2   100'   (5c) Follow the natural mid-height weakness across the Bismark Wall, then gain & follow Bismark until the end of its traverse. Continue RWs round the arête of the buttress to a ledge.
3   80'   (5a) Descend a corner & traverse RWs across the adjacent face, via the prominent horizontal weakness, until a cramped stance in a shallow gully is gained.
4   100'   (5a) Descend for a few feet, then make a long traverse RWs across poor rock to a large belay ledge.
5   90'   (5a) Traverse RWs into pitch 2 of *LGB* & follow that route to belay at the end of its traverse.
6   40'   As for *LGB (pitch 3)*.   (1988)

48   Magical Mystery Tour *(MMT)*   1,100'   VI   **(R)**   ***
The Great Cave to the Promontory: the classic sea-level traverse of the Old Redoubt, linking the cave platform with the rocky promontory over 300yds to the S ↓ . In anything but calm seas this is a very serious & committing proposition. There are virtually no viable escape routes after the first real difficulties, & there is a zawn-swim to finish. Start an hour or so before low tide.
Traverse into & then out of The Great Cave, past the PB cluster at the start of Moonraker. Continue easily along the HWM until

beside an OHing nose. Pass beneath this strenuously at low tide (4c); or take a traverse line 20' higher up (5a & strenuous), then descend to a ledge & belay. Beyond is an OHing buttress. Climb the gully beside it, then traverse LWs on a line 30' above the water (5a, strenuous), descending gradually to a stance. Continue traversing past a cave (the Green Grotto) to the entrance of a much larger cave (the Blue Grotto) which goes right through the headland. The cave mouth is crossed via a swim (& tyrolean for the other members of the party) to gain a promontory. Easy climbing leads up LWs to gain the top of the promontory.   (1967/68)

Variation The Green Grotto 120' VII This has now been connected to the Blue Grotto. Climb the RH wall of the cave to join the Blue Grotto at the long stride across the chasm. *Night vision goggles would aid proceedings immensely.*   (1991)

49 Magical Mystery Tour II 1,150' VII **(R)**   ★★
The Blue Grotto to Cradle Rock Buttress: A difficult & fascinating exploration of one of South Devon's more pleasantly pungent grottoes.
Gain the end of *MMT* either by doing that route, or by abseiling down the Bismark Wall. Step LWs around the rib into the Blue Grotto & follow the RH wall to a bulging section. Move up & follow a slightly descending line of holds LWs to easier ground. Continue to a chasm. Make a rising traverse into this until it is possible to bridge across to a line of holds on the opposite wall *(the Green Grotto pitch joins here)*. Follow these holds down LWs to some ledges. Continue LWs to break through an awkward undercut chimney to slabby rock at the S↓ entrance to the Blue Grotto (sustained 5b). Traverse the slabby cliffs beyond at, or near, the HWM to gain the entrance of a large zawn. Make a descending traverse into this (4b), then go back out along the opposite wall to a ledge 20' above the sea. Move L & down, then steep traversing gains a stance (5a). Climb to the top of a buttress adjacent to the Cradle Rock Buttress descent rake.   (1968)

50 Magical Mystery Tour III 900' V
Cradle Rock Buttress to Durl Head: Essentially an indifferent connection for the rest of the *MMT*, with little worthwhile climbing in its own right.
Start from the foot of the descent rake to Cradle Rock Buttress; A low tide start is essential for the initial boulder-hop to the point just S↓ of Cradle Rock Buttress (the odd passage of 4b); although this has been overcome with some desperate wading & a little climbing if the tides have been misjudged.   (1968)

51 Magical Mystery Tour IV 2,500' VII   ★★
Durl Head to St Mary's Bay: A good, if somewhat demanding conclusion to this mammoth expedition[3].

---

[3] *The time of 2hrs 20mins still stands for doing* **MMT I, II, III** *&* **IV**, *from The Great Cave platform to St Mary's Bay 'dry solo', timing the low tide for Cradle Rock Buttress.*

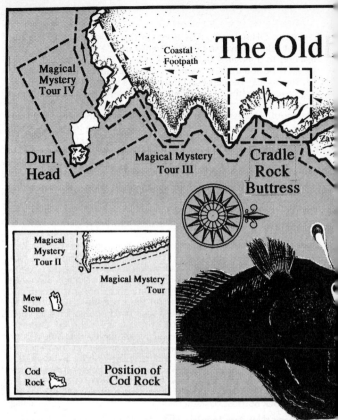

Traverse easily (along the tidal reef beneath the OHs of Durl Head's S ↓ bay) to the first obstacle, the impressive cleft of Dove Cavern. Climb into this on small holds (5b), then climb back out along the opposite wall with similar difficulty. Continue to another technical pitch above a cave (5b) to gain a boulder-filled bay. To leave this, traverse LWs along a series of slabby grooves at a relatively high level (5c) to reach ledges around the corner. The next barrier is a steep shale wall which gives a long sustained pitch (5c), after which, easier climbing leads to another strenuous pitch (5a), gaining the beach of St Mary's Bay. (1969)

CRADLE ROCK BUTTRESS   GR 940 558

Walk along the main coastal footpath which starts about 50yds S ↓

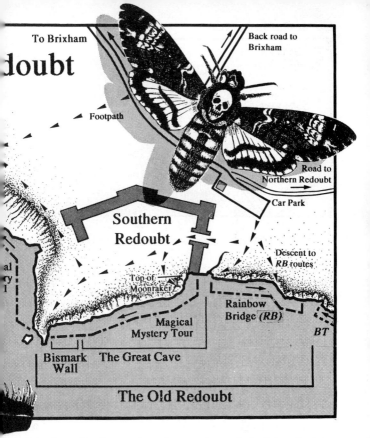

of the Berry Head car park, and passes beneath the S ↓ wall of the Southern Redoubt. Continue past the top of a repulsive-looking zawn until, about 100yds past a stone stile, a path leads down LWs to a wave-cut platform 30' above sea-level. The crag divides into two areas; the Upper Cliff, an amenable venue with a sunny SE↘ disposition, and a good range of mid-grade routes; and the Main Cliff, which is a far more serious crag facing NE↗.

UPPER CLIFF
Overlooking the wave-cut platform is the smaller Upper Cliff, dominated by the sharp arête of Cut-throat.

1 Solstice 80' VS 4c
The obvious groove L of the sharp arête. Start beneath an OH. Surmount the OH & climb the crack above, bearing LWs away from

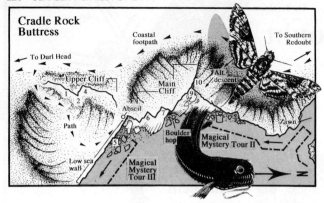

a red chimney. The OH above is climbed on good holds. Finish up
a short wall.   (1980)

2   Cut-throat   60'   E1 5a   *
The knife-edged arête in the centre of the buttress (beware of some
loose rock near the top). Climb a groove in the arête for 20' to a
small ledge. Move up to a small pocket, then barndoor RWs around
the arête to climb steep rock to a large spike. Stand on this to
regain the arête which is followed to the top.   (1970)

3   Tough Luck   50'   E1 5a
Start R of (& higher up the slope than) Cut-throat, just R of a wide
crack. Climb a subsidiary crack to a small TR, then move L into the
main crack. Follow this to exit via a steep corner.   (1983)

4   Good Fortune   40'   HVS 5a   *
Steep climbing up some cracks R of Tough Luck leads, with increasing difficulty, to a good hold atop a projecting block. Several steep
moves remain before topping-out.   (1983)

MAIN CLIFF
The Main Cliff lies to the L (facing seaward) of the wave-cut platform. Approach by a short abseil to boulders which are exposed at
most states of the tide. An alternative approach to the Main Cliff
descends a grass slope which is gained by climbing over the wall
10yds before the stone stile. At the foot of the grass slope a band of
easy-angled slabs lead down RWs to the base of the buttress. This
approach allows the routes on the Main Cliff to be attempted at
high tide or when a mountainous sea is running!

5   Aqualung   40'   E4 6a   †
Start some way L of the abseil descent at a crack which follows the
slanting RH rib of an arch/cave (a low tide start is essential). Strenuously follow the crack LWs until it is possible to reach a PR above

the small capping OH. Surmount the OH, then climb the remaining steep wall to the top. (1992)

6 Sidewinder 60' HVS 5b
Steep climbing on interesting rock, which follows the diagonal line across the L wall of the large blind corner, near the LH side of the Main Cliff. Start L of the corner, beneath a finger-width crack. Follow this until it is possible to step into a shallow niche. Climb up out of this to regain the crack which leads steeply to the arête. Follow this to a sloping ledge (PB). Scramble off LWs or climb the second pitch of Zeta. (1982)

7 Zeta 180' HVS 5b,-
This takes the conspicuous slanting corner above & to the R of Sidewinder. Scramble up some shale slabs to belay beneath it.
1 80' Climb the corner, moving L at 10', then continue direct to a ledge at 40'. Climb the OHing corner above with difficulty. Move up L to a small stance on the arête.
2 100' Descend LWs beneath an OH, then step out L onto a long rambling slab; finish up this. (1968/82)

8 Finn 100' HVS 5a
Take a stance atop the shale slabs, as for Zeta. Follow a ramp up RWs for 10', then step up onto the wall. Trend up LWs for 30' by following the obvious crack (slanting L/R). Continue diagonally RWs until 15' from the top. Traverse LWs for 10' before finishing. Belay well back from the edge. (1969)

Down R of the start to Sidewinder is a deep cave that can be crossed by boulder-hopping across its mouth at most states of the tide (although not in high seas). This leads to the next route:

9 The Pinch 130' E4 4b,6a ★★
An outstanding climb that goes straight up the guts of the leaning headwall. It is spoilt only by the lack of traffic. Start beneath the first corner R of the cave.
1 60' Climb the corner on strange vertically-stratified rock to an OH. Traverse LWs for a few feet, then climb direct to a stance at a large block.
2 70' Climb direct (for 35') to a conspicuous round hole in the face. Continue up to an enormous jug, then move slightly LWs to climb the gently OHing wall to the top. The tree belay is a long way back from the edge. (1969/83)

10 Ganges 100' HS 4a
The larger but less attractive corner to the R of The Pinch. Climb the corner direct, exiting RWs at the top. (1968)

DURL HEAD   GR 940 557

This excellent area is about another five minutes walk S ↓ from Cradle Rock Buttress. It is a minor headland distinguished by a flat,

rocky causeway running out to the 40' high monolith of Durl Rock.
On the N ↑ side of the headland is a steep cliff consisting of two
faces at right-angles to each other. The LH face has a sharply
undercut base, while the RH section is remarkable for its huge
OHs. S ↓ of the headland is a boulder-strewn, box-shaped zawn
which leads to another area of extensive OHs.

NORTH BAY
Descend the seaward face of the headland easily to the HWM, then
skirt the N ↑ base of what is essentially a detached pinnacle, to be
faced by the grossly OHing corner of:

1   Gravity's Angel *(GA)*   60'   E4 5c   ★
Prime your forearms with spinach! Start just R of a horizontal blow-
hole (which can be squirmed through to gain the South Bay at a
speleological Moderate). Climb the steep, discontinuous cracks to
a niche. Follow another crack up RWs before trending back LWs to
a PR. Launch up LWs to a ledge, then crawl onto the summit of the
barely detached pinnacle.   (1986)

2   Man Bites Dog *(MBD)*   80'   E2 5b
To the R of *GA* is a large sea cave whose L edge is split by an
impressive (although repulsive) off-width crack/chimney. Climb
the crack very strenuously for 35' until the angle relents. An even
wider crack leads to the top.   (1973/83)

3   Dog Bites Back   70'   E1 5b
Climb the wall L of *MBD*. Start 3yds L of that route. Climb the
easiest line, via a disjointed set of grooves (& the occasional ledge)
which lead to a grassy exit.   (1986)

4   Star Trekking *(ST)*   100'   E4 6a,-   ★★ †
To boldly go. . . across the mind-boggling ceiling in the cave R of
MBD . . .or not? That is the question. If you are considering it, then
start on the far side of the tidal cave beneath the base of a thin flake
running the full width of the OH.
1   40'   Climb direct to the first PR, then follow the flake out to the
lip of the OH past a further 3PRs. Make some gymnastic moves to
attain a standing position above the lip, & belay.
2   60'   Climb diagonally RWs for 25' until a weakness (trending
R\L) is reached. Follow this to finish.   (1987)

At high tide the following seven routes can be approached by
scrambling down a grassy hollow (N ↑ of the cliff). Traverse LWs
from this, along a series of ledges just above the HWM.

5   La Rage   170'   E2 5b,5b   ★ †
A fine route. Start in the first corner formed by an alcove where the
walls join at right-angles to each other.
1   90'   A rising traverse-line leads out LWs just above the lip of the
cave of *ST*. Powerfully follow this to join *MBD* & belay.
2   80'   A hard move LWs (round the arête) is then followed by a

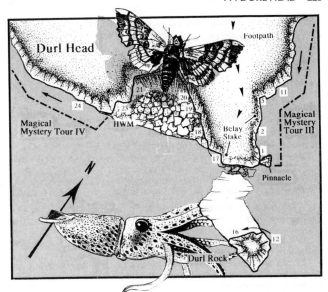

traverse LWs to a short corner which leads to the top. (1986)

6 Chuck Berry 90' E1 5b
An excellent directissima based around *BRW*; perhaps a trifle hard for the grade. Follow La Rage for roughly 20', then strike up the leaning wall to join *BRW* at the base of the L-facing corner (midway through pitch 2); follow *BRW* to finish. (1987)

7 Berry Red Wall *(BRW)* 140' VS -,4b
The far less impressive upper (LWs) traverse-line of the wall. Start as for La Rage.
1 60' Climb the greasy cleft above the belay, & either squeeze through the constriction, or outflank it on the L to gain a ledge above the first OH. Traverse RWs to a TB.
2 80' Move back L, then step down across the chasm onto the red wall. Continue LWs (until level with the belay ledge) around a small corner, then go up for 10' to a good runner. Traverse horizontally LWs, then move up to mantelshelf onto a large ledge. Climb the corner above easily to the cliff top. (1970)

8 Fowler's Dolly Mixture 110' HS -,4a
A morish route, so don't go 'Bertie'. Start as for *BRW*.
1 60' As for *BRW*.
2 50' Climb direct from the belay to step R onto an undercut nose. Move L onto a ledge beneath a corner. Climb the RH wall,

then trend R towards an easy but exposed arête to finish.   (1970)

9   Lady of Shame *(LOS)*   105'   E1 5b,5a   ★
Spectacular for the grade. Begin just R of the start of *BRW*, on ledges beneath the blatant crack in the low OH.
1   30'   Forcefully climb the OHung jamming-crack to a generous TB on the slab above.
2   75'   Move L & step across a cleft to join *BRW*. Follow that route until it deviates LWs, then continue up a vertical crack until a step L leads to some friable ledges. Trend out LWs to finish.   (1978)

10   Lap it Up   80'   E2 5b,5b   †
Enjoyable climbing through the OHs just R of *LOS*.
1   30'   Take the OH R of *LOS* at its widest point, via the obvious crack. Pull over to a ledge & belay in a niche.
2   50'   Climb the obvious roof-crack, then finish past some hollow flakes on the wall above. Belay well back.   (1987)

11   Foaming at the Mouth   100'   E4 4c,5c   ★★★
Believe me, this route will have you doing it as well. It takes the huge OH just R of Lap it Up. Start at a short corner.
1   40'   Climb up through a series of small OHs until a large ledge to the R of the main OH is reached.
2   30'   Reach out L to the base of the wildly OHing crack & launch up inside it! Squirm past 3TRs to make an awkward mantel to gain the belay ledge above.
3   30'   Easy climbing leads off RWs to finish.   (1987)

DURL ROCK
Due to the 'butterfly-effect' of this pinnacle being mis-named (as Cradle Rock) in the previous guide, the route names are not as pertinent as they once were. The routes lie on the clean white wall facing the headland.

12   Bath Time   30'   VS 4b
From the L edge of the face, traverse LWs above the HWM until beneath an OH. Climb this to finish up the crack above.   (1986)

13   Cot Death   30'   VS 4c   ★
Climb the L arête & then the ramp-line, which leads up RWs from it, to gain the summit of the pinnacle.   (1986)

14   Cradle Snatcher *(CS)*   25'   HS 4b   ★
The fine finger-crack in the middle of the wall.   (1986)

15   Lullaby Baby   30'   S
The thin crack in a shallow groove just R *CS*.   (1986)

16   Chi   30'   D
Climb the R edge of the face.   (1992)

SOUTH BAY
The routes inhabit a box-shaped zawn & are described from R to L. Use the same descent as for the N↑ bay, but traverse S↓ or R

(looking seaward) at the HWM. At mid-tide, abseil from the belay stake atop the descent, down the line of Saracen. During high tide the best approach is to abseil down the wall of *CYS* from a belay stake hidden in the grass 50′ further up the slope (near the N ↑ edge of the headland).

17 Saracen 30′ VS 4c
The route lies above the horizontal blow-hole through the headland, & just R of a large low OH. Climb the pocketed wall to a hanging groove. Climb this to top-out just in front of a belay stake on the very tip of the headland.   (1986)

18 Cod Gives You a Stiffy *(CYS)* 40′ E1 5b
Around to the L of the large low OH is a scruffy-looking wall bounded on the L by a loose-looking corner (it is). Start just R of the corner. Climb a short groove, then take the soundest path up the wall R of the shallow loose corner.   (1988)

19 Infidelity 60′ E3 5c
Start 10′ L of *CYS*, below a PR (at 15′) in the bulging RH rib of a wall beyond the loose corner. A thin crack leads past the PR, to a TR. Step R to a crack, then trend LWs up the wall to a scoop. Step RWs up out of the scoop, then finish LWs.   (1987)

20 Up the Aunty 60′ E3 5b
Start atop a large boulder 5yds L of Infidelity. Climb direct to a PR at 25′, then trend up LWs to the base of a shallow scoop, PR. Follow the RH side of this to join & finish up Infidelity.   (1988)

21 Infidel 70′ E1 5b   ★
A fine route which climbs the clean wall opposite Infidelity. Climb the middle of the wall direct, staying R of a shallow ragged crack (hidden PR on R). Pull into a niche, then step down L & traverse LWs along the obvious crackline LWs to the arête. Trend up R & scramble up steep grass to a belay stake.   (1984)

22 Dragnet 100′ VD
Start at a corner 20′ L of Infidel. Take some pegs for belays.
1 35′ Climb the corner to a sloping ledge & belay on the L beneath a large OH.
2 20′ Traverse LWs to a restricted stance in a corner.
3 45′ Move onto the L wall (above a large OH), then make a rising traverse LWs across this to finish. Belay well back.   (1988)

23 Monster Munch 70′ E5/6 6b   ★ †
A bold & committing route in its upper reaches. Start in the middle of the wall, below some multi-tiered OHs, around to the L of Infidel. Easy climbing, up through the initial OHs, leads to a monstrous roof. Arrange some scant protection (in the cracks in the OH), then move slightly L & make a long reach/jump for the lip. Hand-traverse RWs until a strenuous move gains the short finishing corner. Belay to Infidel's stake.   (1990)

24   A Drop in the Ocean   70′   E4 6a   ★★ †
This lies in the centre of a cluster of OHs that start 30yds S ↓ of the
box-shaped zawn, above a tidal reef. The line is distinguished by a
small TR near the lip of an OH.
1   40′   Climb direct to the start of a thin crack in a horizontal OH.
Jam out to the lip past the TR. From the lip, make some strenuous
moves on sloping holds until good jugs can be reached. Belay just
above the lip.
2   30′   Climb diagonally LWs to the top, where an isolated block
well back from the edge is used to belay.   (1987)

COD ROCK   GR 946 559

This is the fin-shaped stack approximately a quarter of a mile E→ of
the Bismark Wall. Its ⟍NW face offers a number of 60′ climbs on
steep, weathered limestone. A boat of some description would
appear to be the only sane method of approach *(unless you happen
to be a cross between Captain Webb and Pat Littlejohn)*. A mooring
PB used to exist just R of the centre of the face, although no-one
has been out there within living memory, so it's probably just a rust
stain by now.

1   Different Kettle of Fish   60′   HS 4a   **(R)**
This lies around the LH corner of the ⟍NW face, & climbs the
obvious corner above a blow-hole.   (1981)

2   Blistez   40′   S   **(R)**
Climb the blatant crack on the LH side of the face.   (1981)

3   Shy Talk   60′   HS   **(R)**
The LH of the three cracklines L of the mooring PB.   (1981)

4   Kittiwake   60′   HS   **(R)**
Climb the central crack of the three.   (1981)

5   Pollocks   60′   S   **(R)**
The RH of the three cracklines L of the mooring PB.   (1981)

6   Grope & Hope *(G&H)*   60′   VD   **(R)**
Climb the crack immediately R of the mooring PB.   (1981)

7   Kaktus   60′   D   **(R)**
Climb the easier ground R of *G&H*.   (1981)

DARTMOOR GRANITE

*When the Moor wind roars
and grey mists veil the tors,
ancient, fleeting shadows plague
the twilight of your mind.*

*For the Wisht Hounds are abroad,
and abandoned by the Lord,
the night becomes a dream,
where no-one hears you scream.*

A.N. Ominous

Mystery and myth are the cornerstones of Dartmoor lore. Perpetuated by fireside yarns in smoky taprooms the length and breadth of
this pagan plateau, these tales become all too real. Often full of
horror, they are tempered with a yokel nous bordering on the
psychotic:

As the full moon waxed 'bove the sleepy hollow that shelters
Warren House Inn, a saddle sore traveller, overtaken by a blizzard,
did beg refuge of the innkeep. Curiosity be the devil itsel' and on
seeing the large chest in 'is room 'e done a bad thing and did peek.
There were not much sleep to be 'ad that night and 'twas a mor-
tified soul did inquire of the landlord the followin' dawn, of the
corpse at the foot of 'is bed. Casual enough, the traveller be told,
"why, 'tis only feyther! 'Twas too cold to take 'im to the buryin', so
mother salted 'im down!".   *(common folklore)*

Many of the fables are more far-fetched; from pixies and hairy
hands, through to carriages of bone drawn by headless horses.
However, the stories relating to the appearance of the various tors
are of a similar nature to Native American Indian or Aborigine
interpretations of geomorphology. For instance, Hingston Rocks
and Heltor are assumed to be the result of King Arthur and the
Devil playing quoits. While Bowerman's Nose supposedly came
into being by the affrontary of Bowerman, a huntsman of some
renown (who was blessed with a large olfactory organ – said to
smell out the wiliest of foxes), when he blundered into a coven of
witches, knocking their ringleader off her broomstick[1]. Run ragged
by the witch, who had changed into a hare, he fell from his horse
into a bog and only managed to keep his nose above the mire. She
turned this to stone and cut off his hounds' heads, scattering them
over the neighbouring hill, thenceforth known as Hound Tor.

---

[1] *It is conjectured that the shaft of a witches broom was used to introduce a concoction of
hallucinogens, via the nether regions (hence flying off the handle). So it is reasonable to
assume that she was a bit upset.*

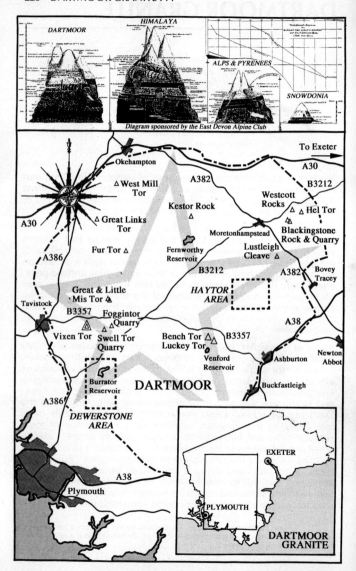

Diagram sponsored by the East Devon Alpine Club

Apocryphal stories aside, climbing on the Moor of a summer's evening is an uplifting experience; from the leafy and sun-dappled slopes of the Dewerstone, to the breeze swept vista atop Haytor. Opportunities for bouldering abound, while the granitic masses of Vixen Tor and Low Man provide some of the most brutally taxing pitches to be found in the Shire.

HAYTOR AREA

The large number of high quality tors which go together to form the Haytor area, are strewn across a rolling plateau which spans between Bovey Tracey and Widecombe-in-the-Moor. Apart from the gems cast liberally along the flanks of Haytor (and Low Man), there are numerous other jewels scattered about the buttresses of Bonehill Rocks, Chinkwell Tor and Hound Tor.

Widecombe hides one of the more infamous hostelries in the Shire, *The Rugglestone*. It is purported to be an earthly portal to Hades through which the locals (burley farmers with extraordinarily thick accents) can move to-and-fro. Paying for a pint ordered from the landlord is also ill advised, as he only accepts souls and refuses to give any change. Eating here can also be a bit of a chore due to the menu consisting of dead goat. . . live goat, and sometimes battered goat.

Thankfully tearooms seem to crop-up with alarming regularity in these 'ere parts. Couple this to the succulent sorbets and tasty tit-bits on offer from the ice-cream vans (in every available layby) during the summer months, and the Moor appears to become a calorific minefield. Therefore a great deal of self-discipline will have to be exercised if you wish to arrive at the crag in any fit state to climb (and you are very sad if you do). For those who succumb to these sinfully glutinous delights, take heart from the knowledge that you couldn't be indulging yourself in finer surroundings.

HAYTOR   GR 757 770

Approach and Access
Haytor is the most prominent tor of the Moor. It can be seen from the A38 quite clearly as a double dome on the skyline (from the summit it is possible to see both Chudleigh and Berry Head on a clear day). When approaching from the N ↑ follow signs to the town centre of Bovey Tracey, from where the Tor is clearly signposted. If approaching from the S ↓, leave the A38 at Ashburton, and follow signs to Widecombe and Haytor. From the car park below the Main Tor a broad, green track leads up to the wide

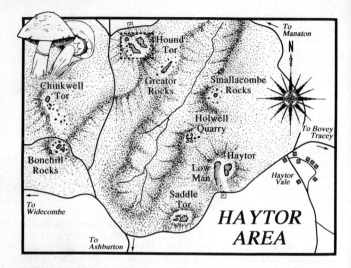

avenue between Haytor's West Face on the R and the seemingly insignificant rock dome of Low Man on the L.

Situation and Character

The Main Tor and Low Man give some of the finest and longest routes on the Moor. Main Tor gives a varied selection of pitches up to 90' in length, while Low Man's West Face presents a broodingly impressive array of climbs up to 150' in height. The rock is rough (due to the large feldspar crystals) and rounded OHs, flakes, cracks and breaks abound.

MAIN TOR

The climbing lies on the West, North and East faces. When approaching up the broad green track the first salient feature is a long, low wall on the R (containing many vicious boulder problems). The routes are described from R to L.

WEST FACE

This is the first climbable face to be seen, having entered the wide avenue between Main Tor and Low Man. Initially the buttresses are very narrow; subsequent buttresses are somewhat broader.

1 Accomplice to Murder *(AM)* 30' HVS 5a

Start below the RH side of the second slim buttress L of the low bouldering wall. An eliminate-style route that attempts to keep out of the crack to the L by climbing its R arête. (1986)

2   Aramis   30'   HS 4a
This is the steep narrow crack just L of *AM*. Climb it to an awkward
exit LWs onto the LH rib. Finish up this.   (1946)

3   D'Artagnan *(DA)*   30'   HVS 5c
A fierce, committing problem. Climb the centre of the wall R of
Aramis finishing up the rib of that route.   (1976)

4   Athos   30'   VD
The crack L of *DA*, moving out R to finish.   (c.1950s)

5   Haggis   40'   HVS 5a   ★
A fine route which requires a committed approach. Climb the
centre of the wall L of Athos to an OH. Pull over this via some small
flakes, then continue over a smaller OH to finish.   (1961)

6   Step Across *(SA)*   50'   D
A contrived route up the slabby sandwiched block L of Haggis.
Climb the slab, then chimney up the gap above to gain the RH wall.
Make a long stride L onto the LH wall, then move out onto the front
face of the buttress to finish.   (c.1950s)

The cracklines either side of the sandwiched slab are D.

7   Bulging Wall   50'   VD
A wandering line (with many variations on its theme). Start below a
flake crack on the RH side of the wall L of *SA*. Climb the flake to a
ledge, then up the wall above by the easiest line.   (c.1950s)

8   Zig Zag   50'   D
Start below the rounded diagonal crack on the LH side of the wall.
Follow this RWs on to the face, then follow the large holds until the
angle eases dramatically.   (c.1950s)

9   Hangover   50'   E1 5a
Start at the base of a crack, 10' L of Zig Zag. Awkwardly gain the
rounded break (via the crack), which is followed LWs for 10' until
beneath some large, hollow flakes leading up LWs. Boldly climb
these with a climactic, long reach to finish.   (1961)

10   Rock Lobster *(RL)*   50'   E3 6b
Climb the blunt arête just L of Hangover's initial crack, then step R
& despatch the wall above with a 'balls-out' move to pass the bulge.
(B-52 fans may want to 'go jump in a crater' later).   (1985)

11   Don't Stop Now   50'   E1 5c   ★
Boulder up the incipient crackline, a few feet L of *RL*, to a desperate
move to gain the rounded break. Climb the wall above direct on
well-spaced holds.   (1980)

*L of Hangover's buttress is a large sloping alcove at half-height,
known as The Meadow.*

12   Letterbox Wall   60'   VS 5b,4b
A satisfying problem topped-off with a piquant wall.

1 35' Start beneath the hanging flakes of Hangover. Gain a standing position on the letterbox flake, followed by some testy moves to the rounded break which leads LWs to The Meadow.

2 25' Climb up the wall above the centre of The Meadow. (1955)

13 Grey Mare's Groove (GMG) 60' D
Pick any line to gain the alcove of The Meadow, then scramble over blocks in the break on the R. (c.1950s)

14 Cobleigh's Chimney (CC) 70' VD
Start below the LH chimney which leads up to The Meadow. Climb this, then follow the steeper chimney on the LH side of The Meadow & finish up the wall above. (c.1950s)

15 Frog's Failure 60' E1 5a
Climb the arête L of CC. Approach with a good deal of caution as there isn't much gear to be had. (1992) †

NORTH FACE
The face is dominated by the clean, mean-looking wall of Rough Diamond. L of this is the unappealing slash of North Face Chimney, followed by a flake-encrusted slab and the smoother wall of Vandal & Ann. The L-bounding breach is taken by East Chimney.

16   Glass Bead Game   60′   E5 6a
Sustained & bold. Gain the sloping platform below the R edge of
the smooth wall L of *CC*. Start below two shallow, parallel & vertical
cracklines 5′ L of the R arête. Climb the LH of the two cracks to the
break, then claw up the smooth wall above to a desperate groove.
Finish up this.   (1985)

17   Rough Diamond *(RD)*   60′   E4 6a   ★★★
A veritable classic. An impetuous start gives way to sustained tech-
nicalities up the main crackline. Follow a thin crack below & L of
the deepest vertical crack in the wall. Where it peters out, scratch
furiously RWs to join the main crack which is followed to the top
without reprieve.   (1979)

18   Rough Justice *(RJ)*   60′   E5 6a   ★★★
A real mind-bender for the vertically challenged (but nothing
special for your average six footer). Boulder up the flared drainage
gully (5′ R of the L-bounding chimney) to gain a steep slab. Trend
RWs to a shallow crack which is followed until it peters out at a PR.
Boldly gain the short slim groove up on the L, from where desperate moves lead up slightly RWs to a hasty exit.   (1983)

Haytor
– North Face –

19 Direct Justice 60' E5 6b
There is more to this than first appears. Start as for *RD*. Layback its
thin crackline & the rounded rib on the L, to eventually gasp up the
remainder of *RJ*. (1984)

20 West Chimney *(WC)* 40' D
Climb the outside of the chimney bounding the RH side of the
huge flake forming the slab of BPS. (c.1950s)

21 North Face Chimney *(NFC)* 50' HS 4b
Underestimating this pitch as a mere graunch will leave you well &
truly scuppered! From the top of *WC* gain the base of its wider
continuation. Gamely struggle into the fissure, which leads to a
ledge on the L. Climb the remaining rock awkwardly up LWs to gain
the summit slabs. (1954)

Below & L of the **RD** *wall is the huge flake of* **BPS***. Both* **BPS** *&*
Central Chimney finish atop the flake, where a descent can either
be made down the easy arête or by traversing LWs & descending **EC***.*
Alternatively finish up **NFC***.*

22 Bridle Piton Slab *(BPS)* 40' D
Any number of lines are possible (at this grade) up the polished &
flake-encrusted slab. (c.1950s)

23 Central Chimney 40' D
Climb the obvious chimney L of *BPS*. (c. 1950s)

24 Vandal & Ann *(V&A)* 80' HVS 5b,5a ★★
A bald first pitch leads to a bold conclusion. Start L of the chimney.
1 40' Climb direct up a steep slab 5' L of the RH arête (passing an

iron spike), then gain a ledge beneath the base of a groove in the bulge of the headwall.
2   40'   Enter the groove awkwardly, then climb it to a delicate exit via the summit slabs.
(1955/59)

25   Little Gem   25'   E1 5b
Approach via pitch 1 of *V&A*, then tackle the head-wall R of pitch 2 of *V&A*. Its difficulty is inversely proportional to the climber's perpendicular length, while the route is graded for a solo ascent (because there's no worthwhile gear).
(1985)

26   Diamond Sky   70'   E2 5b
Very bold at the top. An eliminate but worthwhile line. Start at the foot of an ill-defined rib L of *V&A*. Follow this to a large ledge, then climb the bulging wall above (using a horizontal break), 10' L of pitch 2 of *V&A*.
(1983)

27   East Chimney   (EC)   40'   M
Climb the outside of the chimney which separates the North Face from the East Face.
(c.1950s)

There are two speleological delights hidden within the huge flake of **BPS**. **Green Chimney** *50' (S) is entered via a 25' squeeze from the base of* **EC** *& is usually slippery. While* **Tunnel Chimney** *40' (M) lies deeper still within the flake, & finishes at the top of* **WC**.

EAST FACE
This blends into the North Face, however it can be distinguished from that face by the line of *EC*.

28   Canis   100'   VS 4c   ★
Start beneath a canine-like fang of rock on the NE↗ arête of the Tor. Climb onto the fang, then move up onto the flake in the RH crack. Follow the crack to a ledge & surmount the OH above. A beckoning slab leads precariously to the summit.
(1952)

29   Chimney & Direct   (C&D)   100'   D
Start beneath the chimney L of Canis. Climb this to easy territory beneath the East Face. Traverse LWs to a glacis leading to some obvious flakes & the summit slabs.
(c.1950s)
Variation Known as **Half Nelson** S 4a. Step up LWs from the chimney to gain the flakes direct.
(c.1950s)

30   Superdirect   80'   S
Climb direct up the middle of the slab L of *C&D*.
(1964)

31   Corner Slab   80'   VD
To the L of the slab is a chimney/groove; start beneath this. Follow the fissure for 10', then move out R onto the slab, which is climbed via a bulge to the top.
(c.1950s)

Roughly 350yds NE↗ of Haytor is a disused quarry, enclosing a small lake. On the far side of the amphitheatre, a stream wends its way down to a branch of the old granite railway. Up to the L of where the stream emanates from the quarry there is a short steep brown wall giving the line of:

32 Sandman   25'   E3 5c   †
Better than it looks. Start below the RH side of the face, roughly 2yds L of the arête. Climb the wall direct, to finish 7' further out in space from where you started.   (1993)

LOW MAN

Looking ↙SW from the Main Tor is the dome-shaped summit of Low Man. The characteristic feature of this face is the undercut nature of its base, due to the finer-grained granite eroding at a higher rate than the coarser stuff above.

This is by far and away the finest wall of granite on the Moor. With the sun setting over the ←W horizon it rears up like a shield of beaten bronze, up which only the most adamant of leaders could ever hope to make any headway, let alone reach the summit. To gain the first route descend the rocky slope R of the dome, where the face begins at a short steep wall. The R edge forms the undercut arête of:

1 Screw   50'   VS 5a
Start on a detached block to the L of the arête. Boldly gain the rib above the OH by climbing diagonally RWs from the block. Follow the rib over several bulges to the top.   (1970)

R of Screw is a wide, overgrown crack & R again is a large OH, the L edge of which forms the upper part of **HC**'s *corner:*

2 Honeymoon Corner *(HC)*   60'   S 4a
Gain the top of a pedestal at the foot of the corner. Enter this & follow it artlessly to a large ledge on the R. Move up from the centre of this, then continue LWs around a bulge to follow less strenuous rock to the top.   (1955)

3 Outward Bound *(OB)*   70'   HVS 4c   ★
Photogenically spectacular climbing through the large OHs 10' R of HC. Gaily gambol through the OH on superb flakes to a grassy terrace. Finish up the wall (above the RH end of the ledge), by trending up R & then back L near the top.   (1960)

4 The Flier   70'   E1 5c
A route with brutally rewarding climbing. Climb up to & over the break in the OH 10' R of OB. Continue in the same line for 10' before traversing RWs to follow *RNW* to the LH side of the terrace on *RG*, then finish up *OB*.   (1971)

5 Raven Wing *(RNW)*   70'   VS 4b
Start by a short corner 4yds L of the obvious slash of *RG*. Follow the corner for 10', then swing up L to gain the arête. Climb this to a break, then move L & climb to the terrace of *RG*.   (1967)

Variation 70' E1 5b Start L of the corner, beneath an OH. Surmount this, then step R to join *RNW*.   (1988)

To the R is the vast expanse of the main face. This is bounded on the L by the crack/chimney of **RG** *& on the R by the grimly OHing crackline of Levitation's Direct Start. In between are a profusion of subtle cracks & flakes above the prominent OHs near the base.*

6   Raven Gully *(RG)*   100'   S 4a   ★★
This route is on a par with the Dewerstone's lower grade classics. Start beneath a crack forming the RH side of the line. Gain the slab, via the crack, & move up LWs to the harrowing chimney. Uncouth lurches up this lead to a sloping ledge (optional stance). Climb the easy chimney above, or move L to follow the slab on the outer face of the block to the L.   (1951)
Variation finish 30' VS 4c An exposed delicacy. Start from the top of the easy chimney. Traverse the obvious line RWs onto the main face, until beneath some bulges. Pull over these RWs on small holds to gain the low-angled slabs above.   (c.1950s)

7   Interrogation   150'   E3 6a,5b   ★★★
An uncompromising line giving superlative climbing. It traces a tenuous line up the steep wall to the R of *RG*. Start 6' R of the gully.
1   75'   Gain the apex of a rounded flake, PR. Climb the vague groove above, to gain a horizontal fault & PR. Hard moves lead up L to the start of some blind flakes & another PR. Follow these to where they curve sharply LWs at some projecting holds which lead to a broad terrace on *RG*.
2   75'   Traverse back RWs along the projecting holds to gain a standing position on a narrow ledge, via a fearsomely exposed mantel. Delicate moves RWs lead to a slight groove. Climb this, then follow the summit slabs to the top.   (1964/80)

8   Interrogation Superdirect   150'   E5 6a   ★★★ †
Climb the wall direct, between *RG* & the normal start, to the break at 35'. Join & then follow Interrogation to its fearsome mantel (without deviation out L to belay). Trend up LWs from the narrow ledge, over a bulge, then scratch up the bald slab to the base of a hanging groove. Follow this to the summit slabs.   (1987)

9   Aviation   130'   E1 5b,5b   ★★★
He broke the mould after this one. The route follows a varied & sustained line starting some 30' R of *RG*, beneath a rib leading to an obvious shallow groove (above a bulge).
1   40'   Climb the rib & crack to a groove which leads to a horizontal break. Make an exposed & delicate traverse RWs along this to belay at a granite pancake.
2   90'   Step R & climb through the bulge to gain a rounded groove. Committing moves up this lead to the summit slabs. Belay (well back) to some iron rings.   (1961)

10 Igneous Pig *(IP)* 120′ E3 5c,5c
This climbs through the OH 10′ to the R of Aviation, starting beneath a smooth wall just R of a shallow groove.
1 40′ Climb the clean wall boldly to the OH & some generous undercuts. Surmount the OH using flakes over the lip which lead to a sloping ledge. Continue direct to the stance of Aviation.
2 80′ Step L & climb a flake to where it finishes, then climb the wall to a bulge (poor PR). Traverse LWs beneath the bulge for several feet, then pull over the bulge, via some taxing pulls on large crystals. Saunter up the slabs to finish. (1979)

11 Rhinoceros 140′ E2 5c,5c ★★
Originally entitled **Aviation Direct**. A fine counter-diagonal to Aviation, starting 20′ R of *IP*, beneath a pod-shaped crack.
1 40′ Climb up to the crack in the bulge, & negotiate this, trying to lose as little skin as possible, to the sloping ledge atop

Haytor
– Low Man –

IP's OH. Follow that route to the belay.

2 100' Reverse Aviation's traverse & pull up into a R\L slanting groove. Follow this to the capping bulge & traverse RWs for 10' to a poor PR. A long reach over the bulge gains poor holds which lead boldly up a slab to the top.   (1968)

Variation 2a E5 6c known as **Die Laughing**. From the top of the flake trend up LWs over a blank-looking bulge to join and finish up Interogation.   (1994)

12 Blood Lust 100'   E4 6b
A vicious route, *whose crux sequence was choreographed by no less a vampyre than Count Dracula himself.* Start beneath the tortuously OHing crackline R of Rhinoceros. Attack this in a determined fashion to a dubious but welcome flake on the L. Follow the remainder of the crack, then step R to gain the main horizontal fault. Pull directly over the bulge & continue up grooves & over

bulges until the angle eases.   (1985)

13   Levitation   90'   HS 4b
A pleasantly rewarding scramble up the RH wing of the main face,
where the initial OHs end & some slanting cracklines descend to
the ground. Follow these up LWs to a ledge & continue in the same
line to a flake. Climb the bulges above direct using flakes to bear
LWs, then finish easily.   (1967)

14   Levitation Direct *(LD)*   25'   HVS 5b
Satisfying thuggery through the large OH, some 7yds L of the start
to Levitation. Climb direct to a flake in the OH, from where a
powerful lurch gains a ledge above the OH. Follow a flake/crack to
join Levitation at the bulge.   (1968)

15   Nameless   60'   S
Characterless & frequently slimy *(& therefore a must for all lovers of
esoterica)*. Follow Levitation to the ledge atop the cracks, then
move R & climb the mossy slabs to the top.   (c.1950s)

16   Capstan   40'   VD
Start at a line of weakness L of a large block which abuts the RH side
of the main face. Climb the slab to a cylindrical boss of rock &
continue to the top via a short groove.   (c.1950s)

17   Low Man Girdle   200'   E3 5a,6a,4c   ★
The first two pitches make this a worthwhile excursion. Start as for
Levitation.
1   70'   Follow the cracks up L to the ledge & continue to the flake,
then traverse LWs along the horizontal break to the belay of
Aviation.
2   50'   Traverse LWs by reversing Aviation, passing beneath the
R\L groove of Rhinoceros. Continue to follow the rounded break
LWs to join Interrogation. Make some frantic moves past its PR (in
the horizontal break) to reach some generous holds before moving
down L into *RG*.
3   80'   Follow *RG* to its sloping terrace, & traverse the obvious
wide break LWs, until the crag peters out.   (1964/80)

18   Dehydration   150'   E2 5c,5c
A higher version of the above. Start below a cleft just R of *LD*.
1   75'   Climb up to join Levitation & follow this LWs until it is
possible to belay at the level of the upper traverse-line.
2   75'   Follow the break LWs (across Aviation) to cross Rhinoceros
just beneath its final bulge. Continue L in the same line until it is
possible to gain the flakes at the end of pitch 1 of Interrogation.
Follow this route into *RG* & finish up this.   (1982)

*400yds ↖NW (ie. in the direction of Holwell Quarry) of Low Man is a
track atop a spoil-heap which leads into a small quarry. This contains only one wall of any note, split vertically by a thin crackline
upon which the following route centres itself:*

19   Myrtle Turtle   40'   E3 5b
A boulder-problem start gives way to easier wall climbing leading to, then finishing up, a small corner on the R.   (1987)

SMALLACOMBE ROCKS   GR 755 783

Head due N ↑ from Haytor, passing between the vague hummocks of two quarry spoil-heaps (the LH spoil-heap contains the above route). After crossing the remains of a granite railway, contour the hillside until the boulder-field of the Rocks becomes apparent. The routes lie on the N ↑ face of the main block.

1   Buzzard   40'   HVS 5b
Climb the blatant layback flake to its end, then traverse LWs to continue up a jamming crack.   (1986)

2   Buzzard Direct   35'   E1 5c
Follow Buzzard to the top of the flake, then finish up the desperate wall above.   (1986)

HOLWELL QUARRY   GR 751 778

This quarry dwells within a dank hollow just over half-a-mile ↖NW of Low Man, and is reached by crossing over the old granite railway, then descending a steep slope to regain a lower branch of the line that leads to the quarry mouth. A good deal of fine, dry weather is needed before any of the routes can be contemplated, let alone attempted. Off to the L of the main amphitheatre is a stepped buttress (climbed by Xmandifer) and 30' L of this is a stepped slab taken by:

1   Chryswalke Connection   80'   VS 4b
Follow the slab in its entirety.   (1984)

2   Xmandifer   60'   HS 4a
Start beneath a downward-pointing rock spike in the stepped buttress. Climb direct to a ledge below the final OHing wall, passing a borehole (slot-in PR). Step L around the arête & finish steeply on improving holds.   (1979)
Variation   HVS 5a From the ledge below the OHing wall, place a peg & climb the impending wall direct.   (1983)

3   Spear of Destiny   50'   HVS 5b
This climbs the obvious corner R of Xmandifer. Start up an arête, which leads to the base of the corner. Follow the corner without deviation.   (1984)

To the R is the main bay (whose LH & RH corners are taken by Brief Encounter & Jazoo respectively). There are several thin cracks in the LH wall, which are as yet unclimbed. The following route climbs the first of two cracklines (in the LH wall) over halfway into the bay:

4   A Fall of Moondust   70'   E2 5c   †
Boldly climb the ramp leading into the crackline, which is followed
crunchily to the top.   (1983)

5   Saversnake   70'   E3 5c   †
This follows the next crunchy crackline on the R, which is just L of
an impressively smooth wall.   (1983)

6   Le Dernier Cri *(LDC)*   75'   E4 5c   ★★ †
Although the 2PRs have been stolen & the route is now without any
form of protection, it is still one of the finest quarried wall climbs
on the Moor. Climb the centre of the wall, L of *BE*. *Queues are an
unlikely occurrence on this route.*   (1983)

7   Brief Encounter *(BE)*   60'   VS 4c
This climbs the LH corner at the back of the bay.   (1978)

8   Jazoo   40'   HVS 5b
This is the companion route up the RH corner.   (1983)

9   You May Be the Face I Can't Forget   40'   E4 5c
Possibly the longest route name in the guide. This climbs the centre
of the bijou visage opposite *LDC*, via a series of poor edges, with
the crux at the top & no gear.   (1985)

10   Spasm Chasm   40'   VS 4c
Tackle the gaping crack R of the last 'thingammy'.   (1984)

SADDLE TOR   GR 750 764

A mile further ←W along the road which runs beneath Haytor is a
parking bay, beneath an eminently worthwhile lumplet. The routes
are described by starting beneath the LH arête of the OHung wall
which can be seen from the parking bay.

1   Mezzotinter   20'   E1 5c
Gain the arête from the L & follow it to the top.   (1983)

2   Bjørn Again *(BA)*   20'   E2 6a   ★
Start beneath the widest point of the bulge R of Mezzotinter, &
gamely climb direct to the summit.   (1987)

3   The Funnel   20'   S
There's no light at the end of this one. Swim up the holdless
chimney (via an awkward OHing entry) R of *BA*.   (c.1960s)

4   Foul Bite   20'   E2 5c
A fearsome proposition for those of limited stature. Start R of the
blunt RH arête & finish on the L.   (1984)

5   Firing Squad   25'   S 4a
Start R of Foul Bite. Climb up under a small OH, then move L into a
crack to finish.   (c.1950s)

The crag resumes play on the opposing side of the Tor, where the *dominating feature is the R\L diagonal fissure of Verdigris Cleft. The following route starts some 15' L of this:*

6   Busty Bitch   40'   E4 6b   †
Gird-yur-loins to boulder up the wall to a horizontal break. Step R (partway along ø Bruto's traverse) & cup the obvious pink boss, from where a wild slap leads to the top.   (1988)

7   Verdigris Cleft *(VC)*   40'   HVS 4c
A villainous struggle, run through with metaphysical connotations of good & evil *(where dressed in white, one might emerge severely blackened)*. Follow the evil orifice to its terminus, hopefully summiting in a halo cast by the dying embers of the sun's waning refulgence.   (c.1960s)

8   É Bruto   40'   E1 5b
Follow *VC* until a flared break leads out R to a sloping ledge below a bulging arête. Blindly flail up the arête to finish (people of normal stature may wish to stand on an *#11 Hex* on the slab, to place the vital *Friend* & to reach the holds).   (1985)

9   Don't Tell Emma   40'   HVS 5a   †
To the right of *VC* is a large triangular OH & right again is a large block. Step up to the block & then gain the wall above the OH. Traverse LWs to the arête & finish up this.   (1994)

BONEHILL ROCKS   GR 732 775

A magnificent bouldering venue (dealt with elsewhere) that sports a few, more demanding climbs. The Rocks command a fine panorama from the crest of the hill, overlooking that wonderful conurbation of cream-teaness. . . Widecombe-in-the-Moor.

On the S ↓ side of the Tor is a 30' slab giving a number of worthwhile pitches. Just L of this is a leering face bound on the L by a sharp arête & on the R by a boulder-choked gully (connecting it to the slab).

1   The Umpire Strikes Back   25'   E4 6a   *
Climb the wall just L of the gully, starting at the obvious thin crack. *'Owzat' for a scary solo?*   (1987)

2   You Cannot Be Serious   25'   E4 6b
Chris was & here is the result. Start about 6' R of the sharp arête & climb the wall direct to reach what looks like a loose crystal in the break ('tiz solid actually), then swing up RWs to finish yet another solo offering.   (1986)

CHINKWELL TOR   GR 728 783

There are three tors in close proximity to each other in this area, namely Bell, Honeybag and Chinkwell. They offer a plethora of bouldering opportunities. However, the substantial buttress on the ←W flank of Chinkwell Tor has a splendid crop of extreme pitches.

The buttress takes the form of a large, square leaning tower on the hillside overlooking Widecombe. A rather vegetated climb is given by the break in its ∠SW face:

1   Sphinx   60'   VD
Follow the weed-choked fissure direct.   (c.1960s)

The next climb lies on the ↖NW face of the block.

2   Widecombe Wall *(WW)*   70'   E1   5c   ★
A fine route that has a bite far worse than its bark. Start on the RH side of the wall, beneath a line of flakes which lead to a wide horizontal break. Traverse the break LWs to a short, blind crack in a shallow corner. Follow this to gain a jamming crack on the L, finish up the crack.   (1974)

3   The Fair   50'   E3 6a   ★
An arduous route that bisects the traverse of *WW*. Start beneath a vague crackline some 10' L of the start of *WW*. Take the crack to the break, step R slightly & blast up the unrelenting, flared crack to a capping bulge. Grovel over this & finish RWs.   (1984)

A further 10yds RWs up the slope (from the start of WW) is another smaller wall of granite.

4   Scrumpy Special   30'   E1 5c
Climb the centre of the wall direct on small crystalline nubbins, passing a prominent black chicken-head in a horizontal break (which provides an ingenious wire placement).   (1984)

HOUND TOR   GR 743 790

Approach and Access
This Tor inhabits the moorland plateau NE↗ of Widecombe. It provides panoramic vistas in every direction, most notably providing a splendid view of Low Man. There is a National Trust car park conveniently located at the foot of the Tor. A short walk up the hillside leads to the isolated mass of Perched Block.

Situation and Character
Hound Tor forms a maze-like conglomerate of rocks which on first acquaintance, and indeed numerous others, can leave you with the sensation of being totally lost. Even with a guidebook clenched firmly in your sweaty palm, you still feel like a crucifix-wielding Christian warding off a lion in the Roman Circus!!!

PERCHED BLOCK
When walking up from the car park this is the detached block down and R of the main bulk of the Tor. The RH wall (ie. the one facing

the car park) has a prominent R\L slash, providing the line of Kistvaen Corner. The bulging arête above the start of the groove gives:

1   Dead Dog Rib   35'   E2 5b
Climb the bulging arête immediately above the start of the groove (mistakenly recorded as Fougou in the old guide).   (1985)

2   Kistvaen Corner   40'   E3 6a
Start just around the R arête of the wall. Climb up, then traverse LWs to gain the R\L slanting groove. Follow it to an abominable stretch over the final OH to finish.   (1985)

3   Sheep May Safely Graze   35'   S
Numerous permutations up the zigzagging cracks at the LH end of the wall lead to the final OH (the crux).   (1954)

4   Perched Block Chimney *(PBC)*   25'   M
Climb the deep set chimney without much effort.   (c.1950s)

5   Lichenthrope   25'   E4 6b   †
Scary wall-climbing to the L of *PBC*. An obvious break runs up L/R from the rounded arête on the L. Follow this to a hard move leading to a frantic rockover to the R, onto the only generous foothold on the wall. Wobble up what remains to finish.   (1990)

6   Hob Hound   30'   E2 5c
A serious route. Topping out without becoming airborne is the crux (gulp!). From the start of Lichenthrope climb the rounded crack system just R of the arête.   (1983)

The following route climbs the centre of the bald wall which lies to the L of the arête defining the line of Hob Hound:

7   Toltec Twostep *(TT)*   30'   E5 6b/c   ★★★
A powerful addition, which would not be out of place on a gritstone bluff. However, the fist-jamming in the horizontal break may deter the faint-hearted. Gain the wide break, then climb diagonally RWs to a vague central flake. Stretch out RWs from the top of this, then finish up a slight groove & rounded crack.   (1989)
Variation 30' E5 6c Start R of *TT* & gain the vague central flake direct, via a powerful move on a sloper.   (1994)

8   Suspension Flake *(SF)*   30'   VS 4c   ★★★
A finely honed gem. Start up on blocks to the L of *TT*. Gain the crack above a ledge, from where a bold swing out RWs gains the start of a shallow break which runs diagonally RWs across the wall. Finish as for *TT*.   (1954)

9   Cantilever Direct   25'   HS 4b
Start as for *SF*, but continue direct up the crack.   (1954)

10   Cantilever Crack *(CC)*   30'   VS 4c
Start on the large block at the LH end of the ledge running LWs

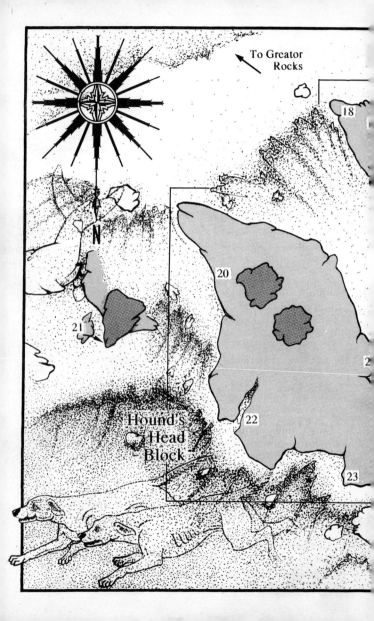

To Greator Rocks

18

20

21

2

Hound's
Head
Block

22

23

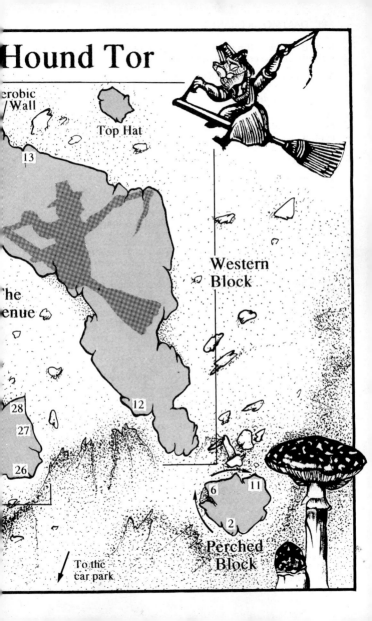

Hound Tor

erobic
/Wall

Top Hat

13

he
enue

28

27

26

12

Western
Block

To the
car park

6

11

2

Perched
Block

from the foot of the crack. Move up & follow a rising L/R traverse leading into the crack. Nip up this to finish.   (1954)

11   Last Flinger   20′   HVS 6a
An extended boulder-problem which climbs the bald wall just L of CC, via a gripping exit.   (c.1980s)

WESTERN BLOCK
From the Perched Block (and clearly visible from the car park) a central avenue separates the two main blocks of the Tor. Western Block is the RH of the pair. Upon entering the avenue an OHing tower on the R gives:

12   Downward Bound   30′   E2 5c   ★
Start on the RH edge of the tower, then follow a line of rounded holds trending LWs up the centre of the wall. Gain & follow a L/R crack to a horizontal break beneath an OH. Traverse LWs until beneath a flake on the lip, which is used to gain the elephant-bum finish.   (1978)

To find the next area, go back down out of the avenue & follow the ←W edge of Western Block, which eventually leads to a steep wall joined at right-angles to the block. This is Aerobic Wall. Roughly 30yds before this area is reached, there is a short wall split by a thin vertical crack giving:

13   Anaerobic Crack   20′   E2 6a
This lies in a shallow, boulder-strewn bay. Thin climbing, in line with the crack, leads to a daring reach to finish.   (1983)

14   Limbo Dancer   30′   E4 5c   ★
A bold line up the LH side of *AW*. Boulder up the wall about 5′ R of where the wall meets Western Block. Blindly reach over the OH to gain rounded breaks which lead to the top.   (1986)

15   Aerobic Wall *(AW)*   30′   E2 5c   ★★
A gymnastic problem protected by *Friends*. Start in the centre of the wall at a thin crack. Follow this to the OH, then grope up the rounded L/R leaning flake, to finish manfully up the rounded breaks above.   (1978)

TOP HAT
This is the isolated 20′ pillar of rock seen when facing towards Haytor from Aerobic Wall. There are a number of excellent problems on its various walls and arêtes (ranging in grade from VD to HVS).

20yds further R of Aerobic Wall is a small bay defined (on its RH side) by the blunt rib of:

16   Little Prow *(LP)*   20′   E1 5b
Climb the rib direct, finishing steeply past two horizontal breaks & a wickedly sloping ledge.   (1984)

17   Prowler   20'   VS 4c
Start as for *LP*, but step out L to gain twin vertical cracks, which are
followed all-too-briefly to the top.   (c .1980s)

*R of **LP** there is a 45 degree OHing wall that turns into a slab giving:*

18   Scorn   20'   E4 6a   ★
An extended boulder-problem that treats most people with disdain. Gain the flake where the wall changes angle to a slab (sling on
flake), then finish via a manic rock-over.   (1993)

HOUND'S HEAD BLOCK
This is the LH mass of Hound Tor. The first route described is
gained by walking up the avenue and turning L. After a further
10yds you are confronted by an obvious smooth, vertical wall,
which is directly below the LH Hound's Head. The central line gives
Full Moon.

19   Teenage Mutant Ninja Slippers   25'   HVS 4c
The LH edge of the wall forms a prow. Climb directly up the prow,
past a suspect flake to finish.   (1990)

20   Full Moon   25'   E3 5c   ★
Climb the centre of the wall to the half-height break *(Friends)*.
Tackle the headwall by insecure crimps on slopers & the odd
crystal.   (1986)

*25yds down & R (looking out) of Full Moon is a prominent Dairylea
Triangle-shaped OH.*

21   Hung Like a Baboon *(HLB)*   20'   E5 6c   ★ †
From the tall boulder opposite the lip of the OH, use a broom-
handle to hook a sling over a tiny flake. . . then dyno for it. A
couple of intense cranks should see you to the top.   (1993)

*30yds R of **HLB** is a dank green gully, the RH wall of which gives:*

22   Slime Time   25'   HVS 5b
Climb the slightly OHing crack, past visceral green algae, to a fierce
pull to gain holds leading up the face above.   (1987)

*A further 25yds R leads to the toe of the block & the rounded edge
of:*

23   Hydraulic Arête   65'   HVS 5b   ★
The rounded arête overlooking the car park. Start from a ledge a
few feet off the ground. Climb an OHing crack to a ledge on the R.
Continue direct, passing two OHs on route for the summit.   (1984)

24   Stegadacea Chimney *(SC)*   90'   D
Start R of Hydraulic Arête. The square-cut chimney is climbed to a
vegetated ledge on its L. Walk 15' LWs & climb the wall on the R,
then the corner of the main block. Step over a rift & climb the front
of the L Hound's Head.   (1951)
Variation S 4a Step RWs from atop the chimney & climb a strenuous

wall to finish up the R Hound's Head.   (c.1950s)

25   Right Chimney *(RC)*   65'   VD
The chimney R of *SC*. Climb the chimney for 20', then follow some cracks to join The Vice. Avoiding the arch, climb direct up the wall to gain a ridge which leads LWs to a large shelf. Step R, then climb the corner above to finish.   (1951)

26   The Vice   65'   VD   ★
1   25'   Climb the slab R of *RC* to awkwardly gain the crack on the R which leads to a large ledge.
2   40'   Climb the crack formed by the large block behind the belay, then step up to gain the summit of the buttress.   (c.1950s)

The remaining routes climb the ←W wall of Hound's Head Block, starting with:

27   Pulpit   60'   D
Climb the slab beneath the Pulpit & traverse LWs to a large ledge. Step back R & make a steep move up to gain the L end of the Pulpit. Finish up the wall above on rounded holds, or up the easier chimney on the L.   (1951)

28   Paddy   50'   M
Start R of the corner leading up to the Pulpit. Climb up L of a small OH to a ledge, then finish up the broken crack above.   (c.1960s)

29   Liars Dice   20'   S
20yds R of Pulpit is a square bay. This route climbs the steep crack splitting the R wall of the bay.   (c.1970s)

GREATOR ROCKS   GR 748 787

These rocks lie quarter-of-a-mile SE↘ of Hound Tor. They are clearly visible from Haytor, from where they look quite impressive. Sadly, on closer inspection, they prove to be rather disappointing. However, some short pitches can be found on the various walls on the S↓ side of the ridge. The ridge itself (which runs W↔E) gives an interesting sortie.

1   Black Fox Wall   35'   VS 5a   †
This climbs the most E→ buttress, which faces toward Leighton Lake. Start at the end of the face, just R of an obvious crack where the rock slants RWs. Climb up to a ledge, & take the wall above direct to an OH. Traverse RWs along a break (on strange holds) to top out.   (1985)

2   Cheese Greator   40'   VD
Near the E→ end of the rocks is a V-shaped recess. Climb the R\L rising diagonal on the L wall of the recess.   (c.1950s)

3   Greator Garbo   35'   M
Climb the R wall of the recess.   (c.1950 s)

4   King Jam   25'   E1 6a   †
An extended boulder-problem. Find the furthest ←W of the two
main piles of rock. Behind an OHung slab there is a large cleft.
Climb a narrow buttress to a horizontal shelf beneath the large
cleft. Bridge up this to finish.   (1985)

MOOR TORS AREA

The great upland plateau of Dartmoor is slowly being rent asunder,
by numerous deep-sided river valleys radiating from its heart.
While making the area scenically dramatic, the river valleys can
prove to be extremely vexing when attempting to get between tors
(ie. there's no such thing as a short-cut on Dartmoor. However, if
there were it would only lead to you becoming another *interestin'*
tale to relate beside a be-pentangled taproom fireside).

Talking of taprooms. . . *The Plume of Feather's* on the outskirts of
Princetown makes for an interesting evening's diversion. The resident proprietor has tacked on a bunkhouse for all the ingrates who
stumble in off the Moor. His doors are thrown open to climbers, as
well as cavers, bikers and hippies who are all treated (with the same
disdain) to excellent food, scrumpy and milk on draught.
Apparently the world famous brew of 'Crippledich' (which every-
one seems to forget about) is only on offer during the Yuletide
festivities.

A number of granite quarries have been lumped in with the tors.
Apart from the odd route, most of the quarries resemble (well to be
honest, they are) dank holes, filled with rotten rock and stagnant
pools. They are not what might be termed 'eminently worthwhile'.
Only a Moorland doyen of trivia would have the 'balls' to say that,
and he'd have had to have had a few 'Crippledichs' before even
uttering the phrase under his breath.

WESTCOTT ROCKS   GR 792 875

From Exeter follow the B3212 toward Moretonhampstead. Just
before Doccombe turn L, signposted Westcott (if approaching
from Plymouth, come off at Bovey Tracey and continue up the A382
to turn R at Moretonhampstead for Doccombe). The hamlet of
Westcott is left via a tortuous LH turn, over a narrow bridge, which
leads to a steep hill. There is a parking bay on the L, just over the
brow of the hill. Walk back along the road to a track (L of the
footpath) which leads across open fields, with a wood to the L.
Contour the edge of the woodland, passing through two hedges
separating the fields. Head for the middle of a heath-like area
which appears after the second field (Hel Tor can be seen very

easily on the opposite hill), and descend a broad earth gully leading to the base of the main block, which lies down to the L.

The Rocks take the form of a sprawling outcrop which provides a feast of untapped bouldering potential, as well as a couple of worthwhile routes. However, it does become very overgrown during the summer. The main block is the largest buttress on the edge, and is distinguished by a striking L/R groove-line in the middle of its tallest face. Descent from the summit is via the notch on its LH side (looking out), leading to a scramble to regain the descent path from the earth gully.

1   Wild Palms   40'   E5 6b   ★ †
Start beneath the LH side of the undercut LH arête of the face. Climb the arête (with scant protection) to a sloping ledge. Pull through the centre of the bulge above to finish easily up the shallow summit slabs.   (1993)

2   Shere Khanage   50'   E3 6a   ★★ †
Start below a short wide crack on the RH side of the face. Climb this to a sloping ledge &, using some curious large nubbins, gain the base of the striking L/R groove. Jam & undercut the seam at the back of the groove, to pull through the bulge at the groove's apex. Finish up the slab.   (1993)

HELTOR ROCK   GR 800 871

One of the lowest tors on the Moor, which is set upon a picturesque hilltop. There is a dedicated parking space at the foot of the only path leading to the Tor. The climbing lies on the ←W wall.

Seen from below, the wall is divided into the North Block & the South Block by a fissure (**Devil's Gully** *(DG)* 40' M).

NORTH BLOCK
To the L of *DG* are three trees, an ash, a rowan and a holly, which prove useful for identifying the routes. Above half-height the face is cleaved by the relatively broad and sloping ledge of:

1   Ash Traverse *(AT)*   60'   E
Start beside the ash tree on the LH side of the block. Follow the sloping ledge system which leads RWs into *DG*; the last move proves to be vexatious.   (1961)

2   Dante   50'   VS 4b
A poor route, taking a direct line up the wall some 15' L of the rowan tree (crossing through *AT*).   (1961)

3   Peck   50'   VD
Climb up onto a ledge (2yds L of the rowan tree). Continue up the steep slab, on rounded holds, to a shallow dent in the bulge. Climb this to a broad sloping ledge & a chockstone. Move up onto the block on the R to finish.   (1961)

4   Beatrice   50'   VS 4c   ★
Start just L of the rowan tree. Follow a vague line of weakness to the sloping ledge. Climb the flake-like dyke through the bulge, then move L to finish.   (1961)

5   Ivy   60'   VD
Start between the rowan & holly trees. Climb the wall by faith-&-friction. Finish by traversing RWs into *DG*.   (1961)

6   Wisht You Were Here *(WYW)*   50'   E1 5b   †
Follow the crack, R of the holly, to the base of a thin crack in the bulge. From the top of this a long stretch up RWs gives access to a break; finish LWs.   (1993)

7   Earth   50'   D
Follow *WYW* to the top of its wide crack, then follow the traverse of *AT* into the gully.   (1961)

SOUTH BLOCK
This is the mound to the R of *DG*.

8   Maximagur   40'   HVS 5a   ★ †
Start 10' R of the gully, beneath a flake. Layback this to an easy slab then gain the base of the steep bulge. Climb this diagonally LWs on distant bucket-holds.   (1993)

9   Quoit Enough   40'   E1 5b   †
Follow Maximagur to the steep bulge. Pull directly over this to a second bulge. Climb up over this keeping to the R of Maximagur, then finish direct.   (1993)

10   Furze   45'   D
Follow Maximagur to the base of the steep bulge. Then traverse 12' RWs to a broken groove. Climb this to finish.   (1961)

BLACKINGSTONE ROCK   GR 786 856

An impressive Tor which on closer inspection is found to be wanting. The long N-facing slab is over 100' long and provides two lines of VD up to the final OH. This is usually skirted either to the L or R as the two lines of weakness through the bulge are both HVS. To the R of the slab is a deep, green chimney, which has been climbed, providing a messy VS. The S ↓ side of the Rock is shorter, but much steeper and gives a number of worthwhile pitches.

SOUTH FACE
The various blocks of the South Face are divided by several deep clefts which form easy descents.

1   Old Peculiar   25'   D
A route of simple means that follows the flake & slab of the second slim buttress L of the main block.   (c.1950s)

2   Spingo   25'   VS 4b
Start at the RH toe of the narrow face just L of the main block.
Climb diagonally LWs to the bulge. Overcome this at a shallow
depression to gain the top.   (c.1960s)

3   Scruttock's Old Dirigible *(SOD)*   65'   S 4b   *
Climb the broad flake-like slash in the LH side of the main block,
then weave drunkenly through some bulges to finish.   (c.1950s)

4   Roger & Out   65'   E1 5c
An inebriated ramble up the bald, steep slab R of *SOD*, finishing as
direct as the lunchtime medicine will allow.   (1993)

5   Adnams Enough   70'   M
Gamely struggle up the broad gully which cleaves the clean sweep
of rock to the R of *SOD*.   (c1950s)

NORTH FACE
Descending (past the antique granite staircase) to the toe of the
impressive slab gains the base of the next route. This starts beneath
a steep flake/crack on the RH side of the slab.

*Both of the following routes have HVS variation finishes over the
capping OH, if the slab has not proved taxing enough fayre.*

6   Pished   120'   VD
A bold nomadic foray on to the nether regions of the LH side of this
granite desert, where the runners are more distant than the nearest
oasis. Skirt the final bulge LWs.   (c.1950s)

7   Right Hand Slab & Chimney   120'   VD
A similar experience to the above, taking the RH side of the slab to
skirt the OHing bulge RWs to exit.   (1945)

8   Green Lipped Chasm   80'   VS
The 'offal' void twixt the slab & narrow finger of rock.   (c.1950s)

BLACKINGSTONE QUARRY   GR 783 857

**The owners have made it quite clear that they do not want people to
climb here**.

This quarry had the ignominious honour of producing all the tomb-
stones for the area. Hopefully nobody will be in the market for one
should they decide to visit *(although the owners may 'plant-one' on
the unlucky soul whose presence is detected)*. The quarry lane lies
200yds down the hill from Blackingstone Rock.

The first five routes are on an OHing wall above the pool (to the L
of the entrance defile), and are approached by abseil.

1   Undertaker   30'   HVS 5a   †
An unprotected line up the wall L of Overtaker. Traverse LWs until
half-way along a ledge just above the water, then gain the ledge

above. Climb a slight groove to finish. (1989)

2 Splosh 30′ E1 5b †
Follow Undertaker to the base of a curving groove (on the R).
Layback this for a few moves, then step out R to a PR & finish direct
via an unorthodox manoeuvre. (1990)

3 Hydrophobia 30′ E4 6a ★ †
The centre of the gently OHing wall. The crux is protected by a
sling over a loose flake (which *might* just stop a dunking). Start 10′ L
of the corner, on the ledge system above the water. Use two loose
holds & a small layaway to gain a sloper & the horizontal break
above (PR). Make a long reach for a jug in the next break, then
finish slightly LWs. (1990)

4 The Link 35′ E3 6a ★ †
A worthwhile route. Follow Splosh to its PR, then traverse the thin
horizontal break RWs to join Hydrophobia at its PR. Finish direct, as
for that route. (1990)

5 Overtaker 30′ E2 6a †
The obvious corner-line bounding the RH side of the OHing wall.
There is a desperate move (at half-height) for people that are not
naturally gifted in the reach department. (1989)

*20yds to the R is a clean steep slab, above a narrow beach by the
water's edge. This is taken by:*

6 Tomb with a View *(TWV)* 40′ E3 6a ★
Start in the centre of the slab. Climb up to the base of some
incipient cracks which start at a slight bulge. A long reach (BR) gains
some thin holds beyond. Trend L to finish. (1989)

50yds R of **TWV** *there is a short compact buttress, about 10yds R of
the edge of the lake. The most obvious feature is the sharp arête of*
BSL.

7 Banshee 25′ E3 6a †
Start just L of the sharp arête, at the base of an OH-capped groove.
Bold climbing up the groove leads to a thin break (PR). Hard moves
past this gain the top. (1989)

8 Banana Split Lady *(BSL)* 25′ E5 6c ★ †
The obvious sharp arête. A desperate & unprotected start leads to a
hard protected (PR) finish. (1990)

9 Strawberry Girl 25′ E2 6a †
Start beneath 2PRs to the R of *BSL*. Climb direct past these, via long
reaches between thin breaks. (1989)

10 Death Knell 20′ HVS 5b †
Just R of Strawbery Girl is a hairline crack leading to a shallow
overlap topped by a loose block. Climb the crack, then finish over
the latent tombstone. (1989)

LUSTLEIGH CLEAVE

GR 772 815

From the centre of Lustleigh follow the road leading S ↓ , straight up a steep hill to a T-junction (Rudge Cross). Turn R and follow the road past Pethybridge and Wayne Farm to arrive at a layby opposite a footpath. Follow this up through a boulder strewn wood to arrive at the edge of a large stretch of heathland.

Lustleigh contains two of the finest cream tea shops in the Shire, however they know their reputation and charge extortionately.

THE NUT CRACKERS
Where the path strikes the edge of the heath turn L, then walk along a vague path for 50yds to gain an exposed rocky platform and the top of a stubby pinnacle. Descend down L of the rocky platform & skirt the base of the pinnacle RWs until beneath an obvious flake/weakness in the front face. The next two routes are described from R to L.

1   Split Pinnacle   60'   VD
Climb the flake to some ledges, then traverse LWs to a corner. Step across this into a chimney. Squirm up this until level with the front block, then traverse LWs over the top of this to an ivy-ridden crack. Follow the crack to the summit block.   (c.1950s)

2   Bamboozled   50'   E3 5c   ★★ †
Around the L arête of the pinnacle is a striking OH split by an off-width crack. Step up to the OH & pull over this using the flake on the RH edge of the offwidth. Follow the wide crack to where it peters out, then trend up RWs, via some desperate crystal-pulling, to gain the summit.   (1990)

E→ of the pinnacle, by about 20yds, is another buttress which is bounded on its RH side by a layback corner. The wall to the L contains the flake/crack of:

3   Polly Wants a. . .   25'   S 4a
Follow the crack, which is not as hard as it looks.   (c.1950s)

4   Short but Sweet   25'   VS 4c
Climb the clean cut layback corner.   (c. 1950s)

RAVEN'S TOR
There are no revelations to be had here, nor is it a mecca for body-machines or sardines (in or out of brine). On the other hand the prow of the buttress may yield a Hubble experience. From the top of the footpath follow the ridge ↖NW for approximately 300yds, where the buttress becomes evident. The next four routes are described from R to L.

5   Sow's That *(ST)*   50'   E3 5c   †
Start atop the large boulder on the RH side of the buttress. Hard moves lead up, then LWs to gain the big diagonal break which crosses the centre of the face. Follow this, then climb the LH rib to

finish up a blunt flake.   (1989)

6   Silk Purse   50'   E4 6a   ★ †
Follow *ST* until beneath a thin crack which is immediately above the
start of the wide break. This is hard to enter & even harder to leave!
Gain the sloping break beneath the large OH & traverse LWs along
it, to join & finish up *ST*.   (1989)

7   The Hog's Back *(HB)*   50'   E5 6a   ★ †
The rounded L-bounding arête of the main buttress. Gain the arête
easily from the L, then boldly climb it to a horizontal break. Follow
the blunt flake above to the top (as for *ST*).   (1986)

8   Piggin' Chimney   40'   S 4a
Some 4yds L of *HB* is a large flake which defines a chimney. Climb
up the chimney inside of the bottle-neck, where the flake meets
the main buttress, by means of "shoulder/knee jambing & rough-
ages". Continue up the wall above to finish.   (c.1950s)

KESTOR ROCK   GR 665 863

This large wart-like tor lies near the road leading to Batworthy
which is about two and a half miles ←W of Chagford, and just over
a mile N ↑ of Fernworthy Reservoir. There are several worthwhile
excursions on a short steep wall (the first wall seen from the
approach path).

Chagford itself holds the added attraction of *Blacks*, a Ruritanian
deli which serves a mouthwatering array of 'bonne bouche',
challenging locally-made pasties, plus continental libations and a
knicker-wetting range of sweets. *The Three Crowns* opposite the
deli, offers more traditional fayre.

1   Perspiration   30'   HVS 5b   †
Climb the OHing nose of rock in the centre of the steep face. Finish
out RWs.   (c.1980s)

2   Brown Oasis   30'   S
Climb the corner R of the nose. Finish up Perspiration.   (c.1980s)

3   Sigg-y Stardust *(SS)*   30'   VS 5b
Start at a large jug on the RH side of the wall. Climb up into a
scoop, then finish direct.   (c.1980s)

4   Wart-ho   30'   VD
Climb the LH vertical weakness R of *SS*.   (c.1970s)

5   Warts'n'All   30'   D
The RH vertical weakness.   (c.1970s)

WEST MILL TOR   GR 587 910

A delightful place for tinkering around on those balmy summer evenings. Essentially it comprises of a long low wall of crisp clean granite, with a number of 20' problems ranging from M to VD and a singularly steep jamming crack of VS 4b near its RH edge. However, the 'tour de force' of the crag is the 100' girdle, which gives a magnificent S 4a.

GREAT LINKS TOR   GR 552 867

Another remote tor. Park up beside the *Fox and Hounds* public house which is to be found on the A386. A rough track leads up on to the Moor. Follow this until the track bends to the L, then strike off up the ridge to gain the Tor after a half-hour walk. The Tor offers short, technical routes and some bouldering. The rock masses comprising the Tor run in line from W↔E, the most ←W of which culminate at a trig point. The routes reside on the next block E→, which is joined to the other block by a rocky saddle. The S ↓ face is dominated by an undercut wall, cleaved by two OHing cracks.

1   Great Flake   25'   VS 4c
Climb the obvious OHung crack at the LH end, starting from a V-shaped niche.   (1985)

2   Lynx   30'   VS 4c
The next crack to the R is harder than it looks.   (1985)

3   Missing Link   30'   E4 6a   †
Still awaits a repeat, let alone an on-sight lead. Protection is difficult to arrange & an abseil inspection is advised. Climb the fiercely OHung wall R of Lynx at its widest point.   (1985)

4   Tenuous Link   40'   VS 5b
At half-height, in the highest point of the wall, there is a short groove. Climb direct to the base of this, then exit from it along the obvious line on the R to gain the top.   (1985)

FUR TOR   GR 588 831

A great place for getting away from it all, being situated in the middle of the nether regions of Dartmoor. Apart from being isolated, it has the added attraction of some fine bouldering and a number of short scrappy climbs (from M to VD) among the blocks that form its maze-like summit.

BENCH TOR   GR 693 717

There are more than a few pearls scattered along its edge, making it a perfect venue for a summer's afternoon. From the car park just S ↓ of Venford Reservoir, walk over the hill to the E→ and contour its E→ slope N ↑ until the cliff edge appears down to the R. The first routes climb the buttress at the top of the slope.

1   Lawbreaker   25'   VS 4b
Start beneath the broad LH arête (of the smooth wall of Hot-shot).
Climb the arête direct to a hard finish.   (1989)

2   Hot-shot   25'   E3 6a   ★ †
The clean wall to the R of Lawbreaker. Start on the R, on top of a
boulder. Step off this LWs in a fearsome position (above lots of
nasty, sharp boulders) straight into the crux. Continue direct, just R
of the arête to a fairly dynamic move to finish (starting direct bumps
up the grade to a terrifying 6b).   (1989)

*The edge becomes more continuous further down the slope, where
it gains more height. The dominant feature is a large, square-cut
groove. The next pitch starts L of this.*

3   Central Buttress *(CB)*   30'   VD
Start on a boulder below the obvious narrow face on the LH side of
the main crag. Step up R to gain large holds, which lead steeply to
the top (R of the crack of *SW*).   (1959)

4   Senior's Wall *(SW)*   30'   VS 4c
Start 5yds L of a square-cut groove, beneath an OH. Climb over
this, then continue up the broken crack above to finish. The hard
moves over the OH can be avoided by climbing the arête above the
boulder (just R of *CB*), then traversing RWs into the crack (reducing
the grade to S 4a).   (1974)

5   Oak Tree Zig Zag *(OTZ)*   50'   VD   ★★
One of the many underrated gems of the Moor, taking the R\L
slanting groove L of a large OH. Start from a block below the centre
of this OH. Climb up to gain a traverse-line beneath the OH, then
follow this LWs to the groove-line which is followed in its entirety
(gaining the groove direct is S 4a).   (1959)

6   Suspended Sentence   55'   HVS 5b
Start as for *OTZ*. Climb up the main groove until a break leads
horizontally RWs on to the main face (about 15' above the OH
mentioned in the following two routes). Finish slightly RWs up the
main face (as for *HW*).   (1989)

7   Judge Dredd *(JD)*   50'   E5 6a   ★★ †
A downright murderous arête. Start as for *OTZ*. Climb into the
main groove until level with the lip of the OH. Follow the flake out
R to the arête, then climb the LH side of this to the capping roof
(bold). Pull up R into a hanging groove, from which thin moves lead
up RWs to a poor break & a rounded finish.   (1989)

8   Hostile Witness *(HW)*   50'   E2 5c   ★★★
A power-packed route which tackles the main face of the Tor after
surmounting the OHs from the L. Follow *JD* to the arête on the lip
of the OH. Continue to hand-traverse the flake RWs to gain a
further flake on the front face. Make an irreversible move off the
flake & follow a crack to just below the top, where a move R yields

an excellent jug to finish on.   (1976)

9   Innocent Bystander   50'   E4 6b   ★ †
The OH & Wall R of *HW* provides the meat of this excruciating
miscarriage of justice. Climb the wall to a crack through the OH,
where vicious jams lead to a break. Continue diagonally RWs up
the wall to finish.   (1979/86)

10   Trembling Wall *(TW)*   40'   VS 5a
Start 7yds to the R of *OTZ* at a break in the RH end of the low OH,
below a prominent dead tree. Climb the slab bearing RWs to the
break in the OH. Climb through this, then continue up the wall
above to finish.   (1974)

11   Ash Chimney *(AC)*   30'   VD
If you are desperate, this climbs the obvious chimney at the RH end
of the main face.   (1974)

12   Kestrel   40'   HVS 5a
Start 3yds R of *AC*, beneath the L face of an arête. Pull awkwardly
onto a mossy ledge, then step R around the arête to gain & climb a
thin crack leading to the ash tree. Climb past the tree & finish up
the bulging wall R of the chimney.   (1987)

13   Monster   50'   E1 5b
Start 4yds R of Kestrel, below a vertical crack. Climb up, then
traverse diagonally LWs along a wider crack to the ash tree. Finish
as for Kestrel.   (1987)

14   Law of Nations   40'   E4 6a   †
Start just R of Monster. Climb into the R\L slanting crack of Monster, but deviate out R onto a projecting foothold in the wall. Finish
up the crack on the L with difficulty.   (1988)

15   Legal Aid   115'   HVS 5a,5b,4a
A R-to-L girdle of the cliff. Start R of Trembling Wall, below a crack
which runs up L of a cruddy groove.
1   40'   Gain the crack, which is climbed to a bulge. Traverse LWs
across the wall to the dead tree on *TW*.
2   40'   Climb to a break in the OH & go through this to a line
which leads L across the wall. Traverse delicately across to the flake
on *HW*, then move up & swing around the corner to a belay in *OTZ*.
3   35'   Follow the obvious line L to join & finish up *CB*.   (1980)

LUCKEY TOR   GR 685 721

Misnamed in the previous guide (and all the other guides come to
think of it) as Eagle Rock. The quickest approach from the A384 is to
park (with the permission of the farmer) at Rowbrook Farm. From
here a number of tracks contour down the hillside to the crag.
However, for a truly memorable day it is better to park at Dartmeet.
A life-affirming walk through deciduous woodland (S ↓ along the

E→ bank of the Dart) ends at the stunning eruption of the crag. Rising dramatically from the uncannily manicured pasture beside the River Dart, it is one of Nature's more discreet *trompe-l'oeil*; appearing to be almost a 100' in height, when in fact it is a mere 40'. That aside it also provides a splendid arena for a day's sporting activity and a picnic.

1   Main Gully   30'   D
Just before the LH side of the crag disappears into the hillside there is a gully which forms the LH boundary of the crag. It is best climbed using the large holds on the RH wall.   (1960)

2   Rocking Block   35'   E1 5b
This climbs a scruffy wall L of Main Gully.   (1986)

3   Ivy Wall   35'   VS 4c
Start just L of the L arête that bounds the front face of the crag. Climb the steep wall via an OHung niche to the top. It is also possible to traverse RWs above the OHs (on rounded holds) & then climb to the top.   (1961)

4   The Eyrie   40'   E2 5c   ★★
A fine route which tackles the line up the arête to the R of Ivy Wall. Climb the steep wall just R of the arête to some ledges below the OH. Move L & pull up into a short crack which leads to a ledge, from where a bulge leads to the top.   (1980)

5   Eagle's Nest   40'   S   ★★
An impressive route for its grade which follows the obvious break in the highest point of the OHs, to the L of the front face. Climb the twin cracks up to the OH, then continue out of the OHung niche by swinging up on huge chockstones.   (1961)

6   Original Route *(OR)*   35'   S
Start up the shallow corner leading up to the RH end of the ledge in the centre of the face. Move delicately RWs from the ledge, then climb up to finish beside a gorse bush.   (1960)

7   Songline   35'   HVS 5a
Start to the R of *OR*, at the base of an open-book corner beneath a long crack in an OH. Climb the corner to the OH & jam out along this using footholds on the R wall. Pull into the next crack leading to another OH. Hard moves past this lead to a hanging corner crack, which is climbed direct to finish.   (c.1990s)

8   Bloodshot   35'   HVS 5b
The roof crack R of Songline. Climb over some large blocks to a ledge, then surmount the OH above via some difficult jamming & laybacking.   (1984)

9   Black Jam Crack *(BJC)*   30'   VS 4c   ★
The narrow crack on the extreme RH side of the main face forms the substance of the route. Start beneath the narrow black groove

from which the crack emerges.   (1961)

10 Black Jam Arête   30'   HVS 5a   ★
Climb the LH arête of *BJC* in its entirety.   (1980)

R of the main face are several cracks & chimneys. On the far R the biggest chimney gives:

11 Right Hand Chimney   30'   D
Climb the large chimney in its entirety.   (1960)

TEMP TOR   GR 666 666

A devil of a place to find, being hidden deep within the SE↘ reaches of the Moor. This wraith-like Tor inhabits the slopes N↑ of the Avon Dam Reservoir, above a pilgrim's path known as Abbot's Way. You'd be a fool to climb here unless you had packed the picnic recommended in the Rescue Notes.

FOGGINTOR QUARRY   GR 566 735

After two and a half miles driving ←W from Two Bridges (on the A384) there is a car park on the L, with a farm track running due S↓ out of it. Cars must be left at this point. A brisk fifteen minute walk leads to a derelict quarry building and the E→ entrance to the Quarry.

The Quarry is in the form of a large secluded amphitheatre, dominated by a crystal clear lake which makes for a refreshing dip on a hot summer's day. At its most E→ extent, the lake passes beneath a clean wall dominated in its top third by a huge quarry bolt (this is the line of Rockface). Further-on, a compact buttress guards the entrance to a subsidiary bay, containing one of the finest crack climbs on the Moor, Limestone Cowboys. The Swan Lake buttress occupies a position directly opposite to this, just above the S↓ shoreline of the lake.

1 Rockface   50'   HVS 5b   ★
A serious route, although the crux is amply protected. Start in the middle of the wall beneath a large quarry bolt at 35'. Climb the wall to a small ledge at 20' (poor PR). Continue direct to a good ledge below the bolt. Finish up the wall on the R.   (1976)

50yds to the R is an OHing wall split by a thin crack, at the entrance to a small bay.

2 Limestone Cowboys *(LC)*   45'   E4 6b   ★★★
Originally aided (**Wicker** A1), but now a taxing free route. Start beneath the RH arête of the OHing wall. Climb the arête to reach a thin break. Traverse LWs along this to gain & follow the vertical crackline to a hard lock-off to finish. (A boulder-problem direct start has been done at hard 6b).   (1985)

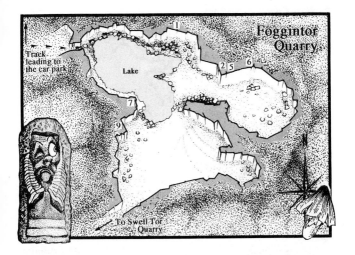

3 Wicked Woman *(WW)*   45'   E3 6a
This climbs the arête to the R of *LC* in its entirety. Staying out of
Wicked proves to be the crux. Start as for *LC*.   (1986)

4 Wicked   45'   HVS 5b
Start at the foot of the arête of *WW*. Climb this for 10', then step R &
climb a fragile flake/crack to the RH arête of the face. Step up to
gain a line of holds leading back L, PR (missing, presumed lost in
action), to regain the LH arête to finish.   (1976)

5 Fogginard   45'   E2 5c   †
Well, bloody desperate actually since the start fell away. Fathom the
inky depths of the gash 4yds R of Wicked, then finish up the
weed-choked crack.   .   (1976/93)

6 Stepladder   60'   HS   ★
Further into the small bay of orange-streaked granite there is
another large quarry bolt at half-height. Start some 10' to the R of
this. Climb to a broad ledge, then follow a shallow groove for 15' to
a horizontal crack on the L. Move diagonally LWs to encounter the
quarry bolt at waist level & then climb straight up the wall above on
perfect holds, just R of a grassy ledge.   (1976)

*The arête of the thin promontory of rock (opposite Wicked) has
been climbed at a rather bold HS 4b. The following three routes are
gained by circumnavigating the S ↓ toe of the lake, to gain a rock
ledge at the base of blank-looking wall.*

7   Swan Lake   35'   HS 4a   ★
Worthwhile. Start on a ledge 15' above the water. Climb the LH
arête of the blank wall, then pull over a small OH to gain a niche.
Step L & make an awkward move to good holds which lead to the
top. Iron stake belays well back.   (1967)

8   Parsifal   35'   E1 5c
Climb directly up the wall L of Swan Lake.   (1985)

9   Saturday Night Finger   40'   VS 5a
This lies on the black wall a little to the L of Parsifal. Climb up &
slightly L to a ledge, then tackle the groove on the L. Overcome the
steep wall above with difficulty.   (1983)

SWELL TOR QUARRY   GR 560 733

Misnamed in the previous guide (and all the other guides come to
think of it. Dartmoor seems to have this affect on guide-book
writers. . . *Who's a clever little sod then? – Ed*) as King's Tor Quarry.
From the E→ entrance to Fogintor Quarry march due E→ (across a
shallow valley and up the neighbouring hillside) to gain the Upper
Quarry workings of Swell Tor. Contour the edge of the Quarry S ↓
to a narrow boggy defile leading into the Main Quarry. Alternatively the quarry can be entered via the Upper Quarry.

The quarry is again in the form of an amphitheatre (aren't they all!)
& the ←W-facing walls remain greasy in all but the driest conditions. The routes are described from R to L, beginning with a clean
wall in the narrow entrance defile.

1   Yer Tiz   30'   E3 5b   †
The RH side of this compact wall is defined by two vague, shallow
grooves. Boldly follow the first which trends up RWs, then climb
the second, which terminates at a projecting block. Skirt the LH
side of the block to finish.   (1992)

2   April Fool   30'   E4 6c   †
An exemplary piece of invented wall craft. Start 10' L of Yer Tiz.
Climb the wall direct (past 2BRs), with a desperate move to gain the
base of the borehole strike (an ascent, let alone a bolt-free ascent,
would seem to be in order).   (1/4/93)

*Directly opposite the entrance of the Main Quarry is the Three
Steps Buttress. Off to the R across a marshy bog is a larger, heavily
kaelonised face whose L edge is taken by the first route in the
Quarry proper (all the routes of the following wall could do with a
heavy dose of cleaning).*

3   Anarchist   80'   E2 5c   ★
Gain a sloping ledge L of the arête (3' off the ground). A series of
thin cracks lead diagonally RWs to a ledge at 40', where a step L
gains a small rib & PR. Finish direct.   (1981)

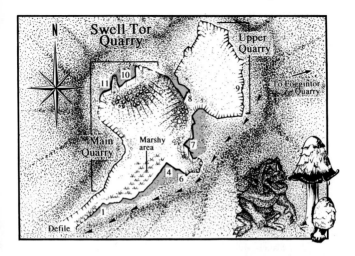

4 Monarchist 70' HVS 5a
Start just L of Anarchist. Climb the weakness which leads up LWs to a vegetated niche. Continue via the overgrown crackline from the top of the niche, passing a loose block after 20'. Follow the crack in its entirety.   (1981)

5 Republican 80' E2 5c
15' L of Monarchist are two diagonal borehole strikes. Climb the glacis to gain the first borehole. Boldly climb this to the second, before moving out R to a diagonal crack leading up LWs past 2PRs (missing presumed AWOL). A series of diminishing steps lead more easily to a mantelshelf finish.   (1985)

6 Tenterhooks 80' HS 4a   ★
Start at the base of a vague corner-line at the LH end of the wall. Climb this for 25' to a vegetated ledge, where a groove leads up R to a more substantial ledge. A series of exposed steps lead up RWs to finish (as for Republican).   (1967)

40' to the L of Tenterhooks there is a tree growing out of a ledge at right-angles. The next route starts behind this.

7 Oblomov 80' VS 4c
Take the cracks R of the tree to a small ledge & PR. Traverse LWs to an iron spike, then climb to another ledge & PR. Follow the short OHing corner above & move L via a ledge, to make a difficult mantel onto a grassy ledge leading to the top.   (1965)

L of Oblomov a series of ramps & ledges lead to the entrance of the

Upper Quarry. The next route climbs the crack just L of the sharp arête of a buttress guarding the LH side of the entrance.

8   Shear Crack   *(SC)*   25'   HVS 5b
A crack snakes from L/R up the buttress, then follows the arête from half-height. Gain & follow the crack in its entirety, with some hard moves to gain the niche & the ensuing arête.   (1992)

9   Sure Swell   30'   S 4a   †
Opposite *SC*, on the E→ side of the Upper Quarry, is another arête (between an OH & a vegetated face). Climb this direct.   (1988)

*Descending from the Upper Quarry back down into the Main Quarry, leads to a scree-slope beneath & some way to the R of the buttress of **TS**. This is gained by contouring the slope for 150' in a ←W direction until beneath the toe of the buttress.*

10   Three Steps *(TS)*   30'   HS 4b
Scramble up RWs from the LH side of the buttress for about 30', then make a long stride L to gain the foot of the slab. Deftly climb up the line of lichen-encrusted scoops to overcome a slight OH with difficulty. Belay well back on the R.   (1965)

11   Lime Street   40'   S
Further L of *TS* is a separate buttress stained by bird droppings. Start just L of the OH pierced by a borehole. Climb to the OH, then make a long stride RWs onto the face to gain a ledge. Continue by a series of mantelshelves, then move L to finish.   (1965)

GREAT AND LITTLE MIS TOR   GR 562 770

A quarter-of-a-mile further ←W of the car park for Fogginter there is another car park on the S↓ side of the road. The Tors are situated roughly a mile N↑ of this car park, and can be reached via a rough track. Although only a small venue, there is enough for an evening's sport. Both Tors lie within an MOD *live-round* firing range. Keep a weather eye open for a red flag flying from the top of Great Mis Tor, which means firing is in progress, and don't touch anything that looks remotely metallic.

LITTLE MIS TOR
A pleasant lump-ette residing 50' to the L of the track, after approximately fifteen minutes of powerful walking!

1   Hidebound   15'   VS
Climb the R arête of the large OH to the top.   (c.1990)

2   Piebald   20'   VS 4c
On the wall facing the radio mast (across the Moor at Princetown) is a flared crack in a bulge. Climb this, then follow a break RWs to gain a groove. Follow this to a rounded finish.   (c.1990)

3 Palomino 20' D
Follow Piebald to the crack, then finish up LWs. (1992)

The hanging rib beneath Palomino gives a boulder-problem of 6b.

4 Hacking 20' VS 4b
Climb the thin crack in a low wall (10' L of the boulder-problem) to
a broad ledge. Tackle the wall above near its RH edge, then finish
via a short flared groove. (1992)

5 Pony Trek 20' HS 4b
Start below the middle of the ←W face, opposite a large square
boulder 45yds to the L of Hacking. Climb the wall, using the RH
arête from time to time. (c.1990)

6 Pale Horse 20' HVS 5b
Climb the centre of the face (10' L of Pony Trek), via a crack at half
height. Finish with a tricky mantelshelf. (c.1990)

GREAT MIS TOR
Follow the track to where it divides in two, then take the LH track
which leads toward the main block of Great Mis Tor. Head toward
the LH side of the block topped by a flag pole, encountering a
hidden wall just before this is reached. The first route climbs the
groove on the RH side of the face.

*The block topped by the flag pole lies approximately 40' to the L.
Directly beneath this is a short wall split at half height by a low OH.
There are a number of boulder-problems ranging from 5b to 6a in
this area.*

7 Mistake 20' D
Climb the groove (containing two cracks) direct. (1992)

8 Remiss 20' HVS 5a
Climb the flake crack which finishes halfway up the RH arête of the
wall. From the top of the crack, finish via the bold wall on the LH
side of the arête. (1992)

9 Misadventure 20' E1 5b
A white streak runs the full length of the centre of the wall. Follow
the LH side of this direct. (1992)

10 Mistory 20' HS 4a
Climb LH side of the wall via the twin cracks. (1992)

VIXEN TOR GR 542 743

Approach and Access
This high quality venue lies just S ↓ of the A384, halfway between
Tavistock and Two Bridges. Cars can be left at a convenient car park
across the road from the Tor, which is a brisk half-mile walk away.

The rocks lie on private land and a walled enclosure surrounds them. **Please use the stile on the ←W side of the enclosure.**

Situation and Character
The first buttress to be seen (which is N ↑ facing) contains the wickedly OHing Torture and Two Way Stretch. To the L is a hidden wall of sheer granite (the East Face), tackled by a fearsome array of desperates such as Sly and Angel of Mercy. Walking to the end of this wall reveals a large savannah of slabland, (Feasibility Study). Returning to the base of Torture leads, via a ←W peregrination, to the top of the gully containing Solus (down-climbing the gully gives an arduous short cut to the base of the vast slab). Continuing ←W from the top of the gully leads beneath the toe of the West Face, to the start of the S-facing walls which begin with a low bouldering wall. Beyond lie the slab routes of Docker's Dilemma and Feasibility Study.

1   Torture   60'   E4 6a   ★★★
A magnificently brutal & intimidating line, that would have any 'new age' man running for his mother's apron strings. Climb the OHing groove awkwardly, then boldly step out R onto a steep slab & an all-too-brief respite before a taxing passage through the fearsomely OHing crack. Exquisite knee-barring on the lip proves to be the crux.   (1979)

The easiest descent is to down-climb the alarmingly polished chimney of **Ordinary Route** *(60' M), a torso-devouring fissure, the lair of which resides just to the R (or ←W) of Torture.*

2   Two Way Stretch   60'   E4 5c   ★★
As fearsome as its neighbour, & pure torture for dwarves whose rack-induced screams can be heard from the road! Follow Torture until a R\L trending line leads to a long reach L to a good shelf. Traverse this RWs, then pull over an OH to gain a standing position. Finish over the bulge above. *Friends* provide good, although hard-won protection.   (1985)

EAST FACE
Around the corner to the L is a rippled wall which sane people rightly dismissed as unclimbable. Sly climbs the RH side of this.

3   Sly   60'   E5 6a   ★★
A bold proposition. Climb the thin crack near the arête, then traverse awkwardly RWs & make a strenuous move to gain a diagonal ramp. Boldly gain the next break (crucial #2½ Friend), then make an awkward move out R to finish. Two sets of medium sized *Friends* are required.   (1987)

4   Angel of Mercy *(AOM)*   60'   E6 6b   ★★★
A thought-provoking route which is adequately protected, although you won't think so when you're on-route *(for the ground)*. Start just L of Sly, directly below a PR in the break at 15'.

Climb up to the break (bold), then make a series of hard moves to the next break (PR & *Rurp*). Continue to the OH & surmount this in line with the white streak above.   (1986)

5   Crunchy Toad *(CT)*   60'   E2 5c
Start 10' L of *AOM*. Climb the wall, via some horizontal breaks, to a rounded flake. Move slightly L & tackle the OH direct.   (1982)

6   Plektron   60'   E1 5b   ★★
Start beneath a L/R slanting gash. Climb this & continue diagonally RWs, then make a hard move to stand on a rounded flake. Move R slightly, then take the OH direct as for *CT* (or, traverse LWs to a glacis then scramble off).   (1969)

7   Radjel   50'   E4 6a   †
Start 15' L of Plektron at an obvious flake. Follow the flake to a bulge which is surmounted using a small undercut. A difficult traverse RWs along a break leads to a diagonal crack which is followed to the top.   (1993)

GULLY WALL
Returning to the base of Torture, a stroll ←W gains the apex of a boulder-choked gully (supposedly the setting for the demise of a witch called Vixana, who used to lure unsuspecting travellers to their deaths in the surrounding bogs. That is until one bright spark borrowed a ring from some pixies, which made him invisible, & pushed the poor dear off the top of the Tor). The ←W-facing wall of the gully plays host to a veritable glut of bulging wall and flake climbs, starting with:

8   Solus   45'   HVS 5b
Step onto the wall & climb past several bulging horizontal breaks. Move R to gain the base of, & then follow, a diagonal break leading to the final block. Finish up the obvious slanting ramp.   (1979)

9   Boris Yeltsin   40'   E4 6a   ★★ †
Start some 5yds R of Solus beneath two suspended flakes (the upper one being reminiscent of the flake on Five Finger Exercise at Cratcliffe Tor). Gain & follow these to the top.   (1991)

10   Old Men   45'   HVS 5b
R again is a perched block in the bed of the gully, beneath which the ground drops away dramatically. Stagger up the prominent line of flakes above the perched block.   (1986)

11   Vendetta   65'   E2 5c   ★
A route with instant exposure. Start atop the perched block at the foot of Old Men. Traverse RWs along the the obvious horizontal line to the rounded arête. Make a hard move round this, then climb the wall above to the top.   (1987)

12   Vixana   40'   E4 6a
Start beneath the perched block, below a steep wall leading to a

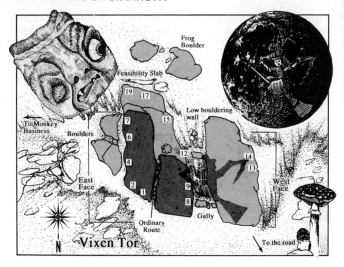

Vixen Tor

staggered crack. Gain the crack, which is followed to the horizontal break of Vendetta. Ascend the bulging wall above direct, via two obvious small pockets, to the next break. The ensuing rounded holds lead unnervingly to the top. (1989)

Either descend the gully to the foot of Commando Crack & the attendant slab routes to its R; or meander ←W from the top of the gully to the West Face.

WEST FACE
The West Face is distinguished by a strident L/R slanting crack.

13 The Fox 30′ HVS 5a
Start some 10yds L of the blunt arête of the low bouldering wall, just R of a wide crack bounding the LH side of the wall. Climb the wall & step L into the crack. Follow it to where it becomes vegetated, then finish RWs. (1979)

14 Bronco Dilator 30′ E2 5c
Start 5′ R of The Fox, below a R\L slanting crack. Climb up to this then follow it. Finish direct through the bulges above. (1986)

The wall drops off in height to the R, terminating in a blunt arête which heralds the onset of a steep, low bouldering wall.

FEASIBILITY SLAB
Further E→ of the low bouldering wall the field of action broadens to encompass not only the desert-like expanse of Feasibility's slab, but also a gawky array of modernist boulders, which provide a feast

of high quality problems. The following two routes emanate from the dark confines of a chimney at the foot of the gully (containing Solus et al) which emerges L of the slab:

15   Commando Crack *(CC)*   90′   VS 4c,4c
A veritable assault course for any latent warmonger, starting with a prodigious off-body-width affair.
1   50′   Enter the chimney to the L of the slab & follow this strenuously to the grass terrace above.
2   40′   Climb the OH, then follow the crack above to bulges which are swarmed over to finish.   (1959)

16   Eureka   90′   E4 6b   ★
A route of delicacy, derived from the brutal depths of *CC*'s fissure. Thrash up the chimney of *CC* to gain a thin crack running out RWs to the arête. Follow the crack to gain the main face of the slab, just above an OH. Climb to the main horizontal break & traverse RWs to the centre of the face. Finish as for *DD*.   (1986)

The centre of the slab is vaguely highlighted by a bald, pale streak that roughly delineates:

17   Docker's Dilemma *(DD)*   110′   E5 6a   ★★★
Tastily bold climbing up the faint pale streak, just L of the slab's centre. Initially carefree climbing leads to a horizontal break, where the angle steepens. From a standing position in the break, pensively work up the 'braille'-covered wall to another horizontal break. Fine climbing up the wall above leads to a wide break. Surmount the awkward OH & bulge above, to finish direct.   (1980)

18   Enigma   90′   E2 6b
A safe eliminate which is squeezed between *DD* & *FS*. Climb the slab between the two routes to a short diagonal crack. Follow this up to the horizontal break, then step R & finish up the wall above the initial crack of *FS*.   (1987)

19   Feasibility Study *(FS)*   120′   E3 5b,6a   ★★
A testing & thoroughly enjoyable excursion up the finest slab on the Moor.
1   90′   Follow *GB* to the break above the flared crack, then traverse this LWs with difficulty. Step up beneath the slight bulge, to gain a rounded flake at its end. Climb this awkwardly to reach the grassy bay & tree belay of Babylon.
2   30′   Traverse RWs along a wide fault for 10′, then pull over the OH to another more vexing bulge (dubious TR), & make a series of tenuous moves directly over this to better crystals leading to the top (in common with *DD*). Finishing up pitch 2 of *CC* reduces the grade to a more amenable E2.   (1978)

20   Green Beret *(GB)*   100′   HVS 5a,4c
An exposed outing which covers some intimidating terrain for the grade. Start beneath a flared crack in the R edge of the slab.

1   60′   Move up the initial slab to a horizontal break, then bear R to the base of the crack. Awkwardly gain this & follow it to a second break, then move R & climb the easy-angled rock above.

2   40′   Climb the R arête of the main block (also the L arête of the East Face), via a boulder problem start.   (1958/79)

21   Thrutch   160′   E4 5a,6a,5c   ★
A pumpy girdle of the Plektron wall. Popeye's forearms would prove very useful.

1   60′   Climb the initial pitch of *GB*.

2   50′   Start up pitch 2 of *GB*, then cross Plektron at its wide, vertical crack.

3   50′   Continue RWs along the next break, past the 2PRs on *AOM*, to a desperate finish up Sly.   (1987)

22   Babylon   100′   VD
There is little to recommend this route, apart from the flora that decorates its entire length (budding botanists will have a field day). Start just R of *GB*.

1   35′   Climb the corner to a ledge, then move L into a chimney which leads to easy ground R of the top part of the face.

2   25′   Follow a stomach-traverse LWs, between the top of the Feasibility Slab & the steep wall above, to gain a grassy bay. Tree belay beneath a chimney.

3   40′   The undercut chimney at the back of the bay.   (c.1950s)

The following two routes lie on a small steep buttress amidst some trees, roughly 50yds R of the Feasibility Study slab.

23   Monkey Business   25′   E3 6a   ★ †
A powerful route which follows a crackline over the LH side of an OH on the front face of the buttress.   (1993)

24   Down the Welly   25′   E5 6c   ★ †
A short but power-packed testpiece. Climb the well protected vague weakness which weaves over the centre of the OH.   (1994)

DEWERSTONE AREA

Situated NE↗ of Plymouth (an ineffable conurbation of concrete and naval prowess) lie perhaps some of the more discreet Moorland Tors, and the major edifice of The Dewerstone.

The tors around Burrator Reservoir play host to a seemingly infinite number of granite bouldering possibilities, while Sheeps Tor has an outlook and friendly disposition second to none. On the other hand, The Dewerstone inhabits a heavily wooded valley (containing the River Plym), which provides a magical, Tolkienesque backdrop to the finest middle-grade climbing on Dartmoor.

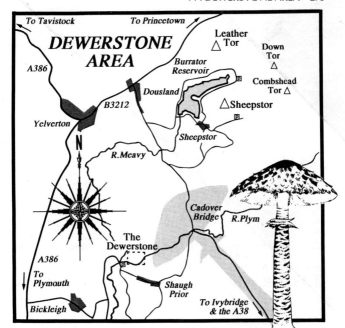

However, even this far flung corner of the Moor has its fair share of devastation wrought by no less a colossus of ghoulishness than the cloven-hoofed and be-horned hunstman, Dewer (an erstwhile Devonian name for the Devil 'imself). Tales abound of his penchant for hounding unbaptized souls. Of course (with material like this to work with) there will always be a classic piece of god-fearing apocrypha knocking about, and it just so happens that. . . an ageing farmer was strolling homewards through the valley late at night somewhat the worse for wear, when he met up with the demon huntsman. Not realising who he was the farmer *(who must have been blind!!!)* asked him what he had caught that day. With a malevolent cackle the huntsman handed over his game bag telling the tired old man to keep it. The farmer stumbled off under the weight of the bag, dreaming of the succulent wildfowl it contained. He called to his wife when he arrived at the cottage "come see what I got for supper". The mother arrived just in time to see her husband unwrap the ruined corpse of their own son.

LEATHER TOR
GR 563 700

Although a minor tor, it does possess a few routes of some worth. It is approached from the Yelverton to Princetown road (B3212), and lies immediately N ↑ of Burrator Reservoir. The routes are on the E→ face, and tend to be greasy in all but the driest conditions. To the L of the main face is a small wall which leads to a subsidiary summit (two VDs take the obvious lines on this).

1   Ivy Bend   25'   VD
Start at the LH end of the main wall below an obvious open groove. Climb this to the top.   (c.1950s)

2   Dies Irae   40'   VS 4c
Start 10' L of the lowest part of the face. Climb direct to an OH which is overcome via a strenuous OHing crack.   (c.1950s)

3   Vae Victus   40'   S
Climb the groove R of Dies Irae. Finish up the arête.   (c.1950s)

4   Troglodyte   30'   S
On the RH side of the face is a small cave. Climb the LH side of this, then move RWs above it to finish up a groove.   (c.1950s)

SHEEPS TOR
GR 565 682

A superbly situated crag that compensates for its lack of height with excellent rock and eminently worthwhile routes for the lower and

middle grade climber. It is approached via the village of Sheepstor, above which another road (signposted The Kennels) leads to within a few hundred yards of the Tor itself. The routes lie on the E→ face. On approaching that face from the road the most obvious formation is the triangular feature of Slab Route. There are three prominent cracks to the L of this, the furthest L being:

1 Play Crack 20′ D
Climb the short crack just R of where the wall peters out, then gain the large L/R diagonal break. Follow the short continuation crack above to some good block belays. (c.1930s)

2 Worker's Wall *(WW)* 35′ HS 4a
Follow the large crack R of Play Crack to gain the diagonal break. Step R & struggle up the wider crack to finish. (c.1930s)

3 Fingerin' 35′ HVS 5b
This climbs the wall immediately R of *WW*, via eliminate-style climbing up blind cracks to gain the diagonal break. Follow this RWs to a crack which leads to the top. (c.1970s)

4 Crack & Chimney 35′ S ★
Start 5′ R of *WW* beneath a curving flake/crack. Follow this to the break, then finish up the fissure above. (c.1930s)

5 Wind Wall 35′ HVS 5a ★★
The finger-jamming crack hanging above the triangular slab. Start 5′ L of the slab. Climb a thin crack, then step R to gain the

finger-jamming crack. Follow this to the diagonal break, then finish up the rounded continuation crack above. (c.1970s)

6   Slab Route   30'   D
Climb the centre of the triangular slab (at right-angles to Wind Wall) in its entirety. (c.1930s)

7   Slanting Crack *(SC)*   25'   S
Climb the crack in the slim wall R of Slab Route. (c.1930s)

8   Mushroom Wall *(MW)*   30'   VS 4c   **
Climb up the steep wall between *SC* & the arête. (c.1954)

The rounded arête provides a bold extended boulderproblem of 5c, if you can stick to it.

9   Omega Crack *(OC)*   30'   VD
Climb the wide crack just R of the rounded arête. (c.1930s)

10   Burdock   30'   HS 4a
Follow the thin crack R of *OC* until beneath an OH. Climb through this, via the continuation crack, to finish. (c.1930s)

11   Overhang Crack   30'   S 4a
Climb the crack & OH just R of Burdock. (c.1930s)

12   Dandelion   30'   S 4a
The last in the trilogy of roof cracks. (c.1930s)

13   Barking Crack *(BC)*   30'   VD
R of Dandelion is a wide corner crack, bounded on the R by a sharp arête. Climb the crack in its entirety. (c.1930s)

14   Sheltered Arête *(SA)*   30'   E1 5b   *
The sharp arête provides a fine, but unprotected route. (c.1970s)

15   Sheltered Wall *(SW)*   30'   E1 5c
Thin face climbing up the smooth wall R of *SA*. Using the arête, or the crack on the R, drops the grade to 5b. (c.1970s)

16   Sheltered Crack   30'   VD
Climb the R-bounding crack of the smooth wall. (c.1930s)

The broken wall to the R contains a number of generally lineless VDs, with the exception of two 5a problems that follow blind, rounded cracks to the R of a projecting block.

17   Girdle Traverse   100'   VS 4c
A L-to-R traverse of the wall. Follow Play Crack for 15', then make a slightly rising traverse RWs to the base of Wind Wall's finger-jamming crack. Step R to gain Slab Route at half-height. Traverse across *MW*, via a horizontal crack, to join *OC* which is followed for a few feet to a ledge running RWs beneath the OHs. Cross the top of *BC* to the obvious break across the top of *SW*, then descend slightly RWs to follow a line of holds just below the top of the lower walls to the R. (c.1960s)

THE DEWERSTONE   GR 539 638

Approach and Access
From the A38, the best approach is via Ivybridge to Cornwood, then follow signs for Shaugh Prior. The car park is on the R, just before the humpbacked bridge that crosses the River Plym. From Plymouth it's best to turn R off the A386 at Roborough (signposted Bickleigh/Shaugh Prior). Just over a mile past Bickleigh, you cross over the River Plym via the humpbacked bridge and park on the L.

From the car park a wooden footbridge leads to a path which contours the hillside, above the LH bank of the River Plym, to the base of the rocks (roughly half-a-mile). The land is owned by the National Trust, who are seriously concerned with the level of erosion. It is probably fair to say that the dustbowl at the foot of Devil's Rock is an ecological disaster, and in the light of this it is imperative that visitors use the dedicated approach path, **remove all** their **litter**, and refrain from overtly disturbing the local environment.

Situation and Character
The main area of the crag is unmistakable, with the 150′ perpendicular face of Devil's Rock rising majestically from the very banks of the Plym itself. To the R of this (hidden in the trees) lie the more isolated buttresses of the Needle, and further R, those of Upper and Lower Raven. These are clearly visible when viewed from the summit of Devil's Rock. The rock is composed of highly weathered granite, encrusted with chicken-heads, large feldspar crystals, and rounded flakes, ribs and OHs.

THE WESTERN ROCKS

These encompass the isolated pinnacle of The Tooth, and the rambling buttresses that go to make up The Tower and Penny Bay. As the name suggests, they form the most ←W extent of The Dewerstone, and are the first buttresses to be encountered on the approach path (barring The Tooth, which involves a minor detour away from the main crag).

THE TOOTH
This sits beside the main footpath, roughly 100yds after the path bends back upon itself, and about 300yds past the approach path which leads to the main area. The route climbs the wall opposite the Tooth.

1   Bruised Heels   25′   E1 5b
A short slab leads up to a thin R\L slanting crack, which is followed to gain the R arête of a groove. Follow this to finish just L of a mini flying arête.   (1987)

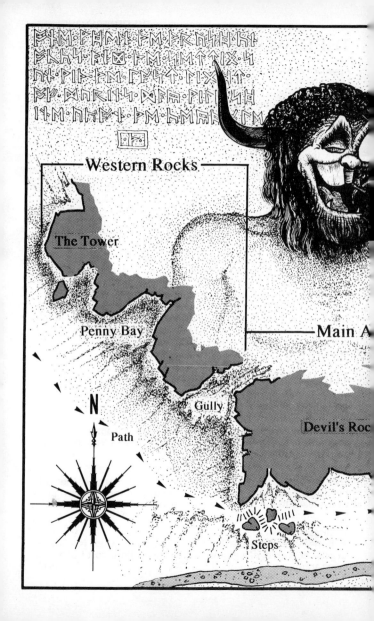

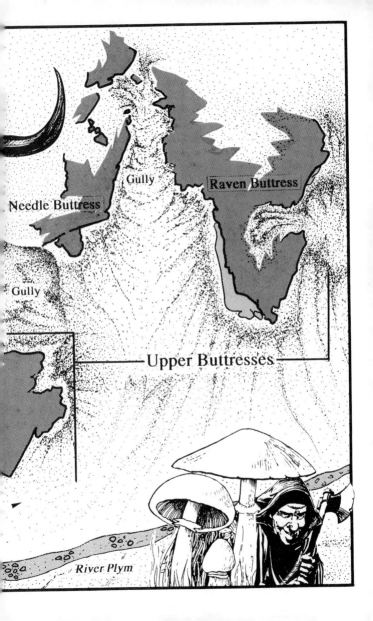

Needle Buttress

Gully

Raven Buttress

Gully

Upper Buttresses

River Plym

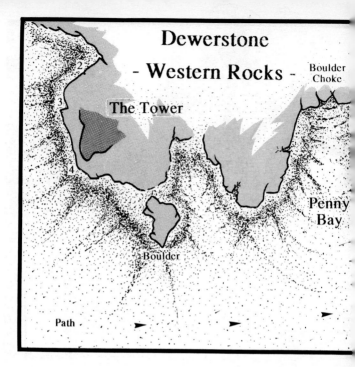

Dewerstone

- Western Rocks -

The Tower

Boulder Choke

Penny Bay

Boulder

Path

THE TOWER
The first buttress (of any consequence) to be seen through the trees above the approach path is The Tower. Its foremost face is characterised by an amazing suspended flake that OHs a narrow slab, and hides a chimney that worms through the bowels of the buttress (Window Slit). The easiest ascent/descent is by climbing the slanting slab on the LH side of the front face, **Tower Stairs** 50′ M. The following route begins in a bay at the back of the buttress.

2 Window Pane   30′   VS 4c
Climb the thin dog-leg crack in a wall tucked behind & L of a prominent groove/crackline on the L wall of the buttress. Using a foot on the gully wall reduces the grade.   (1986)

3 Tower Crack   30′   HS 4b   ★★
A fine jamming exercise (encompassing most aspects of the art). Climb the obvious groove/crackline (on the L face) until it ends, then exit LWs with difficulty.   (c.1950s)

4 Windowsill   40′   S   ★
A fearsome prospect at any grade. Gain & then climb the broad R\L

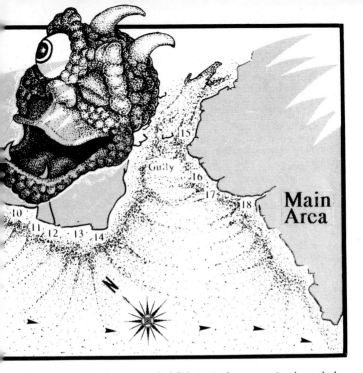

Main Area

cleft (created by the suspended flake), via the conveniently angled tree trunk. Resisting the constant urge to slip out sideways proves both tiring & irksome. (1958)

5 Window Slit 60' VD
For troglodytes & general deviants only. Start at the foot of the slanting slab of Tower Stairs. Climb the slab to gain a narrow cleft. Squirm up this, via an excruciating climax through a constricted hole, to pop-out onto an arête which leads to the top. *Lunatics descend the route headfirst!* (c.1950s)

PENNY BAY
This is a three sided bay of rock 20yds R of The Tower. The back of the bay is a boulder choke, through which a hole runs upwards under an OHing block. This is named, rather unfortunately, The Admiral's Hole. The Chimney outside of this is climbed by **Circle Climb** S 4a.

6 Wobbling Wall *(WW)* 45' E2 5b
An exhausting exercise with hard won protection. Climb the rounded breaks, on the R wall of the bay, to gain a black quartz

vein. Follow this to the bulge above, then undercling LWs to a strenuous exit up the groove in the OH. (1979)

7 Twittering Crack 40' HVS 5a
This is the prominent crack R of *WW*, & L of the obvious niche. It is a lot harder than appearances suggest. Climb the crack, then step out R to the arête & finish via the slab. (c.1960s)

8 Saint's Niche *(SN)* 40' HS 4a
Short & sharp. Climb into the obvious niche & jam up this until it is possible to move R to join *AD* to finish. (1950)

9 Agag's Direct *(AD)* 40' S 4a
Climb the LH side of the slab (R of *SN*), past several tricky mantels, to finish over a testy bulge at the top. (c.1950s)

10 Agag's Slab 40' D
Start in the centre of the slab to the R of *AD*. Move up diagonally LWs, then back RWs to a tree. Trend up LWs to finish. (1950)

*R of **AD** is a mossy slab, & R again is another slab dominated at two-thirds height by a long shallow OH.*

11 Noddy 45' VS 4b
Climb over the initial bulge of the mossy slab, then make some difficult moves up the rib which leads to easier angled rock. Scramble over this to finish. (1980)

12 Goblin 50' VS 4c
Climb the slight depression in the centre of the clean slab (R of Noddy) to the long OH. Traverse LWs for 10' using holds above the OH, then step up L to finish via the upper slab (finishing direct over the OH bumps the grade up to 5a). (1969)

13 Mambo Slab *(MS)* 40' VD
Follow Goblin to the long OH. Traverse RWs onto a tree stump in a corner, then follow the corner to finish. (c.1960s)

14 Caesar's Nose *(CN)* 40' S
Climb the RH side of the slab until it is possible to step R onto the hanging rib. Continue up this to join & then follow a L/R diagonal crack which leads to the top. (c.1950s)

THE MAIN AREA

Roughly 20yds R of *CN* is a short chimney (Pinnacle Chimney), flanked on the L by a 40' wall with a holly tree at half-height, and on the R by two blocky towers which are separated by the rake of Mucky Gully. The two towers are Pinnacle Buttress and Colonel's Arête. R again is the broad, vegetated breach of Main Gully.

15 Hagar the Horrible 35' E3 5c ★
Level with, & 20yds R of the top of *CN* is a short wall with an OH at 20'. Climb the wall to the OH & overcome this at its widest point to

reach a R\L slanting crack. Follow this to the top.   (1986)

16   Holly Tree Wall *(HTW)*   40'   D
Start just to the L of *PC*. Climb the slabby wall which leads to the
holly tree. Move around (or through) this, then climb a chimney on
the R to the top.   (c.1950s)

17   Holly Tree Wall Direct   35'   HVS 5a
Take a direct line to the tree of *HTW*, then climb the nasty wide
crack above with difficulty.   (c.1960s)
Variation E1 5b Known as **Rufty Tufty**. Foot-traverse the L limb of the
tree to gain & follow a flared crack to the top.   (c.1990s)

18   Pinnacle Chimney *(PC)*   40'   VD
A pleasant pitch which climbs the short chimney to the pinnacle,
then the steep LH wall to the top.   (1949)

18a   Troy   40'   HVS 4c   †
R of *PC* the side of the pinnacle forms a narrow wall. Climb this to a
layback up the RH side of the pinnacle. Finish as for PC.   (1994)

19   Pinnacle Buttress *(PB)*   120'   D   ★
A good introductory climb, escapable throughout, but with a finely
positioned last pitch. Start below a chimney at the foot of the
buttress.
1   40'   Struggle up the chimney, then scramble to block belays.
2   20'   Climb up just R of the arête to a large ledge on the L.
3   30'   Step off a wobbly block to gain, then climb an exposed wall
to a ledge below the pinnacle.
4   30'   Move R above an OH, then move up to a small ledge on
the arête of the pinnacle & follow this to the summit. Either jump or
climb across onto the final wall.   (1949)
Variation 4a 30' HS 4a Move R below the OH, then tackle this at its
widest point to join the original route on the arête.   (c.1950s)

20   Pinnacle Buttress Direct   110'   HS 4a,4a
A series of variants on the parent route giving good climbing. Start
L of the tree beneath the block at the foot of the buttress.
1   85'   Climb the face of the block, then move round the R arête.
Scramble up to some rock steps which lead to a steep crack. Climb
this, with difficulty, to a wide ledge.
2   25'   Follow the crack (above the ledge) to the top of the pinnacle, then jump across the gap to gain & finish up the short wall
beyond.
Variation 2a 25' Move out L from the ledge & climb to another
ledge, from which the summit block is easily reached.   (c.1960s)

21   Mucky Gully *(MG)*   110'   D   ★
This route seems to have tidied its act up a bit. It climbs the
groove/gully between *PB* & *CA*.
1   40'   Follow the corner of the gully, or the R wall, to a N&TB
beside a flake on a narrow ledge.

2   70'   Continue up the gully to a large chockstone. Climb over this, then continue up the RH wall to finish.   (1894)

22   Reverse Cleft   120'   S -,4a,-
A good exposed crack climb. Start at the foot of *MG*.
1   40'   As for *MG* to its N&TB on the narrow ledge.
2   50'   Move up to a prominent crack on the R & follow this (with difficulty) to a tree belay.
3   30'   Climb the front face of the summit block, then hop across the gap behind it to gain the top.   (1949)

23   Colonel's Arête *(CA)*   130'   VD   ★★
A good climb. Start below an earthy wall just L of Main Gully.
1   30'   Climb the earthy wall & scramble to a belay beneath a crack.
2   25'   Move L, then gain a ledge on the arête. Follow the arête to a large ledge.
3   45'   Climb up past a tree to the foot of a short crack. Climb this, moving R at the top. Climb over a rocking stone on the arête to gain a tree belay.
4   30'   As for Reverse Cleft *(pitch 3)*.   (1948)

24   Colonel's Cavort   125'   HS -,4a,-
A series of variations on *CA*. Start beneath a wide crack formed by a detached block R of the foot of *MG*.
1   50'   Climb the crack, then traverse RWs to the ledge above pitch 2 of *CA*.
2   45'   Climb up just L of the arête to a ledge. Climb the yummy off-width above to a ledge & belay.
3   30'   As for Reverse Cleft *(pitch 3)*.   (c.1960s)

25   The High Traverse   45'   VD
The traversing this short pitch contains is worth the effort (best done as a continuation to *CA*). Traverse RWs from the stance below pitch 4 of *CA* to reach a ledge OHung by an imposing black wall topped by a roof. Step R & climb a short groove, then traverse delicately RWs until clear of the OH. Climb direct to a tree, then scramble to the top.   (1949)

MAIN GULLY
This is the wide forested gully which is almost totally overgrown. Care should be taken in the middle section of the gully due to loose rock and (when wet) dangerous muddy slopes. The L wall gives a few short routes which are in the process of revegetating.

26   Dark Cleft   40'   VD
Start three-quarters of the way up the gully below a large chimney in the L wall. Halfway up the chimney deviate RWs, move up, then step back L into the chimney to finish.   (c.1950s)

27   The Echo   45'   HVS 5a
This has totally overgrown with slime & moss. The route would

need a damn good clean before you could even think about climbing it. Start beneath a finger-crack (which has totally disappeared!) to the L of Dark Cleft. Climb this to a ledge, then layback an edge on the R to the top.   (1977)

28 Kernow 40′ S
Start R of the large chimney of Dark Cleft, below a deceptively easy-looking wall. Climb this to an OH, then move L & make a difficult move over it to finish.   (c.1960s)

29 If I Should Fall. . . *(ISF)* 40′ E3 5c
Start up & R of Kernow, atop a pointed block 10′ L of a dead tree. Hand-traverse RWs to gain a standing position on a horizontal fang of rock, then climb the OHing arête above to finish.   (1992)

30 Sayonara 40′ HVS 5a
Start atop the pointed block, then climb up the wall L of *ISF*. Follow the arête to finish.   (1992)

A recent rockfall has left the following route in a diabolical state:

31 The Tunnel 25′ D
Start near the top of the gully, beneath a large projecting block. Climb over this to enter the fissure behind. Emerge from the bowels of the cliff 15′ higher & severely chastened.   (1949)

DEVIL'S ROCK
Gorged (almost to bursting) with middle grade gems, this is the premier arena of the crag. The large rambling terrace forming the top LH section of Devil's Rock is known as The Meadow, while the most obvious feature on the LH side of the main wall is the clean-cut corner of Central Groove. To the R of this is an OH & steep headwall taken by Gideon, while the obvious fist-jamming crack is taken by Climbers Club Direct (which joins the Ordinary route at an OHing niche).

32 Wrath of Grapes *(WG)* 165′ E3 5c,5b
1 50′   Climb the arête L of the start of Vineyard, moving L to gain some undercuts on the wall. Continue directly up the wall to a ledge & belay.
2 55′   As for Vineyard *(pitch 2)*.
3 60′   Climb the groove for a few feet, then traverse RWs onto a wall, via tourmaline holds. Continue direct up the wall to finish up the black flakes in the OH of *IH*.   (1988)
Variation 1a 50′ E3 6a Known as the **The Grapevine**. Climb direct up the wall to join *WG* at the undercuts.   (c.1980s)

33 Vineyard 165′ VS 4a,4b,-
R of Main Gully is a clean wall bound on the R by a large block. Start just L of this.
1 50′   Climb the steep wall using the obvious cracks to gain a niche at half-height, then follow a crack to a tree belay (the LH groove can also be climbed to reach the same point).

2   60′   Make a rising traverse LWs along a sloping ledge to an earthy groove. Follow this & a short slab to a tree belay in The Meadow.

3   55′   Climb the short layback crack (on the L) to join High Traverse, then climb up to the large black OH & traverse RWs under this to finish up a short groove past a tree.   (1952)

The OHing black wall & roof above pitch 3 of Vineyard is breached by:

34   Inkspots Hangover *(IH)*   40′   HVS 5b   ★
Hard for the grade. The best approach is to follow Vineyard, or bag two for one & do *WG*. Start below the LH end of the OH. Climb the flake in the wall which leads to the OH. Traverse RWs until it is possible to gain (& flail up) a series of black flakes leading to a rounded groove on the lip; finish up this.   (1962)

35   Pinkspots Headache   40′   E1 5b
An even harder version of the above. Follow *IH* to the OH, but breach it to the L of the black flakes, *bon chance*.   (1985)

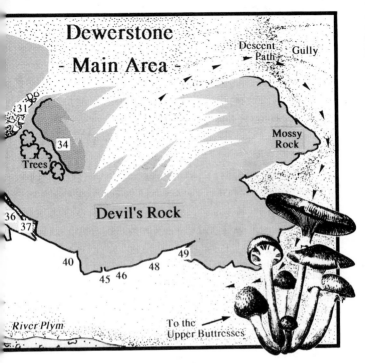

36 Cretin's Cavort *(C'SC)* 60' HVS 5a
. . .has been shortened from the original 3 pitches to 1. Start atop the large block (at the foot of the wall) to the R of Vineyard. Climb the steep wall just L of the arête on widely-spaced holds to a tree belay (protection is hard won). (1962)

37 Leviathan 75' VS 4c ★★★
Superb climbing up the groove in the blunt arête R of Vineyard. Gain the top of the large block beneath the groove, then follow this to where it fades. Move up R to a bulge, then traverse RWs to gain & climb up the arête to finish on the ledge above; tree belay (abseil off). Taking the bulge direct provides a dirty HVS 5a. (1957)

38 Extendable Arms 155' E1 5c,5b ★
A steep eliminate line between Leviathan & Vala. The second pitch climbs the large bulge R of The Meadow.
1 75' From the base of Leviathan swing onto its RH arête & follow this to a ledge. Continue over a small OH to gain the LH end of another OH, then follow the arête to a tree belay.
2 80' Move R, then climb broken rock above the corner of *CG*,

until beneath an OH. Climb the hanging wall above this to gain a crack, which leads easily to the top.   (1979)

39   Vala   160'   HVS 5a,4a,5b   ⋆
Exhilarating climbing for the grade. It climbs the stepped OH to the L of CG. Start as for that route.
1   75'   Climb to the bollard of *CG*, then layback onto the steep wall beneath the OH. A long reach over this leads to increasingly large holds until the tree belay is attained.
2   60'   Walk up LWs (passing behind a flake) until beneath a small OH. Climb this to gain The Meadow, then walk up RWs to a tree belay (to the L of pitch 2 of *CG*).
3   25'   Step down L & climb an OH between two chimneys, then finish up a slab (this pitch is rarely repeated).   (1963)

The wall between Vala & **CG** *has been climbed at a very eliminate E1 5c (known as* **Return from the Kurds***).*

40   Central Groove *(CG)*   160'   HS 4b,4b   ⋆⋆⋆
One of the best routes of its grade in the country. It takes the magnificent corner on the LH side of Devil's Rock.
1   80'   Climb the wall to the foot of the groove/corner. Follow this on generous holds to the capping OH, then traverse RWs on black plate-like flakes to an airy stance on the arête.
2   80'   Climb the short wall above to gain a ramp. Follow this diagonally RWs to a wide ledge (optional stance). Finish up the obvious hanging corner above the ledge, via laybacking & secure fingerlocks (good block belays).   (1949)
Variation 2a 80' HS 4b Worthwhile. After traversing the ramp climb up to, & then around a bulge L of the hanging corner. Continue up a crack to reach the top.   (c.1980s)

41   Scimitar   170'   E1 5b,4b   ⋆
Steel fingers & a cool head are *de rigueur*. After skirting the large OH it rushes up the R wall of *CG*.
1   90'   Start at the foot of the short wall beneath *CG*. Climb this to step R onto a slab leading to the OH. Traverse LWs under this (past a PR) until a desperate layback gains the bald wall beyond. Climb this direct to the airy stance atop the arête.
2   80'   As for Central Groove *(pitch 2)*.   (1968)

42   Scimitar Direct   90'   E1 5b   ⋆⋆
Follow Scimitar to the base of the slab, then climb the thin crack which leads direct to the LH end of the OH. Pull up past the OH, step R to the arête, then continue up this (PR) for a magnificently airy runout. Finish as for Scimitar.   (c.1980s)

43   Fruitflancase   155'   E1 5a,4c,5a   ⋆⋆
A fine pitch that tackles the LH jamming crack in the headwall above the OH (R of *CG*).
1   85'   Follow Scimitar to the top of the slab below the OH, from where awkward moves lead up RWs to gain the base of the crack.

Pete Bull on Toltec Twostep (E5 6b), Photo. Nick White

Ken Robinson on Wind Wall (HVS 5a) Photo. Nick White

Follow this in conjunction with the crack on the L to a small bulge. Belay on a ledge above this (on its LH side).

2   70′   Trend up LWs over broken rock to a short rounded crack. Climb this to gain a ramp which leads to the base of the final corner of *CG*. Step L, then climb the rounded crack in the OHing wall. Finish up the slab above.   (1969)

44   Gideon   155′   E1 5b,5a   ★★
A good route for budding extreme leaders to cut their teeth upon *(remember that he or she who hesitates on the crux is lost!)*.

1   85′   Follow Scimitar to the OH. Move around this, then step R to gain the RH crack (above a spike). Climb the shallow groove above to good jugs. Continue more easily to a ledge (bollard belay).

2   70′   Climb the narrow crack above the belay to the wide ledge below the final corner of *CG*. Finish up the corner.   (1962/69)

45   Energy Crisis *(EC)*   80′   E4 6a
A hard problem taking the OH & thin crack in the R edge of Scimitar's slab (in need of a good clean). Climb to the OH, then overcome this direct (using a fang-like flake on the lip) to gain & follow the thin crack & arête. Finish up Gideon.   (1978)

46   Climbers' Club Direct *(CCD)*   160′   HVS 5a,4c   ★★★
A stunner. It takes the bull by the horns, & follows the crackline that soars direct up the guts of the crag. Start 20′ R of *CG*.

1   70′   Climb to the small OH split by a wide crack. After hard moves to enter the crack, follow it to an OHing niche. From the top of this, step out L using holds above the bulge, to gain the bollard belay of Gideon.

2   90′   Climb the obvious V-groove to the capping OH (overcome by bridging) to gain a crack leading to a spacious niche. Step L & follow the steep continuation crack to the top.   (1936)

47   Climbers' Club Super Direct *(CCS)*   40′   E1 5b
Usually damp (graded for dry conditions). Climb the appealing, although desperate line of thin discontinuous cracks in the wall R of *CCD*. The object is to get to the hanging flake without falling off. Belay in the niche of *CCD*.   (1957)

48   Ultimate Eliminate   150′   E2 5c,5b
1   85′   Follow *CCSD* then gain & climb the R arête of Gideon. Follow this to its belay.

2   65′   Climb diagonally RWs to reach a large flake R of *CCO* (on the skyline of the buttress when viewed from the belay), & layback this to finish up the arête of the buttress.   (1986)

49   Piglet Wall   40′   E5 6b   ★
A test piece, being both technical & on the bold side for the grade. Start 10′ R of *CCSD*, & just L of a shallow arch. Climb the wall trending RWs to a lunge for a flat edge at the base of a shallow black groove. Mantel onto the flat edge, then continue up the

groove (bold). Belay on the traverse of *CCO*.   (1985/91)

50   Climbers' Club Ordinary *(CCO)*   170'   VS 4b,4a,4b   ★★
Start in an earthy gully R of the shallow arch.
1   75'   Climb up to gain a line of footholds leading out diagonally LWs to a flake. Traverse LWs under an OH into a large niche. Move up the groove, then swing R into a smaller groove which leads to the bollard belay of Gideon on the L.
2   70'   Climb the obvious V-groove to the OH. Move R & up, then back L to gain the continuation crack which leads to a shallow niche. Traverse LWs on good holds to reach the wide ledge below the final corner of *CG*.
3   25'   Finish up the final corner of *CG*.   (1935)

51   Globe & Laurel   145'   HVS 4c,5a
As well as being disjointed, it is in dire need of more traffic. It climbs the rounded cracks to the R of *CCO*. Start in the niche just L of the earthy gully.
1   80'   Climb out of the niche RWs to cross *CCO*. Traverse RWs below the OH, then move up to turn the OH by a long stride L to a good foothold. Swing L & climb a short groove, then continue LWs to the bollard belay of Gideon. (It is possible to climb straight over the OH above the large flake at a slightly harder grade).
2   65'   From the ledge below the bollard, tiptoe RWs into a groove & layback up this to a ledge on the R. Move up to easier rock which leads to pitch 4 of Route B. Finish up this.   (1959)

52   Bee Line   100'   HVS 4b,5a
A filler-in of little merit. Start as for *CCO*.
1   50'   Climb the earthy wide crack (above the start of *CCO*) to gain the second stance of Route B.
2   50'   Step L, then follow the cracks in the rounded arête until level with the top of the chimney on the R. Traverse LWs to a ledge on the main face. Easier climbing leads to the ledge below pitch 4 of Route B. There are numerous ways of finishing (take your pick. . . & *maybe a shovel*).   (1965)

53   Route B   150'   HVD   ★
A scrappy start leads to a fine, exposed final pitch. Start R of the earthy gully, beneath the centre of a large block.
1   30'   Climb over a bulge & move LWs (beneath an OH) into a short groove, then follow this to the top of the block.
2   25'   Climb over some blocks to a tree (belay).
3   45'   Move L along a ledge, then climb a shallow chimney to exit RWs. Climb the wall above to a large ledge. Belay on its RH side.
4   50'   Traverse LWs along the ledge, then move on to the main face. Climb a short groove, moving R at an OHing nose of rock, then go up & LWs above the nose to finish.   (1949)
Variation 1a 40' HS 4b Climb over the bulge, then move R beneath the OH to climb a short groove.   (c.1950s)
Variation 4a 50' Climb the flake behind the belay, then move L to

join the parent route on the OHing nose.   (c. 1950s)

54 Knucklecracker 100' HS 4a,4a
A game of hide-&-seek in the trees R of Route B yields an unpromising buttress. Start just L of a crack, below a mossy groove on the extreme RH side of the buttress.
1   50'   Climb the groove & the slab above to a tree belay.
2   50'   Walk down LWs along a narrow ledge until beneath a crack. Climb this, then move L onto a narrow slab. Follow this & the slabs above to the top.   (1964)

GIRDLE TRAVERSES
There are three main lines, but others are possible.

55 The Admiral's Traverse 270' VD
A route which takes an impressive line (from L to R) across the top of Devil's Rock. Start at the beginning of The Main Area, at the base of *HTW*.
1   40'   Climb the slab of *HTW*, then cross over *PC* & belay to the large chockstone.
2   40'   Move out R across the wall to belay on *CA*, beneath pitch 4 of that route.
3   20'   Descend for a few feet, then cross the top of Dark Cleft to belay in Main Gully.
4   30'   Descend Main Gully to a holly tree belay level with the ledge at the top of pitch 1 of Vineyard.
6   60'   Traverse RWs over broken rock above *CG*, until a ramp leads up RWs to the wide ledge beneath the final hanging corner of *CG*.
7   40'   Move down RWs until it is possible to make a short exposed traverse to a crack (*CCO* reversed). Continue RWs to the edge of the face, then go round to belay as for Route B.
8 40' As for Route B *(pitch 4a)*.   (1949)

56 Cornish Reprieve 290' HVS 4b,4b,5a,4a,-   ★
A fine L-to-R traverse for the middle grade climber. Start at the foot of Vineyard.
1   50'   As for Vineyard.
2   80'   Climb RWs across the wall to the arête of Leviathan. Move up & around the arête, then traverse RWs across a steep wall into *CG*. Descend this to a restricted stance at a good TB.
3   70'   Traverse across the RH wall to a ledge on the arête, then move up & R (past an antique PR) to gain a diagonal break which is followed to the bollard belay of Gideon.
4   50'   Climb the V-groove of *CCO*, then go R & up to the belay ledge of Route B.
5   40'   As for Route B *(pitch 4)*.   (1963)

57 Lateral Thinking 175' E1 4b,5c,4c   ★
An airy R-to-L traverse that has a short sharp crux.
1   45'   Follow *CCO* & belay in the OHing niche (above *CCD*).

2   60'   Move L out of the niche. Make a hard move to gain the crack of *EC*, then follow this to the spike of Gideon. Traverse LWs, just above the lip of the OH, then belay in *CG*.

3   70'   Traverse LWs to the stepped OH on Vala, then continue into Leviathan. Traverse across the wall of *C'SC*, then climb up to the tree belay of Vineyard (abseil off).   (1978)

THE UPPER BUTTRESSES

R of Devil's Rock and high in the trees are two ridge-like buttresses. These are separated by a wide tree-filled gully, at the top of which is a bluff of rock (La Bête Noire). The LH ridge is Needle Buttress, and is distinguished by a clean narrow buttress topped by a pinnacle. Raven Buttress to the R is much larger, although it is split by The Saddle at half-height (which divides the Upper from the Lower Buttress).

NEEDLE BUTTRESS

The cracks just L of the LH arête are taken by Needle Arête, whilst Camel follows the arête more closely. The front face is taken by Cyclops, whilst the crack R of this gives the line of pitch 2 of Scorpion. The gully wall supports a number of routes which are usually wet and overgrown. Below Needle Buttress there is a short layback crack which leads to a tree-covered ledge below the buttress proper.

58   Cleopatra   100'   VS 4c
This starts roughly 30' L of the cracks in the arête of *NA*. The pitch is described intact although it is better to do the first part of Portal (to avoid the mossy slab). Climb the slab, then scramble up to some cracks in a short wall (optional stance). Make a hard move to gain a narrow ledge, then finish up the groove above.   (1981)

59   Portal   120'   S -,4b
Start 15' R of Cleopatra, & just L of the layback crack (which leads to the tree-covered ledge).

1   40'   The short wall leads to a mossy slab & a belay on a sloping ledge (best done on a dry day).

2   80'   Climb the wall L of the arête by bearing L to an OHung recess. Move out of this on the R, then take a diagonal line LWs over the slab, finishing via twin cracks.   (c.1950s)

60   Needle Arête *(NA)*   120'   VD   ★★
An open route with a fine second pitch. Start at the base of the layback crack just R of Portal.

1   30'   Climb a cracked ramp onto the tree-covered ledge.

2   60'   Take the easy slab above to where it steepens, then follow a crack just L of the arête to a short corner. Hard moves up this lead to a traverse RWs (past a spike) to a tree.

3   30'   Ape up the wall behind the tree (using the odd branch if you're so inclined) to a clumsy traverse LWs around the arête to

gain & follow a groove to the summit.   (1949)

61   The Camel   100'   HS 4a,4a
Worthwhile climbing with an exposed finish. Start beneath a blunt rib on the tree-covered ledge above pitch 1 of *NA*.
1   60'   Climb the slab above, via the rib, to an arête below where the slab steepens. Move up & R onto a smaller slab which is followed to the tree belay of *NA*.
2   40'   Climb above the tree to a thin LWs slanting crack. Follow this to move onto the LH arête of the buttress. Climb the arête, then finish up the edge of the Needle.   (1964)

62   The Stitch   90'   E1 5b,5a
An eliminate line between The Camel & Cyclops (pitch 1 is poorly protected). Start at the foot of the arête just R of The Camel.
1   60'   Climb the slab to where it steepens, then follow a line of weakness R of The Camel to a horizontal break. Move R, then climb up before moving back L onto the slab of The Camel. Follow this to the tree belay.
2   30'   Just R of the tree is a rounded crack; follow this past a PR, then continue direct to a narrow OH. Overcome this, then move L to gain the summit of the Needle.   (1976)

63   Cyclops   100'   HVS 4c,5a   ★
To the R of The Stitch is a slab with a small tree on it.
1   70'   Climb the slab, then hand-traverse RWs to a small pointed block. From atop this, make a rising traverse LWs on rounded holds to a flared crack leading to the tree belay of NA.
2   30'   Take the rounded crack (as for The Stitch) to the PR, from where a crack (leaning L/R) leads out RWs to a hidden foothold. Move up RWs into a short groove & finish up this.   (1964)

64   Scorpion   100'   HS 4b,4b
A disappointing route. Start beside two oak trees which are below a short earthy crack.
1   70'   Climb the crack until beneath a short wall, from where delicate moves RWs lead to a grassy recess. Follow a rake up LWs, then move back R to a tree belay.
2   30'   The corner/groove above leads to the top.   (1958)

65   Final Touch *(FT)*   100'   E1 5c
Follow Scorpion to the grassy recess, then move out RWs & follow the curving line of cracks to a horizontal break. Pull onto a ledge containing a large flake, then climb directly up the wall above to the RH arête. Move L to gain & then overcome a bulge (on good holds) to reach the top.   (1979)
Variation start   E3 6a   Start R of the tree at the base of Scorpion. Climb a thin L/R slanting crack (awkward) to a break, then continue direct (bold) to join *FT*.   (c.1980s)

The wall to the R leads into a broad gully (which separates Needle Buttress from Raven Buttress). This wall contains a number of green delicacies that it would be advisable to clean, prior to an ascent. Starting from the L they begin with:

66 Exaltation 70' HVS 5a
Follow the long wide crack R of *FT* to where it peters out at a small niche. Step L into the continuation crack which leads (mossily) to a dishevelled & fern-encrusted exit.   (1968)

67 Babylon 60' S 4a
R of Exaltation is a mossy groove slanting up R\L. Follow this (with some difficulty), then excavate a path through the leafy tresses of fern to the hanging gardens above.   (1960)

68 Winnet 40' HVS 5a
Start below the shorter wall at the RH end of the face, 3yds L of a tree (beside a blunt flake) at the base of a L/R diagonal crack. Follow the crack to a thin mossy ledge, then finish direct up the wall, via a vague crack & some dubious earth ledges.   (1976)

69 Shades of Green 165' HVS 5b,5a
A girdle of Needle Buttress from L to R. Start as for The Stitch.
1   75'   Follow The Stitch to the break, then move R & continue traversing RWs until it is possible to climb up to the tree belay of Scorpion.
2   90'   Step around the corner to a flake, then step down onto a horizontal break & follow this into Babylon. Descend for a few feet, then hand-traverse RWs to the base of Winnet.   (1978)

At the head of the gully behind Needle Buttress there is a small bluff of rock containing four routes.

70 In Extremis *(IE)* 30' HVS 5a
On the LH side of the front face (L of a chimney) is an undercut groove. Climb this in its entirety, then finish RWs. The temptation to escape RWs at half-height is almost justifiable (except for the tortuous jamming this entails).   (1958)

71 Left Chimney *(LC)* 20' D
Climb the chimney R of *IE*.   (c.1955)

72 Crème Brulée 45' E4 5c   †
Start below the arête R of *LC*, & L of the obvious ramp/corner of *LBN*. Climb the arête direct until it is possible to join the OHing groove of *LBN*. Finish direct up the LH wall.   (1994)

73 La Bête Noire *(LBN)* 45' E1 5b
Start R of *LC*, below a steep ramp leading up RWs to an OH. Once beneath the OH, traverse LWs to a short corner & a hard move to gain a short finger-crack which leads to the top.   (1960/77)

Above the bluff are some exacting boulder-problems on an outcrop of small boulders. These are adjacent to the ancient remains of an Iron Age fort which provides extensive views of the Moor beyond.

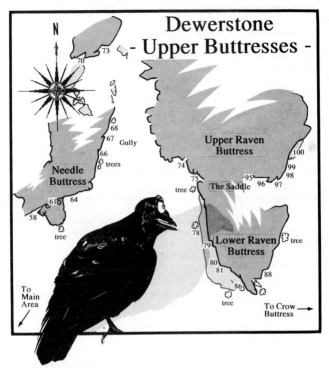

Dewerstone
- Upper Buttresses -

RAVEN BUTTRESS

The RH side of the broad gully R of Needle Buttress is dominated by the sloping bulk of Upper and Lower Raven Buttress. For the sake of convenience the ←W faces (or LH walls of both buttresses) are described first. Apart from the first climb described, the routes either start from part-way up, or begin beneath, a vegetated rake that runs L/R up to The Saddle (a feature which separates the Upper Buttress from the Lower Buttress). The front of the Lower buttress is characterized by three tiers of slabs & OHs which give the line of Spider's Web.

74   Right Chimney   20'   D
This lies on the RH side of the gully, opposite *LBN*.   (c.1955)

75   Sloppy Gully *(SG)*   130'   D
From the base of the vegetated rake that leads to The Saddle, a vague groove can be seen disappearing into the foliage that bounds the LH side of the wall. Follow this, past various curios (birds nests etc.), to the top.   (1950)

76 The Bewilderness *(TBW)*   100'   E1 5b,5b   †
A logical, although wandering line up the clean wall R of *SG*. Start
just below the top of the easy access rake to The Saddle, beside a
R\L curving crackline.
1   70'   Step L into a crack (below the bollard of Yogi). Climb it,
moving L to hard moves which lead up to a hard traverse LWs into
an overgrown sentry box. Climb up out of the sentry box, then
follow a crack which leads to the corner stance at the end of pitch 1
of Yogi (P&NB).
2   30'   Traverse LWs along a break (beneath a blank wall) to a hard
mantel onto a series of flakes which lead to some good finger
holds. Traverse LWs along a blind break (hard to protect), then
finish beside a tree (used for aid on the first ascent).   (1993)

77 Yogi   120'   HVS 5b,5c   ★
A cunning, though worthwhile companion to *TBW*. Start at the top
of the easy access rake to The Saddle.
1   80'   Surmount the bulge above, then move up to a bollard on
the R (huge bird's nest). Move L until it is possible to climb steeply
to a stance & tree belay.
2   40'   Move L to a small ledge on the steep blank wall, then climb
up to a crack, which leads (past a sapling) to the top.   (1964/77)

78 Valhalla Wall *(VW)*   100'   HVS 4b,5a
Start by a tree (below the short lichenous wall of the access ramp)
25' R of *SG*.
1   40'   Climb the short wall, then cross a mossy slab. Move
diagonally RWs to a rounded flake, after which a slab leads to the
tree belay (in common with *FTW*).
2   60'   From the top of the flake move up RWs on a line of
footholds to a horizontal break (PR). Traverse RWs to the arête,
then climb slabs to the top. Alternatively you can climb direct from
the PR, up the steep wall to the top (harder).   (1962)

79 Fly on the Wall *(FTW)*   100'   HS 4b,4a   ★
The line follows the dog-leg weakness up the LH side of Lower
Raven Buttress. Start 20' down the slope from *VW*. Climb up onto
the access ramp & belay below a small tree in a groove.
1   50'   Climb past the tree into the groove, then follow this to a
slab which leads to a tree belay by a flake.
2   50'   From the flake, step up LWs onto a ramp leading to an OH
(PR). Trend RWs beneath the OH to reach a wide crack. Follow this
awkwardly, then finish up some easy slabs.   (c.1960s)

80 Brown Legs   100'   E1 5b
A poorly protected trouser-filler. It climbs the corner R of *FTW*,
then tackles the wall above (just R *VW*). Finish by crossing *VW*, then
overcome the OH above to finish.   (1986)

81 Imperialist   110'   HVS 5a,4c   ★
A fine route which follows the vague arête R of *VW*. Start in a

recessed corner just L of the slabs at the foot of Lower Raven Buttress.

1   40'   Climb the corner for 10', then swing onto a slab beneath an OH. Move L, then climb a short wall onto another slab. Move R to a stance (PB).

2   70'   Move back LWs into an OHung niche. Climb up this, then move LWs onto an arête. Follow this to easier ground which leads on to the finishing slabs.   (1969)

82   Black Widow   110'   E1 5b,5a
A strenuous route up the obvious OHing crack above *ST*.

1   50'   Climb the polished L edge of the slab of *ST* to gain a niche (this point can also be reached by climbing large flakes in the wall L of the slab's edge). Move out R to gain the crack, then follow this strenuously to a slab (P&NB).

2   60'   Climb the crack above, which leads out R from the niche to join SW. Finish as for that route (take care, as there is some loose rock on this pitch).   (1979)

83   Silken Thread *(ST)*   60'   HVS 5a
A deceptively easy-looking route which can be used to start *VW* or *FTW*. Start below a line of weakness just L of the centre of the slab. Follow the obvious crackline to the OH. Traverse LWs, then turn the OHs by an awkward move to gain a slab which leads to the tree belay of *VW*.   (1958)

84   Smash or Grab   130'   E3 6a
A highly eliminate line that wanders through the OHs of Lower Raven Buttress.

1   60'   Climb the slab (L of *ST*), then tackle the OH above direct to gain the stance & PB of Imperialist.

2   70'   Climb the OH above the belay, then continue through some overlaps to a hard finish through the final OH.   (1986)

85   Tarantula   50'   HVS 5b   ★
An impressive direct start to *SW*. Follow *ST* to the OH, then move R & up to the OH. Pull over this onto a narrow ledge on the slab above, then step L to the PB of Imperialist.   (1969)

86   Spider's Web *(SW)*   150'   HVS 5a,5a   ★★★
A classic route of the crag, involving some intricate route-finding & a delicate final pitch. Start by a tree R of *ST*.

1   60'   Climb the slab to an OH. Traverse RWs to a groove (tricky), then follow this for 10'. Swing L (via a rounded flake) onto a slab, then continue L to a PB (in common with Imperialist).

2   90'   Climb straight up behind the belay to a small slab. Step delicately RWs onto another slab, then move R again until it is possible to climb to an OH. Traverse LWs beneath this to the L arête, from where an easy slab leads to the top.   (1959)

Variation 1a 60' VS 4c Climb the clean buttress R of the normal start direct to the smooth groove of the parent route.   (c.1960s)

87   Shelob   130'   E1 5b,5a
A direct (& serious) line up Lower Raven Buttress, which finishes direct over the final OH. Start as for *SW*.
1   50'   Follow *SW* to the OH & overcome this on dubious-sounding holds. Move up, then L to the belay of Imperialist.
2   80'   Step back R & gain a groove, which leads up to a tree below the final OH. Surmount this via a crack, then belay to the tree above (unrepeated since a key hold fell off the crux).   (1981)

88   Mango Corner   90'   VS 4c
Far better than it looks. To the R of *SW* is a square-cut corner. Start beneath this. Climb the corner direct, on doubtful rock, until beneath a slab. Move onto this & climb up to the OH above. Step up, then L onto a slab; tree belay.   (1964)

89   Boris   80'   VS 4c
Start just R of Mango Corner. Climb the wall & groove to an OH. Move L, then surmount this by a long reach.   (1981)

Upper Raven Buttress is delineated by The Saddle, which is reached via the grassy rake at the foot of Sloppy Gully; or from the wide tree-filled gully on the E→ side of Lower Ranger Buttress (which defines the upper limits of that buttress). The large OH is skirted by **RF**, *while the large nose R of this provides the crux of Randy.*

90   Back to Nature   45'   VS 4c
Start as for *RF*. Gain cracks in the arête L of *RF*, & follow them to finish up the easier-angled rock above.   (1981)

91   Snoopy   60'   E2 5b
Climb the OHing wall & the nose of rock L of *RF*, taking care with the loose-feeling nose.   (1985)

92   Raven Face *(RF)*   65'   VD   ★
Start at the highest part of The Saddle. Climb over bulges until beneath an OH. Traverse RWs below this to a groove which leads to the top.   (1949)

93   Randy   80'   VS 4c,4c
A somewhat unprotected although worthwhile route. Start below a well defined groove R of *RF*.
1   50'   Follow the groove, moving delicately out RWs where it finishes, to belay on *RF* (L of a prominent nose of rock).
2   30'   Climb up RWs & pull up onto the square-cut nose. From here a few moves up a slanting groove lead to the top.   (1969)
Variation 1a 80' 4b Known as **Yosemite**. Start R of Randy. Follow a diagonal line up RWs to the tree belay on Armada, then follow a line back L (via a niche) to the belay on *RF*.   (1969)
Variation 2a 30' HVS 5b Known as **Safe Sex**. The initially good holds lead to a committing finish. From atop the nose of rock move RWs & finish direct up the wall.   (1993)

94 Cyberpunk 80' HVS 5a,4c †
A direct, although eliminate line up the steep slab between Yosemite & Armada. Start beside a curved tree 20' R of Randy.
1 50' Climb gingerly up a short mossy corner (behind the tree), then follow cracks which lead onto a slab. Climb direct up the slab, passing some overlaps at half-height. Surmount a final bulge to reach the tree belay on Armada (on the R).
2 30' Climb pitch 2 of Armada for 15', then traverse LWs along a break to gain the top of a protruding block (the nose). Finish as for Randy or Safe Sex or God knows how many other variations that exist on this miniscule piece of rock!!! (1993)

95 Armada 110' HS 4a,4a ∗
An interesting pitch up the vague corner roughly 10yds R of *RF*. The second pitch is a rather brutal chimney. Start below the groove, some way down the path from The Saddle.
1 60' Climb into the groove & follow it, over an OH, to a tree. Move up & R to a large ledge; tree belay.
2 50' Follow the constricted chimney to the top. (1952)

96 Bolshevik 110' HVS 5b,4a
Start below the buttress, between Armada & *CC*..
1 70' Climb the buttress for 20' to a blank-looking slab on the R, then follow this to an OH. Step L, then climb the OH to a tree, from where a short wall leads to another tree on a terrace.
2 40' Gain a square-cut corner R of the stance, then climb the wall R of the chimney of Armada. (1969)

97 Corner Chimney (*CC*) 95' HVS 5a
The obvious chimney R of Armada. Start below the lowest part of the buttress, underneath a tree 15' above the ground. Climb to the tree, then step up behind this into a chimney. Move R, then go up to a V-groove. Enter this from the L (awkwardly), then climb the crack above to a ledge. Either climb direct to a tree, or scramble off easily to the R. (1957)
Variation start VS 4c (Avoids the unpleasant wall below the tree). Climb a line of holds which lead up LWs into the corner. (c.1950s)

98 Grunting in the Gutter 90' E1 5b
Start between *CC* & *DS*, below an OH. Negotiate the OH, then layback up the arête to a small ledge. Move up, then swing L around some blocks to gain a groove. Pull up over the capping OH & finish up the wall above. (1987)

99 Dragon Song (*DS*) 90' E3 6a ∗∗
A fine route. Start below an OH, just R of *CC*. Pull RWs out of the OH, then climb a crack to a diagonal break. Move up & R to a horizontal break (PR removed). Make difficult moves up to gain good holds. Step R & gain the V-groove. Follow this, then finish via a R\L diagonal line on the slab above. (1979)
Variation A far more sustained finish which puts the route firmly at

the top of its grade. From the better holds above the PR (missing), step L to gain a deep RWs trending crack. A wild swing up LWs gains a good hold & a tricky mantel to finish.   (c.1990s)

100   Dangler   70'   E1 5b   *
A rather bold route which follows a devious R-to-L line across the wall. Start in the shallow corner 30' R of CC. Climb up to a niche below an OH. Move out L, then climb through the V-groove to the niche above. Exit out L from the niche, & climb the slab above to the terrace.   (1969)

101   Apparition   70'   HVS 5b
This takes a direct line from the first OH of Dangler. Follow Dangler to the niche below the OH. Climb straight up cracks to a R\L slanting crack. Climb this up to, & then over, an OH. Finish direct up the slab above.   (1979)

102   Nibelung   150'   E1 5b,5b,4c
A good diagonal line which starts at the foot of Dangler, & finishes as for Randy.
1   40'   Follow Dangler to the horizontal break, which is followed LWs to CC. Belay in the groove below the OH.
2   60'   Step down & across into Bolshevik, then descend to a steep slab below an OH. Cross to the bottom L corner of the slab, then swing around into Armada. Belay to the small tree.
3   50'   Climb the chimney of Armada for 6', then use a sloping ledge on the LH wall traverse LWs to gain the nose of rock on pitch 2 of Randy. Finish up that route.   (1976)

CROW BUTTRESS

This lies about 500yds upstream from the Main Area, and can be seen from the top of Devil's Rock as a pinnacle of rock protruding through the trees. The buttress is rather overgrown and the climbing is characterless. The best reason to visit the area is for the superb bathing pool (just upriver), which can take the sting out of a hot summer's day. There is also a slabby waterfall providing a slide, and a rope swing is usually hanging around.

103   Semiramis   45'   S 4a
This is the obvious crackline about 15' L of the L arête of the steep E-facing wall.   (1970)

104   Moral Fibre *(MF)*   45'   VS 4c
Climb the L-bounding arête of the face to the OH, then pull out RWs to a small alcove. Regain the arête, but move back onto the face (from a ledge) & finish up a crack.   (1970)

105   Cracking Plant *(CP)*   40'   VS
This is the wide crack just R of the arête.   (1970)

106 Flange 40′ VS 4b
The thin crack R of *CP* presents a technical layback to start, which
soon eases off.   (1970)

107 Doctor of Physick 40′ VS 4b
Climb direct past the remains of a tree stump, then continue up a
delicate wall (R of Flange).   (1970)

108 Lather 40′ S 4a
This climbs the crack near the broken RH side of the face.   (1970)

109 August Weed 100′ S 4a
A girdle (of sorts). Scramble up to a square chimney 6yds L of
Semiramis. Climb the chimney, then traverse RWs under an OH to
a ledge on *MF*. Cross over to another ledge near the top of *CP*, then
go around the arête easily to a small slab. Continue moving RWs to
Lather, then step up & continue traversing RWs (with difficulty) to a
holly tree. Finish up the wall above.   (1970)

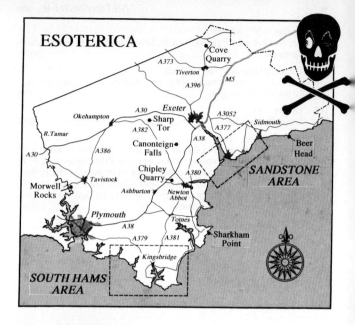

ESOTERICA

Esoterica, now there's a word to conjure with. Monsieur Roget had a veritable field day with it. Obviously in the grip of a violent attack of Pythonesque humour ("I didn't expect the Spanish Inquisition"), he went to town on esoterica's link with the occult. Reading between the lines, he accuses esoterica of allegorical anagog, with perfidiously clandestine and cabbalistic overtones, no doubt just to throw de Torquemada's ghost off the scent.

In a different way, but with exactly the same ends in mind, climbers have employed the term *esoteric* as a smoke screen for the highly contagious *Crag X* syndrome. Thus giving it its totally unjustified connotations of shit rock, poor gear, bad landings (and so on). It is a shame such a stigma has been attached to the term by the climbing world, for its meaning, "of or pertaining to information intended for the initiated" *(a sort of deliberately cultivated air of obscurity if you like)* is elitist enough, without having to go to such extraordinary lengths of dissuasion.

Now I've been around a bit, and I've seen a few things in my time, and the one thing that makes me really suspicious is when you hear someone dismiss a crag or an area as *esoteric*. Because generally they ain't giving you the true benefit of their knowledge (they being the initiated, and you being a lowly comer-in). So here goes, a major exposé; the inside lane on Devon's most well kept esoteric secrets.

SANDSTONE AREA

It has been remarked upon before that the sandstone cliffs of the Shire, are not a patch on their antipodean counterparts (unless you consider The Twelve Apostles to be among the premiere crags of Australia, and being of a discerning nature you wouldn't). However, what they forego in stability they make up for with their distinctive sense of adventure. An Alpine mentality, coupled with the kind of courage it takes to win a Victoria Cross, would still be insufficient qualifications to repeat some of the following feats of derring-do, perpetrated in the days of yore (and not so yore).

Often referred to locally as Devonian Desert Rock, there have been to date, no known instances of climbers dying of thirst on any of

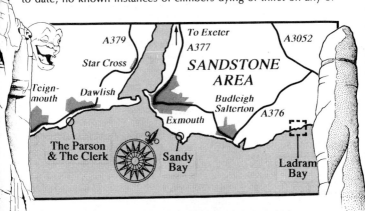

the routes. For it is possible to quench a dry throat by merely grabbing a glutinous lumpette of rock and squeezing it until fresh *East Devon Mineral Water*® droplets run down into your mouth. However, mirages have been reported aplenty (*usually induced by a cocktail of class A substances, which many of the leading exponents in the field use for courage*) manifesting themselves in apocryphal phrases like "what a superb route; sound rock; good gear all the way; bomber belays; and that was a path!"

LADRAM BAY   GR 096 850

This unique area consists of a number of offshore sea stacks and dramatic headlands composed of New Red Sandstone. This stuff does not readily lend itself to protection, so go prepared. A selection of *ice pegs* and *drive-ins* add some semblance of normality to the affair. However, for the impecunious among you, six inch nails have been used to good effect (*if only in the construction of your own coffin*). The absence of substantial belays on the summits of the pinnacles necessitates the use of simultaneous, or see-saw abseils.[1]

1   Big Picket Rock   140'   VI   ***
The classic of the area. It can be approached from either Ladram Bay, or Sidmouth, at low tide. Start under the S↓ face, below a cave.
1   60'   Climb up LWs via an easy ledge system, then go back RWs to gain the cave.
2   30'   Climb up out of the RH side of the cave, exiting RWs onto a steep wall using some chipped holds (now eroded to desperate slopers) to gain & follow a ledge RWs to a stance.
3   50'   Traverse RWs & climb a groove to the summit plateau, where a summit book eagerly awaits. (The ledge at the end of pitch 2 has given up the ghost. It is therefore advisable to run pitches 2 & 3 together, unless a hanging stance is preferred).   (1971)

2   The Reddlemen   730'   IV/A1   **
A sporting, Fowleresque adventure which scales the arête/prow of High Peak. This is the headland directly behind Big Picket Rock. Therefore use the same approach details.
1   130'   Start 15' L of a prominent hole & climb up to a ledge at 20'. Traverse RWs, then climb up a wall followed by two short corners using direct aid (about 24 *snargs* or *warthogs*). Axes would prove useful to gain a grassy ledge between the two corners (*in-situ* stake & "possible belay").
2   150'   From a stake & snarg belay on the R, traverse easily LWs & up to the summit of a block, topped by a bird's nest (IV). Aid up the wall (A1) in a splendid position. Climb the crumbling mud gully on the R (IV) to an *in-situ* stake belay (or tree belay higher up).

---
[1] *In extreme circumstances people have been known to abseil off the ubiquitous flora atop the stacks. . . cabbage plants!!!*

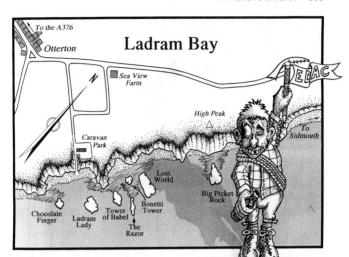

3 & 4 300' Walk up easy-angled mud/grass. Exit via a final thorny thrash to gain a hawthorn tree belay (I).
5 150' Glimpse over the 400' drop to the L, then scamper gaily through the badger sets to the top. (1991)

3 Lost World 60' V-
Unlike the film, a helicopter is not required to gain the summit plateau, although it could be considered as a preferable alternative to climbing. Start below the S ↓ side of the seaward face.
1 30' Climb the steep wall, exiting LWs past the remains of a 6" nail, to gain a large shelf.
2 30' Climb the corner/crack above the stance to gain some easy mud slopes which lead to the forested summit *(the last known sanctuary of the dwarf Brassicae alpina)*. (1971)

4 Bonetti Tower 80' VI-
Although not quite in the same footballing league as its alpine namesake, it is a game effort (although quite possibly an own goal) from one of the stalwarts of the East Devon Alpine Club. Start below the seaward face.
1 40' Negotiate the seaward slab *(the Brown Spider reached via the Hinterstoisser paddle, after which retreat is impossible due to the tide)* to a stance beneath a prominent corner.
2 40' Climb the corner with great care & difficulty. (1971)

5 The Razor 90' V-
Sweeney Todd's first & only addition.

1   20'   Climb the short wall of the seaward arête.
2   40'   Traverse LWs by means of an undignified stomach-crawl,
then climb the wall above to some specious ledges.
3   30'   Climb the corner above to gain & finish up the earthy arête
leading to the cut-throat summit. It would be advisable not to
see-saw abseil from this, if a close shave is to be avoided. Return to
the second stance to retreat.   (1971)

6   Tower of Babel   50'   IV
Un pinnacolo "il cui toco pu spingersi in alto fino al cielo;"   Genesi XI.
Fanger‹ unter der aufs meer hinaus felswand an.
1   30'   απϐδκγ ϖφδ σδκδφαβιυ πϖδδμ ςαι ρπηκε ϖφδ γησηκδ
ηκμιδκδκϖ λε α πητ ηκϐφ κατι ελφ αηγ ϖφδκ ειηγδ ιδεϖ ϖλ α
μριμηϖ πϖακϐδ.
2   20'   דקט דבקע היד הבהיש דמפּתהג היד קד בהצבצּג עאצמו היד בּימעג
ידבּאה היד עעא וץ הטאההטצּאע היד דצהקוּצצּג הבהיד דמד. (MCMLXX I)

7   Ladram Lady   60'   III
Approach by boat. Climb the seaward wall for 15' to a large ledge.
Walk L, then scramble up steep mud to the summit. *The wearing of
galoshes to negotiate this final obstacle will only elicit scorn &
ridicule from the yokel grimpeurs, who reserve theirs for more
taxing fayre like Caveman.*   (1968)

8   Chocolate Finger   80'   V+
Start on the S ↓ side of the pinnacle near the second obvious nose
of rock sticking out of the pinnacle.
1   50'   Follow a ledge system leading up to the prominent platform at two-thirds height.
2   30'   Climb the wall above easily. *Lavatorial humour is strictly
forbidden on the throne [damn] summit.*   (1971)

SANDY BAY   GR 036 798

This lies between Exmouth and Budleigh Salterton. To the ←W of
Straight Point is a double stack in close proximity to the cliff face.
The N ↑ portion of the stack forms a natural arch. Traverse from
Sandy Bay to the ledge at the base of the pinnacles.

1   Kamin Number 5 *(KN5)*   50'   III
This climbs the narrow chimney between the stacks, & although it
looks daunting, it is in fact *tres imbecile*. Follow the chimney by
back-&-footing, then bridge up the final part of the chimney to
either of the twin summits. Descend by see-saw abseil over the
natural arch through the higher stack.   (1972)

*There are a further two routes on the promontory between KN5 and
Sandy Bay. The first climbs a sandy chimney in the short LH wall of
the ill-defined zawn (the RH wall of which runs out to meet the*

pinnacles which form KN5):

2   Sandpit Chimney *(SC)*   40'   HVS 4c   †
Start beneath the obvious chimney in the short wall opposite *KN5*.
Squirm up the sandy orifice, then either belay well back from the
edge, or bring a couple of stakes to belay with.   (1994)

*The seaward face of the short promontory has a wave-cut ledge just
above the HWM. The following route ascends the corner/crack at
the LH end of this ledge:*

3   Jam Today   40'   E1 5b   †
Purported to be an excellent (if somewhat sandy) jamming crack,
which happens to be blessed with good protection. After nego-
tiating the thought-provoking finish, a belay can be arranged in the
cracks at the top of *SC*.   (1994)

THE PARSON & THE CLERK   GR 961 747

The Parson is a large stack which leans against the cliff between
Dawlish and Teignmouth. The Clerk lies further offshore, and is
generally reached by swimming. However, the more industrious
may wish to employ a boat. The classic approach to the Parson is
more involved.

There is a steep narrow lane at the S ↓ end of Holcombe (on the
A379) which descends to the sea. Follow this to the beach, then
find the nerve to enter the railway tunnel which burrows through
the headland for approximately 400yds (and is frequently used by
both Intercity 125s and local sprinters). Abseil down the embank-
ment on the far side of the tunnel to gain the beach, then traverse
to the foot of the landward wall opposite The Parson. Climb the
wall to a ledge with a handy, rusty spike. From there, lasso a similar
spike on The Parson proper. Upon gaining the stack, traverse LWs
to the seaward face.

1   The Parson   140'   VIII-   ***
Bold & serious but a classic all the same, which demands a cool
head & a skilful use of rubble.
1   50'   Climb the seaward arête to some large ledges under an
enormous OH.
2   50'   Traverse RWs to a mud slope below a prominent corner
which leads to a saddle. No belay.
3   40'   Climb the nerve-wracking rubble wall above to the summit. Jump to the mainland & pray to God the landowner does not
raise Cain for trespassing.   (1971)

2   The Actress   40'   VII+   †
From the second stance of The Parson climb the OHing prow above
on its landward side. It is possible to bridge against the stack near
the top. (A dangerous variation climbed by mistake).   (1989)

3   The Clerk   60'   IV
There is a curious hole at two-thirds height.
1   40'   Climb the ⟋SW arête to a shoulder beside the hole
(thread the hole for a belay).
2   20'   Climb the arête above to the summit.   (1974)

SOUTH HAMS AREA

This is a place to get away from it all. Late morning starts, a lunch
time session in the *Hallsands Hotel* near Start Point (the crab-
stuffed french-sticks are fresh and cheap, also check-out the
mural painted in the gents. . . it's enough to bring tears to your
eyes), can be followed by getting lost down leafy lanes to find the
crag. The rock is weird greenstuff and not above suspicion, but
the alcohol numbs the fear factor and doubles the number of
holds to go at (however, it also means twice as many seem to fall
off).

In fact the beer in this neck o'the woods can get quite cosmopolitan. Choices range from *Morlands Old Speckled Hen* (a full-
bodied Cotswold delight, weighing-in at a healthy 5.2%), through
Marstons Merrie Monk (a strong ochre colour, achieved by
straining through antique habits to ferment its heady 4.2%), to
Adnams Broadside (a distinctive bitter, with a smoky after taste
that packs a punch at 4.4%). In fact you would be better off
packing a real-ale directory rather than a climbing guide to this
area.

PILCHARD COVE   GR 843 465

These shale cliffs are situated near the village of Strete, half-way
between Dartmouth and Torcross on the A379. There is a car park
about a mile S↓ of Strete, at the N↑ end of the aptly named
Slapton Sands. The climb takes the prominent groove up the LH
side of a smooth slab at the N↑ end of the Cove. There are two
things to beware of in this vicinity; (1) there are little stone shelters around the base of the route. Don't let curiosity get the better
of you, as the cove is a veritable viper's nest of naked old men
*(who are nutty, but sadly lacking in the dextrously-balanced
department)*; (2) when topping-out take especial care to watch
where you are going, as there are *real* adders up there.

1   Pilchard Groove   110'   HS 4b,4a
1   80'   Climb the prominent & clean-cut corner just beyond a
vast steep grassy cwm. The corner has become vegetated, so
climb the L arête of the groove (which is much finer) to a stance &
NBs near the apex of the groove.

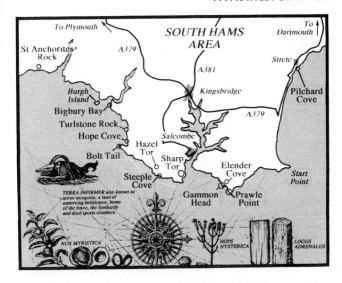

2   30'   Pull around the RH arête to gain a tottery ledge. Traverse RWs to some block belays (taking care not to follow the friable rock into one of the stone shelters).   (1979)

PRAWLE POINT   GR 772 350

From Kingsbridge follow the A379 E→ toward Torcross. At Chillington turn S↓, following signs for East Prawle. Drive through the centre of the village (stopping only at the magnificent tavern of *The Pig's Nose* for a quickie), then follow information signs leading down to the car park at Prawle Point.

Either (1) coasteer ←W until stumbling upon the rock arch around which the routes are based, or (2) follow the footpath to the disused coastguard lookout, then descend a steep grassy gully directly beneath it to where the arch comes into view. Looking S↓ from atop the arch, it is possible to see the striking corner-line of Mental Block on Gammon Head, and the rocky ridge of Sharp Tor in the distance.

When standing on top of the arch, there is a square-shaped zawn on the L. The first route takes the LH & shorter subsidiary wall adjacent to this.

1   Amorok   25'   HS 4b   †
Although short, this climb follows the perfectly formed crackline in

the wall adjacent to the L arête of the square-cut zawn.   (1991)

2 Astral Arête *(AA)* 60′ S 4a   ★★ †
Gain the arête R of Amorok by traversing RWs along the HWM.
Follow the arête throughout, then finish by scaling the OHing
crenellations. Traversing RWs 12′ from the top to finish up the
corner reduces the grade to VD.   (1991)

3 Flying Saucers *(FS)* 60′ S   ★ †
Approach via *AA*, then continue to traverse RWs along the HWM
until gaining the centre of the LH wall (of the square-cut zawn).
Climb direct up the amazing pock-marked wall. Finish
direct.   (1991)

4 Moomin & the Toxic Waste 75′ HVD   †
This climbs the obvious corner formed by the LH wall & the back-
wall of the zawn.   (1991)

5 Ned's Atomic Dustbin 70′ S 4b   †
Start on the landward side of the arch (opposite *FS*).
1 50′ Climb a slab to the OH of the arch, then step L to a
diagonal crack. Traverse RWs above the lip of the arch (& beneath
an awkward overlap). Continue easily to a huge TB.
2 20′ Follow the steep cracks (above the stance) LWs to an 'eye'
through the rock. Continue in the same line to the top.   (1991)

6 Drowning Witch 50′ E5 6a   †
A route of great dodgyness. Start in the black corner where the E→
side of the arch meets the dark-coloured stratifications which rise
up out of the sea on the landward face. Climb between the two
rising L/R diagonal cracks until the angle relents. Finish easily up
the seaward arête.   (1991)

*E→ of the arch is another wall bound on its RH side by a level
platform (about 40′ above the HWM). A diagonal fault runs from the
base of the arch to the platform, passing beneath a large OH. Just
before the platform is reached, you step across the top of a square-
cut groove. The following three routes begin at the base of this, on
boulders that are wave-washed at high tide.*

7 Loop de Lip *(LDL)* 70′ HVS 5b   †
Start by traversing the HWM RWs from the arch to gain the sea-
washed boulders at the base of the square groove. Climb the LH
wall (just R of the arête) to the diagonal fault. Move up to the RH
side of the OH above, then hand-traverse LWs across the lip for 5′
to pull onto the wall. Either take the wall direct, or trend up LWs to
follow huge pockets up the rib to the top.   (1993)

8 Safe Surfer *(SS)* 70′ S 4a   ★
Follow *LDL* to the base of the square groove. Climb the LH corner/
crack to the diagonal fault, then continue up the hanging groove-
line above. Finish out LWs to avoid the OH.   (1991)

9   Cabarête   70'   HVS 5a   †
This climbs the OHing R arête of the hanging groove of *SS*. Follow
that route to the diagonal fault. Climb the OHing start of the arête,
on good pockets, to a spike at half-height. Continue up to the
capping bulge, then finish direct through this.   (1993)

*For the fervent coasteers among you, the coastline from the disused
coastguard lookout to Gammon Head provides an exciting outing.
There are a couple of breathtaking slime slides down greasy slabs to
pass Black Cove:* **Prawle Crawl** *3,500' Grade IV (1989).*

ELENDER COVE   GR 767 357

From East Prawle follow the signs which lead to the car park at
Prawle Point, but at the top of the second steep descent to the car
park continue across the road onto a muddy track. Turn into the
second field on the R and park.

Follow the coastal footpath ←W for about 600yds to a path leading
down into Elender Cove. Roughly 100yds up the slope there is a
steep ivy-covered slab up which both of the following routes
climb; there is a niche at half-height on the L edge of the slab.

1   Whispering Doom   70'   HVD
Start 5' in from the LH arête of the slab. Climb up to, then step L
into the niche. Traverse RWs for 10', then climb straight over two
bulges to a ledge on the R. Step back L & continue over some more
bulges to a good block belay 15yds back from the edge.   (1971)

2   A Product of Civilisation   70'   HS 4b
Start 15' L of the R edge (between the third & fourth patches of ivy
from the L). Climb direct to a slight OH (poor runner). Tackle the
OH direct, then continue in the same line on holds that are barely
adequate. Join & finish up the previous route.   (1971)

GAMMON HEAD   GR 766 356

Use the approach details of Elender Cove until above the beach.
Beyond the cove there is a rocky spur jutting seaward. Follow the
path until atop this, then continue along a thin track which follows
the ridge (past a sharp dip) to reach a rocky outcrop. Descend
diagonally LWs down the steep seaward slope (beyond the outcrop) to another outcrop above the sea. This is the top of the crag.
Either abseil in, or zigzag down the grassy cwm on the R. The
routes are described from R to L.

1   Meathead   40'   E2 5b   (no stars) †
Climb the crack in the wall 40' to the R of the dramatic corner-line
of *MB*. Step R to finish.   (1989)

2   Mental Block *(MB)*   100'   E5 6a   ★★★ †
The *pièce de résistance* of the Hams. Climb the stunning corner-

line, passing the eponymous block at half-height. There are 4PRs, however their combined holding power would (without any shadow of doubt) still see errant future ascensionists buried beneath the block, should it decide to go 'mental'. (1989)

3   Battle of the Bulge   40′   E2 5c
L of the L arête of *MB* the cliff drops in height dramatically. This route tackles the butchly-bulging, although scrappy wall, via a pathetic *in-situ* TR. (1988)

SHARP TOR   GR 729 367

Follow road signs for Salcombe (A381), then take the turn-off for South Sands. Either park in the non-residents car park (cheap), or park in the NT car park for Sharpitor Museum (expensive), where the coastal footpath begins. Take the lower footpath, passing through the heavily wooded slopes that mask Sharpitor Rocks. The bold outline of Sharp Tor (which descends the ridge in a Ramshawesque silhouette), becomes visible from the first set of steps.

The rocky ridge bisects the path at another set of stone steps. To the R of these there is a wall bound on the R by a deep corner/groove. The first four routes are based upon this wall & the groove.

1   Look Sharp *(LS)*   55′   VS 4c   †
The L rib/arête of the wall starts by the first step. Climb it on curious pinch-grips to a small ledge at half-height. An awkwardly-angled groove heads up R\L. Gain this, then finish up the true arête if you dare. The descent is obvious. (1993)

2   Erazor Flake   55′   S 4a   ★ †
Climb the centre of the wall R of *LS* on immaculate rock, to gain & follow the obvious flake-line (block belays up to the R). (1993)

3   Hades   60′   S 4a   †
Follow the deep corner/groove to the capping bulge. Bypass this on the L (using a hollow-sounding flake), then follow another flake on the LH wall to top-out. (1993)

4   Flying Arête   50′   VD   ★ †
Follow Hades until an obvious traverse out RWs, along a line of flakes/pockets, gains the arête. Follow this to the top. (1993)

The following route starts at the top of the stone steps, beneath a dramatically-positioned leaning buttress that forms a needle's-eye with the ridge.

5   Hair of the Dog   65′   E2/3 5b   ★ †
A slim pillar rises up from the path towards a bulging headwall. Climb the elegant groove up the LH side of the pillar to a small ledge. Step up diagonally LWs to a slim groove, & follow this boldly to the summit. (1985)

Dave Turnbull on Ultramontane (HVS 5a) Photo: Andy Grieve

Ken Palmer on The Wave (6b) Photo. Wendy Palmer

Descend the stone steps & follow the path to a stone bench. Just L of the bench a faint path heads up to a buttress with a clean-cut OH jutting out of its RH side.

6   Four Strong Winds   120'   S 4b   ★ †
A slight L/R leaning groove splits the LH face from half-height, leading to a hole below the summit. Climb the LH side of the wall beneath the groove, then follow this to the hole. Crawl through this & belay on the crest.   (1992)

STEEPLE COVE   GR 705 367

Follow the A381 S↓ from Kingsbridge to Marlborough. Take the road to Soar then follow a footpath S↓ to the Cove, where there is a boulder-bridge leading out to a sea stack.

1   The Steeple *(TS)*   80'   S
Climb the landward facing wall of the pinnacle (beyond the boulder-bridge), then traverse RWs onto the seaward face. Finish up this (lots of loose rock).   (1970)

2   Steeple Slab   300'   VD
Start below a vague line of weakness, roughly in the middle of the grassy slab which faces the pinnacle. Climb straight up the slab, with no protection & a poor belay at half-height.   (1982)

The next stack is roughly 300yds SE↘ of Soar Mill Cove. Approach by descending an earthy gully directly opposite the stack. Continue (via a boulder-bridge) to gain a platform on the seaward face.

3   Erotica   75'   HS
A route to titillate the serious loose rock pervert. Climb an open groove on the R to gain a niche. Move L, then climb direct to the summit. Descent is by simultaneous abseil. . . *spuff!!!*   (1977)

HAZEL TOR   GR 699 379

This tor, near Salcombe, has some routes of dubious worth scattered along the faces of the two dominant pinnacles. The first two routes climb the wall which faces some houses across the valley:

1   Delicatessen   35'   VD
Start at the base of the LH slab. Climb the centre of the slab, then finish over the blocks above.   (1971)

2   Hush Puppy   65'   VD
Begin at the base of a steep slab, just L of the main tower.
1   15'   Climb the slab trending LWs. Belay on the R.
2   50'   Traverse LWs around a corner. Step onto the main face, then climb this direct to a belay.   (1971)

3   Spiral Tower *(ST)*   55'   VD
1   15'   As for Hush Puppy.

2   20'   Traverse RWs along a sloping ledge, then belay around the corner in a gap between the towers.
3   20'   Climb the SE↘ tower until it is possible to traverse to the ↖NW tower to finish. (Descend by reversing pitch 3, then continue down between the towers & the main wall).   (1971)

4   Piper at the Gates of Dawn   85'   VD
Start towards the LH end of the steep wall facing the cove.
1   55'   Climb the L edge, which OHs for for the last 5'. Move R for 20' along a ledge, & belay at its extreme RH end.
2   15'   Traverse RWs around the corner. Belay in the gap between the two towers (in common with *ST*).
3   15'   Move back LWs & climb the wall to finish.   (1971)

BOLT TAIL   GR 667 397

From Marlborough follow signs to Hope Cove. Either follow the coast path ←W, or coasteer in the same direction (Grade III with a singularly taxing patch of grade V) to a semi-island/reef called The Bury Stone. The descent lies down a gully just S↓ of some large boulders lying between The Bury Stone and the cliff, while the climbs lie on the cliff facing the Stone.

1   Flaked Out   85'   VS 4c,4c
Start opposite the col on the Stone, below a layback crack.
1   50'   Climb up to, then follow the crack diagonally RWs until the wall OHs. Climb past a R-facing bulge, then mantel onto a ledge. Continue up LWs to a ledge & belay.
2   35'   Traverse LWs, passing a corner & then an OH, to gain another corner. Climb up to a sharp arête, then finish by traversing across the slab on the L.   (1970)

2   Helter   80'   S
Start 30' R of the previous route. Climb a slab diagonally RWs by the easiest line.   (1970)

HOPE COVE   GR 674 406

The only route lies on the impressive-looking slab some 400yds N↑ of the village of Outer Hope. Approach via the beach.

1   Hopeful   140'   S
Climb the centre of the slab to a horizontal break, then follow a shallow depression. Climb a grassy groove to finish.   (1983)

THURLSTONE ROCK   GR 674 414

Drive through the village of Thurlestone and follow the road down toward the beach. Park where the road takes a sharp turn to the L. The arch of Thurlstone Rock is clearly visible, and is but a brief barefoot promenade away through the sand.

1   The Thurlstone   70'   HS/A1 *(or XSlippery)*
Start below the seaward face of the arch. Lasso a suitable knob to gain the drier rock above, then follow your nose to the summit. Descent is via simultaneous abseil.   (1981)

BIGBURY BAY   GR 660 433

Some 3 miles S ↓ of Aveton Gifford (on the A379) there is a round-about; take the exit marked Bantham. Drive straight through Bantham to the public car park in the sand-dunes.[2] Boulder-hop E→ around the point, to be confronted by a huge hand sticking straight out of the sea (reached at mid/low tide).

1   Bantham Hand *(BH)*   30'   VS 4b   ★★
Start from a ledge on the seaward edge of the pinnacle. Step out L onto the steep slab & trend LWs to the base of a depression in the middle of the face, then climb straight up to the summit ridge. Descend either by simultaneous abseil. . . or jump!!!   (1974)

2   Antipodeans Afoot   35'   HS 4a   ★ †
Start below the landward arête of the pinnacle. Make a rising traverse RWs along the natural line leading towards the depression on *BH*. Climb the wall L of the depression to the summit.   (1991)

St ANCHORITE'S ROCK   GR 591 473

This isolated rock is situated between Mothecombe and Noss Mayo, and lies above the coastal footpath.

1   Jude the Obscure *(JTO)*   30'   HVS 5a   †
The first wall encountered from the footpath. Climb the centre of the wall, taking the bulge above the shallow recess direct.   (1991)

*Over the fence (R of **JTO**) is a descent into the quarry beyond. The following two routes are described from R to L.*

2   Far from the Madding Crowd *(FMC)*   60'   HVS 4c
Start below a large steep slab. Climb the RH side of the slab via thin cracks to a steep groove, which leads to a juggy finish.   (1981)

3   Don't Mess with Tess   60'   E2 5b   †
Start below a shallow groove on the LH side of the wall/slab. Climb this direct to join & finish up *FMC*.   (1991)

---

[2] *Hidden deep within the dunes is a curious cottage straight out of the rhyme of "The Old Woman Who Lived In A Shoe".*

MISCELLANEOUS

Now (strangely enough) in the twisted world of semantics, some have argued (in language akin to estuarine English: ie. extremely filthy and delivered through a wide mouth) that miscellany is a term specifying "an area of knowledge even more inaccessible than that of esoterica". From a climbing perspective this hypothesis would seem to hold a good deal of rubble. So what follows is not only the best *mish* but some of the finest *mash* around, and you'll have to have more than an acquired taste to cope with most of it.

LUNDY   GR 135 450

Lundy is an arch example of miscellaneous esoterica. It is recorded in Arthurian Legend as the "Isle of Glass" (it has a preponderance for disappearing behind a veil of sea-haze). Even Edward II got lost sailing to Lundy. He ended up landing on the coast of Wales where he got a red hot poker up the back passage for his trouble (what a bummer). The island is now cloaked in an almost impenetrable fog of *Crag X* syndrome, to such an extent that within the most elite circles of esotericists it still carries a certain cachet. Of course it goes without saying that it will never catch-on as a popular venue. This is due to the masonic handshake nature of the information needed to get there (and the Machiavellian cloak and dagger-like machinations of the climbers who actually get to land upon its mythical shoreline!!!). So all-in-all it's hardly worth mentioning.

COVE QUARRY   GR 952 202

This has the dubious honour of being the N↑ most banned climbing venue in the guide. Therefore the following route is recorded just to keep the records straight. The quarry lies 4 miles N↑ of Tiverton on the A396, above the village of Cove. Turn L at the post office, then follow the road to the top of the quarry. The quarry rim is adjacent to the road, and is defined by a large number of very stout trees.

1   On the Rink of Disaster   140'   E6 6b   ★★★ †
This takes a fine line up the tallest & cleanest slab near the L end of the quarry. Start at the base of a shallow corner below a PR at 30'. Climb to the PR, then down-climb for 10' to an obvious large pocket. Climb out RWs, then continue direct (via shallow pockets) before traversing back LWs to another PR. Awkward moves gain another PR & so on to the final PR (beside a large pocket). Skate up the slab above on improving holds to a good nut slot below the final desperate moves.   (1988)

BEER HEAD

GR 228 879

The chalk sea cliffs to the ←W of the picturesque fishing village of Beer provide Devon's answer to the horrifying exploits perpetrated by certain deranged individuals on the White Cliffs of Dover. Early explorations by Roman quarrymen gave way to the rather more romanticized 'smuggler period' when colourful characters such as Jack Rattenbury utilized the cliff paths and caves to land and store contraband from France.

It should be noted that the chalk sea cliffs lie within the boundaries of an area designated as **Heritage Coastline**, most of which has an SSSI (Site of Special Scientific Interest) rating. This is an environmentally senstive area and, as such, **climbers should avoid disturbing both the vegetation and the seabirds** (especially during the main spring nesting period).

In the unlikely event of any further developments here, it should be noted that there is a locally established ground-up ethic; therefore **climbers should only hand-drill placements should they be absolutely necessary.**

THE TRAVERSE

The sea traverse around Beer Head from either Beer or Branscombe (with a return over the cliff footpath) is a splendid outing at low water. This involves moderate climbing, boulder-hopping and a fine bit of back-and-footing in a through cave behind the seaward-jutting buttress. The entrance to this feature is gained via a 6' wall and then descending a blow-hole if traversing ←W from Beer (traversing E→ proves to be farcicially easy). By half-tide, and following the dry-feet ethic, the climbing required becomes much harder. High tide is probably desperate, or for strong swimmers only! Training shoes and dogs are de rigueur, leave the gear behind but carry enough cash for a pub meal at either end.

THE STACK

The impressive foreshore stack in the landslip has probably had ascents, but is best avoided due to it being in a Roraima-like position in the midst of a jungle-like zone of botanical delights. An additional disincentive is the recent large rockfall which it overhangs and would seem destined to join in the near future.

THE GROT

The grot slope to the left of the main headland provides some mixed entertainment (in full ice regalia. . . *naturellement*) with a pitch of grade III and then one of IV leading to some boiler-plate slabs. However, these have as yet proved to be an insurmountable obstacle due to the dusting of loose earth which overlays them *(this is probably the East Devon equivalent of ideal powder-skiing conditions)*. A good *in-situ* warthog marks the top belay, and points the way to anyone demented enough to want to complete this project.

THE MAIN WALL
The main wall of the headland provides the most fun with the following route proving to be a real hand-pulled-beer nasty of a climb on interestin' rock:

1 Hair of the Dog   380'   VI+   ★★★ †
Start under the highest point of the headland, towards the RH side of the impressive white wall (& L of a large corner/gully system). It is advisable to carry a selection of Hex's (7-11), several long angle pegs, 10-15 assorted warthogs &/or snarg drive-ins, lots of slings & biners, the odd pair of etriers, & some hammer axes.
1   50'   5b   Climb up into the open flinty chimney & exit RWs to belay on a pedestal jutting from a small cave (stake belay).
2   40'   5a   A short sandy stomach-traverse L leads to a steep wall & a flakey crack. Exit RWs to a ledge & stake belay at the foot of a ramp.
3   80'   5c/A1   Free climb the corner/ramp until it steepens & aid (in the RH wall) is required to reach a large ledge & ample belays.
4   60'   5a/A2   Move R & then aid back L (2 *in-situ* warthogs) over the bulge to gain a small corner/crack above the stance. Free climb this to gain a ledge (stake belay).
5   150'   4c/I   Move RWs up to a ledge (PR) & climb the slabby wall above until it is possible to move into a grass/earth gully. Trend RWs up this to gain the sanctuary of a solid stile belay (axes proove useful for the final section)   (1994)

SHARP TOR   GR 728 898

This is an inexplicable outcropping of shale on the N ↑ tip of the Moor, hence its exclusion from the Dartmoor Granite section. The best approach is via the road from Moretonhampstead to Whiddon Down (A382). At the bridge over the River Teign (by *Mill End Hotel*) there are a couple of signposted footpaths running E→. The Fisherman's Path is the lower of the two, and proves to be a rather tedious approach. The Hunter's (or upper) Path is the better of the two. Depart from the path at the main scree chute which leads interminably to the foot of the first buttress. The general tedium of the routes, the fact that the buttresses are degenerating to detritus, and the copious quantities of bramble and gorse (to say nothing of the heat in the summer), make the routes less than ideal entertainment. For the hardy few who persist to this point, there are three buttresses. From L to R these are West, Central and East Buttresses (the first two separated by the scree chute of Great Gully).

GREAT GULLY WALL
The Central Buttress is topped by an upper wall, while Great Gully Wall is the tier beneath.

1   Wall Climb   65'   S 4a
Climb a groove L of a loose OH. A shallow cave provides a rest,

while the loose L/R diagonal weakness leads to the top.   (1947)

2 Great Gully Groove 40' VD
To the L of Wall Climb is another groove. Climb the RH wall of this
in its entirety.   (1947)

EAST BUTTRESS WALL
The upper part of East Buttress finishes at a large square block,
known to esotericists as The Eyrie.

3 Brown Wall 75' VD
Climb the L wall of the groove leading to The Eyrie.   (1947)

4 Gorse Groove 40' D
Climb the actual groove.   (1947)

5 East Crack 70' S 4b
A route which has the heady distinction of being the best on the
Tor. Climb up the square-cut runnel L of Brown Wall. Finish up the
groove/crack above, which is easier than it looks.   (1947)

CANONTEIGN FALLS   GR 832 824

The crag lies in a thickly wooded valley on the ←W side of the River
Teign, near Canonteign House, and is on private land owned by
Lord Exmouth. It is debatable whether the climbing warrants either
the tedious tax-free approach through dense brambles and rotting
tree trunks, or the expenditure of *mucho dinero* to enter through
the gentrified portals of the estate. The rock is igneous, akin to
dolerite and plastered in moss due to the waterfall that cascades in
a pale imitation of:

1 Niagara 150' VD
The old waterfall stopped running for a while when its leat was
breached. Sadly, the cascade is now flowing again, although the
three alpinists of the Shire are ecstatic for reasons that will become
apparent. Start beneath a groove on the LH side of the face.
1 30' Climb the open groove on good holds to a grass ledge
(PB).
2 50' Move R along the ledge for several feet, then climb the
steep wall R of a crack, on small holds. Continue past a large tree to
a terrace stance.
3 40' Climb up to a tree on the L edge of the terrace. Move R into
a groove which is followed pleasantly to the next ledge.
3 30' From the ledge climb up the break in the R side of the final
tower to gain the summit.   (1965)

2 Psycho 150' VS
A climb with some excellent (wet) sections. Some 20' to the R of the
base of Niagra is a very steep wall.
1 30' Climb the steep wall, via a shallow recess, to a ledge (PB).
2 50' Layback up a flake to the large OH above. Turn this on the

R by pulling up on widely-spaced, but good incut holds. Continue over easy ground to the terrace above (PB).

3   40'   The OH above is split by an obvious layback crack which looks difficult but is surprisingly easy. Climb the crack, then continue up to the ledge below the final tower.

4   30'   Take the final tower just L of centre, climbing up on small incuts (PR). Pass the final OH by traversing LWs.   (1965)

3   I Sick Hell   150'   III/IV

In the mists of a distant winter, an unheard of & unexpected thing happened. . . *ice*. The line is blatantly apparent when in condition. Probably not repeatable this millenium *(the same would appear to be true of the other two routes)*.   (1987)

CHIPLEY QUARRY   GR 807 722

This lies 4 miles ←W of Newton Abbot on the A383 near Bickington. On the current map it resides under the "p" in Chipley (OS Sheet 191: *hopefully the map will not be out of date before this guide appears*). The face opposite the quarry entrance is composed of igneous rock, and reaches a maximum height of 80'.

1   Dynomight   65'   E1 5a

Start below the tallest part of the face. Climb the centre of the wall (boldly), past a couple of poor PRs, until it is possible to make a RWs escape onto a large belay ledge.   (1989)

2   Isca   60'   E1 5b

This climbs the crackline (slanting R\L) some 10' to the R of Dynomight. Follow the crack until under an OH (PR). Step L with difficulty, then layback the crack for a few feet until better holds lead to a large ledge. Tree belay well back.   (1983)

3   A Few Dolerites More   60'   E3 5b

Climb direct up the wall, from the base of Isca's crack, until beneath the OH (PR – missing). Make a hard move to gain the sloping ledge above. Continue boldly on small holds to the top. Tree belay well back from the edge.   (1989)

4   A Fist Full of Dolerites   55'   VS 4c

Start 10' L of a quartz-lined pocket. Climb to the top bearing RWs to pass the OH (TR).   (1989)

5   Ivy Route   45'   HS 4a   ★

Gain the quartz-lined pocket, then bear RWs to climb a rib for 15'. Step R onto a large ledge & continue direct up the easy wall to finish. Tree belay well back.   (1983)

6   Hijo de Puta   50'   E4 6b/c   †

Start 5' R of the quartz pocket, beneath a shallow OH. Climb direct to this then scratch up the wall to join Ivy Route. Step L & continue boldly to the top (no gear. . . whatsoever).   (1989)

7   Doing a Dalby   40′   VD
Climb the prominent crack 15′ L of the corner bounding the RH
side of the face.   (1983)

8   Dalby   40′   VD
Climb the short wall between the crack & the corner.   (1983)

9   Ascent of Silage   45′   VS 4b   †
Start in the corner R of Dalby. Climb to a small ledge, then move
out R & climb past a tree to the top.   (1989)

SHARKHAM POINT   GR 937 546

Well off the beaten track. This place is so *miscellaneous* even the
Devonians steer well clear. It is the headland S ↓ of St Mary's Bay,
where the limestone changes to rock of a curious green and slabby
nature. The climbing lies on the S ↓ side of the point, on a slab of
rock called (surprisingly enough) The Green Cliff. This is the landward side of a steep narrow (and tidal) zawn. The cliff is dominated
by two L/R diagonal seams of iron ore.

1   Rusty Road   100′   S 4a
The LH seam. After a delicate start (just L of the seam) continue
along the seam for 40′ until beneath a groove above an overlap.
Gain this direct, then take a zigzag line through the overlaps above
until easy rock on the R leads to the top.   (1979)

2   Rusty Road To. . .   100′   S 4a
The RH seam. Where the vein peters out weave up through the
steeper rock above to the top.   (1992)

3   Traversty   150′   S 4a,4a
A girdle of The Green Cliff from L to R which follows the prominent
fault at half-height. Start on a commodious ledge directly above the
cave at the back of the zawn.
1   100′   Traverse RWs to a groove which is descended gingerly to
an obvious break beneath an OH. Follow this delicately RWs to a
large niche, then step up & continue to traverse to where a step-
down leads to a second, smaller niche & belay.
2   50′   Step R, then make a strenuous pull through a break in the
bulge. Continue diagonally RWs to the top.   (1979)

*There are several pinnacles littered around the tip of the point, the
largest of which provides a jolly jape at low tide. On top of the
headland is an extensive refuse tip. About 200yds inland from this is
a small limestone outcrop (that shouldn't be here according to the
geologists) split by a crack:*

4   Happy Camper's Crack   40′   VS 4c
Very steep, although well protected. Fight through the vegetation
to a small cave at the base of the wall. Step up R, then L into the
crack, which is followed to the top.   (1968)

MORWELL ROCKS

Approach and Access
This area lies along the heavily-wooded E→ bank *(if there were any justice in the world it would have been on the ←W bank)* of the valley surrounding the River Tamar, below Gunnislake and just off the A390. The access situation at Morwell is ridiculous at present, with the landowner (Tavistock Woodlands) charging £5 per capita for a day's climbing. To be honest with you the climbing isn't worth paying tuppence for, let alone five quid.

If approaching the N ↑ end of the Rocks, park in a layby a quarter-of-a-mile uphill from the river (on its E→ side). Walk back down the hill to find a footpath which follows the Devon riverbank S ↓ to the first buttress.

The routes are described from N ↑ to S ↓ (& from L to R).

Situation and Character
Due to the heavily-vegetated nature of the hillsides, and the loose appearance of the cliffs themselves, many have been deterred from climbing here and rightly so. However, the persistent few may find the odd choice pitch (although it is a needle-in-the-haystack scenario).

GUNNISLAKE BUTTRESS
This lies about 400yds down the track. Much higher up and further to the R is Chimney Rock, which is hard to see from the track but can be seen very well from the other side of the river *(which isn't a fat lot of good really, considering the river is over 50' wide at this point)*.

1   Cerebus   120'   VD
A poor, vegetated route. Start just up R of the lowest rocks & L of a large bramble patch.
1   60'   Climb for 25', then step R into a shallow recess above the brambles: *a slip here could have serious consequences.* Bear L to a stout oak tree & belay.
2   60'   Traverse LWs (up over a projecting ledge), then move R into a chimney & follow it to the top.   (1958)

2   Quickening Pulse   110'   HVS 4c
A reasonable route which follows the crest of the OHing buttress R of Cerebus. Scramble to a ledge in an Ohung bay (PB). Climb direct, then bear R to an OH. Move L to gain an arête & follow this, stepping R into a shallow groove to finish.   (1979)

3   Thor   80'   VS 4c
A short-lived route of dubious worth. Start by scrambling up to a tree R of a crack. Climb the obvious inset corner.   (1958/79)

4   Damaged Goods   70'   HVS 5a
Climb the crack in the wall R of Thor to an OH. Surmount this to

gain good holds above, then trend up LWs, before heading back up RWs to finish.   (1979)

5   Odin Your Tea's Ready   100'   HVS 4c
An intimidating route up the wall that forms the RH-flanking face of the buttress, *wash your hands before starting*. Climb the wall direct, past a sapling, to a short OHing groove which gains a large ledge. Step L onto the arête to finish.   (1979)

UPPER CLIFF
Between the top of Gunnislake Buttress and Chimney Rock is an isolated face containing an OHing groove-line.

6   Haunted People   85'   HVS 5a
Gain the base of the groove (by climbing over some friable rock), then follow it to a capping OH. Step RWs & traverse to the arête which is followed to the top.   (1979)

CHIMNEY ROCK
The broken ←W face of the tower gives a number of grotty Diffs. The best feature of the buttress, however, is the superb view of the Tamar Valley from its summit. The ridge seen breaking through the trees downriver gives a heavily overgrown route, **Soupçon** 200' VD. Follow the well defined ridge in three pitches. However, the first pitch is rather artificial.

7   Overhanging Crack   50'   S
Higher up in the trees above Haunted People is a small crag split by a central chimney. This is a daunting prospect for all but the most devout masochist. . . if taken direct.   (1958)

WEIR BUTTRESS
If there is a showpiece here, then this is it. Its selling point is that it is directly above the path. It lies just over 100yds further S ↓ from Gunnislake Buttress.

8   Limping Home   130'   VS 4b,4b
A girdle-traverse of the buttress. Start at a tree on the LH side of the wall, L of an OH.
1   100'   Move up & out R onto the wall (above the OH) at a prominent loose block. Traverse RWs across the wall, then gain height to reach a tree belay.
2   30'   Traverse RWs to finish above some grass slopes.   (1978)

9   Palace of Skulls *(POS)*   100'   E3 5b   ★
A serious route. Start with a desperate scramble from the track to a small ledge below an OH in the centre of the front face of the buttress. Climb up LWs to the base of a steepening wall. Make a long reach L to a good hold, & attack the steep wall direct.   (1979)

10   Vacancy at the Vatican   100'   HVS 4c   ★
There always seems to be a little pall of smoke drifting off the top this route. Start as for *POS*. Climb up LWs, then step R & climb to a

break. Move L & surmount a bulge to reach a groove which leads to a tree. Step L again & climb past another tree to finish.   (1978)

11   Love is like Anthrax   130'   VS 4c

A bold route on dubious rock. Start as for *POS*. Step R onto a ramp-line & follow this to exit out RWs onto a pile of rocks on a ledge. Step up to reach a groove, then step out RWs & climb direct over an OH to finish.   (1979)

12   Tiptoe   120'   HS 4b

Follow a line up the R edge of the buttress. Start R of the R edge & scramble up what rock there is until beneath the OHs at the top of the wall. Butcher an exit L through the tree.   (1958)

The track continues through a cutting to a fork. The lower track passes through a gate into a meadow, from where the buttresses on the wooded slopes ahead can be seen clearly. High up on the L is Pinnacle Buttress, which has no climbing potential. Directly ahead, in line with the track, is Main Buttress (the largest face on view), followed by Summit Buttress, which is on the skyline. Rising from the track beyond the bend in the river, are Blasted Buttress & then River Buttress, with the cluster of A, B & C Buttresses behind them.

MAIN BUTTRESS

There is only one reasonably good route on the face.

13   Spinal Column   200'   S -,4a,-,4a

Start from the lowest rocks in the trees.

1   20'   Climb a short wall on the R edge of the buttress to the top of a detached block.

2   80'   Climb a rib slightly to the R, then go straight up on good holds, without deviating out LWs.

3   50'   Scramble up heather to the base of a steep tower.

4   50'   Turn the OH above on the L, then climb the tower to a ridge leading up into the hillside.   (1958)

SUMMIT BUTTRESS

This is split in two by a ledge at half-height. The lower face gives a number of inconsequential routes (VD to S), while the upper face yields two pitches of only slightly better quality.

14   Fern Chimney   40'   D

A deeply-vegetated cleft which faces up the valley. Climb the chimney, then move out onto the mid-pitch ledge. Climb the wall above to finish.   (c.1950s)

15   Cleaver   80'   S 4a

This is the prominent crack. Make an awkward move to gain the crack from the L, then follow it easily to the top.   (1959)

BLASTED BUTTRESS

The wall is close to the river, which means it has the attendant attraction of easy access. The routes are on reasonable rock with the first starting L of the centre of the wall.

16   Good Day Sunshine *(GDS)*   100'   E1 5b   †
Climb the steep wall to a ledge, via a pocket at 25'. Continue up thin cracks to a small OH, then finish up the steep wall above. Good tree belay (& thorny descent).   (1987)

17   Perfecto   100'   VS 4b
A good pitch, although it lacks protection low down. Start just R of *GDS*. Climb the wall direct on good, but hollow-sounding holds. Move R to an oak tree in a groove, then traverse LWs for 10' to a crack which is followed to the top.   (1958)

18   Seasons in the Sun *(STS)*   80'   VS 4b   †
Start just R of Perfecto. Climb the steep wall on large holds for about 20' to reach a flake-crack. Continue RWs to a groove & climb this, then the wall above (bearing LWs) to finish at the highest point of the wall.   (1987)

19   Lazing on a Sunny Afternoon *(LSA)*   100'   HVS 5a   †
Start R of *STS*, below a flake/crack growing a small oak tree at 30'. Climb the wall (past a PR) to gain the flake. The wall above is climbed direct to a tree-covered ledge, from where a step R leads to another wall & an OH, before the top is gained.   (1987)

20   Sunshine Superman   60'   E2 5c   †
Further R of *LSA* is a small hole, just above ground level, beside a broken diagonal crack. Climb up to a PR, then go over a bulge & up the wall above to a break. Move R, then climb the bulging wall above to the top.   (1987)

MIDDLE BUTTRESS
This is just to the R of Blasted Buttress.

21   Continuation Wall *(CW)*   95'   S 4a
Start a few yards above the top of Blasted Buttress. The wise will take their own pegs. A horizontal traverse RWs leads to a bramble-infested ledge, then continue direct to another to a ledge. Finish up the wall above.   (c.1950s)

22   Pine Top   120'   VS 4b,4b
An unpleasant-looking prospect, which fully realises that potential. It takes a R/L diagonal line up the obvious fault. Again pegs should be carried, although in this case the wise would do well to keep walking.
1   80'   Climb the steep narrow shelf which leads up LWs for 70', then step L to a small platform & PB where the face steepens.
2   40'   Climb the LH corner above the belay, which is both loose & awkward. Continue in the same line to the top.   (1958)

23   Impertinent Robin   140'   VS 4b
A L-to-R girdle of the cliff at two-thirds height which is serious, although not technically demanding. Start as for *CW*. Step R onto a

grassy ledge, then climb diagonally RWs to another ledge. Descend a ramp to gain an open groove. Follow this to exit RWs via a scramble to gain the belay.   (1979)

A BUTTRESS

Above Middle Buttress are three crags at varying heights on the hillside (A Buttress is clearly seen on the L). These buttresses can be reached more easily from a forestry track that contours the crest of the hillside. This can be reached easily from Morwellham, or by following a path that leads direct through the woods from the layby on the A390.

24   Jollity Farm   110'   HVS 4c,5a   †
Start 10' L of the clean arête in the centre of the cliff.
1   80'   Climb up past a PR at 20' to a ledge on the L, then move LWs to a crack. Move up & L to a corner, then traverse RWs across the hanging slab to an arête which leads to a tree belay.
2   30'   Climb the centre of the wall above (PR) to the top. Scramble to a tree belay.   (1987)

25   Aerial Ballet *(AB)*   100'   E2 5b,4c   ★
A good route which follows the clean-cut arête.
1   70'   Climb a thin crack R of the arête, then step L onto a small foothold. Climb direct to an OH, exiting L over it to a grassy belay ledge.
2   30'   Climb the prominent crack to finish.   (1979)

26   Monkey Puzzle *(MP)*   90'   VS 4b,4b   †
Start 10' R of *AB*.
1   60'   Climb up to a vegetated ledge & small holly tree at 30'. Move slightly R, then climb up to another vegetated ledge.
2   30'   Follow the steep crack & arête above, making use of the trees near the top.   (1987)

27   Daylight Saving   80'   HVS 4c
A poor route which attempts to follow the arête 10' R of *MP*. Climb a groove, then move over onto the RH wall. Trend diagonally RWs to the arête, then climb the OHing rock above (direct) to an unpleasant grassy finish.   (1979)

B BUTTRESS

Just above and to the R of the last crag, there is a buttress with an obvious overlap at half-height, and a ledge with a tree in the bottom RH corner. The next route starts here.

28   Quiet River *(QR)*   70'   VS 4c
Climb straight up a thin crack to the wall below the OH. Tackle this on its LH side, then exit RWs onto the final slab.   (1979)

29   The Entertainer   70'   E1 5b   †
Start at the base of *QR*. Climb the thin crack, then move up to the centre of the OH. Pull over this (PR) & continue up the slab above to the top.   (1987)

C BUTTRESS
This lies just above and to the L of the last cliff.

30   Cold Finger   40'   E1 5a   †
Start 40' L of the OHing arête & just L of a grass-filled gully. Climb up over a bulge, then continue up slabs to a TR at 20'. The steep wall above leads to good finishing holds.   (1987)

31   Maybe Tomorrow *(MT)*   80'   HVS 5a
Start below the obvious groove. Climb this to a tree, then move R to finish direct up the final wall.   (1979)

32   Cream Egg *(CE)*   80'   HVS 5a   †
Start just R of *MT*. Climb the steep wall on generous holds to a flake crack. Move L & up to a jammed block & TR. Step L again, then continue direct (PR) to the top.   (1987)

33   Cold Grief *(CG)*   100'   E1 5b   ★
The OHing L arête (via some exciting moves). Start 10' R of *CE*. Steep moves gain a ledge, then traverse LWs until beneath a slanting groove (PR). Climb direct to the LH end of an OH. Pull over this to good holds which lead to a ledge below a steep crack. Climb the wall R of this, stepping into the crack to finish.   (1979)

34   Points of View   100'   E2 5b   †
Follow *CG* to its first ledge, then traverse LWs for a few feet until below an overlap. Pull over this on the R, then move slightly L & up to a PR below a second overlap. Climb this on the R, then step L & continue up the wall to a large ledge. Finish direct up the wall above the ledge. Tree belay.   (1987)

RIVER BUTTRESS
The last cliff on the track beside the river is the most impressive to look at in the area.

35   Divine Inspiration *(DI)*   150'   VS 4c
The L arête of the face. Start on the track, beneath the centre of the buttress. Climb a R\L slanting fault-line which leads to the L edge of the buttress, via loose rubble. Gain the arête, then follow it until level with a horizontal break leading RWs to an exposed wall; finish up this.   (1978)

36   Salvationist   150'   S 4a
The easiest line up the wall.
1   70'   Follow *DI* to the top of the fault, then move out R into a shallow corner & follow this to a ledge in the middle of the face below an oak tree.
2   80'   Climb the steep wall above to the base of a grassy groove (30' up to the R). Follow this easily to a large ledge below the final OH. Move R to avoid this, & finish up the summit block.   (1958)

37   Ultramontane   130'   HVS 5a   ★
The central crack, which cleaves through the bulges at 40', gives a

striking line. Start as for *DI*. Climb onto the slanting fault, then gain a shallow groove which leads to a pillar on the L. Move up & follow a crack through the OH to the belay of Salvationist. Climb direct up the face above, until beneath the crowning OH. Traverse strenuously LWs for 8', then step back R onto a nose of rock & climb the summit block to the top.   (1959)

38 Thought Process   140'   HVS 5a,5a
Start 10' R of the last route.
1   50'   Climb direct to a bulge (place a peg). Trend up slightly RWs to a niche, then traverse back LWs to climb through another bulge to gain the belay of Salvationist.
2   90'   Step L & climb directly up the thin wall to a large ledge. Finish as for Ultramontane.   (1979)

SEA-LEVEL TRAVERSING

There are over five miles of traversing (that's 24,000' or, put another way, it would be like climbing eight horizontal El Cap's) above the warm inviting waters of the Gulf Stream, as they swirl and eddy their way to intermingle with the salty Adam's ale of the English Channel.

Apart from being one of Devon's more unique offerings, sea-level traversing also enjoys a modicum of popularity. The heady combination of exploration, wide variety of situations, bizarre techniques and the ubiquitous safety net of the sea, has garnered a steadfast group of coasteering cogniscenti. Their founding father, E.C. Pyatt, more or less treated this radical off-shoot of alpinism with the disdain of a First World War general. He commented that "to successfully overcome some of the more difficult sections of the Devon coastline, a plentiful supply of coasteers would be needed" (no doubt to be employed as veritable cannon-fodder against the Maginot Line-like defences of the Old Redoubt etc).

Coasteering is an all-weather pursuit, even though we are not all all-weather participants. Cold rough seas, and shorter days can make some traverses much more serious in winter. It is essential that a party should be able to get itself out of trouble. Ideally all its members should be reasonably strong swimmers, or be self-possessed enough to sacrifice themselves for the good of the group, *"I'm just going for a short paddle. I may be gone some time"*.

The traverses are described as a graded list. They appear in greater detail in the main text.

Rainbow Bridge 810' VIII+ **(R)** ★★★
Perhaps the ultimate pinnacle on the coasteering agenda (if Bob can forgive yet another *non-sequitur*). There aren't enough superlatives in the English language to do this route justice, and it isn't even polished. (page 200)

Gulliver's Travels 470' VIII- **(R)** †
Rainbow Bridge has an alter ego, and ironically enough it traverses the *sinister* side of the Old Redoubt. On-route analysis of the route name could have your grey matter spinning with analogies; "am I a tiny thing caught up in something far too big for my tiny thing to contemplate"; or, "am I a giant thing moving across tiny things, and if they are so tiny why do they keep snapping-off?". Only they who dare will know the truth. (page 216)

The Kraken   500'   VII+   ★★

> *Below the thunders of the upper deep;*
> *Far, far beneath in the abysmal sea,*
> *His ancient, dreamless, uninvaded sleep*
> *The Kraken sleepeth: faintest sunlights flee*
> *About his shadowy sides: above him swell*
> *Huge sponges of millennial growth and height;*
> *And far away into the sickly light,*
> *From many a wondrous grot and secret cell*
> *Unnumber'd and enormous polypi*
> *Winnow with giant arms the slumbering green.*
> *There hath he lain for ages and will lie*
> *Battening upon huge seaworms in his sleep,*
> *Until the latter fire shall heat the deep;*
> *Then once by man and angels to be seen,*
> *In roaring he shall rise and on the surface die.*
>
> *The Kraken – Tennyson*

A gentle boulder-hop lulls the unwitting punter into a false feeling that the route is totally overgraded, whereupon the beast awakes in the form of an unexpurgated voyage across the exposed features of a tortured face. Escape is of a highly unstable nature.   (page 98)

The Magical Mystery Tour (I, II, III and IV)   5,650'   VII   **(R)**   ★★★
A veritable Titan in the realm of traverse-dom, all other crabwise forays being mere minnows in comparison. This epic, of heroic proportions, unfurls itself along a stretch of begrottoed coastline to alight upon the mistily enchanted shores of St Mary's Bay. The name only goes partway to doing the route full justice.   (page 216)

The Watchtower   700'   VII-   ★★★
"There are many here among us who feel that life is but a joke. . . ", well this route will leave you feeling like the metaphorical lost sock in the Laundromat of oblivion, if you get the wrong conditions. It supplies the full gamut of coasteering experiences, with its centre piece being Thunderhole – a dripping orifice that comes alive in a large swell, spouting spume like the monstrous blowhole of a land-locked leviathan.   (page 167)

Morning Town Ride   6,800'   VI-
A seemingly never-ending odyssey, which ducks and dives over and around headlands, buttresses, boulders and rockpools (even avid aerobics buffs would be found wanting for puff on this one). A bottle of oxygen could come in handy.   (page 142)

Pinnacle Traverse (and continuation)   560'   VI-
Technical vignettes, interposed by yawning zawns and the odd boulder-hop make this a fine introductory experience to the more advanced levels of choppy-water avoidance-craft (CWAC). The initiated will probably find that the difficulties fall as easily as water

off a duck's back.   (page 151)

Barnacle Traverse (and continuation) 600' VI-
A consumately choreographed crustacean crunch, clandestinely combining countless callous and cripplingly cruel crimes connecting co-habiting coves (*we know a song about that don't we children!?!*).   (page 195)

Five Star Traverse 1,400' V+
It is quite extraordinary to be able to step off the bus and begin an odyssey such as this from the heart of a modern metropolis, and people don't even so much as bat an eyelid. However, it fails to live up to the quality suggested by its title.   (page 169)

Quality Street 230' V+   ★★
An excellent initiatory excursion, which should whet the appetite for more of the same. The organically sculptured rock decorating the entire length of the wall, between Arch Zawn and the beginning of the Coastguard Cliffs, would have brought tears of joy to the likes of Barbara Hepworth and Henry Moore.   (page 187)

Prawle Crawl 3,500' IV
More of an eccentric promenade than a serious coasteering proposition. Although a couple of the steeper-angled slabs are covered in luminescent green algae, which can add a keen edge to the fear factor when sliding diagonally across them.   (page 311)

Brixham to Berryhead 2,400' IV
Even with the added dimension of a high tide start, the route provides little in the way of technical interest. So while you're dabbling with the un-technical crux sections, your mind can wander. Inventing spurious tales of climbing above doom-laden waters, surreptitiously patrolled by the Nautilus, while Captain Nemo demonstratively thumps out a surly rendition of Bach's Toccatta and Fugue in 'D' minor. . . is one way of whiling away the mundane footage.   (page 177)

Plimsoll Line 200' IV-   ★
A perfunctory undertaking, the quality of which improves exponentially the further the tide rises up the wall (or during a large swell). However, the bubble of enjoyment can burst with a resounding 'plop', should you become embroiled in the seventh wave.   (page 150)

The Long Traverse 350' III   ★★
A sea-level stroll that could have you stranded in the Sanctuary, should you mis-time the tides. Its selling point is the fact that it affords a superb view of the Sanctuary Wall, and provides some exemplary ledges from which to throw yourself head-first into the sea (beware the pedalos).   (page 142)

BOULDERING

Devon isn't renowned for its bouldering, but there again it isn't really known for its climbing either, so there's not much of a surprise there. Thus it may come as a bit of a shock to learn that the Shire has some, let alone a lot. However, all this good news has to be tempered with the knowledge that this is bouldering Devon-style.

Put away all hopes of discovering another Fontainebleau, Spofforth, or Cressbrook (or indeed bouldering fantasy of fantasies. . . Kyloe-in-the-woods). The following venues are far more Devonian affairs than that, for there are few advocates of this form of self-indulgence S↓ of Bristol (possibly due to the lack of bog-walls). Therefore don't be put off by the esoteric nature of what follows, for it is dedicated to those with an aptitude for something different.

LIMESTONE

Limestone bouldering in the Shire has been well and truly over-shadowed by the exploration (and indeed exploits) of the Dartmoor Doyens. This oversight is slowly being redressed, and the areas included represent a mere fraction of the true potential.

One side-effect of bouldering being taken more seriously is the sad demise of the once ubiquitous sight of be-wellied youths flailing-up-a-sweat on the Gully Wall at Chudleigh. You can imagine that for those of us privileged enough to witness such a spectacle, it comes as quite a shock to realise just how much the face of climbing has changed – a sort of clinker-nailed galosh meets the latest sponsored-sticky-rubber scenario (why did the Nineteen-eighties have to come to an end?)

SIDMOUTH ★★★ GR 125 870

Possibly the best *en plein air* wall in the country. The climbing is on an extensive seawall ←W of the seafront. The showpiece is a magnificent sweep of limestone blockwork, sculpted by the wind and the sea into a pocketed vertical playground.

Top-rope problems abound up to the dizzying heights of 6c/7a, while the traversing on the limestone and the sandstone would satisfy the most devout celebrant of the pump – the finest is a round-trip starting on the RH side of the limestone top-roping wall and traversing to the first alcove-like cave in the sandstone, come back out of the cave via a lower-level traverse before regaining the upper weakness leading back to the limestone wall, which is reversed to its RH side (French 8a). Another feature to look out for is an unlikely looking mantelshelf midway along the sandstone which extends LWs from the alcove-like cave. It's been done once, but has rebuffed all other attempts at a repeat, which would make it definitive B3 on the John Gill bouldering scale.

CHUDLEIGH   ★★★   GR 864 788

The first choice for the locals, and reasonable by anybody's standards. There are a couple of draw backs, the bouldering is getting a bit polished and could be considered bold if you're a 'jessie' (low-level traverses abound).

Pixies Hole – This is an extensive area, similar in design to a cellar board. There are an inordinate number of problems (let alone variations) between the base of Albatross and the arête of Dream On. However, the majority of problems are based upon the excessively steep wall just L of the barred cave entrance.

The Gully – Some 15yds R of the gully (extending up to the base of Space Buttress), and directly below the arête of White Edge, is a steep corner in an alcove. The corner itself gives a sustained 6b, while the bulge (and wall) R of the corner has held out for decades (*a possible contender for double figures on the Hueco scale?*). The rest of the bouldering is up in the gully itself. Ferociously exposed would seem to be the only apt description for the problems on this wall, even by Chudleigh's standards. This steep wall is littered with jugs, slopers, mono's, riglettes and smears, and it's criss-crossed by a large number of pumpy circuits.

Cow Cave – The LH side of the cave has an excellent low, low-level traverse on undercuts which has spawned numerous variations. The RH side of the cave has a fairly hairy R-to-L traverse which finishes up at the end of a flake-crack in the middle of the cave roof (6a).

Above Wogs – Directly atop the finishes of Wogs and Black Death, there is a small bay of OHing rock, which supports an inordinate number of problems considering its modest size.

AUSEWELL ROCKS   GR 735 718

These are very strange (and purportedly) natural limestone outcroppings on the summit of a hill 1½ miles ↖NW of Ashburton. They provide some light-hearted bouldering for a summer's evening. Access is from a grassy parking bay backed by two gates, on the minor road E→ of the rocks (GR 741 717). Climb over the RH gate and follow a forest track for a brisk ten minute walk which gains an open heath, from where the Western Block becomes visible (no climbing potential as such). The Central Block is a 100yds further on, where there are a number of reasonably clean and moderately hard problems. The Eastern Block is a 100yds further on and provides the meat of the harder bouldering (it is similar in nature to the Cumbrian Bowderstone). Some very hard problems emanate from a cave under its ←W prow, while its S↓ face has a clutch of fine wall problems.

RIVER DART ROCKS ★ GR 743 668

Opposite the entrance to Bulley Cleave Quarry there is a parking bay beside the river. Follow the path beside the river until the bouldering becomes evident. It takes the form of a low wall, which culminates in a vicious stack of OHs at the hotel end of the path. This is a great venue for top-roping, while the potential for low-level traversing is mind-boggling. However, the rock needs a good clean. At one point the base is severely undercut by about 30'. A line of flakes and pockets decorate the full length of this low level roof, which goes by the name of **The Pulveriser** (5c).

ANSTEY'S COVE ★★ GR 935 650

There are a few bouldering possibilities in the Cove, the best being at the base of The Mitre (revolving around slopers, the odd pocket and some sharp breaks). There are also a few problems to be had around the base of The Lynch. However, the best of the bouldering is reserved for the low-level traverser: Might & Main to Crook Bruce (5c, if you use everything); Might & Main to The Mightiest (6a/c, depending on how low you can go); Rawhide to Devonshire Cream (6a, ending with a fine pull through the bulge to gain the start of Devonshire Cream); Groove & Slab to Acheron (6b). For those willing to walk a little further the reward is the finest traverse of the bunch. It lies in a hidden gully up behind the café and weighs in at a pumpy French 7c.

PLYMOUTH – THE HOE AREA ★★★ GR 475 538

Plymouth's saving grace (from a climbing point of view) is the smörgåsbord of bouldering oppurtunites which abound within its city limits. These are based on or around the Hoe, and to be honest a more fitting setting could not be found.

1 Mayflower Walls – These lie above Cliff Road and directly below the Mayflower Post House Hotel. Essentially the walls are used for stamina training, however the area known as The Arches gives some good problems up to 25' in height. On the footpath above and behind The Arches there is a further wall which provides a 60' traverse on crimps (5a/b).

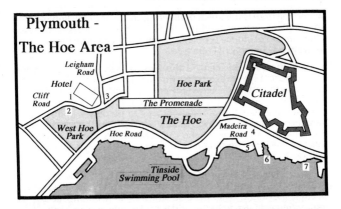

2 West Hoe Park – Directly below Cliff Road is a real gem of an urban crag. A few strategically placed belay anchors along the crest of this S ↓ facing wall, would ensure that it became the premiere training facility within the city limits. Alas the city council takes a dim view of its local climbing fraternity's use of the park.

There is a desperate 6c low-level traverse with numerous variations coupled with a smattering of vertical problems. However, the crags most profitable use would be as a top-roping venue. To date only one such route has been done, which is a credit to the Heath-Robinsonesque ingenuity of the locals. They used a sturdy automobile *(probably a Ford Escort van)*, parked on the road above the crag as a top-rope anchor and **Rambles After Dark** (6b) came into being.

3 Grand Hotel Wall – is a considerably more sustained traversing proposition compared to the neighbouring Mayflower Wall. Starting opposite the hotel entrance (in Leigham Street) traverse around the edge of the building, then attempt to pass an awkwardly placed street sign. The ensuing uphill section is topped-off by the crux.

4 Madeira Wall – A fine sweep of limestone blockwork runs parallel to Madeira Road for three hundred yards, below the Citadel. The finest section lies between the two sets of steps, and plays host to innumerable problems of 5b and upwards. The steps below the Citadel provide an extended problem in the shape of **Deckchair Arête** (5c), while the arch gives a good 5b problem over its apex; the traverse between the white door and the arch is a stiff 6a for those without deft footwork.

5 Tinside Wall – Descending the seaward steps from the Madeira Wall reveals the splendid sight of some multi-coloured Victorian bathing huts. Lurking beneath the huts and beside the Tinside swimming pool is the finest bouldering area in the city. Replete with an excellent array of boulderable features and traverses, the area offers some very fierce problems ranging in grade from the very easy to the heady heights of French 8a.

6 Springboard – Adjacent to the Tinside Wall is a natural grotto which sports a sea-level traverse through a cave system. The obvious line along the walls and across the entrance and exit roofs of the cave weighs in at 5c, so it's best attempted at high tide (the meshed-scaffolding across the entrance proves to be only a minor inconvenience). **Banana Sandwiches** (5b) traverses around the pillar between the entrances to the cave and **Freddy Fishcake** (bold 5c) follows the large undercut flake rising up through the first cave entrance.

7 High Dive – To find this area follow a path from Madeira Wall towards the Sailing Club, before which another sea-filled grotto becomes evident. The traverse consists of climbing across an impending wall (6a) with the odd wave lapping at your heels. If the traverse-line is followed beyond an undercut prow the ensuing groove gives hard 6b climbing to gain the top.

GRANITE

If you can muster together the required amount of skin for an evening, let alone a day, of bouldering on the Moor then the portals of a novel experience should swing wide for you.

Dartmoor hasn't really been a buzz-word in bouldering circles. . . up until now that is. Admittedly, it doesn't have the same ring as gritstone in that it doesn't conjure up an image of an immaculate series of moves on perfect elemental rock, under an azure canopy on a day when every inhalation turns your lungs to ice while your breath looks like you're a chain-smoker (and fingers feel like they're pregnant with radiators). Well, after a late autumn day's bouldering on Combshead Tor that will be how you explain it to the uninitiated, and of course you'll be able to wear that smug smile reserved for such an occasion.

WESTCOTT ROCKS   GR 792 875

The full potential of this venue has yet to be realised. The bouldering possibilities appear to be limitless, but the locals seem loathe to put the work in to get the place up to scratch. The boulders lie along the edge of a wooded escarpment, and form a gritstone type edge. It boasts an array of novel features such as a bouldering gallery, and a half-pint granite version of The Cornice at Water-cum-Jolly.

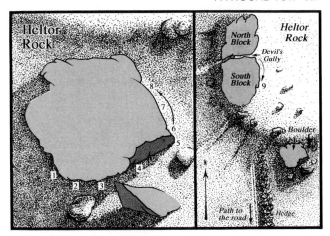

HELTOR ROCK ★   GR 800 871

Heltor's saving grace as a climbing venue is the boulder which overlooks the approach path on the walk up to the tor. After ticking the standard problems it becomes a playground limited only by your own imagination.

- ☐ **1** 3a Rippled rib
- ☐ **2** 4b Wall via rounded breaks
- ☐ **3** 5b Wall on slopes
- ☐ **4** 6a The OH direct
- ☐ **5** 5c Arête
- ☐ **6** 5c Low level traverse
- ☐ **7** 5b Rippled wall
- ☐ **8** 5a Wall
- ☐ **9** 5a Rounded break on E face of South Block

HOUND TOR ★★   GR 743 790

The complexity of the tor does not readily lend itself to either a written or illustrated description. Suffice it to say that the bouldering is there and most of it is superb, although it takes a seasoned eye to spot it. Of particular note is the face of a fin-shaped boulder to the ←W of the toe of Western Block; a boulder with a very low OH opposite Aerobic Wall which begins with a front lever (and goes by the name of **Skin-graft**), and has the attendant attraction of being a Plymouth 5c (there is no higher accolade for a problem); and finally there is an alcove R of the start of Liar's Dice which has spawned innumerable eliminates.

BONEHILL ROCKS   ★★★   GR 732 775

Undoubtedly one of the most popular granite bouldering areas in the Shire, and rightly so. The only drawback is that it is very popular with the tourists as well. This sad state of affairs is due to Widecombe being less than a hefty stones throw-away, but the aggravation of grockels under-foot can be off-set by the compensating indulgence of a post-pump gorging at the finest cream tea hostelries in the world. . . well maybe not the world, but they are close to hand.

There is far more bouldering here than this short resumé can do justice to – and the potential for harder stuff is mind-boggling – however, the problems contained herein represent the cream of the more independent lines.

- ☐ **1** 5b LH side of steep slab
- ☐ **2** 5c Middle of slab
- ☐ **3** 6a RH side of slab
- ☐ **4** 4c Groove & horizontal crack
- ☐ **5** 3a Low level traverse
- ☐ **6** 5c Traverse thin break (joining 7 boosts the grade to 6b)
- ☐ **7** 5c Centre of curved scoop (bum-drag start)
- ☐ **8** 5b RH rib of curved scoop
- ☐ **9** 6a Arête R of 8 (direct)
- ☐ **10** 6b R-to-L traverse of block via thin break (finish up 9)
- ☐ **11** 5b Rib (via rounded breaks)
- ☐ **12** 3b Jamming crack
- ☐ **13** 5b Wall R of crack
- ☐ **14** 4b Wall (begin at small flake)
- ☐ **15** 5c Rounded arête (plus LH wall)
- ☐ **16** 5b L-to-R traverse of break (mantel finish)
- ☐ **17** 6a Steep wall via lunge for flake (join 16)
- ☐ **18** 6c OHs & rough breaks (even harder with thin LWs traverse to start)
- ☐ **19** 3a Multiple lines up the slab
- ☐ **20** 5b Sharp arête (bold)
- ☐ **21** 5c RH arête & wall
- ☐ **22** 5c Rippled wall direct
- ☐ **23** 6a Rising LWs traverse of wall on breaks (finish direct)
- ☐ **24** 6b Direct start to 23
- ☐ **25** 6b OH & bald wall above (bold)
- ☐ **26** 5c Superb crack through OHs (bum-drag start)
- ☐ **27** 4c Jamming-crack
- ☐ **28** 5c Rounded rib & LH wall
- ☐ **29** 6c Centre of wall (project)
- ☐ **30** 5a Flake
- ☐ **31** 5b R-to-L traverse along break (finish up 30)

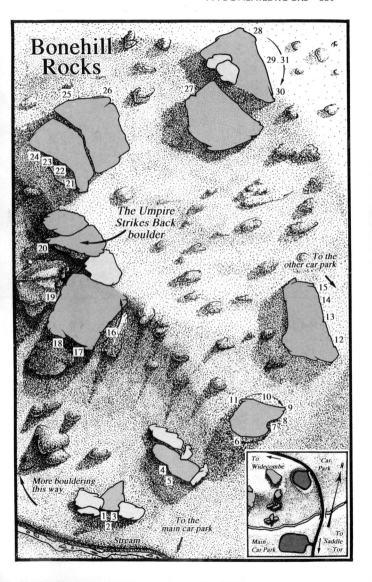

Bonehill
Rocks

The Umpire
Strikes Back
boulder

To the
other car park

More bouldering
this way

Stream

To the
main car park

To
Widecombe

Car
Park

Main
Car Park

To
Saddle
Tor

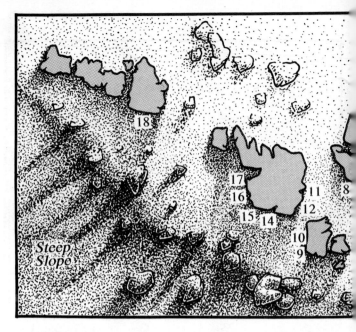

COMBESTONE TOR ★★

GR 671 719

In direct contrast to Lustleigh Cleave, the bouldering at Combestone Tor lies about 10yds from the parking bay. These ill-frequented and exposed boulders are set against the scenic backdrop of the steep-sided valley containing the River Dart. The boulders can provide a pleasant end-of-the-day burn after a visit to either Luckey Tor or Bench Tor.

- ☐ **1** 4b Rounded rib (direct)
- ☐ **2** 6a Low level traverse
- ☐ **3** 2a Wide crack
- ☐ **4** 5b Wall
- ☐ **5** 5c RH side of OH
- ☐ **6** 5a LH side of OH
- ☐ **7** 4c Arête
- ☐ **8** 4a Wall
- ☐ **9** 4c Arête
- ☐ **10** 3c Wall
- ☐ **11** 3a Runnel in slabby wall
- ☐ **12** 3b Slabby Wall
- ☐ **13** 4b Rounded arête

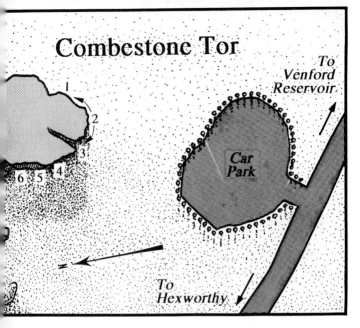

Combestone Tor

To Venford Reservoir

Car Park

To Hexworthy

- ☐ **14** 5b Rippled wall
- ☐ **15** 4a Groove
- ☐ **16** 3a Rib
- ☐ **17** 5a Wall
- ☐ **18** 5b Wall & breaks

MANATON ROCKS ★★ GR 746 816

Another excellent granite venue, with a wide variety of bouldering opportunities (and potential). Park-up by the village church, and follow a path on the far side of the graveyard. This leads up onto a wooded ridge. Contour the wooded hillside L of the path, where the bouldering becomes apparent.

The first problem is a vicious jamming crack (formed by two large boulders meeting), on the RH side of a steeply OHing prow with a thin crack running up it.

- ☐ **1** 4c Jamming crack
- ☐ **2** 6a Thin crack
- ☐ **3** 5b Wall
- ☐ **4** 6a RH rib of slabby wall
- ☐ **5** 5b Middle of mossy wall

Manaton Rocks

Open heathland

Woodland

Stone wall

Approach path

LUSTLEIGH CLEAVE ★★ GR 772 815

A fanatical devotion to exploration can be richly rewarded on this picturesque ridge, high above the River Bovey. The words "infinite possibilities" spring to mind for the optimists, while the word "nightmare" could easily replace "possibility" for those of a more morose nature. Walking in ever increasing circles around the two climbing areas of Raven's Tor and The Nut Crackers will yield a

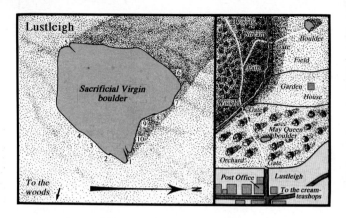

good percentage of the problems (or not as the case maybe).

For those who like their bouldering to be less fraught, the Sacrificial Virgin boulder (GR 781 816) is the obvious alternative. Wend down the short road beside the Post Office in Lustleigh and amble through the orchard (containing the May Queen boulder) to follow a footpath through some woods – trending RWs. After five minutes the boulder becomes apparent as a large lump in the middle of a field. Public rights of way are uncertain hereabouts, so be discreet and if challenged be courteous.

- ☐ **1**   5b   Cracks in LH rib of OHung scoop
- ☐ **2**   5c   Wall via all holds possible
- ☐ **3**   6a   Wall just L of rounded lump
- ☐ **4**   6b   Wall L again (without lump)
- ☐ **5**   3a   The descent
- ☐ **6**   5c   Wall R of rounded rib
- ☐ **7**   6b   RH bounding rib of OHung scoop
- ☐ **8**   6b   **Desire** – Flake & RH wall (bold)
- ☐ **9**   6b   OH direct (still to be soloed)
- ☐ **10** 5c   Wall (on nubbins)

VIXEN TOR   ★★   GR 542 743

A selection of boulders, resembling fossilised monsters, occupy the rocky meadow below the toe of the Feasibility Study slab. They sport features of an incredibly aggressive nature, so you'd be wise to tape-up or retire to the low bouldering wall (between the slab and the West Face). There are some very technical problems here, the low-level traverse of the wall (R-to-L) has only recently been done at 6c.

The crack through the OH on Frog Boulder goes at 6a although some of the Plymouth locals would have you believe it to be a path at 5a, while the wall to its R has a number of variations – the easiest being 5c.

COMBSHEAD TOR   ★★★★   GR 587 688

Superb bouldering, although you'll probably get pissed-off by the walk-in (a mountain bike does take the sting out of it). The most direct approach is to park in the large parking bay at the NE ↗ end of Burrator Reservoir, from where a track runs virtually all the way to the tor.

Just below the summit is the isolated pinnacle of Cuckoo Rock, which provides some taxing problems. The other blocks in close proximity to Cuckoo Rock also provide a myriad concentration of boulderable features in the shape of hanging corners, sharp arêtes, thin faces, cracks and slabs.

Contouring back along the ridge to Down Tor opens up a veritable feast of further potential. However, it will take more than a casual afternoon's fossicking through the jumbled clitter to find the best problems.

☐	**1**	5c	Hanging groove
☐	**2**	4c	Slabby rib
☐	**3**	6a	Mossy crack, mantel & slight groove
☐	**4**	4a	Ribby arête
☐	**5**	6a	RH side of sloping arête
☐	**6**	6c	Thin wall
☐	**7**	5c	Sharp arête
☐	**8**	6a	Crystal wall
☐	**9**	6a	Diagonal cracks leading to slab (bold)
☐	**10**	3a	Slab
☐	**11**	5c	RH side of R arête of the slab
☐	**12**	4b	Crack in arête
☐	**13**	4c	Wall
☐	**14**	4b	Arête
☐	**15**	5a	RH side of arête & slight runnel
☐	**16**	6b	Wall direct on sloping breaks (still to be soloed)
☐	**17**	6a	Arête (bold)
☐	**18**	6c	Low level traverse
☐	**19**	6a	Rounded arête
☐	**20**	5b	Wall between arête & crack
☐	**21**	5a	Crack
☐	**22**	6b	Arête & hanging flake
☐	**23**	4c	Crack
☐	**24**	6c	Wall between crack & arête (project)
☐	**25**	5c	Arête direct
☐	**26**	5a	RH side of arête
☐	**27**	5b	Crack

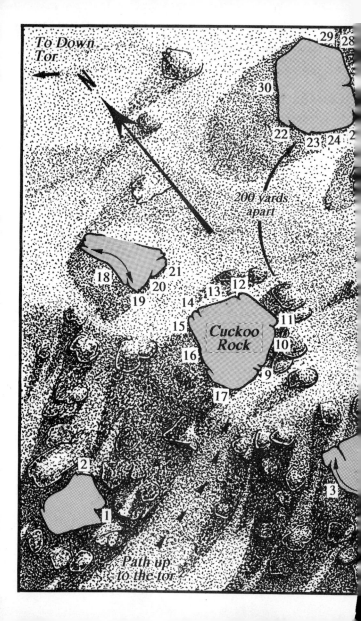

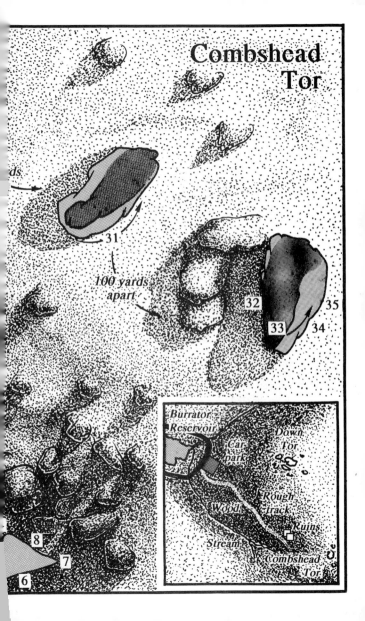

Combshead
Tor

ds →

31

100 yards
apart

32 35

33 34

8

7

6

Burrator
Reservoir

Car
park

Down
Tor

Rough
track

Wood

Ruins

Stream

Combshead
Tor

☐	**28**	5c	Arête & RH wall
☐	**29**	6b	Wall direct
☐	**30**	7?	Wall (project)
☐	**31**	6b	L-to-R low level traverse of break under bulge
☐	**32**	6c	Undercut & dyno for flake
☐	**33**	6b	Traverse of block via break & slopes, finish up 34 or 35
☐	**34**	5b	Mantel
☐	**35**	5b	Flake & slab

MISCELLANEOUS

Not content with the bountiful supply of natural bouldering offered by the leafy dells, pungent grots and windswept moors of the Shire, the indolent locals have taken to buildering. Needless to say, this activity is not going to be documented here. What is on offer is a pumpy sandstone venue in the shape of Exmouth, and a superb series of steep low-level traverses at Downderry.

EXMOUTH   GR 021 799

Some very pumpy problems and traversing can be had at the end of the Marine Drive. Park near the turning circle at the end of the beach, where most of the bouldering is immediately obvious. The LH part of the wall sports a rounded L/R diagonal ramp. Followed to the break at 15' this gives a forearm-numbing 6b. To the R there is a 6b over a bulge at a short, weeping crack. R again there is a 5c/6a problem over a juggy bulge that can be extended into a pumpy RWs traverse. (After a storm the shingle can get washed away leaving a powerful low level traverse; it also increases the grades of the other problems).

Further R are several OHs that give scary 5c problems. Around the corner, the bay extends toward Sandy Bay, where numerous fallen boulders can be enjoyed at your own discretion.

DOWNDERRY   ★★★   GR 330 538

Although part of Cornwall, Downderry was overlooked in the North Devon and Cornwall guide, which was a bit remiss really, so to undo such a heinous error here is an unexpurgated review.

There are a number of ways to reach Downderry; either turn S ↓ off the A38 at Trerulefoot and head for Seaton – or catch the Torpoint ferry (from Plymouth) and head for Seaton. Either way you end up on the B3247. Park-up at a small parking bay in the middle of several tortuous hairpin bends just E→ of Downderry, and descend a slippery mud path to gain the beach. The bouldering begins some 400yds along the beach (which is a haunt for flaccid male naturists in the summer).

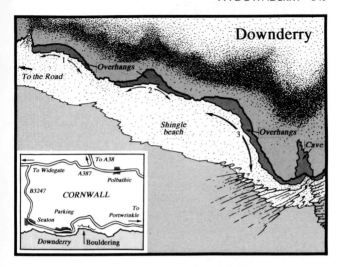

The traverses are very reminiscent of the bouldering at Criccieth on the Lleyn Peninsula, and are incredibly pumpy. There are also a number of vertical problems centred around the cave at the end of the final traverse. If you're still not impressed then attempt to connect problems 1, 2 and 3.

- ☐ **1** 6b **The Wave**
- ☐ **2** 6b **The Undercut**
- ☐ **3** 6b **The Promontory**
- ☐ **4** 5c **Cave Traverse** – the rail on the RH side of the cave

FIRST ASCENTS

The following listing is as detailed and comprehensive as the present level of documentation will allow. If anyone can shed any further light over the copious number of blanks, be it a name or date then please contact either the author, editor or the publisher.

Many of the earlier routes have been re-documented to give their ascentionists due credit. In the case of whole aid routes being climbed free (or the odd aid-point being eliminated), then these details are listed twice: (a) in *italics* under the original first ascent date; (b) as a full entry under the date of the First Free Ascent (FFA); First Dry Ascent (FDA); First Winter Ascent (FWA). This has been done to present a clearer perspective of how events unfurled chronologically. By the same token Bolt Free Ascents (BFA) have been treated in the same fashion.

Variations, although credited with a separate date (where applicable) in the text, are dealt with under the same entry as the original First Ascent date.

The abbreviations *(AL)* and *(VL)* indicate alternate and varied leads respectively.

The presence of only one name does not indicate a solo ascent.

1894	**Main Gully / Mucky Gully**	Walter Parry Haskett-Smith, Scott Tucker.
1923	**Wogs** I.B.Prowse.	
2/9/35	**Climbers' Club Original**	David Cox, Rennie Bere *(by the original finish)*.
27/9/36	**Climbers' Club Direct**	Robin Hodgkin, David Cox. *After pitch 1 they followed what is now the Ordinary. Pitch 2 was climbed by G.Whittaker (in September 1950), as part of the Superdirect. The top crack was first climbed direct by John Deacon in 1959 as part of Globe & Laurel.*
13/10/45	**Right Hand Slab & Chimney** Tony Moulam.	
18/5/46	**Aramis** Tony Moulam.	
1947	**Brown Wall / East Crack / Gorse Groove / Great Gully Groove / Wall Climb** Tony Moulam.	
7/48	**Colonel's Arête** Jim Moulton, *Skinner* Saunders *(solo)*.	
22/1/49	**Route B** Keith Lawder, Bob Higgins *(VL)*.	
28/1/49	**Pinnacle Buttress / Pinnacle Chimney** Bob Higgins, Keith Lawder *(VL)*.	
28/1/49	**The Tunnel** Keith Lawder.	
5/2/49	**Central Groove** Jim Simpson.	
5/2/49	**Needle Arête** Jim Simpson *(solo)*.	
26/2/49	**Raven Face** Bob Higgins.	
30/4/49	**Reverse Cleft** Bill & Bob Higgins *(AL)*.	
1949	**Admiral's Traverse** Keith Lawder, G.Whittaker, Bill Higgins. *This name originally referred to the short traverse on pitch 3 but the name is now used for the complete girdle in recognition of the exploration of the crag done by Admiral Lawder. The pitches were climbed at different times by those mentioned.*	
1949	**The High Traverse** Keith Lawder, Bob Higgins.	
25/6/50	**Agag's Slab** J.D.Derry.	
23/7/50	**Saint's Niche** J.Goss.	
9/12/50	**Sloppy Gully** R.Smith, J.Goss.	
1951	**Pulpit / Right Chimney / Stegadacea Chimney** Jack Denton.	
1951	**Raven Gully** Tony Moulam. *Someone has at last come forward to claim the prize awarded to the Higgins brothers, which they say was not theirs to claim.*	
8/1/52	**Canis** Tony Moulam.	
1/6/52	**Vineyard** Frank Dowlen, J.Smith *(VL)*. *Pitch 1 was originally a separate route called Leviathan. Due to some confusion this name later became used for another pitch. The variation start was climbed by Andy McFarlane, Deryck Ball in 1969.*	

1/6/52 **Armada** J.Smith, Frank Dowlen *(VL)*.

7/54 **Cantilever Direct** Jack Denton.
16/8/54 **Cantilever Crack / North Face Chimney** Jack Denton.
16/8/54 **North Face Chimney** Jack Denton.
16/8/54 **Suspension Flake** Geoff Sutton.
26/8/54 **Sheep May Safely Graze** Geoff Sutton.
8/54 **Mushroom Wall** Geoff Sutton.

18/9/55 **Letterbox Wall** Jack Denton.
10/55 **Ann** Geoff & Ann Sutton.
11/55 **Honeymoon Corner** Geoff & Ann Sutton *(newly weds)*.

1/5/57 **Corner Chimney** Barry Page, P.C.Henry.
9/57 **Leviathan** Tom Patey. *The direct finish to pitch 1 was climbed by Andy McFarlane, Deryck Ball in 1969.*
1957 **Climbers' Club Superdirect** Barry Page.

3/58 **Scorpion** Tom Patey.
4/58 **Windowsill** Tom Patey.
8/9/58 **Green Beret** Tom Patey. *Pitch 1 added by Pete O'Sullivan, A.Cloquet, M.Wilson on 11/5/79.*
9/58 **Salvationist** Tom Patey.
4/11/58 **In Extremis** Tom Patey.
8/11/58 **Spinal Column** Tom Patey.
9/11/58 **Perfecto** Tom Patey.
16/11/58 **Pine Top** Tom Patey.
17/11/58 **Silken Thread** Tom Patey.
12/58 **Thor** Tom Patey, Eoin Sloin *(1pt)*. FFA Pete O'Sullivan, B.Rossiter in 1979.
12/58 **Cerebus / Overhanging Crack / Tiptoe** Tom Patey, Eoin Sloin.

1/59 **Cleaver** Tom Patey.
5/59 **Spider's Web** Tom Patey, Barry Page, P.C.Henry. *The present finish was added by John Jones.*
6/59 **Commando Crack / Ultramontane** John Zeke Deacon, Tom Patey, Vivian Stevenson. *Pitch 1 of Commando Crack was added in October 1959 by Tom Patey.*
7/59 **Vandal** Tom Patey. *This was combined with Ann to form the route Vandal & Ann.*
30/9/59 **Globe & Laurel** John Deacon, S.Jarvis, Vivian Stevenson *(3pts)*.
1959 **Central Buttress / Oak Tree Zig-zag** Andrew Borwick.

4/60 **Original Route / Main Gully** Cliff Fishwick, G.Seale.
30/6/60 **Outward Bound** Tom Patey.
7/60 **Barn Owl Crack** Tom Patey, R.Grant, S.Bemrose.
7/60 **La Bête Noire** R.Griffith, Mike Rabley *(1pt)*. FFA Pete O'Sullivan, Chris George in 1977.
7/60 **Right Hand Chimney** Cliff Fishwick.
7/60 **Scar** Nev Hannaby, Tom Patey. *Pitch 1 added by Frank Cannings in September 1962. Direct finish added by Pete Biven in June 1966.*
8/60 **Babylon** Mike Rabley, Brian Shackleton.
9/60 **Loot** Nev Hannaby, Eric Rayson. *Named because a prior would-be ascentionist left some swag behind. Misnamed as Lute for 30 years!*
11/60 **Guy Fawkes Crack** Nev Hannaby, Eric Rayson.
11/60 **Inkerman Groove** Eric Rayson, Nev Hannaby. *Direct variation by Andy McFarlane, A.Pearson 18/9/71.*
11/60 **The Slot** Nev Hannaby.
1960 **Chudleigh Overhang** Tom Patey *(1pt)*. He traversed off L after the first pitch. FFA in 1961 by Pete Biven, Jim Braven. The modern finish was added by Frank Cannings, John Taylor, A.R.Thompson on 12/6/65.
1960 **Sarcophagus** Tom Patey. *Variation done a few years later.*

1/61 **Reek** Eric Rayson, B.Waistell, Nev Hannaby. *They probably did* **Spearhead** *at the same time.*
3/61 **Machete Wall** Eric Rayson. *Named after the implement used to defoliate the route & definitely the hardest undertaking in Devon at the time.*
3/61 **Sisyphus** Tom Patey, Jim Braven.
14/5/61 **Ivy Wall** Barrie & Pete Biven, Cliff Fishwick. *The RH finish was added by Frank Cannings in 1964.*
5/61 **Black Jam Crack / Eagle's Nest** Pete Biven, Cliff Fishwick.
6/61 **Great Western** Nev Hannaby, Eric Rayson. *Pitch 4 added by Pete Biven, Jim Braven in November 1961.*

8/8/61	**Evening Buttress** Dave Bassett.
8/61	**Never on Sunday** Dave Bassett, Alex Allen.
7/9/61	**Red Crack / Thursday Rib** Dave Bassett.
11/9/61	**Crystal Corner** Alex Allen, L.Message.
12/9/61	**Hawkin's Climb** Alex Allen, L.Message.
9/61	**Aviation** Dave Basset, Harry Cornish.
13/10/61	**Captain's Corner** Dave Bassett, Alex Allen, L.Message.
16/10/61	**Abbott's Way** Dave Bassett.
1961	**Ash Traverse / Beatrice / Dante / Earth / Furze / Ivy / Peck** Pete Biven, Cliff Fishwick.
1961	**Brer Fox / Brer Rabbit** R.Moodie, R.Gammage.
1961	**Haggis** Robin Shaw.
1961	**Hangover** Joe Barry.
1961	**Squirrel** Jim Braven, R.Gammage.
1/62	**Valhalla Wall** Mike Rabley, Brian Shackleton.
19/5/62	**Inkspots Hangover** Dave Bassett, Joe Barry.
7/62	**Combined Ops** Pete Biven, Barrie Biven, Cliff Fishwick, Jim Braven.
7/62	**Oesophagus** Barrie Biven, Jim Braven.
7/62	**Stalactite** Pete Biven, Jim Braven. **Stalactite Direct** *was rumoured to have been done the same year, although somewhere along the line the 'golot' (a type of bolt) fell out & the route became overgrown. Renamed* **Grim Reaper** *after the BFA by Nick White on 10/5/86.*
12/62	**Gideon** Mike Rabley, John Jones *(1pt).* *FFA by Len Benstead, Dennis Morrod in 1969.*
1962	**Cretin's Cavort** Mike Rabley.
1962	**Eastern Girdle / South Face Girdle** Pete Biven, Jim Braven.
1962	**The Long Traverse** John Worsley. *The HVS escape pitch was added by Pete Biven in 1964.*
31/3/63	**The Notch** Frank Cannings, Dennis Morrod, Jim Braven.
3/63	**Tropic of Capricorn** Pete Biven, Jim Braven.
7/4/63	**Ben Gunn** Frank Cannings, Denver Rainford.
7/4/63	**Tropic of Cancer** Frank Cannings.
12/9/63	**Cornish Reprieve** Pat Mellor, Bob Moulton.
21/12/63	**Dripdry** Frank Cannings, Denver Rainford. *Pitch 2 was added by Brian Housely, Brian Neely on 27/3/66. FFA of first pitch by Pat Littlejohn in 1982. FFA of pitch 2 by Dave Cope on 4/3/85.*
1963	**Vala** Brian Shackleton, Pat Mellor.
2/64	**Green Mantle** J.Brooks, R.Cockran. *The variation was also done at the same time, by J. & R.Brooks.*
2/64	**Nexus** Pete Biven, D.Horley.
22/2/64	**Smoke Gets in Your Eyes** Frank Cannings. *Reduced to 1pt & then FFA by Pete Leedell in February 1971.*
29/2/64	**Leap Year Finish** Frank Cannings, A.R.Thompson.
3/64	**Sexus** Pete Biven, D.Horley.
2/4/64	**The Dial** Frank Cannings, A.R.Thompson. *The variation finish* (**Crescendo**) *was climbed by John Taylor in April 1967.*
4/64	**Plexus** Pete Biven, D.Horley. *Mr Biven was obviously doing some light reading at the time.*
5/64	**Thornifixion** Pete Biven, D.Horley. **The Rosy Exit** *was done by Pat Littlejohn, Steve Dawson on 9/4/67. The Miller collection is now written in stone. Bob (the editor) assures me that this is a suitably (pen)insular comment.*
9/8/64	**Superdirect** Frank Cannings, Pete Badcock.
21/8/64	**Interrogation** Frank Cannings, Pete Badcock *(6pts).* *FFA & direct start (1pt) by Pat Littlejohn in 1971. The aid on the direct start was eliminated by Mick Fowler in 1980.*
25/10/64	**Low Man Girdle** Frank Cannings, Pete Badcock *(aid).* *FFA by Mick Fowler in 1980.*
10/64	**Caveman Rock** Pete Biven, W.Reilly.
10/64	**Colossus** Pete Biven, D.Horley, W.Reilly, P.Raven.
1/11/64	**Cyclops** Frank Cannings, Brian Shackleton.
1964	**The Camel** Brian Shackleton, John Jones *(AL).*
1964	**Dulux** Pete Biven, D.Horley.
1964	**Grey Tower / The Ridge** Pete Biven *et al.*
1964	**Knucklecracker** Brian Shackleton.
1964	**Mango Corner** John Jones, Brian Shackleton.
1964	**Yogi** John Jones, Brian Shackleton *(1pt).* *FFA by Pete O'Sullivan, Chris George in 1977.*

1/65 **Devil's Elbow**   R.Cockram, Steve Dawson.
7/2/65 **Niagra**   Pete Biven, D.Horley, P.Raven.
14/2/65 **The Spider**   Frank Cannings, Pete Biven. *The main pitch was originally done by Frank Cannings, Tony Thompson on 9/4/64. Pitch 1 was climbed later (with the addition of Pete Badcock) on 8/11/64.*
28/2/65 **Logic**   Frank Cannings, P.Badcock, A.Thompson. *Variation start (***Dream On***) added by Pat Littlejohn (solo) in 1971.*
2/65 **Gagool**   Ian McMorrin, W.Reilly.
2/65 **Sickle**   Pete Biven, P.Raven.
28/3/65 **Nimrod**   Frank Cannings, B.Housley.
4/4/65 **Psycho**   Al Alvarez, Pete Biven *(AL).*
11/4/65 **Titan / Ivy League**   Frank Cannings, Frank Stebbings. *FFA of pitch 3 of Titan by Chris Nicholson on 27/4/84 & named* **Pig's Ear.**
5/65 **Three Steps**   Roger Binns.
16/5/65 **The Fly**   Frank Cannings, Joe Raven. *This was the date of the final complete ascent. Pitch 1 was originally called Renaissance, & climbed by Pete Biven, Jim Braven on 6/10/62. Pitch 2 was first climbed by Frank Cannings et al on 9/4/64.*
5/65 **Decembrist / Hammer / Jacobin / Kulak Groove / Sickle** Brian Shackleton, R.Widdows.
6/65 **Prometheus**   Pete Biven, Frank Cannings *(VL).*
10/6/65 **Scorpion**   Frank Cannings, Pete Biven.
14/6/65 **Bachillinus**   Bob Moulton, Nick Allen *(AL).*
6/65 **Andromeda**   Pete Biven, D.Horley. *Variation done by Chris Bonnington, Pete Biven in September 1965.*
6/65 **Hammer**   Brian Shackleton. *The variation was climbed in March 1965 by S.Abbot, P.Raven, Pete Biven.*
6/65 **Lime Street**   Roger Widdows, Brian Shackleton.
6/65 **Oblomov**   Brian Shackleton, Roger Widdows.
16/9/65 **The Track**   Frank Cannings, A.Thompson. *Variation by Ed Grindley on 7/10/70.*
22/9/65 **Cygnus**   Pete Biven, Frank Cannings.
28/9/65 **Geminii I**   Frank Cannings, Pete Biven.
9/10/65 **Octobrist / Party Line**   Brian Shackleton, Bob Moulton *(AL)*
9/10/65 **Trotsky**   Bob Moulton, Brian Shackleton *(AL).*
10/10/65 **Geminii II**   Pete Biven, Jim Braven, A.Clarke.
10/10/65 **Little Subtleties**   Steve Dawson, L.Elton.
10/10/65 **Orion**   Brian Shackleton, Bob Moulton *(AL)*, Pete Biven.
17/10/65 **Rock House Corner**   Brian Shackleton.
13/11/65 **Bolshevik**   Bob Moulton, Graham Gilbert *(AL).*
13/11/65 **Sunday Express**   Graham Gilbert, Bob Moulton *(AL).*
21/11/65 **Leo**   George Lowe, Phil Bennett. *Originally known as Bristol Harp. Renamed* **The Mane Man** *on the FFA by Nick White on 15/11/88. Direct Start (Aid), added by Steve Dawson, D.Rogers on 12/3/67.*
26/12/65 **Highway '65**   Frank Cannings, D.Walls.
28/12/65 **Central Pillar**   Frank Cannings, Pete Biven.
1965 **Bee Line**   Brian Shackleton, Roger Hemes.

29/1/66 **Götterdamerung**   Brian Neely, L.Elton, Steve Dawson
20/2/66 **Obstreperous**   Denver Rainford, Brian Housley. *FFA as a top-rope problem by Nick White in September 1986. Led by Ken Palmer on 18/6/91.*
27/2/66 **Tantalus**   Andy Powling, Brian Neely (2pts). *Pitch 1 & FFA by Brian Wilkinson, Andy Gallagher on 14/4/79.*
5/3/66 **Route '66**   Steve Dawson, L.Elton.
3/66 **Valkyrie Rib**   Brian Neely, L.Elton.
4/4/66 **Concerto**   Frank Cannings, Andy Powling *(2pts). FFA by Steve Bell on 23/3/79.*
16/4/66 **Tristan**   Pat Littlejohn, Steve Jones. *Pat's first foray into the world of newrouting.*
4/66 **Tar Baby**   Steve Dawson, P.Butler. *The finish had been done before by L.Elton, John Jones in December 1965.*
4/66 **White Edge**   Pete Biven, Ian McMorrin *(AL).*
1/5/66 **Panga**   Ian McMorrin, Pete Biven *(AL 2pts). FFA by Steve Bell, Bruce Woodley 27/6/79.*
14/5/66 **Black Death**   Denver Rainford, E.Phillips *(AL-13pts of aid). Climbed with 1pt in 1980 by Paul Dawson. FFA by Pat Littlejohn in 1982.*
23/5/66 **Port Tack**   Pete Biven, Cliff Fishwick.
30/5/66 **Central Slabs / Gulliver**   Pat Littlejohn, Steve Jones.
5/66 **Bolero**   Andy Powling, Pat Littlejohn, Brian Neely.
3/6/66 **Main Mast**   Frank Cannings, Pete Biven.
3/6/66 **Ropeway**   Pete Biven, Frank Cannings.
10/6/66 **Slipway**   Pete Biven, Cliff Fishwick.
6/66 **East Gully Wall**   Pete Biven, Jim Braven.

7/66	**Perseus**	Ian McMorrin, Pete Biven.
8/66	**Gretel**	Steve Dawson, Brain Neely.
8/66	**Hansel**	Brian Neely, Steve Dawson.
9/9/66	**Genesis**	J.Paterson, Brian Shackleton, J.Jones.
9/9/66	**Noebbles Buttress**	J.Jones, Brian Shackleton, J.Paterson.
25/9/66	**Diana**	Pete Biven, John Hammon, Ian McMorrin.
25/9/66	**Grey Wall Eliminate**	Frank Cannings, Andy Powling.
25/9/66	**Garden Wall Eliminate**	Frank Cannings, Pete Biven *(AL)*.
8/10/66	**Nemesis**	Pat Littlejohn, Steve Dawson *(1pt)*.
25/12/66	**Christmas Corner**	Frank Cannings, Pete Biven.

18/3/67	**Raven Wing**	Frank Cannings, Pete Biven. *Variation start by Jon Gandy in 1988.*
9/4/67	**Yggdrasel**	Steve Dawson, Pat Littlejohn.
30/4/67	**Red Monk**	R.Crawshaw, D.Rogers.
30/4/67	**Schizophrenia**	I.Staples, Steve Dawson *(AL)*.
1/4/67	**West End**	Pat Littlejohn, Steve Dawson, John Hammond.
4/67	**Barn Owl Variant**	Brian Neely, Andy Powling.
4/67	**Levitation**	Andy Powling, Pat Littlejohn.
7/5/67	**Chastity Corner**	Pat Littlejohn, D.Rogers, R.Crawshaw.
7/5/67	**Ruddy Corner**	R.Crawshaw, D.Rogers, Pat Littlejohn.
21/5/67	**Mayday**	Brian Neely, Pat Littlejohn *(AL)*.
21/5/67	**Tree Root**	Jeff Jones, John Fowler.
29/5/67	**Gates of Eden**	Steve Dawson, John Hammond.
29/5/67	**Swan Lake / Tenterhooks**	Pat Littlejohn, Steve Jones.
2/6/67	**Diamond Rib / Rubber Soul**	Pete Biven, Cliff Fishwick.
3/6/67	**Nardley Stoad's Climb**	John Hammond, Ann Kellow, John Fowler.
3/6/67	**Nest Egg**	T.Lindop, E.Phillips *(AL)*.
9/6/67	**Love Not War**	John Hammond, T.Lindop *by the original finish. Present finish added by Brian Neely on 18/6/67.*
10/6/67	**Last Exit to Torquay**	Pete Biven, Al Alvarez.
13/6/67	**Midas Touch**	Frank Cannings, Pat Littlejohn, Pete Biven.
13/6/67	**Pinnacle Traverse**	Pete Biven *(solo)*.
17/6/67	**Triton**	Pete Biven, Frank Cannings.
18/6/67	**The Pearl**	Frank Cannings, Pat Littlejohn *(AL)*, Pete Biven.
18/6/67	**Tobacco Road**	Frank Cannings, Pat Littlejohn, Pete Biven.
23/6/67	**Tremor**	Pat Littlejohn, John Taylor.»PG«
6/67	**Ancient Mariner**	Pat Littlejohn, Ron Littlejohn.
8/7/67	**The Bead**	Frank Cannings, Fred Stebbings.
9/7/67	**Gargantua**	Frank Cannings, Pat Littlejohn.
15/7/67	**Neptune**	Pete Biven, Frank Cannings, Pat Littlejon.
15/7/67	**Slithy Tove**	Frank Cannings *(solo)*.
16/7/67	**Mighty Atom**	Pat Littlejohn, Brian Neely.
20/7/67	**Five Star Traverse I / Plimsoll Line**	Pat Littlejohn *(solo). The variation to Plimsoll Line was added by P.Way (solo) on 22/2/80.*
23/7/67	**Pantagruel**	Frank Cannings, Pat Littlejohn *(AL 3pts). FFA Pat Littlejohn, Ed Hart 28/12/77.*
25/7/67	**Coup de Grâce**	Pat Littlejohn, Brian Housley.
26/7/67	**Discuss the Thoughts of Chairman Mao**	John Hammond, Pat Littlejohn *(AL)*.
29/7/67	**Swing Low**	Pat Littlejohn, Frank Cannings *(AL)*.
30/7/67	**Readymix**	Pat Littlejohn, Brian Neely, John Hammond.
31/7/67	**Fandangle**	Pat Littlejohn, John Hammond.
7/67	**Evening Arête**	John Fowler, Frank Stebbings.
7/67	**Two Stroke Banana**	Pat Littlejohn, Steve Dawson.
3/8/67	**Crinoid**	Pat littlejohn, Pete Biven *(1pt). FFA by Pat Littlejohn some time later.*
6/8/67	**Moonraker**	Pete Biven, Pat Littlejohn *(VL)*.
12/8/67	**Osram**	Pat littlejohn, Brian Neely.
20/8/67	**Mighty Cheese**	John Fowler, John Hammond *(AL)*.
3/9/67	**Barbican**	Frank Cannings, Pete Biven *(5pts). They escaped up the belt of slabs after pitch 2. Final pitch added on 1/6/68, by Pat Littlejohn, John Hammond. FFA by Pat Littlejohn in 1977.*
9/9/67	**Barnacle Traverse**	John Fowler, Fred Stebbings *(climbing solo)*.
9/9/67	**Ruddigore**	Andy Powling, John Fowler, Frank Stebbings.
23/9/67	**The Ultimate Trundle**	Pete Biven, Trevor Peck.
1/10/67	**Quantum of Solace**	Brian Neely, John Hammond *(AL)*.
3/10/67	**Pikadon**	Pete Biven, Frank Cannings *(AL)*.
5/11/67	**St Gregory the Wonder Worker**	Mark Springett, Pete Biven *(AL)*.
24/12/67	**Enterprise**	Pat Littlejohn, Brian Neely.
31/12/67	**Magical Mystery Tour**	Rusty Baillie, John Cleare *(aid used on high section & rescued before the final section by Pete Biven via a rope & prussik). FFA by Frank Cannings, Pete Biven on 3/1/68.*

31/12/67	**Merlin Rocket**	Pat Littlejohn, Andy Powling.
3/1/68	**Magical Mystery Tour**	FFA by Frank Cannings, Pete Biven.
27/1/68	**Acheron**	Pat Littlejohn, Ed Grindley, John Taylor.
27/1/68	**Romeo & Juliet**	Brian Neely, E.Phillips *(AL)*.

9/2/68   **Penny Lane**   Pat Littlejohn, John Hammond *(1pt). The original line took the start of Mortality Crisis (using a filed-down penny as a rurp for aid. The route now takes most of the line of Apollo done by Pete Biven, Ian McMorrin (AL) in March 1966. FFA by Steve Bell, J.Grubb on 31/3/79.*

9/3/68   **The Spy**   Pat Littlejohn, John Hammond *(1pt). FFA by Ed Hart in 1973. Pitch 1a climbed by Pat in 1992.*

12/3/68   **Cinqtus**   Pete Biven, Dennis Kemp *(VL-2pts). FFA was sometime during the 1980s.*

17/3/68	**Hermeda**	Ed Grindley, R.Gibbs, John Hammond.
30/3/68	**The Cope**	Frank Cannings, A.Thompson.
30/3/68	**Incubus**	Pat Littlejohn, Pete Biven *(AL)*.

30/3/68   **The Mitre**   Frank Cannings, Pete Biven, Pat Littlejohn *(1pt). Modern Finish added by Pat Littlejohn, John Hammond on 5/1/69. FFA by Steve Bell, Bruce Woodley on 22/9/79.*

31/3/68	**MMT III**	Pete Biven, Frank Cannings, A.Thompson.

31/3/68   **Zeta**   Frank Cannings, Pete Biven *(AL-4pts). FFA by Bruce Woodley, Brian Wilkinson in 1982.*

5/4/68	**Barnacle Traverse Continuation**	Pete Biven, Frank Cannings.
5/4/68	**Lost Arrow**	Frank Cannings, Pete Biven *(AL)*.
6/4/68	**Binky / Neanderthal**	E.Hammond, John Fowler, Fred Stebbings.

6/4/68   **Goddess of Gloom**   Frank Cannings, Pete Biven, Mark Springett. *Variation on pitch 2 climbed by Pete Biven, Mark Springett on 3/3/68.*

6/4/68	**Oggie**	John Fowler, G.Radway, Frank Stebbings.
20/4/68	**Crooked Man**	Ed Grindley, R.Gibbs, Pat Littlejohn.
5/5/68	**Flying Fifteen**	Pat Littlejohn, John Hammond.
5/5/68	**Swashbuckler**	John Hammond, Pat Littlejohn.
18/5/68	**Ichor**	Pat littlejohn, John Hammond.
18/5/68	**Krapp's Last Fake**	John Hammond, Pat Littlejohn.
2/6/68	**Animals are People**	John Hammond, Pat Littlejohn.

3/6/68   **Jumping Jack Flash**   Ed Grindley, P.Christie. *Variation start added by John Fowler, Sue Crosse, G.Higginson in June 1969.*

9/6/68	**High & Dry**	Ed Grindley, Pat Littljohn *(AL)*.
13/6/68	**Exaltation**	Paul Leedel, Martin Chambers.

16/6/68   **Grip Type Thynne**   Pat Litlejohn, John Hammond, John Fowler. *The variation finish (Jaywalk) was climbed by Pat Littlejohn, John Hammond on 19/1/69.*

21/6/68	**Epoc**	Ed Grindley, John Fowler.
21/6/68	**Gut Bucket**	John Fowler, Ed Grindley.
23/6/68	**Lethe**	Ed Grindley, John Fowler. *Variation finish added by S.Woolard in 1981.*
29/6/68	**Fake's Last Krapp**	Pat Littlejohn, John Hammond.
30/6/68	**Seguidilla**	Pat Littlejohn, Ed Grindley.
30/6/68	**Twang**	Pat Littlejohn, Ed Grindley *(AL)*.

6/68   **Rhinoceros (Aviation Direct)**   Jim Collins. *Not the Californian but a Londoner who for the last 22yrs has contested Pat Littlejohn's claim to this FA (which finished up Aviation). Pat named the route Rhinoceros & claimed it on 14/5/71 – the date on which Littlejohn reascended pitch 1 & added an independent pitch 2 with Sam Whimster. The variation, Die Laughing, was added in 1994 by John Gaskins .*

7/68	**Ganges**	John Fowler, Fred Stebbings.
3/8/68	**Scimitar**	Pat Littlejohn, John Fowler.
21/8/68	**Quality Street**	John Taylor, Pat Littlejohn *(VL)*.
19/10/68	**Happy Camper's Crack**	Pat Littlejohn, John Fowler.
2/11/68	**Era**	Ed Grindley, G.Higginson.
23/11/68	**Morning Town Ride**	Ed Grindley, G.Higginson, E.Hammond.

6/12/68   **Cocytus**   Ed Grindley, Pat Littlejohn *(AL 2pts). FFA by Pat Littlejohn, Dave Garner in 31/5/76.*

14/12/68	**Aornis**	Ed Grindley, Pat Littlejohn.
22/12/68	**Moonshot**	Pat Littlejohn, John Hammond.
26/12/68	**Jeckyll & Hyde**	Pat Littlejohn, John Fowler.

28/12/68   **The Watchtower**   Pete Biven, Frank Cannings, Mark Springett *(by swimming Thunder Hole – this was free climbed with 1pt by Keith Darbyshire, Hugh Clark in 1972). The variation mentioned in the text was the original finish. The new finish was soloed by Pat Littlejohn on 12/9/91.*

1968	**Barnacle Traverse Continuation**	Pete Biven, Frank Cannings.

1968	**Five Star Traverse II** Pete Biven, Mark Springett.	
1968	**Ladram Lady** John Fowler *(solo)*.	
1968	**Levitation Direct** Pat Littlejohn, Steve Jones.	
1968	**MMT II** Pete Biven, John Fowler, Pat Littlejohn.	
1968	**Pinnacle Traverse Continuation** Pete Biven, John Fowler.	
25/1/69	**End Crack** Ed Grindley, G.Higginson.	
25/1/69	**Eubulus Williams** Ed Grindley, G.Higginson, C.Byrne.	
25/1/69	**Ramshackle** Ed Grindley, G.Higginson *(AL)*.	
1/2/69	**Brass Bound Crack / Sabre Tooth** Ed Grindley, G.Higginson.	
2/2/69	**Tiny Tim** Pat Littlejohn, Ed Grindley, John Hammond.	
5/2/69	**Ferocity** Ed Grindley, G.Higginson *(AL aid)*, E.Hammond.	
14/2/69	**Magic Carpet Ride** Pat Littlejohn, Ed Grindley *(VL)*.	
15/2/69	**Sacrosanct** Pat Littlejohn, Ed Grindley *(AL)*, Pete Biven. *The free version of pitch 1 was added by Steve Jones in October 1974 - originally followed pitch 1 of Cinqtus.*	
22/2/69	**Rainyday** Ed Grindley, C.Byrne. *FFA By Chris Nicholson, Mark Courtier on 28/4/84.*	
23/2/69	**The Lynch** Pat Littlejohn, Ed Grindley *(aid)*. *A rare Littlejohn aid route. FFA by Nick White on 23/10/87.*	
22/3/69	**The Meadfoot Girdle** Ed Grindley, G.Higginson *(1pt)*. *FFA by Pete O'Sullivan 5/8/79.*	
30/3/69	**Siddaw Bwurda** John Hammond, Pat Littlejohn.	
4/4/69	**Dreadnought** Frank Cannings, Pat Littlejohn *(AL)*. *FFA by Pat Littlejohn in 1977.*	
5/4/69	**The Seventh Circle** Frank Cannings, Pat Littlejohn *(VL)*, Pete Biven.	
13/4/69	**Blood** Pat Littlejohn, John Fowler, Frank Cannings.	
13/4/69	**The Hood** Pat Littlejohn, Frank Cannings *(3pts)*. *FFA Pat Littlejohn, C.King 28/10/77.*	
19/4/69	**Dangler** Len Benstead, Dennis Morrod.	
19/4/69	**Neophron** Pat Littlejohn, Steve Jones *(2pts)*. *FFA by Steve Bell, John Grubb in 1979.*	
19/4/69	**Randy** Ian Duckworth, R.Ward, R.Watson. **Yosemite** *was climbed the same day by Len Benstead, Dennis Morrod. The fact that this route & Randy cover much the same piece of rock, & were climbed on the same day, has caused endless confusion to the last three guidebook writers – especially this one!* **Safe Sex** *was added by Paul Birchell, Tim Dennell on 21/10/93.*	
27/4/69	**Bolshevik** Len Benstead, Dennis Morrod.	
11/5/69	**Finn** Pat Littlejohn.	
11/5/69	**Little John** Ed Grindley, G.Higginson.	
14/5/69	**Imperialist** Len Benstead, Dennis Morrod.	
25/5/69	**Pegs' Progress** G.Higginson, Deborah Hansen-Bay *(aid)*. *FFA by Bruce Woodley in 1983.*	
25/5/69	**Snoopy** Pete Biven, Pat Littlejohn *(AL)*, Steve Jones.	
26/5/69	**The Pinch** Pat Littlejohn, Steve Jones. *Pitch 1 climbed earlier by John Fowler. FFA by Pat Littlejohn, Tony Penning in 1983.*	
4/6/69	**Caliban** Ed Grindley, T.Lewis, Deborah Hansen-Bay.	
7/6/69	**Plektron** Pat Littlejohn, John Fowler. *Variation finish added by Steve Bell, J.Grubb on 20/6/79.*	
7/6/69	**White Queen** G.Higginson, Ed Grindley, Deborah Hansen-Bay.	
8/6/69	**Gilded Turd** Pat Littlejohn, John Hammond *(AL)*, Pete Biven, Ed Grindley.	
14/6/69	**Iconoclast** Pat Littlejohn, Ed Grindley.	
19/6/69	**Bloodhound** Pat Littlejohn, Steve Jones.	
19/6/69	**The High Traverse** Pat Littlejohn, Steve Jones *(AL)*.	
28/6/69	**The Magus** Pat Littlejohn, Ed Grindley *(AL)*, Pete Biven, G.Higginson.	
29/6/69	**All that Fall** Pat Littlejohn, Ed Grindley, G.Higginson.	
6/7/69	**Safari** Pat Littlejohn, Pete Biven *(VL pitches 1-5)*. *Completed by Pat Littlejohn, Ed Grindley on 2/11/69.*	
27/7/69	**The Rainbow** Pat Littlejohn, Steve Jones.	
23/8/69	**Quiver / Zen** Pat Littlejohn, Steve Jones *(VL)*.	
28/8/69	**Goblin** B.Hocken, P.Gross.	
7/9/69	**Slipshod** Pat Littlejohn *(solo)*.	
14/9/69	**Fruitflancase** Andy McFarlane, Deryck Ball *(VL)*.	
21/9/69	**Little Wonder** John Fowler, Sue Crosse.	
21/9/69	**St Jude** Pete Biven, Judie Herbert.	
21/9/69	**White Rabbit** P.Gross, R.Crossley.	
28/9/69	**Gilgamesh** Ian McMorrin, Pete Biven *(AL)*.	
9/69	**Cross Route** C.Ross, Sue Crosse, Pete Biven.	
9/10/69	**Cleavage** S.Chadwick, D.Wright *(AL)*.	
11/10/69	**Girdle Turd** Ed Grindley, G.Higginson *(AL)*.	

10/69	**Gugu Wack** John Hammond, Sue Crosse, John Fowler.
1/11/69	**The Odyssey** Pat Littlejohn, Ed Grindley *(AL).*
1/11/69	**Ulysses** Pat littlejohn, Ed Grindley *(reclimbed on 19/5/89 after rockfall by Nick White).*
9/11/69	**Mars** Pete Biven, Alison Chadwick, P.Owens. *Pitch 1 led by Ed Grindley, P.Christie in May 1969.*
11/69	**Just One More** C.Byrne, M.Tracey *(VL aid). FFA by Martin Crocker (renamed* **Just Revenge***)on 4/5/86.*
12/12/69	**Gangway** T.Cotter, P.Marrow.
27/12/69	**Tarantula** Deryck Ball, Andy McFarlane.
1969	**Brewery Arête / Diamond Lil** Andy McFarlane, Deryck Ball.
1969	**Brixham to Berry Head Traverse** Pete Biven, John Fowler.
1969	**The Kraken** Pete Biven, Ed Grindley, John Fowler *(a rope move was used to overcome the technical climbing, which was climbed free by Pat Littlejohn (c.1970s) when he added the pitches leading into LQP).*
1969	**Gideon** FFA by Len Benstead, Dennis Morrod.
1969	**MMT IV** Pete Biven, John Fowler, Dick Isherwood. *This ascent involved two tyroleans, which Pat Littlejohn dispensed with when he soloed it (c.1970s).*
5/1/70	**Rockets** T.Cotter, S.Chadwick *(AL).*
1/70	**Loner** T.Cotter, S.Chadwick.
22/2/70	**Median** Pete Biven, Ed Grindley, Alison Long, Moira Owens.
4/4/70	**Boo Bah Plost** John Hammond, Pat littlejohn *(VL).*
19/4/70	**Dust Devil** Pete Biven, Steve Jones *(2pts). FFA by Pete O'Sullivan, Chris George on 18/6/78.*
19/4/70	**Yellow Rurties** Pat Littlejohn, John Hammond *(VL).*
25/4/70	**Incubus Direct** Pat Littlejohn, Ed Grindley *(2pts). Pat did the FFA in the same year, but via a different start. . . which fell down.*
2/5/70	**Screw** Ed Grindley, John Fowler.
28/5/70	**Cut-throat** Pat Littlejohn, Pete Biven, John Hammond.
28/6/70	**Arncliffe** Ed Grindley, Meg Burrow.
9/8/70	**Fowler's Dolly Mixture** John Fowler, Sue Crosse.
11/8/70	**Sahib Ibizi** P.Gross, P.Crossley.
16/8/70	**Armadillo** R.Crossley, P.Gross.
23/8/70	**King Crab** Frank Cannings, Pete Biven, Pat Littlejohn.
23/8/70	**Last Wall of the Castle** R.Crossley, P.Gross.
27/8/70	**Steppenwolf** P.Biven, I.Holwell. *Pitches 1-3 by Ed Grindley, Pete Biven (AL), G.Higginson on 18/10/69. Pitches 4-5 by Ed Grindley, M.Tracey, D.Milner, C.Byrne on 25/10/69. Variation finish added by Pat Littlejohn, H.Clarke in September 1974. An atypical piece of Littlejohn on-route ingenuity (he used a dodgy peg as a handhold). The finish is still unrepeated.*
18/9/70	**Titus Groan** R.Crossley, P.Gross.
20/9/70	**Berry Red Wall** John Fowler, Sue Crosse, John Hammond.
9/70	**Salt** C.Ross, John Hammond *(VL),* S.Willard.
4/10/70	**Melinda** Pat Littlejohn, Charles Wand-Tetley.
18/10/70	**Graunching Gilbert** Keith Darbyshire, A.Millar.
25/10/70	**Beggar's Banquet** Ed Grindley, Pat Littlejohn *(AL).*
1/11/70	**Seaworm** John & Sue Fowler.
1/11/70	**Sloop** Pat Littlejohn.
3/11/70	**Stag Party** Charles Wand-Tetley, A.Millar.
8/11/70	**Home Brew** C.Gimblett, P.Harper. *Variation start by Ed Grindley, Meg Burrow on 18/4/71.*
15/11/70	**The Equation** Pat Littlejohn, Charles Wand-Tetley *(2pts). FFA by P.Newman, Steve Bell on 8/10/78 (pitch 3 was climbed at a lower level than the aided version). Pitch 3 climbed along the original route on 3/3/87 by Nick White, Clark Alston.*
7/12/70	**Winterlude** Frank Cannings, Pete Biven *(AL).*
14/12/70	**Paranoid** Ed Grindley, A.Miller.
20/12/70	**Foos Won't Moos** John Hammond, C.Ross.
1970	**August Weed / Cracking Plant / Doctor of Physick / Flange / Lather / Moral Fibre / Semiramis** P.Williams, J.Baker, P.Crossley, P.Gross *(mix & match any combination of the aforementioned).*
1970	**Flaked Out / Helter** B & M.Rossiter.
1970	**Perseus Direct** Ed Grindley.
1970	**The Steeple** Keith Darbyshire, John Fowler, Pete Biven.
9/1/71	**Deadline** Pat Littlejohn, Steve Jones.
10/1/71	**Labyrinth** John Fowler, Sue Fowler, E.French.
1/71	**Iron Butterfly** Charles Wand-Tetley, Benny Goodman *(AL),* G.Higginson *(aid). The big band leader (?) comes out of retirement to help with this magnum opus aid-route. FFA by Steve Mayers in September 1990 & called* **Cocoon***.*

2/71	**Smoke Gets in Your Eyes**	FFA by Pete Leedell.
2/3/71	**The Curse**	Martin Chambers, F.Hayton, Nigel Gifford *(VL)*. *Completed after six days of effort.*
27/3/71	**Crocodile**	Pat Littlejohn, Charles Wand-Tetley.
3/71	**Opus Dei**	Ed Grindley, A.Millar.
1/5/71	**The Flier**	Pat Littlejohn.
22/5/71	**Rastus**	Charles Wand-Tetley, John Fowler.
28/5/71	**East of Eden**	Sam Whimster, Charles Wand-Tetley. *FFA by Bruce Woodley, Simon Lee in July 1985 & called* **Beast of Eden.**
9/8/71	**Delicatessen**	G & R.Woolver.
9/8/71	**Hush Puppy / Piper at the Gates of Dawn / Spiral Tower**	R & G.Woolver.
11/8/71	**A Product of Civilisation / Whispering Doom**	R & G.Woollver.
2/9/71	**Combat**	Pat Littlejohn, Steve Jones.
18/9/71	**Inkerman Groove Direct**	Andy McFarlane, A.Pearson.
9/71	**Chocolate Finger**	Pete Biven, John Fowler.
11/71	**Big Picket Rock**	Pete Biven, Keith Darbyshire, John Fowler.
11/71	**Bonetti Tower**	Keith Darbyshire, Alison Onyskievich, Pete Biven.
11/71	**Lost World**	Pete Biven, John Fowler, Alison Onyskievich.
11/71	**The Razor**	John Fowler, Alison Onyskievich.
11/71	**Tower of Babel**	John Fowler, Keith Darbyshire, Pete Biven. *For all those desperate enough to sort out the gobbledegook here is the translation for the route: A pinnacle ". . .whose touch may reach unto heaven;" Genesis XI. Start beneath the seaward face. 1.30'. Ascend the venerably steep wall using the divine implement of a 6" nail for aid, then glide L to a pulpit stance. 2.20'. Climb the final corner to the summit, where ". . .the Lord did there confound the language of all the earth" – Genesis XI.*
12/12/71	**The Exile**	Pat Littlejohn, N.Townsend.
1971	**Interrogation**	FFA by Pat Littlejohn *(by the original line which started up Raven Gully).*
1971	**The Parson**	Keith Darbyshire, Pete Biven, John Fowler, S.Nicholls.
1/72	**Tremulous Traverse**	T.Cotter, Andy McFarlane *(AL).*
2/72	**Mac's Route**	Andy McFarlane, Deri Ball, S.Chadwick.
4/72	**Central Route**	T.Cotter, P. De Mengle.
20/8/72	**The Quaker**	Pat Littlejohn, Steve Jones *(1pt).* FFA by Mick Fowler in September 1979.
8/72	**Left Edge / Lunatic**	T.Cotter, S.Chadwick.
11/72	**Kamin #5**	Keith Darbyshire, John Fowler.
1972	**The Watchtower**	FDA (1pt) Keith Darbyshire, Hugh Clarke.
2/73	**Black Ice**	Pat Littlejohn, Keith Darbyshire. *The start described was added by Bruce Woodley in 1983, while the variation start was put up by Steve Bell, Roger Mear on 9/9/79. Originally the route began up Grip Type Thynne.*
2/73	**Man Bites Dog**	Keith Darbyshire, Hugh Clarke *(1pt).* FFA by Brian Wilkinson, Bruce Woodley in 1983.
3/73	**Moving Target**	Pat Littlejohn, Frank Cannings.
22/10/73	**Ruby in the Dust**	Keith Bentham, C.Gimblett.
10/73	**Rainbow Bridge**	Andy McFarlane, Deryck Ball *(VL 8pts).* *The first 250' or so had been climbed before (largely on aid), by Pete Biven, Mark Springett in 1968 & called Bathos. Pitches 2,7,12,& 13 added by Keith Darbyshire, Pat Littlejohn (VL) & aid reduced to 1pt over two days in the spring of 1974. Pitch 6 climbed free by Crispin Waddy (solo), in the winter of 1989. Entire route done free (solo) in September 1991 by Nick White.*
1/11/73	**Band of Rusty Gold**	Keith Bentham, C.Gimblett.
7/11/73	**Normal Hero**	Keith Bentham, C.Gimblett *(2pts).* FFA by Mick Fowler in 1981.
20/11/73	**Transference**	Keith Bentham, C.Gimblett.
1973	**The Spy**	FFA by Ed Hart.
1974	**Ash Chimney**	Iain Peters.
1974	**Bantham Hand**	John Fowler, S.Nicholls, Chris Gibson.
1974	**The Clerk**	John Fowler.
1974	**Seniors Wall / Trembling Wall**	Iain Peters, Dave Garner.
1974	**Widecombe Wall**	Keith Darbyshire.
30/11/75	**Small Change**	Pat Littlejohn, Dave Garner.
21/12/75	**Gremlin / Hornet**	Pat Littlejohn.
23/4/76	**Hostile Witness**	Pat Littlejohn, Dave Garner.
4/76	**Groove & Slab**	Pat Littlejohn, Dave Garner.
29/5/76	**Fear of Flying**	Pat Littlejohn, Dave Garner.
4/7/76	**Nibelung**	Pete O'Sullivan, A.Pearson. *Pitch 2 added by Pete O'Sullivan, Steve Bell on 10/7/79.*

6/7/76	**Stepladder / Wicked** Pat Littlejohn, Dave Garner.
10/7/76	**Snakecharmer** Pat Littlejohn, Dick Broomhead *(1pt)*. *FFA by Pete O'Sullivan, Chris George in 1978.*
10/7/76	**The Wake** Pat Littlejohn, Dick Broomhead.
29/7/76	**Foginnard / Rockface** Pat Littlejohn, Iain Peters. *Fogginard was reclimbed after a rockfall in 1993 by Tim Dennell.*
4/8/76	**The Stitch** Pete O'Sullivan, D.Blackler, Simon Cook.
4/8/76	**Winnet** Pete O'Sullivan, D.Blackler, Simon Cook, A.Pearson.
8/76	**The Bat / Olympia / The Wild Bunch** Chris Gibson, Pete Leedel.
16/10/76	**Revolver** Steve Bell, Chris Gibson.
11/76	**Astral Traveller** Chris Gibson, Steve Bell.
1976	**D'Artagnan** Pat Littlejohn *(solo)*.
16/1/77	**Erotica** John Fowler, Sue Fowler, Steve Bell.
14/4/77	**Crook Bruce** Pat Littlejohn, Charles Wand-Tetley. *Reclimbed in 1991 by Nick White after rockfall.*
1/5/77	**Imperial Wall** Chris Gibson, Anthony Morley.
4/8/77	**Yardarm** Pat Littlejohn, Dave Roberts.
28/10/77	**The Hood** FFA by Pat Littlejohn, C.King.
10/77	**The Echo** Pete O'Sullivan, Chris George.
10/77	**Zuma** Pat Littlejohn, Chris King.
16/11/77	**Strictly Private** Pete O'Sullivan, A.Cotter.
30/12/77	**Hot Lips** Pat Littlejohn, Ed Hart *(AL)*.
22/12/77	**The Lonely Hold / The Long Slide** Pete O'Sullivan, A.Cotter.
28/12/77	**Pantagruel** FFA by Pat Littlejohn, Ed Hart.
1977	**Barbican / Dreadnought** FFA by Pat Littlejohn.
1977	**La Bête Noire / Yogi** FFA Pete O'Sullivan, Chris George.
4/3/78	**Storm Child / Crêpes Suzzettes** Brian Wilkinson, Andy Gallagher.
4/3/78	**Sea Slip / Flambé** Andy Gallagher, Brian Wilkinson.
22/4/78	**Stratagem** Brian Wilkinson, Andy Gallagher.
4/5/78	**Brief Encounter** Simon Cardy, A.Clarke. *FWA Bruce Woodley in December 1981.*
6/6/78	**Dumnonia** Pete O'Sullivan, Chris George, A.Cotter. *Pitch 2 added by Andy Gallagher, I.Richards in June 1979.*
18/6/78	**Dust Devil** FFA Pete O'Sullivan, Chris George.
21/6/78	**Shades of Green** Pete O'Sullivan, Chris George.
10/8/78	**Vacancy at the Vatican** Pete O'Sullivan, T.Carter.
24/8/78	**Limping Home / Divine Inspiration** Pete O'Sullivan, T.Carter.
8/78	**Aerobic Wall** Simon Cook.
8/78	**Downward Bound** Simon Cook, D.Massey.
16/9/78	**Energy Crisis / Lateral Thinking** Pete O'Sullivan, Chris George. *Energy Crisis was previously climbed with aid as a direct start to Gideon.*
21/9/78	**Feasibility Study** Pete O'Sullivan, A.Cotter, Chris George. *Pitch 2 added by Pete O'Sullivan, M.Wilson in December 1979.*
5/10/78	**Lady of Shame** Pete O'Sullivan, B.Rossiter.
8/10/78	**The Equation** FFA by P.Newman, Steve Bell.
10/78	**Hot Ice** Kev Buckley *(solo)*.
1978	**Snakecharmer** FFA by Pete O'Sullivan, Chris George.
27/1/79	**Extendable Arms** Pete O'Sullivan *(unseconded)*.
3/2/79	**Impertinent Robin** Pete O'Sullivan, Julian Maund, M.Wilson.
3/2/79	**Aerial Ballet / Maybe Tommorrow** Pete O'Sullivan, Julian Maund.
3/2/79	**Quiet River** Pete O'Sullivan, Julian Maund, M.Northcott
10/2/79	**Odin Your Tea's Ready** B.Rossiter, Pete O'Sullivan.
10/2/79	**Quickening Pulse** Pete O'Sullivan, B.Rossiter.
17/2/79	**Haunted People / Love is like Anthrax / Palace of Skulls** Pete O'Sullivan, M.Wilson.
20/2/79	**Cold Grief** Pete O'Sullivan, M.Dunning.
25/2/79	**The Fox** Pete O'Sullivan, M.Wilson.
17/3/79	**Broadside / Jim Jam / Squall** Brian Wilkinson, Andy Gallagher.
17/3/79	**Cloudburst / Sirocco** Andy Gallagher, Brian Wilkinson.
23/3/79	**Concerto** FFA by Steve Bell.
30/3/79	**Hidden Groove** Brian Wilkinson, Andy Gallagher.
31/3/79	**Damaged Goods** Pete O'Sullivan, M.Wilson.
31/3/79	**Penny Lane** FFA by Steve Bell, J.Grubb.
2/4/79	**Pilchard Groove** Damian Carrol, Dave Viggars.
7/4/79	**Cunard Line / Traversty** Brian Wilkinson, Andy Gallagher.
8/4/79	**Black Widow** R.Bennet, M.Dunning.
14/4/79	**Tantalus** FFA by Brian Wilkinson, Andy Gallagher.

20/4/79 **Igneous Pig**   Steve Bell, J.Grubb. *Pitch 2 was given an independent finish by Nick White, Steve Thorpe in 1984.*
10/5/79 **Daylight Saving**   Pete O'Sullivan, M.Wilson.
19/5/79 **Rusty Road**   Brian Wilkinson, Andy Gallagher.
27/5/79 **Ikon**   Pat Littlejohn, Pete O'Sullivan.
27/5/79 **Saturn Five**   Steve Bell, J.Grubb.
11/6/79 **Hot Fun**   Pete O'Sullivan, H.Cripps, A.Cotter.
26/6/79 **Twilight**   Andy Gallagher, I.Richards.
27/6/79 **Panga**   FFA by Steve Bell, Bruce Woodley.
3/7/79 **Meadow Fly**   Andy Gallagher, I.Richards.
6/7/79 **Green Ranger**   Andy Gallagher, P.Haworth.
7/7/79 **Rough Diamond**   Pat Littlejohn, Pete O'Sullivan.
8/7/79 **Apparition**   Pete O'Sullivan, Steve Bell.
8/7/79 **Dragon Song**   Steve Bell, Pete O'Sullivan.
9/7/79 **Haphazard**   Andy Gallagher, G.Richards.
10/7/79 **Final Touch**   Pete O'Sullivan, Steve Bell.
25/7/79 **Relay**   G.Lodge, B.Day.
7/79 **Innocent Bystander**   Roger Mear, A.Hughes *(climbed with aid over the OH). FFA by Ken Palmer, Nick Hancock on 14/8/86.*
5/8/79 **The Meadfoot Girdle**   FFA by Pete O'Sullivan.
17/8/79 **Xmandifer**   N.Crowhurst, S.Crowhurst. *Variation finish added by Andy Winfield, J.Pym in 1983.*
19/8/79 **Pathos**   Pete O'Sullivan, Julian Maund.
8/9/79 **Rocketman**   Steve Bell, S.Marriott.
9/9/79 **Samurai**   C.Bryant *(unseconded).*
22/9/79 **The Mitre**   FFA by Steve Bell, Bruce Woodley.
30/9/79 **Gagool Direct / Solus**   Steve Bell, Roger Mear.
9/79 **The Quaker**   FFA by Mick Fowler.
4/10/79 **Thought Process**   Pete O'Sullivan, Roland Perriment.
6/10/79 **Depth Charge**   Mick Fowler, Arnis Strapcans *(AL). Pitch 1 had been climbed before by Arnis Strapcans in November 1976. The quote at the start of the route is Arnis' description.*
21/10/79 **Pastoral**   Andy Gallagher.
8/11/79 **Farewell to Arms**   Iain Parsons, Roger Mear.
18/11/79 **Demeter**   Andy Gallagher.
1979 **Neophron**   FFA by Steve Bell, J.Grubb.
1979 **Thor**   FFA by Pete O'Sullivan, Vivian Stevenson.
1979 **Torture**   Nipper Harrison, J.Edwards.
1979 **Wobbling Wall**   Julian Maund.
20/1/80 **False Alarms**   Pete O'Sullivan, Julian Maund *(2pts). FFA by Gordon Jenkins, Keith Marsden in 1981.*
3/80 **Anti-matter**   Pete O'Sullivan, Chris Gibson.
3/80 **Grand Slam**   Pete O'Sullivan, Chris George.
4/80 **The Eyrie**   Pete O'Sullivan.
4/80 **Legal Aid**   Pete O'Sullivan, Roger Mear.
4/80 **Uncul-patter**   Steve Bell, Chris Gibson.
5/80 **Call to Arms**   Steve Monks, Ed Hart. *Pitch 2 added by Steve Lewis, John Codding in 1983.*
5/80 **Lip Trip**   Mick Fowler, Andy Meyers *(AL).*
21/6/80 **Solstice**   Andy Gallagher, Stuart Bondi.
20/7/80 **Calcite Diamond**   Chris Nicholson, Andy Gallagher.
7/80 **Liaison with Lenin**   Bruce Woodley, Martin Glaister, J.Brooks.
7/80 **Mass Murderer**   Paul Dunwell, Dave Lassasso. *The first route bolted for free-climbing on Torquay limestone. The first bolt-free ascent was by Pat Littlejohn (solo) in 1985. The route has now been degeared (being outside the bolting accepted area).*
10/80 **Bismark**   Mick Fowler, John Codding.
1980 **Black Jam Arête**   E.Holt, Dave Thomas, Nick Hancock.
1980 **Cash Investment / Drake's Circus / Mayflower / Night Club / Traffic Jam / Traffic Lights**   D.Nicholls.
1980 **Charlie Chaplain Walks on Air**   Paul Dawson *et al.*
1980 **Docker's Dilemma**   Paul Dawson.
1980 **Don't Stop Now**   Paul Dawson.
1980 **Famine**   Steve Bell, Roger Mear, Bruce Woodley.
1980 **Interrogation / Low Man Girdle**   FFAs by Mick Fowler.
1980 **Noddy**   A.Cotter, S.Deeming.
25/1/81 **The Long Goodbye**   Pete O'Sullivan, Dick Swindon.
4/81 **Cod**   Chris Nicholson, Andy Gallagher.

17/5/81	**Vista** Andy Gallagher, Dick Thorns.
25/5/81	**Buzby** Chris Nicholson, Andy Gallagher.
31/5/81	**Third Time Lucky** S.Woolard, A.Holburn.
23/6/81	**Weeble** Andy Gallagher, Pete Way.
6/81	**Anarchist** Iain Peters, A.Clark.
6/81	**Monarchist** Iain Peters, Don Sergeant.
6/81	**Izitso** Andy Gallagher, Pete Way.
11/7/81	**Far From the Madding Crowd** Nick Hancock, Andy Grieve.
12/11/81	**The Thurl Stone** Nick Hancock, Andy Grieve.
1981	**Back to Nature** J.Wyatt, Nick Hancock.
1981	**Black Death / Dripdry** FFA by Pat Littlejohn *(pitch 1 of Dripdry).*
1981	**Blistez / Different Kettle of Fish / Grope & Hope / Kaktus / Kittiwake / Polloks / Shy Talk** N.Hearn, M.Stapleton.
1981	**Boris / Cleopatra / Shelob** Dave Thomas, Nick Hancock.
1981	**Brec to the Vag** D.Nicholls.
1981	**False Alarms** Gordon Jenkins, Keith Marsden.
1981	**Zeta** FFA by Bruce Woodley, Brian Wilkinson.
29/5/82	**Sidewinder** Bruce Woodley, Brian Wilkinson.
12/6/82	**Steeple Slab** J.Bebb, Nick Hancock *(AL)*, Andy Grieve.
7/82	**Dehydration** Bruce Woodley, Keith Phillips.
11/82	**Caveman** Andy Meyers, Mick Fowler *(AL). By far & away the most audacious route in Britain for the time.*
1982	**Aggravation / Hands Off Argentina / 19th Nervous Breakdown** Robbie Warke.
1982	**Crunchy Toad** Steve Lewis, M.Lyndon, C.Jones, Mick Fowler.
29/1/83	**Afterglow** Chris Nicholson.
23/2/83	**Jericho** Pete Bull, N.Green.
3/83	**Hopeful** S.Deeming, Pete O'Sullivan, P.Howarth.
4/83	**Hob Hound** Bruce Woodley, Martin 'Minky' Parry.
4/83	**Pig's Might Fly** Chris Nicholson, Bruce Woodley.
29/5/83	**Blonde Bombshell** Pat Littlejohn, Tony Penning.
29/5/83	**Madness** Pat Littlejohn, Tony Penning. *The end of of an obsession. This was the day Pat finally solved the crux pitch. Pitches 1 & 2 were done with Hugh Clarke in 1979.*
30/5/83	**Tough Luck / Good Fortune** Tony Penning, Pat Littlejohn.
30/5/83	**The Pinch** FFA by Pat Littlejohn, Tony Penning.
5/83	**Back Brain Stimulator** Andy Winfield.
5/83	**Prime Time / Splash Down** Pete Bull *(solo).*
6/83	**Bird Scarer / Total Control** Pete Bull, N.Green.
6/83	**A Fall of Moondust** Chris Nicholson, Bruce Woodley.
6/83	**Jazoo** Chris Nicholson.
6/83	**Saversnake** Bruce Woodley, Chris Nicholson.
3/7/83	**Blinding Flash** Pat Littlejohn, Tony Penning.
3/7/83	**Flashdance** Pat Littlejohn, Tony Penning, Pete Cresswell.
8/83	**All Because. . . / Sunkiss** Bruce Woodley, Brian Aplin.
8/83	**Man in Black / Milky Bar Kid** Bruce Woodley, Alistair Whyte.
8/83	**The Big 'Y'** Bruce Woodley, Brian Wilkinson.
8/83	**Burning Bridges / Sunset Boulevard** Bruce Woodley, Keith Phillips.
8/83	**Crunchie** Bruce Woodley *(solo).*
8/83	**Malteaser** Keith Phillips, Cath Rolfe.
19/9/83	**Douglas Fairbanks Jnr.** Pete O'Sullivan, M.Dunning.
9/83	**Dirt Eater** Bruce Woodley, Ian Day, N.Oxton.
9/83	**Le Dernier Cri** Bruce Woodley, Alistair Whyte, Martin Parry. *On the first ascent two 8' foot slings were attached to the top PR & a tree limb was also dynoed for (this may or may not still be there, the PRs certainly are not).*
4/10/83	**Rough Justice** Pete Bull *(unseconded). The start described was soloed by Pete Bull on 18/5/85. Originally the route began by traversing RWs out of North Face Chimney.*
16/10/83	**Saturday Night Finger** Andy Winfield, M.Lane.
10/83	**Isca** Nick Biven, T.Bowdler.
11/83	**Dalby** Nick Biven *(solo).*
11/83	**Doing a Dalby** T.Bowdler *(solo).*
11/83	**Ivy Route** T.Bowdler, Nick Biven.
1983	**Anaerobic Crack** Chris Nicholson *(solo).*
1983	**Charlie Don't Surf / Depression / Slippin' & a Sliding / Suburbia** Pete O'Sullivan, B.Rossiter, S.Deeming.
1983	**Diamond Sky** Pete Bull *(solo).*
1983	**Man Bites Dog** FFA by Brian Wilkinson, Bruce Woodley.
1983	**Mezzotinter** Steve Thorpe *(solo).*

1983	**Pegs' Progress** FFA by Bruce Woodley. *The variation finish was climbed at the same time.*	
1983	**South Face** Roger Greatrick.	
29/1/84	**Praline / Saline** Nick White, Mark Courtier.	
5/2/84	**Aquiline** Nick White, Mark Courtier.	
2/84	**The Final Taxi** Pete Bull, Nick Tetley.	
2/84	**White Edge – Concerto** Nick White, Steve Thorpe.	
3/3/84	**Plind Pew / Tied Line** Nick White, Brian Wilkinson.	
3/3/84	**Placebo** Brian Wilkinson, Nick White.	
3/3/84	**Ray Zazorn** Nick White *(solo)*.	
4/3/84	**Dumb Blonde** Chris Nicholson, Nick White.	
3/84	**Up the Creek** Pete Bull *(solo)*.	
1/4/84	**Big Jim** Chris Nicholson, Ian Day.	
2/4/84	**Blue Monday / Devonshire Cream** Chris Nicholson, Nick White. *Chris perfects the airborne retreat.*	
2/4/84	**Date With the Devil / Devil's Advocate** Nick White, Chris Nicholson.	
9/4/84	**Tendonitis** Dave Cope, B.Frampton.	
11/4/84	**Mukdah's Wall** Bruce Woodley, Keith Phillips.	
13/4/84	**Desparête** Bruce Woodley, Martin Parry.	
13/4/84	**Major Tom** Chris Nicholson *(unseconded)*.	
14/4/84	**Caius / Semi-detached** Bruce Woodley, Simon Lee.	
14/4/84	**Chryswalke Connection / Spasm Chasm / Spear of Destiny** Andy Winfield, M.Corser, R.Stowell.	
17/4/84	**Infidel** Brian Wilkinson, Martin Parry.	
23/4/84	**Phoenix on Fire** Robbie Warke.	
27/4/84	**Pig's Ear** Chris *'Flinger'* Nicholson *(unseconded)*. *FFA of pitch 3 of Titan.*	
28/4/84	**Clotted Cream** FFA by Chris Nicholson, Mark Coutier. *Previously an aided route called Rainyday by Ed Grindley, C.Byrne.*	
20/5/84	**Foul Bite** Steve Thorpe *(solo)*.	
5/84	**American Express** Chris Nicholson, Nick White. *A closely contested duel at the time.*	
5/84	**Smokey Joe** Nick White, Chris Nicholson.	
6/84	**Hydraulic Arête** Pete O'Sullivan, I.Thomas.	
6/84	**Megatarts / Stratatarts** Nick White *(solo)*.	
11/7/84	**Sly Boots McCall** Nick White, Mark Courtier. *The Variation was done the same year by Nick White, Chris Nicholson.*	
7/84	**Alpha One** Robbie Warke, *Bunny* Warren.	
7/84	**Biko** Rik Meek, Robbie Warke.	
11/8/84	**Bloodshot** Andy Grieve, Nick Hancock.	
20/8/84	**Before the Storm** Robbie Warke *(unseconded)*.	
1984	**Direct Justice** Kit Wilkinson *(unseconded)*.	
1984	**The Fair / Scrumpy Special** Bruce Woodley, Alistair Whyte.	
1984	**Little Prow** Iain Peters *(solo)*.	
1984	**Telescopic Arms** Ken Wallis.	
4/3/85	**Dripdry** FFA by Dave Cope *(pitch 2)*.	
9/3/85	**Rock Lobster** Kit Wilkinson, Ken Wallis, Pete Bull.	
19/4/85	**Highly Strung** Nick White, Phil *Peebo* Barber.	
26/4/85	**Ground Control / Space Odyssey** Bruce Woodley *et al*.	
3/5/85	**Me Thane** N. & C.Crowhurst.	
4/5/85	**Mortality Crisis** Nick White, *'effing'* George Szuca.	
5/5/85	**Molyslip** N. & C.Crowhurst.	
8/5/85	**Glass Bead Game** Chris Nicholson, Mark Courtier. *The budding buddha meets the age of feuilleton.*	
8/5/85	**Snoopy** Andy Greive.	
8/5/85	**Two Way Stretch** Nick Hancock, Pete Saunders.	
9/5/85	**. . .king Hell** Chris Nicholson, Nick White.	
11/5/85	**Stepping Out** Kit Wilkinson, Pete Bull.	
15/5/85	**Piglet Wall** Chris Nicholson, Nick White. *The direct finish was added by Ken Palmer in 1991.*	
18/5/85	**Blood Lust** Nick Hancock. *This route became steeped in gore from spirited failures by the likes of Nipper Harrison, Pat Littlejohn, Chris Nicholson & Pete O'Sullivan, who all ended up with deep puncture marks in the same place on the same hand.*	
18/5/85	**Little Gem** Pete Bull *(solo)*.	
6/6/85	**Republican** Iain Peters, Pete O'Sullivan, D.Butterick.	
30/6/85	**Lynx** J.Barker, Pete O'Sullivan.	
30/6/85	**Tenuous Link** Pete O'Sullivan, J.Barker.	
30/6/85	**White Life** Nick White, Pete Bull.	

18/7/85	**Great Flake** Iain Peters *(solo)*.	
18/7/85	**Missing Link** Pete O'Sullivan, J.Barker.	
20/7/85	**Junior Leader** C. & N.Crowhurst *(AL)*.	
25/7/85	**Dead Dog Rib** Iain Peters, Pete O'Sullivan. *Recorded as Fogou in the previous guide.*	
27/7/85	**Kistvaen Corner** Pete O'Sullivan, Iain Peters. *Previously top-roped in the mid-1950s.*	
7/85	**Beast of Eden** Bruce Woodley, Simon Lee.	
12/8/85	**Pinkspots Headache** Nick Hancock, Andy Grieve.	
17/8/85	**Into the Groove** Dave Cope *(unseconded). A whiff of the Peak, now sadly degeared. Climbed bolt-free by Ken Palmer on 18/6/91.*	
8/85	**Equipoise** Bruce Woodley, K.Poulter.	
9/85	**Hair of the Dog** J.Barber, Pete O'Sullivan.	
9/85	**Parsifal** Pete O'Sullivan, J.Barber.	
9/85	**Torbay or not Torbay / Torquey** Chris Nicholson. *Torquey has now been superseded by More Steam, Bigger Women.*	
15/10/85	**Limestone Cowboys** Chris Nicholson, Nick White. *Another protracted 'gun-fight' at high-noon.*	
15/10/85	**You May Be the Face. . .** Chris Nicholson *(solo)*.	
1985	**Black Fox Wall / King Jam** Robbie Warke.	
1985	**É Bruto** Steve Thorpe *(unseconded)*.	
1985	**Mass Murderer** BFA by Pat Littlejohn *(solo)*.	
15/2/86	**Out on a Limb / Golden Dive** Nick White, Pete Bull.	
2/86	**Suicide** T.Dudley, P.Slater.	
17/3/86	**Gorillability** Kit Wilkinson, Pete Bull.	
21/3/86	**Window Pane** R.Steward, Andy Skillabeer.	
3/86	**Ikhnaton / Itsacon** Robbie Warke *(unseconded)*.	
3/86	**Kermit's Evening Special** Robbie Warke, Bunny Warren.	
3/86	**The Lumpy Universe** Chris Nicholson *(unseconded)*.	
3/86	**Sea Slater** Robbie Warke *(solo), apparently done before.*	
3/86	**Squonk** Robbie Warke, Bunny Warren.	
19/4/86	**Hagar the Horrible** Ken Palmer, Nick Hancock.	
19/4/86	**Ultimate Eliminate** Nick Hancock, Pete Saunders *(AL)*.	
23/4/86	**Darling Nikki** Nick White, Dick Thorns.	
30/4/86	**The Hog's Back** Chris Nicholson, Iain Peters. *The crux was soloed with an ab-rope close to hand.*	
1/5/86	**Mayday** Andy Turner.	
4/5/86	**Just Revenge** Martin Crocker, J.Robertson.	
5/5/86	**Mitre Direct** Martin Crocker.	
10/5/86	**Grim Reaper** Nick White, Dick Thorns.	
7/6/86	**Dog Bites Back** Ken Palmer, Andy Grieve.	
7/6/86	**La Rage** Andy Grieve, Ken Palmer.	
12/6/86	**Smash or Grab** Andy Grieve, Nick Hancock.	
15/6/86	**You Cannot Be Serious** Chris Nicholson *(solo)*.	
17/6/86	**Limbo Dancer** Ken Palmer, G.Butler. *An unusually bold offering from Ken. The Moor appears to bring out his reckless side.*	
5/7/86	**Full Moon** Ken Palmer *(unseconded)*.	
11/7/86	**Renegade** Nick White, Pete Bull.	
15/7/86	**Bath Time / Cradle Snatcher / Cot Death / Saracen** Nick White, Clark Alston.	
15/7/86	**Lullaby Baby** Clark Alston, Nick White.	
16/7/86	**Old Men** Iain Peters, Pete O'Sullivan.	
18/7/86	**Gravity's Angel** Nick White, Clark Alston.	
25/7/86	**Nervous Laughter** R.Pomeroy, I.Forsyth.	
29/7/86	**Bronco Dilator** Andy Grieve, Nick Hancock, Ken Palmer, Pete Saunders.	
29/7/86	**Eureka** Pete O'Sullivan, Pete Saunders. *A route discovered in the bath?*	
7/86	**Hell's Teeth** Nick White, Jerry Grogono. *The variation was climbed on the same day.*	
14/8/86	**Innocent Bystander** FFA by Ken Palmer, Nick Hancock.	
5/9/86	**Wicked Woman** Nick Hancock, Andy Grieve, Ken Palmer.	
21/9/86	**Accomplice to Murder** D.Hughes, D.Wyrwoll.	
28/9/86	**Angel of Mercy** Ken Palmer, Pete Saunders. *The most intimidating route on Dartmoor.*	
1986	**Brown Legs** Pete Donnithorne, Tessa Meen.	
1986	**Buzzard** M. & L.Johnson.	
1986	**Buzzard Direct** L.Johnson *(unseconded)*.	
1986	**Rocking Block** L. & M.Johnson.	
1986	**Army Dreamers** Pat Littlejohn. *Pitch 1 was climbed by Robbie Warke, Andy Turner in 1987.*	

17/1/87   **I Sick Hell**   FWA Chris Reece, Nick Hancock *(AL)* Andy Grieve, Graham Butler, Ant Wot *(what?)*.
24/1/87   **Charlie**   Nick White, Pete Bull.
30/1/87   **Lazing on a Sunny Afternoon**   Paul Donnithorne, Tessa Meen.
14/2/87   **Good Day Sunshine / Sunshine Superman**   Paul Donnithorne, Tessa Meen.
14/2/87   **Seasons in the Sun**   Tessa Meen, Paul Donnithorne.
18/2/87   **Sirens of Titan / Timeless Skies / Time Passages**   Paul Donnithorne, Tessa Meen.
20/2/87   **Jollity Farm**   Paul Donnithorne, Tessa Meen, L.Welsh.
21/2/87   **The Entertainer**   Paul Donnithorne, Tessa Meen.
21/2/87   **Monkey Puzzle**   Tessa Meen, Paul Donnithorne.
22/2/87   **Points of View**   Paul Donnithorne, Tessa Meen.
9/3/87   **Cold Finger**   Paul Donnithorne, N.Ashcroft.
9/3/87   **Cream Egg**   Paul Donnithorne, Tessa Meen.
15/4/87   **Thrutch**   Andy Grieve, *'grunting'* John Corber.
23/4/87   **Sly**   Andy Grieve, Nick Hancock.
29/4/87   **Myrtle Turtle**   Chris Nicholson *(solo)*.
4/87   **Slime Time**   Nick White *(solo)*.
3/5/87   **Bruised Heels**   A.Williams, K.Brown.
12/5/87   **Seventh Seal / Whoremoans**   Nick White, Andy Turner.
13/5/87   **Odysseus or Bust**   Nick White, Clark Alston.
14/5/87   **Banzai**   Nick Hancock, Andy Grieve. *The variation was climbed on 26/8/88 by Nick White, Bjørn Aikman.*
19/5/87   **Up the Styx. . .**   Nick White, Andy Turner.
25/5/87   **Interrogation Superdirect**   Nick White, Andy Turner. *Direct start added by Mark Edwards in April 1990.*
28/5/87   **Hart of Darkness**   Nick White, Andy Turner, Rik Meek.
31/5/87   **Chuck Berry**   Ken Palmer, Andy Grieve.
3/6/87   **Garth**   Andy Grieve, Nick Hancock *(& not Ken Palmer). Hand placed logs & threads, but the car-jack was left in the boot.*
14/6/87   **Star Trekking**   Ken Palmer, Andy Grieve. *The route was aided first by Andy at A2 – he would also like to make it known that he aided many of Ken's routes before the FA dates shown.*
19/6/87   **Thread Flintstone**   Ken Palmer, Andy Grieve.
20/6/87   **Foaming at the Mouth**   Andy Grieve, Ken Palmer.
20/6/87   **Lap it Up**   Dave Thomas, Andy Grieve, Ken Palmer.
21/6/87   **Look Back in Anger**   Nick Hancock, Andy Grieve, Ken Palmer.
26/6/87   **Musical Women #2**   Nick White, Andy Turner.
27/6/87   **Espionage**   Nick White, Rik Meek.
27/6/87   **Schweinhund**   Nick White *(unseconded)*.
28/6/87   **Orpheus**   Robbie Warke *(unseconded). A knotted hanging rope was used for protection on the FA.*
6/87   **Bjørn Again**   Bjørn Aikman *(solo)*.
6/87   **Crystal Pockets / Midget Gem**   Nick White *(solo)*.
6/87   **Melange**   Nick White, Pete Gardner.
1/7/87   **Kestrel**   C.Steel, Ed Heslam.
2/7/87   **A Drop in the Ocean**   Andy Grieve, Ken Palmer.
20/7/87   **Killer Queen**   Nick White, Dave 'Guts Training' Barrell. *Some holds still remain intact.*
22/7/87   **Cream Topping / Sole Fusion**   Nick White, Dave Barrell.
29/7/87   **Boogie on Down**   Andy Grieve, Ken Palmer.
29/7/87   **Little White Lie**   Ken Palmer, Andy Grieve. *The direct start was done in June 1991 by Pete Bull, Jon Gandy.*
7/87   **Enigma**   Pete O'Sullivan, N.Crowhurst.
7/87   **Vendetta**   Pete O'Sullivan, D.Bell.
25/8/87   **The Minor Tour / Thesaurus**   Nick White, Pete Gardner.
5/9/87   **Shadow Beast**   Nick White *(unseconded)*.
12/9/87   **Captain Scarlet**   Simon Lee *(solo)*.
11/10/87   **Monster**   Ed Heslam.
23/10/87   **The Lynch**   FFA by Nick White *(unseconded)*.
26/10/87   **Infidelity**   Nick White, Simon Lee.
1/11/87   **The Creaming Dream / White Winds**   Nick White, Pete Gardner.
3/11/87   **One Way Street**   Paul Donnithorne, L.Welsh.
4/11/87   **Big Bills**   Paul Donnithorne, L.Welsh.
4/11/87   **Hazardous Traverse / A Poke in the Hole**   Nick White, Rik Meek. *Fire-pokers were found to offer excellent protection in the old shot-holes.*
4/11/87   **Spear & Jackson**   Rik Meek, Nick White.
5/11/87   **Boltin' Hazard / The Black Streak**   Nick White, Rik Meek.
5/11/87   **Grunting in the Gutter**   Paul Donnithorne, J.McArdle.
5/11/87   **Loose Grit**   Rik Meek, Nick White.

7/11/87	**Blight Delight**	Paul Donnithorne, L.Welsh, Tessa Meen.
7/11/87	**Rawhide**	Nick White, Pete Gardner, Andy Turner.
10/11/87	**Peggy Potato**	Paul Donnithorne, Tessa Meen.
1987	**Arch Temptress / Beak Roamer / Chicken Head / Dance on Dinkies. . . / Duckless in Torbay / Ducks Might Fly / Last Duck to Bombay / Something Ducky / Widespread & Hipless** Robbie Warke, Andy Reid.
1987	**Atheist / Harvestman / Poetic Justice** Robbie Warke, Rik Meek.
1987	**Atropos / Boss Hogg / Undertow / White Rasta / Wind Bandits** Rik Meek, Robbie Warke.
1987	**Crispy Duck,. . . / Torbay's Fowl Community** Andy Reid, Robbie Warke.
1987	**Death of King Edward** Paul Donnithorne.
1987	**Stuff the E5s** C.Smith, N.Ayres, Wendy Sampson.
1987	**Trespass** Robbie Warke (solo).
1987	**The Umpire Strikes Back** Chris Nicholson (solo).
5/1/88	**Rum Truffle** Rik Meek, Robbie Warke.
16/1/88	**Let Your Fingers do the Walking** Nick White, Bjørn Aikman.
1/88	**Captain Flint** Robbie Warke (solo).
21/1/88	**Blood & Sand** Rik Meek, M.Aspinall.
26/2/88	**Lamia / Slipperman / Supernatural Anaesthetist** Robbie Warke (unseconded).
1/3/88	**On the Rink of Disaster** Dave Thomas, Pete Bull.
2/3/88	**Complete the Asterisk** Martin Crocker (unseconded).
3/88	**Empire of the Sun** Nick White, Pete Bull, Andy Turner. The direct start was climbed by Pete Oxley in March 1993.
3/4/88	**Free the Spirit** Martin Crocker, Nigel Coe. A number of drilled PRs were used on the FA. BFA by Dave Thomas on 4/1/89.
3/4/88	**The Mightier** Martin Crocker (unseconded). Originally done by stepping out R to the arête (at 6b), it was climbed direct by Dave Thomas on 10/6/88.
4/4/88	**Photo Thirty-six / Three Dozen Valium** Martin Crocker, Gordon Jenkins, Nigel Coe.
23/4/88	**Wages of Fear** Nick White, Andy Turner.
24/4/88	**Crosstown Traffic** Nick White, Andy Turner.
28/4/88	**Call of the Wild** Pat Littlejohn, Nick White. An earlier gear-stripping attempt almost had the pair swan-diving into the boulder-strewn zawn-bed.
28/4/88	**False Gods** Nick White, Pat Littlejohn.
29/4/88	**Underwhelmed** Pat Littlejohn, Nick White.
4/5/88	**Nebulous Crab** Pete Bull, Clark Alston, Nick White.
6/5/88	**How the Mighty Fall** Nick White, Mike Barnes.
6/5/88	**The Web** Robbie Warke (unseconded).
8/5/88	**Heathen Man** Martin Crocker (unseconded).
8/5/88	**Up in Arms** Nick White, Mike Barnes (variation done on the same date).
21/5/88	**Wrath of Grapes** Paul Twomey, A.Williams.
30/5/88	**More Steam, Bigger Women!!!** Nick White (unseconded). Supersedes Chris Nicholson's route Torquay, by extending it to the top of the buttress.
5/88	**Wilma** Nick White.
1/6/88	**Yabba Dabba Doo** Bjørn Aikman, Clark Alston (AL).
8/6/88	**Brittle Road to Freedom** Dave Thomas, Nick White (AL). A patented cure for constipation.
10/6/88	**End of an Era / Time Bandits** Nick White, Dave Thomas.
12/6/88	**Sure Swell** S.Scarbro (solo).
30/6/88	**Surprise** L.Johnson (unseconded).
6/88	**Absent Friends** Rik Meek, Simon Woodhall.
6/88	**Long John** Rik Meek, Robbie Warke.
6/88	**Raph Skrøtöms Septic Toenail** Bjørn Aikman (solo).
15/7/88	**Napalm** Jon Gandy (solo).
17/7/88	**Battle of the Bulge** Dave Turnbull, Andy Grieve.
18/7/88	**The Shroud** Dave Turnbull, Andy Grieve.
4/8/88	**South Seas** Dominic & Jon Gandy.
4/8/88	**Ship's Biscuit** Jon & Dominic Gandy.
7/8/88	**Shooting Stars** Pete Bull, Andy Turner.
28/8/88	**Croix de Guerre / Grooverider** Nick White, Pete Bull.
30/8/88	**Ash Tip Slab / Bin Bag** Emma Alsford, Paul Donnithorne.
30/8/88	**Waste Disposal** Paul Donnithorne, Emma Alsford.
8/88	**Bearing Down** Nick White, Pete Bull.
8/88	**Busty Bitch** Dick Scratcher, Raph Skrøtöm.
8/88	**Cream Team Special / Walking Tall** Pete Bull, Nick White.
8/88	**Le Hazard** Nick White (unseconded).
8/88	**Supercalorific** Nick White, Pete Bull.
1/9/88	**Hunt the Dump** Paul Donnithorne, Emma Alsford.

2/9/88	**Keep Britain Tidy** Emma Alsford, Paul Donnithorne.
2/9/88	**Tin Can Alley** Paul Donnithorne, Emma Alsford.
5/9/88	**Veins** Paul Donnithorne, Emma Alsford.
19/9/88	**Scone-on. . . (the Cream Tea Slayer)** Nick White, Clark Alston.
19/9/88	**Tapes of Wrath** Clark Alston, Nick White *(AL)*.
2/10/88	**Dragnet** Dominic & Jon Gandy *(solo)*.
2/10/88	**Up the Aunty** Nick White, Jon Gandy.
10/88	**Out of the Cauldron** Jon Gandy, Justin Moat.
2/11/88	**Big Bird** Nick White, Dominic & Jon Gandy. *Variation done by Jon Gandy in 1993.*
2/11/88	**Rubble Trouble** Jon Gandy *(solo)*.
6/11/88	**Gulliver's Travels** Dominic & Jon Gandy. *Pitches 1-3 climbed on this date. The continued adventures, or pitches 4-5 completed on 13/11/88. As yet the route remains unrepeated & unfinished. . . any takers?*
15/11/88	**The Mane Man** Nick White *(unseconded).* The FFA of the second half of the aid route Leo.
19/11/88	**Law of Nations** Martin Crocker *(unseconded)*.
6/12/88	**Agent Orange** Jon Gandy, Nick White.
4/12/88	**La Crème** Nick White *(unseconded)*.
11/12/88	**Walking on Sunshine** Jon Gandy, Chris Waite.
17/12/88	**Satanic Traversities / Ramming Speed** Nick White, Pete Bull.
17/12/88	**Salmon Run** Pete Bull, Nick White.
18/12/88	**No Hold's Barred** Nick White, Pete Bull.
27/12/88	**Cod Gives You a Stiffy** Simon Lee, Bruce Woodley.
30/12/88	**Beware the Sphinx** Pete Bull *(solo)*.
30/12/88	**Born Toulouse / The Impressionist / Monet For Old Rope** Nick White, Pete Bull.
30/12/88	**Freudian Gymslip** Pete Bull, Nick White.
12/88	**Great Dane / Spurting Wildly** Nick White *(solo)*.
12/88	**Raph's Route** Pete Bull *(solo)*.
1988	**Morpheus / Opium Eater** Robbie Warke *(unseconded)*.
3/1/89	**Lunar Sea** Nick White, Dave Thomas.
4/1/89	**Man O'War** Nick White, Dave Thomas.
10/1/89	**Graf Spee** Frank Ramsey, Adrian Gostick (1 rest point). *FFA by Nick White, Pete Bull on 14/1/89.*
14/1/89	**Arc Royale** Nick White, Pete Bull.
18/1/89	**Assana / Boulder Dash / Down with his Pants / Follow the Yellow Gouttes-d'eau / Hanging Rib / Over the Rainbow / Oz Court / Wizard** Nick White, Jon Gandy.
22/1/89	**Auk** R.Earle, L.Johnson.
1/89	**Warspite** Robbie Warke *(unseconded)*.
1/2/89	**Tasty Snappers** Jon Gandy, Nick White.
18/2/89	**Sandshoe Shuffle** Crispin Waddy *(solo). A typically informal ascent. Climbed on-sight in the pouring rain, in a pair of leaking desert boots!*
2/89	**Cry Creamdom** Nick White, Andy Turner.
2/89	**Rainbow Bridge** FFA (of pitch 6) by Crispin Waddy *(solo)*.
26/3/89	**Barney Rubble** Robbie Warke *(unseconded)*.
26/3/89	**Mental Block** Andy Grieve, Nick Hancock.
8/4/89	**Overtaker** Dominic & Jon Gandy.
8/4/89	**Undertaker** Jon & Dominic Gandy.
19/4/89	**A Fistful of Dolerites** J.Privett, D.Nicholls, T.Ridell.
19/4/89	**Ascent of Silage** T.Ridell, D.Nicholls, J.Privett.
19/4/89	**Dynomight** D.Nicholls, J.Privett.
19/4/89	**A Few Dolerites More** J.Privett, D.Nicholls. *(The above four routes were originally bolted. Disgusted doyens of Moor tradition, Dick Scratcher, Raph Skrøtöm, Tessa Tickle, removed the bolts & climbed them clean in November 1989.)*
20/4/89	**Toltec Twostep** Pete Bull *(unseconded). A technical breakthrough for the Moor. The variation start was climbed by Ken Palmer in May 1994.*
24/4/89	**Meathead** Clark Alston *(unseconded)*.
21/5/89	**Death Knell** Jon Gandy *(solo)*.
21/5/89	**Strawbery Girl** Dominic Gandy.
23/5/89	**Sod the Cosmos. . .** Robbie Warke, Wendy Sampson.
29/5/89	**Wildebeest** Dave Thomas *(unseconded)*.
30/5/89	**The Gambler** Pete Bull, Andy Turner.
1/6/89	**Might & Main** Nick White, Bruce Woodley.
2/6/89	**Sun of Righteousness** Dave Thomas *(unseconded)*.
4/6/89	**Avenged** Nick White *(unseconded)*.
17/6/89	**Rise'n'Shine** Dave Thomas, Nick White. *The variation Rye'n'Shy was done the same month.*

6/89	**Banshee**	Nick White, Dominic Gandy.
6/89	**Tomb with a View**	Dominic Gandy *(unseconded)*.
6/89	**Barking Mad**	Mdme Blavatsky & party.
2/7/89	**The Cider Soak**	Nick White.
17/7/89	**Silk Purse / Sow's That**	Nick White *(unseconded)*.
10/8/89	**Suspended Sentence**	Paul Twomey, S.Scarbro.
16/8/89	**The Earthsea Trilogy #3**	Nick White, Dave Thomas. *The concluding episode of an epic route which takes in; the arête at Dyers Lookout, North Devon &; the groove on the Parthenos, Lundy.*
20/8/89	**Junebug**	Nick White, Pete Bull.
8/89	**The New Stone Age**	Dave Thomas, Crispin Waddy. *Pitches 4-5 done a couple of days before, starting up Depth Charge by Dave Thomas, Nick White.*
8/89	**Terra Cotta**	Dave Thomas *(solo)*. *The infamous soloing of Caveman to boot (on pitch 3 of Caveman a hold almost pulled off. Neil Foster took a 40' fall when it disintegrated on the following ascent. Although pitch four had been worked off an ab-rope, Dave forgot about the rope stretch & had to re-work the crux while soloing.*
6/9/89	**Vixana**	Andy Grieve, Nick Hancock, Ken Palmer, Pete Saunders.
9/89	**The Corner**	Pete Bull, Paul Sandys.
9/89	**New Paths / Pommie Granite**	Nick White *(unseconded)*.
9/89	**Warpath**	Pete Bull, Nick White, Dave Thomas.
10/89	**Peak 8b**	Ken Palmer, Nick White.
10/89	**Therapeutic Structures**	John Dunne *(unseconded)*.
10/89	**Trism**	Nick White, Pete Bull.
10/89	**A Moment Spent Talking**	Dave Thomas, Nick White.
10/89	**Honour Bright**	Nick White *(solo – the variations were soloed the same day)*.
11/11/89	**Hot-shot / Lawbreaker**	Nick White *(solo)*.
11/11/89	**Judge Dredd**	Nick White *(unseconded)*.
4/12/89	**Pebbles**	Nick White, Clark Alston.
12/89	**Football Graveyard**	Nick White, Clark Alston.
1989	**The Actress**	Ken Palmer, Nick Hancock.
1989	**Prawle Crawl**	Nick White, Clark Alston *(solo)*.
1989	**Hijo de Puta**	Dominic Gandy *(solo)*.
1989	**Starless & Bible Black**	Robbie Warke.
1989	**Supermousse**	Dave Thomas.
2/2/90	**There She Blows**	Nick White *(unseconded)*.
6/2/90	**Roar Like Sushi**	Nick White *(unseconded)*.
11/4/90	**Monster Munch**	Ken Palmer *(unseconded)*. *Climbed on-sight. A rare occurrence these days!*
15/4/90	**Albatross**	Pete Bull, Nick Tetley.
28/5/90	**Arêtez Vous / The Invisible Man**	Pete Bull, Simon Cook.
28/5/90	**Waffle Supremacy**	Dave Thomas *(unseconded)*.
10/6/90	**Flaming Drambuie**	Dave Thomas, Pete Bull. *Originally this climbed the initial wall of Courvoisier. It now begins up a pitch first climbed by Pat Littlejohn, Nick White on 1/1/89. The Variation finish was climbed by Dave Thomas, Jon Gandy on 21/7/90.*
21/7/90	**Basking Shark**	Pete Bull, Dave Thomas.
7/90	**Carbon Paper**	Jon Gandy, Pete Bull.
5/8/90	**Banana Split Lady**	Jon Gandy *(solo)*.
8/8/90	**Lichenthrope**	Jon Gandy *(unseconded)*.
15/8/90	**Island Racer**	Jon Gandy, Mathew Ruiz.
8/90	**Thug'n'ell**	Jon Gandy *(unseconded)*.
9/9/90	**Hydrophobia**	Nick Biven, Karl Strange.
15/9/90	**Splosh**	Nick Biven, Pete Stapley.
15/9/90	**The Link**	Nick Biven, Karl Strange.
25/9/90	**Quick Dip**	Mark Campbell *(solo)*.
9/90	**Captain Buttwash**	C.Willis, D.Nicholls, J.Privett.
10/90	**Cocoon**	Steve Mayers *(unseconded)*.
16/11/90	**Tuppence**	Ken Palmer.
1990	**Aqua Marina / Stingray / Troy Tempest**	Nick White *(solo)*.
1990	**Bamboozled**	Simon Cook.
1990	**Chainsaw Massacre**	Gary Blake.
1990	**Courvoisier**	Dave Thomas.
1990	**Deadly Assassin**	Jon Gandy.
1990	**Hidebound / Pale Horse / Piebald / Pony Trek**	Paul Twomey *(solo)*.
1990	**Teenage Mutant Ninja Slippers**	J.Privett.
18/4/91	**Bam Bam**	Nick White, Jon Gandy.
4/91	**Avante-garde**	Nick White.

4/91	**Blazing Apostles** Nick White, Mark Campbell.	
5/91	**Antipodeans Afoot** Nicky Sunderland, Nick White.	
5/91	**Don't Mess with Tess / Jude the Obscure** Nick White, Nicky Sunderland.	
3/6/91	**A Fisherman's Tale** Ken Palmer. *The hardest 'thang' South of Hubble (excepting Chimaera)?*	
18/6/91	**Obstreperous / Into the Groove** FFA & BFA (respectively) by Ken Palmer *(unseconded).*	
6/91	**The Mightiest** Jon Gandy *(unseconded).*	
6/91	**Spud** Jon Gandy, Pete Bull.	
17/8/91	**Losing My Religion** Nick White, Ken Robinson.	
18/8/91	**Threadbare** Nick White, Ken Robinson.	
23/8/91	**Boris Yeltsin** Andy Grieve *(unseconded).*	
27/9/91	**Waterline** Mark Campbell, Rob McCloud.	
9/91	**Amorok / Astral Arête / Flying Saucers** Robbie Warke *(solo).*	
9/91	**Drowning Witch** Robbie Warke *(unseconded).*	
9/91	**The Green Grotto / Look, Before You Leap** Nick White *(solo).*	
9/91	**Into the Fire** Nick White *(unseconded).*	
9/91	**Moomin & the Toxic Waste** Wendy Sampson *(solo).*	
9/91	**Ned's Atomic Dustbin** Justin Davey, Robbie Warke, Anna King.	
9/91	**Safe Surfer** Robbie Warke *et al.*	
10/91	**Ancient Eyes / Carreg / Casablanca / Cruise of a Lifetime / Dzirnavas / Legin** Steve Scadden, Len Carr.	
10/91	**Bus Stop / Clapier-dans-fils / Jewel / Laugharne / Oje / Sai Qot / Silver Cufflinks / Tulang Kecil** Steve Scadden.	
10/91	**Lost Identity** Steve Mayers *(unseconded).*	
20/10/91	**Mulinos** Len Carr, Steve Scadden.	
25/10/91	**The Reddlemen** Bruce Woodley, Gary Hamel. *A bad boy Bosch was carried on the FA.*	
30/10/91	**Caribbean Blue** Ken Palmer, Mark Campbell.	
11/91	**Asante Sana / Balta Maja / Katalyn / Leavitt / Meditations / The Ultimate Postcard** Steve Scadden *(solo).*	
1991	**Songline** Tim Dennell.	
1991	**Songs from the Wood / Weasel the Wizard** Robbie Warke, Steve Pack, Andy Medworth.	
1991	**Woodland Bop** Robbie Warke *(unseconded).*	
23/2/92	**Sayonara** T.Catterall, J.Harrington.	
16/3/92	**If I Should Fall. . .** T.Catterall, J.Harrington.	
9/4/92	**Kill your Idol** Nick White, Jared McCulloch.	
19/4/92	**Call of Nature** Nick White, Jared McCulloch, Mark Campbell.	
4/5/92	**Fine, Little Hands** Steve Scadden, Len Carr.	
21/5/92	**Piracy** Steve Scadden *(solo).*	
30/5/92	**Rusty Road To. . .** Steve Scadden *(solo).*	
7/6/92	**Little Heart** Steve Scadden, Len Carr.	
7/6/92	**Oozy in My Pocket** Mark Campbell.	
13/6/92	**Chi** Steve Scadden *(solo).*	
14/6/92	**Waiting For Charlie** Mark Campbell *(unseconded).*	
28/6/92	**Sun's Rays** Steve Scadden, Chris Thomas.	
3/8/92	**Amoebic Plunge** Rob McCloud *(unseconded).*	
16/8/92	**Balls of a Child** Martin Crocker *(unseconded).*	
2/9/92	**Mistory / Remiss** Pete Bull *(solo).*	
2/9/92	**Hacking / Misadventure / Mistake / Palomino / Shear Crack / Yer Tiz** Nick White *(solo).*	
9/92	**Dog's Bolx / Git a Rat Up Ya** Jon Gandy, Pete Bull.	
9/92	**Frog's Failure** Jon Gandy.	
9/92	**Savage** Steve Mayers *(unseconded).*	
9/92	**Witches Tit** Jon Gandy, Robert Lincoln.	
10/92	**Jehovah Kill** Robbie Warke *(unseconded). Now de-geared & awaiting a reascent.*	
1992	**Aqualung** Robbie Warke *(unseconded).*	
1992	**Arapiles, Oh Arapiles** Nick White.	
1992	**Et Tu Brutus** Nick White, Pete Bull.	
1992	**Gus Honeybun** Ken Palmer, Mark Campbell.	
1992	**Four Strong Winds** Robbie Warke, A.King, C.Solway.	
1992	**Have a Good Flight** Nick White *(unseconded).*	
1992	**Red Centre** Nick White.	
26/1/93	**Maximagur / Quoit Enough / Roger & Out / Wisht You Were Here** Nick White *(solo).*	
23/3/93	**White Dwarf** Jon Gandy *(unseconded).*	

1/4/93	**April Fool** Ian Parnell. *Totally fictitious, happy birthday Ian!*
4/93	**Cabarête / Erazor Flake / Flying Arête / Hades / Look Sharp / Loop de Lip** Nick White *(solo)*.
6/5/93	**Harlem Rude Boy / Me & My Magnum / You Know the Score** Nick White, Mark Campbell.
8/5/93	**Porno For Pyro's** Mark Campbell, Nick White.
12/5/93	**Suicide Blonde** Nick White, Mark Campbell.
15/5/93	**Radjel** Andy Grieve *(unseconded)*.
20/5/93	**Hardcore** Nick White, Mark Campbell.
10/6/93	**Breathless / Gothic** Nick White, Ken Robinson.
6/93	**Monkey Business** Sean Hawken, Andy Grieve, Steve Golley.
6/93	**Sandman** Ian Parnell, Paul Twomey.
6/93	**Scorn** Paul Twomey.
6/8/93	**Wild Palms** Nick White *(solo, with hanging rope)*.
6/8/93	**Shere Khanage** Nick White *(unseconded)*.
15/9/93	**Vicious Delicious** Nick White, Clark Alston.
21/10/93	**The Bewilderness / Cyberpunk** Tim Dennell, Paul Birchell.
23/10/93	**St Mongo** Jon Gandy, Pete Bull.
11 93	**Return to Earth** Ian Parnell, Andy Sheahy. *Climbed on-sight.*
1993	**Hung Like a Babboon** Ken Palmer *(unseconded)*.
26/3/94	**Poppy** Ken Palmer *(unseconded)*.
/94	**Down the Welly** Ken Palmer *(unseconded)*.
10/4/94	**Oh Brother!** Clarke Alston, Ian Parnell.
10/4/94	**Raw Umber** Ian Parnell, Clarke Alston.
19/4/94	**Troy** P.Birchell, J.Miles.
22/4/94	**Crème Brulée** Paul Twomey, Ali Wade, *Mad* Jim Adamson.
4/94	**The Cabinet of Doctor Caligari** Ian Parnell, Dave Henderson.
2/5/94	**Uncertain Smile** Mark Campbell.
5/94	**Rave to the Grave** Clark Alston.
14/6/94	**Don't Tell Emma** P.Birchell, S.Coombe.
10/7/94	**One Step Beyond** Ian Parnell *(unseconded)*.
25/8/94	**Hair of the Dog** Bruce & Annmarie Woodley. *Early attempts utilized much aid and fixed ropes but a bold foray by Derek Ryden & Clark Alston resulted in the freeing of pitches 1,2 and the addition of pitch 4 – benightment stopped them completing the route via the more direct chimney line. Clark Alston returned with Ian Parnell on 15/10/94 to do the first "one push" and the first "free as it can be" ascent.*
27/8/94	**Sandpit Chimney** Jim Cheshire, Derek Ryden.
27/8/94	**Jam Today** Derek Ryden, Andy Turner & Mark Lee.

INDEX

Several route names are duplicated within the text, so it is necessary to put abbreviated crag names next to the relevant climbs: *(C)* – Chudleigh; *(BC)* – Babbacombe Crags; *(BH)* – Beer Head; *(D)* – Dewerstone; *(HLQ)* – Hooe Lake Quarry; *(HT)* – Hound Tor; *(OR)* – Old Redoubt; *(RQ)* – Radford Quarry; *(ST)* – Saddle Tor; *(SH)* – South Hams; *(VT)* – Vixen Tor; *(WR)* – White Rock.

RESCUE NOTES

SEA CLIFF AREAS: **In a dire emergency contact the Fire Brigade by dialling 999**, and quote the exact six figure grid reference for the crag you are climbing on (written after the title of each cliff). They are responsible for cliff rescue. They liaise with the Coast-guard Service for information on the nature of the cliffs in question. Therefore clearly state the exact location of the accident and give any other information which might affect the method of rescue (sea-level evacuation is often conducted by lifeboat). However, there was one exceptional circumstance. A party from Exeter University became well and trully plastered to The Parson, while trying to climb it in the teeth of a hurricane! The daring evacuation by helicopter necessitated the winch wire having to be drifted-in under a large overhang, while being buffeted by gusts of wind in excess of 100 mph. Needless to say the national media had a field day with the story.

You'll generally find that Joe Public is genuinely concerned for your well being, especially when they notice a brightly coloured body hanging in the middle of (to their limited experience) mind-bendingly dangerous terrain. So don't be so surprised, or indeed pissed-off when the Coastguard comes to spoil your fun. Again prevention is better than that infamous cricketing phrase, the Coastguard stopped play (due to *iggerunt furineerz* neglecting to contact them).

A dire emergency in the case of sports climbers excludes broken finger-nails and 'flappers'. As aggravating as these can be, they don't warrant a trip to hospital so just chill-out.

INLAND AREAS: **In a dire emergency contact the police by dialling 999** and quote the exact six figure grid reference for the crag you are climbing on (written after the title of each cliff).

While climbing ... the inland crags, it is generally prudent to carry a picnic compose: of garlic, holy water, and bread (of the sacramental variety) -wooden stakes are optional, although a good idea for Dartmoor. Drinking in taverns with pentangles (usually drawn in blood) on the walls is an ill-advised occupation. If you do get into trouble of this kind, I recommend leafing through the phone book for anyone bearing a name ending with Van Helsing.

ABBREVIATIONS

L	- Left
LH	- Left-hand
LWs	- Leftwards
R	- Right
RH	- Right-hand
RWs	- Rightwards
L/R	- Left to Right
RL	- Right to Left *(Note: The stroke indicates the direction of the break, crack, or fault)*
OH	- Overhang
OHing	- Overhanging
OHung	- Overhung
†	- Unrepeated
PR	- Peg Runner *(Note: If the word peg appears, you have to place it)*
PRs	- Peg Runners
PB	- Peg Belay
BR	- Bolt Runner *(and so on, as for PR).*
TR	- Thread Runner *(and so on, as for PR).*
NB	- Nut Belay
HWM	- High Water Mark
N ↑	- North(ern/*erly*)
S ↓	- South(ern/*erly*)
E→	- East(ern/*erly*)
←W	- West(ern/*erly*)

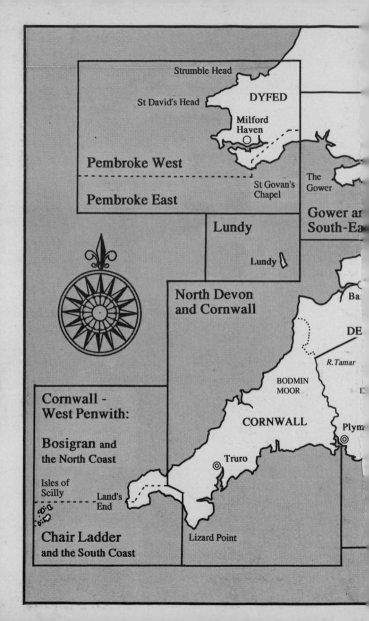